T0192208

Communications in Computer and Information Science 1494

More information about this series at http://www.springer.com/series/7899

Zhiping Cai · Jian Li · Jialin Zhang (Eds.)

Theoretical Computer Science

39th National Conference of Theoretical Computer Science, NCTCS 2021 Yinchuan, China, July 23–25, 2021 Revised Selected Papers

Editors
Zhiping Cai
National University of Defense Technology
Changsha, China

Jian Li
Tsinghua University
Beijing, China

Jialin Zhang
Chinese Academy of Sciences
Beijing, China

ISSN 1865-0929 ISSN 1865-0937 (electronic)
Communications in Computer and Information Science
ISBN 978-981-16-7442-6 ISBN 978-981-16-7443-3 (eBook)
https://doi.org/10.1007/978-981-16-7443-3

This Springer imprint is published by the registered company Springer Nature Singapore Pte Ltd.
The registered company address is: 152 Beach Road, #21-01/04 Gateway East, Singapore 189721, Singapore

Preface

The National Conference of Theoretical Computer Science (NCTCS) has become one of the most important academic platforms for theoretical computer science in China. So far, NCTCS has been successfully held in more than 20 regions of China, providing a place for exchange and cooperation for researchers in theoretical computer science and related fields.

NCTCS 2021 was hosted by the China Computer Federation (CCF) and organized by the Theoretical Computer Science Committee of China Computer Society and the College of Computer Science and Engineering of North Munzu University. It took place during July 23–25, 2021, in Yinchuan, Ningxia. This conference invited famous scholars in the field of theoretical computer science to give presentations, and it included a wide range of academic activities and showed the latest research results. In total, 397 people registered for NCTCS 2021, of which 353 authors submitted 145 papers (67 papers were finally accepted). We invited 82 reviewers from colleges and universities to undertake the peer review process (single blind), where the average number of papers assigned to a reviewer was five and the average number of reviews per paper was three. All papers were managed using the online submission system (CCF Consys), more details can be seen on the conference website: https://conf.ccf.org.cn/TCS2021.

This volume contains 14 of the accepted papers, which have been arranged under five topical headings (Information Hiding, Data Detection and Recognition, System Scheduling, Time Series Prediction, Formal Analysis).

The proceedings editors wish to thank the dedicated Program Committee members and external reviewers for their hard work in reviewing and selecting papers. We also thank Springer for their trust and for publishing the proceedings of NCTCS 2021.

September 2021

Zhiping Cai
Jian Li
Jialin Zhang

Organization

General Chairs

Xiaoming Sun	Chinese Academy of Sciences, China
Wenxing Bao	North Minzu University, China

Program Committee Chairs

Zhiping Cai	National University of Defense Technology, China
Jian Li	Tsinghua University, China
Jialin Zhang	Chinese Academy of Sciences, China

Steering Committee

Xiaoming Sun	Chinese Academy of Sciences, China
Jianping Yin	Dongguan University of Technology, China
Lian Li	Hefei University of Technology, China
En Zhu	National University of Defense Technology, China
Kun He	Huazhong University of Science and Technology, China

Program Committee

Juan Chen	National University of Defense Technology, China
Jianxi Fan	Soochow University, China
Qilong Feng	Central South University, China
Xin Han	Dalian University of Technology, China
Kun He	Huazhong University of Science and Technology, China
Zhaoming Huang	Guangxi Medical University, China
Lvzhou Li	Sun Yat-sen University, China
Zhanshan Li	Jilin University, China
Hao Liao	Shenzhen University, China
Qiang Liu	National University of Defense Technology, China
Xingwu Liu	Chinese Academy of Sciences, China
Zhengyang Liu	Beijing Institute of Technology, China
Lei Luo	National University of Defense Technology, China
Rui Mao	Shenzhen University/Shenzhen Institute of Computing Science, China
Zhengwei Qi	Shanghai Jiao Tong University, China
Feng Qin	Jiangxi Normal University, China
Guojing Tian	Chinese Academy of Sciences, China

Gang Wang	Nankai University, China
Nan Wu	Nanjing University, China
Mengji Xia	Institute of Software, Chinese Academy of Sciences, China
Mingyu Xiao	University of Electronic Science and Technology, China
Tao Xiao	Huawei Theoretical Computer Laboratory, China
Huanlai Xing	Southwest Jiaotong University, China
Yicheng Xu	Shenzhen Institute of Advanced Technology, Chinese Academy of Sciences, China
Jinyun Xue	Jiangxi Normal University, China
Tian Yang	Central South University of Forestry and Technology, China
Yitong Yin	Nanjing University, China
Peng Zhang	Shandong University, China
Yong Zhang	Shenzhen Institute of Advanced Technology, Chinese Academy of Sciences, China
Zhao Zhang	Zhejiang Normal University, China
Cheng Zhong	Guangxi University, China
Xinzhong Zhu	Zhejiang Normal University, China
En Zhu	National University of Defense Technology, China

Additional Reviewers

Chau Vincent
Kerong Ben
Dongbo Bu
Qingqiong Cai
Shaowei Cai
Yongzhi Cao
Pei Chen
Yujia Chen
Zhigang Chen
Zhiguo Fu
Lengxiao Huang
Shenwei Huang
Zhiyi Huang
Haibin Kan
Qian Li
Wenjun Li
Huawen Liu
Renren Liu
Tian Liu
Xiaoguang Liu
Xinwang Liu
Zhendong Liu
Lv Shuai
Bo Ning
Dantong Ouyang
Haiyu Pan
Zhiyong Peng
Jiaohua Qin
Feng Shi
Xiaoming Sun
Chang Tang
Zhihao Tang
Changjing Wang
Meihua Xiao
Yun Xu
Yan Yang
Yu Yang
Penghui Yao
Mengting Yuan
Chihao Zhang
Jia Zhang
Xiaoyan Zhang
Changwang Zhang
Zhengkang Zuo

Contents

Information Hiding

Data Detection and Recognition

System Scheduling

Time Series Prediction

Formal Analysis

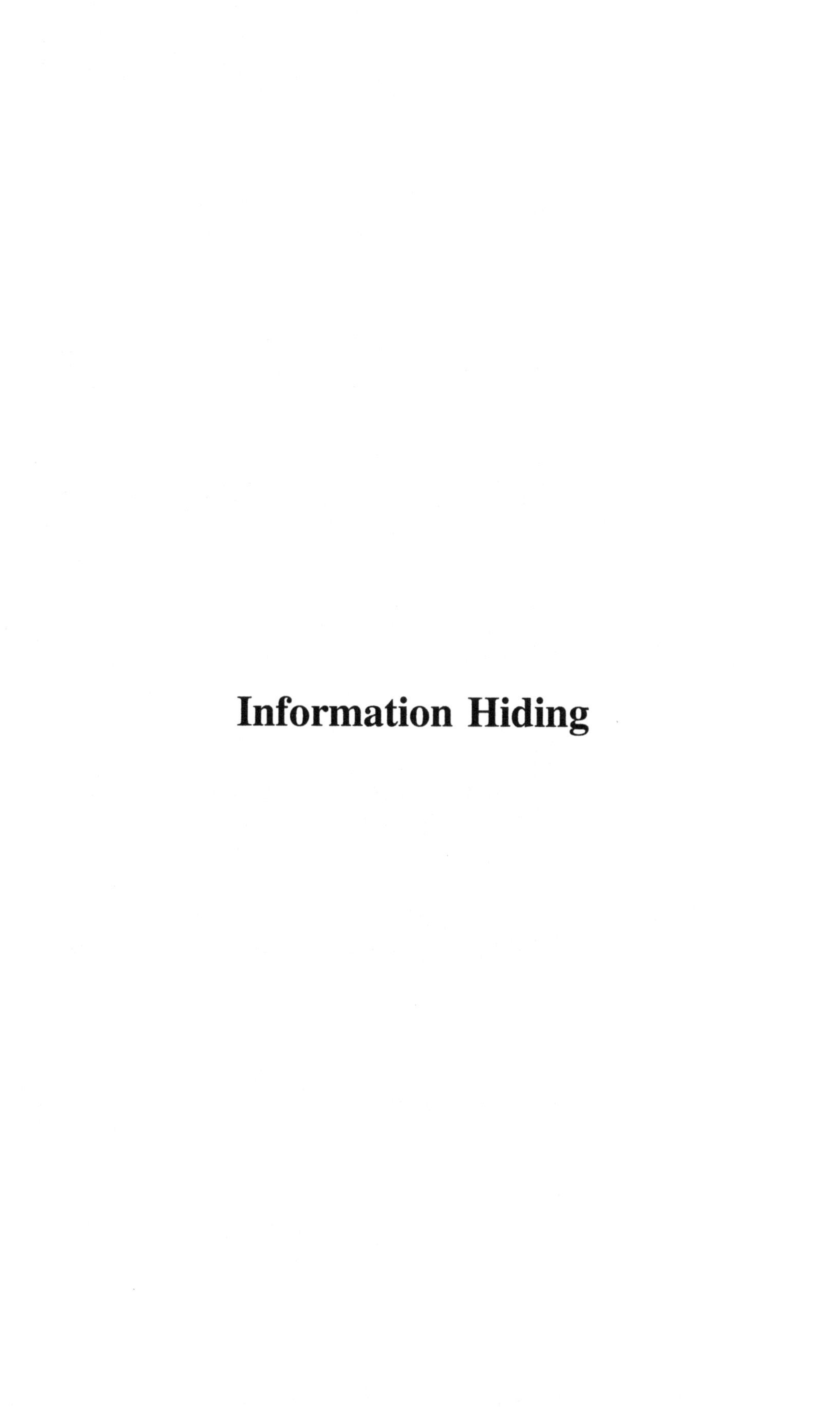

Information Hiding

Research on Adaptive Video Steganography Algorithm for Clustering and Dispersing DCT Coefficient Difference Histogram

Kun Han[1], Ke Niu[1,3(✉)], Shuai Yang[2], and XiaoYuan Yang[1]

[1] College of Cryptographic Engineering, Engineering University of PAP, Xi'an 710086, Shaanxi, China

[2] College of Information Engineering, Engineering University of PAP, Xi'an 710086, Shaanxi, China

[3] Institute of Cipher Engineering, No. 1, Wujing Road, Sanqiao Town, Weiyang District, Xi'an 710086, Shaanxi, China

Abstract. Histogram migration is a method of the information hiding, the advantage of traditional data hiding has large amount of data, but there are many problems, such as poor security and embedding rate changes. The reason is that generate invalid migration when embedding data. The histogram has a larger numerical range after migration. An optimization algorithm is proposed for this problem. Through data difference, Spread out The range of coefficient modifications. The deformation dispersed in each coefficient domain. Then through the K-Means algorithm, according to the number of embedding build suitable embedded space, the embedded fields are evenly distributed throughout the whole video. Finally, the data uniformly embedded through aggregation and dispersion. Through the peak signal-to-noise ratio (PSNR), structural similarity (SSIM), security and bit growth rate tests. Compared with the two similar algorithms, the bit growth rate decreased by 0.14% on average and the detection error rate increased by 0.2% on average under the same embedding capacity and PSNR and SIMM basically remained stable. Experimental results show that the proposed algorithm can effectively improve the security of video steganography and improve the situation of bit rate increase.

Keywords: Video information hiding · Adaptive · DCT histogram convergence and dispersion · High security

1 Introduction

Digital steganography is a technology that uses a large amount of publicly available multimedia data in the network as a carrier and embeds secret information in it so that its presence is not perceived, thus achieving covert communication. Network-based steganography initially embeds information on digital signals of graphics and sound. In

Fund Projects: National Natural Science Foundation (61872384).

Z. Cai et al. (Eds.): NCTCS 2021, CCIS 1494, pp. 3–14, 2021.
https://doi.org/10.1007/978-981-16-7443-3_1

recent years, with the development of communication transmission technology, bandwidth and compression advances, digital video with larger amounts of data is more suitable as a carrier to hide information. Compared to pictures, audio and text data, video, as one of the current mainstream traffic media, can embed a large amount of information, and there are few steganalysis algorithms specifically for video, video steganalysis is relatively difficult, and the hidden channel established in the video is more difficult to be cracked. In addition the video compression standard is more complex compared to graphics, it has more modulation points, motion vector information in the video compression domain, DCT coefficients, intra-frame inter-frame prediction patterns, video entropy coding can all be used as information embedding location. Among them, the way based on DCT coefficient embedding has the characteristics of large embedding capacity, controllable video quality and high security [1], which is one of the mainstream methods of video information hiding at present, and there have been many valuable research results [2–4].

Traditional hiding algorithm research focuses on embedding capacity and robustness. Huang Jiwu et al. [5] proposed the concept of human visual system (HVS) threshold in the watermark embedding process, when the threshold is less than the human HVS contrast threshold, it is difficult for human vision to perceive the presence of the signal, which provides a visual basis for controlling the embedding capacity and selecting the embedding location when embedding information. Lin et al. [6] proposed the concept of human visual system (HVS) threshold in the process of watermark embedding by providing a visual basis in order to The algorithm not only maintains better visual quality, but also significantly improves safety. The histogram shifting-based information embedding method in the luminance component has more advantages in terms of embedding capacity and is widely used in video steganography. The hiding algorithm based on differential histogram panning [7, 8] ensures algorithmic security by dispersing the range of histogram variations while maintaining a large embedding capacity. On this basis, Tang Hongqiong et al. [9] corrected and selectively embedded by adjusting the symbols to avoid distortion, providing some ideas for optimising embedding methods. However, histogram-based panning algorithms are generally used for reversible information hiding techniques without considering their security, and there are problems such as serious histogram distortion during the information embedding process. In this paper, we try to design a steganography algorithm based on DCT coefficients by using histogram panning to reduce histogram distortion and solve the embedding location and capacity while improving the algorithm's resistance to steganography analysis through difference and k-means algorithms.

2 Theoretical Framework of the Algorithm

2.1 Analysis of Embedding Position

The DCT transform is a signal processing method for transforming spatial domain images into the frequency domain. Since the vector basis of the DCT transform has no correlation with the signal content, the DCT transform of a two-dimensional signal can be achieved by two one-dimensional DCT transforms and fast algorithms exist, it is widely used in the video compression process and has been applied to the field of information hiding [10]. In this paper, based on the traditional histogram translation, the amount of histogram translation is optimised by aggregating and dispersing the difference of AC (Alternating Current) coefficients in the DCT matrix and synthesising the embedding space. By analysing the quantized AC coefficients in the first 50 frames of the seven videos of foreman, highway, container, grandma, hall, mother-daughter and salesman, it can be found that excluding the DC (Direct Current) coefficients, the low-frequency AC coefficients a_{12}, a_{21}, and a_{22} occupy most of the non-zero values (Table 1). To analyse the overall video quality variation, this algorithm selects a21 and its adjacent a_{22} values, which have the most non-zero values of AC coefficients in the DCT block, as the difference coefficients in the experiment. The 4 × 4 chunking pattern in H.264 video corresponds to a more complex region of texture where the coefficients are modified to have a lower impact on the visual quality of the video.

Table 1. The number of non-zero values each position in 350 frames

AC factor	Non-zero value quantities	AC factor	Non-zero value quantities	AC factor	Non-zero value quantities
a_{12}	4742	a_{21}	4943	a_{22}	3920
a_{13}	3747	a23	3086	a_{31}	3377
a_{32}	2861	a_{33}	2405	a_{14}	1864
a_{24}	1587	a_{34}	1119	a_{41}	2218
a_{42}	1414	a_{43}	1080	a_{44}	563

The histogram of the difference statistics obtained by differencing the DCT coefficients of a 50-frame video clip is shown in Fig. 1. Compared with direct embedding using the original DCT data domain, the embedded data is more dispersed after differencing, and its data range can be extended by up to 40%. Excluding the edge and some all-zero data, the difference range $t \in (\beta, \alpha), \alpha = \max(a_{21} - a_{22}), \beta = \min(a_{21} - a_{22})$ basically satisfies the normal distribution of $N(u, \alpha^2)$.

Through the experiment, it can be seen that after the prediction and compression of the video data, most of the DCT differences are 0, i.e. the expected value u is close to 0. There is a certain amount of non-0 data in the low-frequency DCT differences, which provides an embedding space for the information. In this paper, we use the 4 × 4 DCT matrix coefficients in the low-frequency coefficient differences to embed the information, and balance the relationship between hidden capacity and invisibility through the selection of embedding position and size.

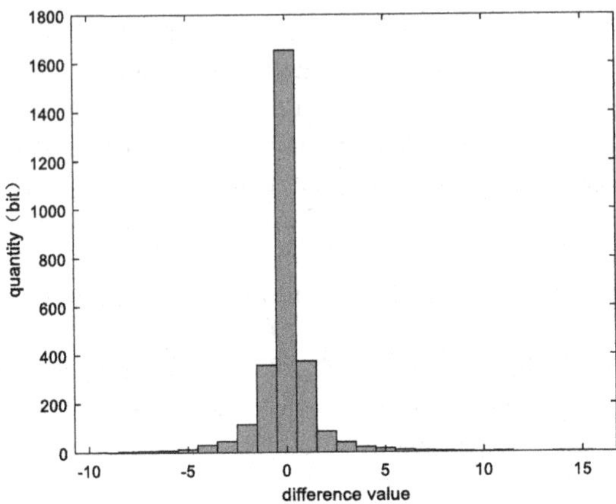

Fig. 1. Difference histogram of DCT coefficients for 50 frames of video

2.2 Histogram Aggregation and Dispersion

Histogram aggregation and dispersion is the process of converging the differences of two coefficients in the same group of the histogram by adjusting the coefficients through translation.

In the DCT coefficient matrix, let the low frequency AC coefficients $a_{21} - a_{22} = t$, $t \in (\beta, \alpha)$ range can be used as the embedding space. Before embedding the data, the embedding space needs to be aggregated, by modifying the AC coefficients so that one of the difference coefficient domains is all aggregated into another difference coefficient domain (called the aggregation domain), forming an empty domain and an aggregation domain as the space for embedding the data.

$$f(x)' = f(x-1) + f(x)\ if\ x > 0 \tag{1}$$

$$f(x)' = f(x+1) + f(x)\ if\ x < 0 \tag{2}$$

Take x and $x - 1$ as the coefficients of the embedding information and use the method of Eq. (1) to translate when the embedding domain is greater than 0, and vice versa using the method of Eq. (2). Aggregation operation on the corresponding DCT coefficient difference histogram in Fig. 1, Make the histogram empty at $x = 2$ to obtain as shown in Fig. 2, get the empty space $f(2)_0'$ of $x = 2$ and the aggregation region $f(1)'$ of $x = 1$ after that Overflow caused by too large or too small values of a11 is considered during aggregation and can be solved by determining the positive or negative of the embedding domain and choosing the larger value minus 1 or the smaller value plus 1. Let the coefficient $a_{21} - a_{22} = t$ differential front range $a \in (m, -m)$, Determine the magnitude of a_{21} and a_{22} based on the positive and negative values of t, if difference t is positive, $a_{21} > a_{22}$, means a_{21} is eternally greater than $-m$, or a_{22} is eternally lesser than m; if difference is negative, $a_{21} < a_{22}$, means a_{22} is eternally greater than $-m$, or a_{21} is eternally lesser than m. If difference t is positive, choose $a_{21} - 1$ or $a_{22}+1$; if difference t is negative, choose $a_{21}+1$ or $a_{22} - 1$. That is, regardless of the size of the

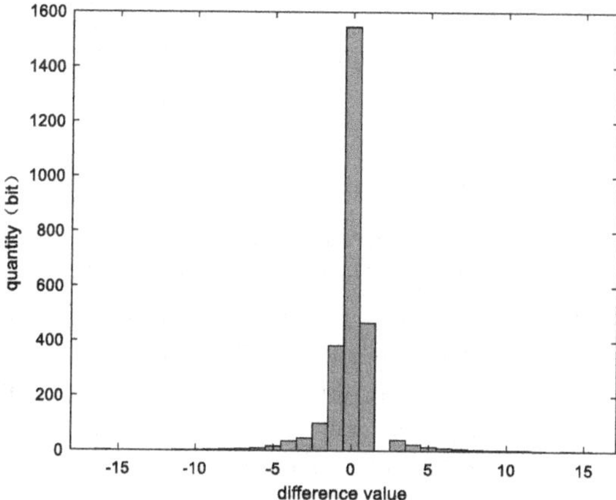

Fig. 2. Histogram after aggregation

difference range, the method of subtracting 1 from the larger value and adding 1 to the smaller value can be used to keep a within the original range $(m, -m)$ effectively solving the problem of overflowing values.

2.3 Optimal Embedding Volume

In the data embedding, the overall data panning will greatly affect the correlation between the graph and the data, when analyzing the individual video embedding volume, the optimal value of this video embedding volume should be calculated in advance. Let the overall total available space be $f(x) + f(x-1)$, and if the data in both regions are embedded, this will result in a theoretical number of embeddings at difference factors x and $x-1$ after translation $f(x)' \approx f(x-1)' \approx (f(x) + f(x-1))/2$. In order to maintain the original shape of the histogram, the number of pans should be proportional to the original data, i.e. the panned data and the embedded data should be kept at the same magnitude in order to maintain the consistency of the DCT statistical properties in the global and local data dimensions and to achieve a balanced overall data. Let the amount of data with difference x and $x-1$ before aggregation be $f(x)$ and $f(x-1)$, in obtaining the null field of the difference histogram $f(x)'_0$ by translating $f(x)$, the number of pans out at the difference x is $f(x)$, to maintain the original shape of the histogram the amount of data to be panned back should be $f(x)$, in this case, if the 1 and 0 in the embedded data D are distributed with uniform and equal probability, the optimal total number of embeddings is $2f(x)$. Let $\rho = f(t+1)/f(t)$ be the embedding rate when the difference x, through experimental analysis, $f(t+1)/f(t)$ range mostly in the 0%–30% interval. That is, the optimal number of embeddings is when the embedding rate is $\rho \approx 0.15$, irrespective of the video characteristics.

Under the optimal embedding rate, the DCT coefficient translation should be adapted to the total amount of embedding space to ensure that the information embedding position is evenly distributed throughout the carrier, when the data to be translated is $f(x)$, the embedded data is embedded by the optimal amount $2f(x)$, and the total amount of data after aggregation is $f(x) + f(x-1)$, if $g = (f(x) + f(x-1))/(2f(x))$, then the histogram properties should be optimally maintained by embedding 1 bit of data per g carrier coefficients.

2.4 K-Means Algorithm Improvements

K-means algorithm has a good effect for extracting the region prime and region classification, and can obtain the cluster class of the sample faster. The algorithm establishes the embedding space with the same size and irregularity of the embedded sample value, which provides a better idea for the algorithm in this paper on the adaptive embedding amount. In this paper, the K-means algorithm is modified for the adaptive embedding of the algorithm in this paper, and the basic idea is that after initially determining a centroid e, by calculating the distance U_{i} between each data point and the centroid in steps and iteratively subtracting them to obtain an ensemble $U_{\mathrm{i(min)}}$, obtain a sufficient number of cluster classes Y with distances from the centroid within a threshold value u, make all dates into $\left|e - U_{i(\min)}\right| \le u$, the exact calculation of the iterations is shown in Eq. 3, where $f(t)$ is the number of each value of the difference coefficient. e is the centroid, $U(\mathrm{t}_i)$ is the value obtained. The specific steps in the algorithm to obtain the cluster class P are as follows:

$$U(t_i) = |e - f(t)| \tag{3}$$

Step 1: Determine the number of bits of information to be embedded W and the number of video frames p, to ensure data security and diversity in the choice of embedding domains, choose frame c as a fixed embedding domain, means that embed e bits of data into frame c on average.
Step 2: Determine the overall embedding domain based on the number e and the fixed number of frames c, calculate the values that should be embedded within the fixed number of frames e, make $e = W \times c/p$.
Step 3: Create a histogram for each c frame and calculate the number of values for each domain of the histogram within each c frame, $f(t)$.
Step 4: Using $f(t)$ as a sample, iterate through the K-Means algorithm to obtain the cluster class $F(x) = \{f(x_1), f(x_2)...f(x_n)\}$ with the smallest distance as the embedding space, centered on the value of e.

3 Algorithm Design

3.1 Information Embedding

The algorithm uses the histogram to cluster and disperse the embedding information in the DCT difference coefficient domain adaptively. The difference value of DCT coefficients in the P-frame of the compressed video is counted to obtain the histogram information, and the information is used to aggregate and transform each data in the embedding domain to obtain a histogram with spare bits, and then the DCT matrix after the embedding information is formed by dispersing the embedding, and the compression is completed to obtain the embedding information of the laden dense video, the process is shown in Fig. 3, and the detailed process is as follows:

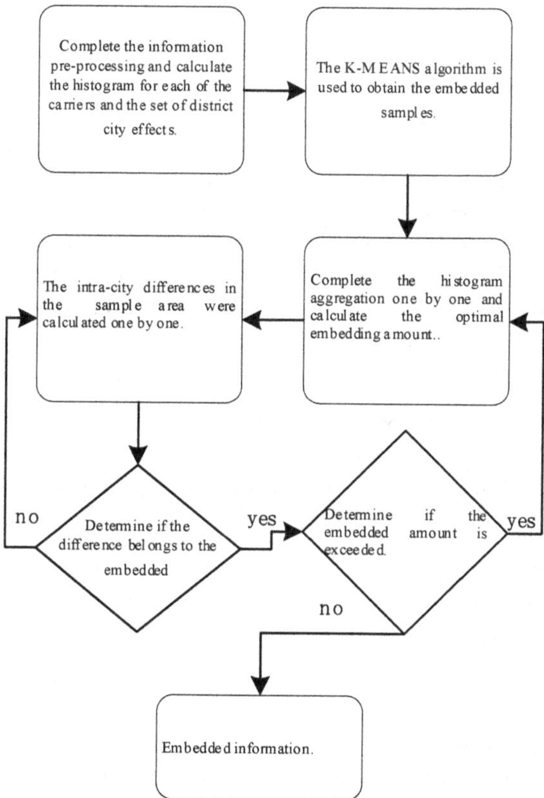

Fig. 3. Embedded processes

Step 1: Information pre-processing;

First, the information to be embedded $D_1(d_1, d_2, \ldots d_n, d_{n+1}, \ldots)$ is binarized to obtain the binary data $D_1(d_1, d_2, \ldots d_n, d_{n+1}, \ldots)_2$; Pre-processing of data using chaos disruption, with chaos disruption parameters stored as keys.

Step 2: Statistical carrier video acquisition of embeddable domain sample space;

Count all 4×4 DCT coefficient matrix $a_{21} - a_{22}$ data to obtain the difference histogram within c frames of data, and sample the number of differences within each group distance of the difference histogram, let the number of each difference in the histogram be $f(t)$, then the optional embedding position is $F(\mathrm{t}) = \{f(t_2), f(t_3) \ldots f(t_n)\}$, where the domain of $t \notin (-1, 0, 1)$ is used as the sample value for the cluster analysis.

Step 3: Embedding domain selection by K-Means algorithm;

Get the embedding field based on the size of the embedding data and the number of frames available. With e as the central point, by $F(\mathrm{t}) = \{f(t_2), f(t_3) \ldots f(t_n)\}$, find the cluster in the sample area that meets the minimum distance from the centroid $F(x) = \{f(x_1), f(x_2) \ldots f(x_n)\}$, where $(x_1, x_2 \ldots x_m) \in (t_1, t_2 \ldots t_n)$, and $W = 2\sum_{i=1}^{m} f(x_i)'$, and W is the total number of bits of information to be embedded.

Step 4: Difference histogram aggregation;

Aggregation of regions $f(x)$ and $f(x-1)$ of cluster class $f(x_i)$, to obtain empty domain $f(x)'_0$ and aggregated domain $f(x-1)'$, Use of airspace and aggregated domains as areas to be embedded.
Step 5: Optimal embedding;

On the basis of steps 1–4, the number of embedding is calculated according to $f(x)$. The number of embedded domains after embedding is equal to the number of such domains before aggregation, that is, $f(x)'' = f(x)$, he information is embedded through the Table 2 algorithm on the basis of uniform embedding, where $f(x)''$. is the amount of secret-carrying data after embedding, and Keep is to keep the original data unchanged, because in the embedding process is changed from a larger difference to a smaller one, so there is no problem of overflow.

Table 2. Embedding method

Embedded area	Embedded values	Embedding method	Embedded domain range
$f(x-1)''$	$d_n = 1$	$a_{12} - 1$	$x \geq 0$
$Keepf(x)''$	$d_n = 0$		$x \geq 0$
$f(x-1)''$	$d_n = 1$	$a_{12} + 1$	$x \leq 0$
$Keepf(x)''$	$d_n = 0$		$x \leq 0$

Step 6: Information embedding;

With the Table 2 algorithm, translation $f(x_n)'$ the secret data fields $f(x_n)''$ and $f(x_n - 1)''$. The algorithm embeds the information into the DCT coefficients while balancing the data $f(x-1)$ and $f(x)$.

3.1.1 Information Extraction

The information extraction process is the opposite of the embedding process, where the length of the embedded data W, the number of frames corresponding to the video p, and the key and fixed value c, are determined before extraction to establish the central value e.

Step 1: The date e embedded within each c-frame is obtained by $e = W \times c/p$, the DCT coefficients are extracted to form a difference histogram, and the corresponding embedding domain is then obtained using the K-means algorithm. As the algorithm recovers the original data volume of the histogram during the embedding process, the embedding domain can be obtained by the same method.
Step 2: Parse the difference histogram, calculate the difference and corresponding embedding information in the embedding region one by one, extract the fixed position difference t in the domain of $t+1$ and t according to the most optimal embedding method, set d as the embedding value to be extracted, and determine $d = 0$ or $d = 1$ according to $t = x$ or $t = x - 1$.

Step 3:
Obtain the corresponding message sequence, decode the data $D_1(d_1, d_2, \ldots d_n, d_{n+1}, \ldots)$ according to the inverse chaos disruption of the parameters according to the key, and finally complete the message extraction.

4 Analysis of Experimental Results

The experiment used MATLAB 2019a as the experimental platform, and seven videos of foreman, highway, container, grandma, hall, mother-daughter and salesman were steganographically written to test their invisibility and bit growth rate, security and embedding capacity.

4.1 Invisible and Bit Growth Rate Analysis

The algorithm uses peak signal-to-noise ratio (PSNR) and structural similarity (SSIM) to measure video quality. The peak signal-to-noise ratio (PSNR), structural similarity (SSIM) and code rate variation are calculated by embedding information on seven sample videos under the optimal embedding capacity of the algorithm in this paper and comparing them with similar algorithms (PPA algorithm) [11] and (±1DCT coefficient algorithm) [12], and the results are shown in Table 3.

The visual invisibility of this algorithm is higher than that of the ±DCT algorithm in Ref. [11], and comparable to that of the PPA algorithm in Ref. [10]. In terms of code rate increase, the bit growth rate of this algorithm is lower than that of the ±1DCT algorithm in Ref. [11], with an average reduction of 0.41%, and slightly lower than that of the PPA algorithm in Ref. [10], with an average reduction of 0.13%, as shown in Fig. 4.

4.2 Embedded Capacity and Security Analysis

In this paper, we refer to the steganalysis algorithm of image DCT domain [13], and use the overall DCT coefficients as the experimental object to exploit the feature that the steganographic modification of quantization parameters may cause perturbation to their correlation. Using six video sequences such as carphone, each sequence selected 299 frames of embedding information, in the case of the optimal embedding rate at $x = 2$, comparing the security of the algorithm of this paper under the conditions of the optimal embedding rate, the embedding capacity of the three algorithms is shown in Table 4, according to the experimental data can be seen, the video itself characteristics and algorithm embedding volume has a greater correlation, different videos in the same security under the embedding volume gap, but Except for the video with poor video differential effect, the algorithm in this paper has an advantage in the overall embedding capacity, and the average embedding capacity is larger than that of PPA and ±1DCT algorithms.

In order to test the algorithm security, the PPA and ±1DCT algorithms were kept within the optimal embedding rate range with the proposed algorithm in this paper for comparison test, and the GFR-MAX features and FLD integrated classifier in the

Table 3. Analysis of experimental results

Video sequences	Algorithms	PSNR/dB	SSIM (%)	Bitrate growth (%)
Foreman	Raw video	38.9191	0.8610	–
	±1DCT CA	36.9898	0.8121	0.3932
	PPA	38.9188	0.8606	0.1116
	This paper	38.9094	0.8605	0.1453
Highway	Raw video	40.0287	0.7826	–
	±1DCT CA	40.0267	0.7811	0.0542
	PPA	40.0276	0.7826	0.0762
	This paper	40.0275	0.7822	0.0428
Container	Raw video	38.6897	0.7527	–
	±1DCT CA	37.4375	0.7533	0.9125
	PPA	38.6873	0.7527	0.5188
	This paper	38.6882	0.7527	0.5940
Grandma	Raw video	39.3438	0.7437	–
	±1DCT CA	37.4013	0.7459	0.8265
	PPA	39.3427	0.7437	0.1983
	This paper	39.3424	0.7437	0.0468
Hall	Raw video	39.3652	0.8061	–
	±1DCT CA	37.7634	0.8042	0.6521
	PPA	39.3647	0.8061	0.8360
	This paper	39.3546	0.8061	0.2719
Mother-daughter	Raw video	40.1202	0.7715	–
	±1DCT CA	38.3245	0.7717	0.9432
	PPA	40.1196	0.7715	0.1375
	This paper	40.1173	0.7715	0.0134
	±1DCT CA	36.3930	0.9164	0.2972
	PPA	38.0547	0.9159	0.2170
	This paper	38.0586	0.9159	0.0450

literature [14] were used for detection. The first 100 frames of the four videos of carphone, bridge-close, akiyo and coastguard were used as training samples, and the last 199 frames of the 10 videos of bridge-close, bridge-far and claire were used as test samples. The test results are shown in Fig. 5, and the detection error rate is significantly higher than that of the PPA and ±1DCT algorithms in the optimal embedding rate range of this paper's algorithm, i.e., it has better security.

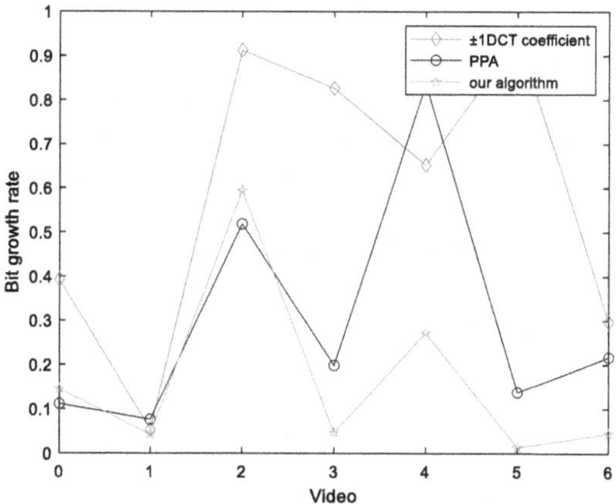

Fig. 4. Bit growth rate

Table 4. Maximum embedding amount

Embedding quantity (bit)	±1DCT algorithms	PPA algorithms	Paper algorithm
Carphone	990	1160	1270
Highway	1130	1040	814
Foreman	900	1090	1508
Coastguard	1380	1260	3138
Hall	970	1080	850
Mother-daughter	920	940	448

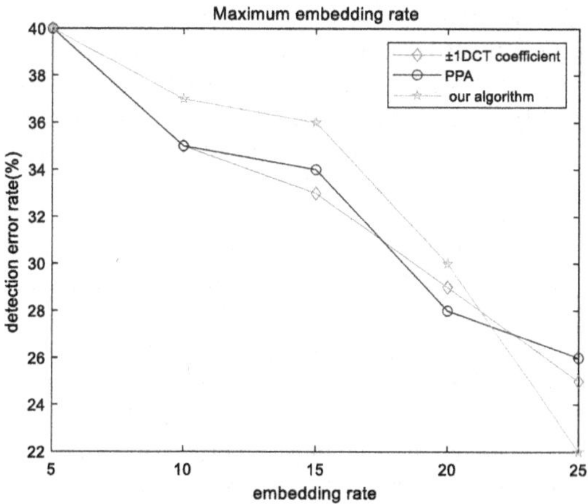

Fig. 5. The error rate of test

5 Conclusion

This paper proposes an adaptive algorithm based on cluster analysis and DCT difference clustering for video steganography. The core idea is to establish a suitable domain for data hiding by matching the size of the hidden data and the carrier DCT difference data, and to use histogram clustering to reduce the wide range of histogram variations and effectively maintain the overall stability of the histogram. The algorithm in this paper has the advantage of smaller bit growth rate and higher security while maintaining a certain embedding capacity.

References

1. Senthilkumar, C., Gayathri Devi, K., Dhivya, M., Rajkumar, R.: A novel method on enhanced video security using steganography. Int. J. Recent Technol. Eng. (IJRTE) **9**(1) (2020)
2. Shi, H., Sun, T., Jiang, X., Dong, Y., Xu, K.: A HEVC video steganalysis against DCT/DST-based steganography. Int. J. Digit. Crime Forensics (IJDCF) **13**(3) (2021)
3. 毛学涛.基于 H.264/AVC 视频的信息隐藏技术研究. 兰州:西北师范大学 (2020). Mao, X.T.: Research Infomation Hiding Technology Based on H.264/AVC Video. Northwest Normal University, Lanzhou (2020)
4. Baziyad, M., Rabie, T., Kamel, I.: Toward stronger energy compaction for high capacity DCT-based steganography: a region-growing approach. Multimed. Tools Appl. (2020, prepublish)
5. 黄继武,施云庆 DCT 域图像水印:嵌入对策和算法. 电子学报 **28**(004), 57–60 (2000). Huang, J.W., Shi, Y.Q.: Image watermarking in DCT: anembedding strategy and algorithm. Chin. J. Electronica **28**(004), 57–60 (2000)
6. Lin, T.J., Chuang, K.L., Chang, P.C., et al.: An improved DCT-based perturbation scheme for high capacity data hiding in H.264/AVC intra frames. J. Syst. Softw. **86**(3), 604–614 (2013)
7. Kang, J., Kim, H., Kang, S.: Genuine reversible data hiding technique for H.264 bitstream using multi-dimensional histogram shifting technology on QDCT coefficients. Appl. Sci. **10**(18) (2020)
8. Qi, W., Li, X., Zhang, T., et al.: Optimal reversible data hiding scheme based on multiple histograms modification. IEEE Trans. Circuits Syst. Video Technol. **PP**(99), 1 (2019)
9. 唐洪琼,钮可,张英男,杨晓元.自适应二维直方图平移的视频可逆隐写算法. 信息网络安全 (09), 106–110 (2019). Tang, H.Q., Niu, K., Zhang, Y.N.: Reversible data hiding in videos based on adaptive two-dimensional histogram modification. Netinfo Secur. (09), 106–110 (2019)
10. Rathi, S., Talmale, G.: Review on discrete cosine transform based watermarking for compressed digital video. In: IEEE 2015 International Conference on Industrial Instrumentation and Control (ICIC), Pune, India, 28–30 May 2015, pp. 327–331. IEEE, New York (2015)
11. 周霈,李芝棠,钱立云.基于余数分类的视频隐写算法. 华中科技大学学报(自然科学版) **44**(z1) (2016). Zhou, P., Li, Z.T., Qian, L.Y.: Steganographic algorithm based on remainder classification. J. Huazhong Univ. Sci. Technol. (Nat. Sci. Ed.) **44**(z1) (2016)
12. 南秀.基于±1DCT系数的H.264视频隐写算法研究. 武汉:华中科技大学 (2015). Nan, X.: The Research on Steganography Algorithm Based on ±1DCT Coeffcients for H.264 Video. Huazhong University of Science and Technology, Wuhan (2015)
13. Yi, Z., Yang, C., Luo, X., et al.: Steganalysis of content-adaptive JPEG steganography based on the weight allocation of filtered coefficients. In: IEEE International Conference on Communication Software & Networks. IEEE (2017)

Coverless Image Information Hiding Based on Deep Convolution Features

Jiaohua Qin[1,2](✉), Jing Wang[2], Jun Sun[1,2], Xuyu Xiang[2], and Lin Xiang[2]

[1] Hunan Applied Technology University, Changde 415000, Hunan, China
[2] College of Computer Science and Information Technology, Central South University of Forestry and Technology, Changsha 410004, China

Abstract. The coverless information hiding technology proposed in recent years does not need to modify the carrier image and has good anti-detection ability. However, the existing coverless information hiding technology has the problems of low hiding capacity and poor robustness. To solve this problem, this paper proposed a coverless image information hiding algorithm based on deep convolution feature, which mainly constructs the mapping relationship between image feature and secret information through deep convolution neural network to realize covert communication. Firstly, the sender learns the category features of the image by training the depth convolution neural network, and extracts the depth feature descriptor on this basis. Then, the depth feature descriptor is mapped into a binary sequence to obtain the hash code of each type of image. Finally, according to the inverted quadtree index, the image consistent with the secret information is retrieved for encrypted transmission. After decryption, the receiver inputs the carrier image into the shared deep neural network for classification, and the corresponding class hash code is searched and connected in turn to obtain the secret information. Compared with the traditional method, this method has higher steganography capacity and stronger robustness.

Keywords: Deep learning · Coverless image hiding · Deep CNN · Hash

1 Introduction

The coverless information hiding technology was first proposed in 2015. Compared with traditional image steganography, coverless steganography does not modify or add any content of carrier information, but establishes a specific relationship between the carrier and the secret information based on the attribute characteristics of carrier to realize the transmission of secret information. Therefore, coverless steganography has a strong ability to resist steganalysis, even if the secret carrier is intercepted, it cannot be cracked and analyzed. However, coverless steganography still has problems such as poor robustness and low hiding capacity.

Deep learning simulates the learning behavior of the human brain through neural networks, and performs feature learning during the modeling process, so as to reduce the semantic loss caused by traditional features and show super computing power. This

Z. Cai et al. (Eds.): NCTCS 2021, CCIS 1494, pp. 15–30, 2021.
https://doi.org/10.1007/978-981-16-7443-3_2

paper applies deep learning to the field of information hiding, and uses the excellent performance of deep neural networks to provide a new solution for coverless information hiding.

2 Related Work

In August 2015, Zhou Zhili et al. [1] proposed the new concept of "coverless information hiding" for the first time at the first International Conference on Cloud Computing and Security. The so-called "coverless" does not mean that there is no carrier, but directly uses the rich feature information contained in the image itself, such as the brightness value, color, texture, edge, contour and high-level semantics of the image pixels to map the secret information to the carrier image. Compared with traditional image steganography, coverless steganography can achieve the goal of secret information loading without modifying the carrier.

The existing coverless image hiding steganography can be divided into two categories according to steganography principles: coverless image steganography based on mapping rules and coverless image steganography based on image synthesis.

The coverless image steganography based on mapping rules was first proposed by Zhili Zhou et al. [1]. In literature [1], each image is divided into 9 pieces to represent 8-bit pixels, the feature sequence is calculated through the relationship between the pixel mean values of adjacent blocks, and the feature sequence and secret information are mapped to each other for information hiding. But there is also the problem of small capacity. Zheng et al. [2] proposed an image steganography based on invariant features. The feature sequences used in this method are generated by invariant features, which enhances the robustness of the system. Recently, Yuan et al. [3] proposed a coverless image steganography based on invariant features and Bag-of-Features. Compared with literature [1, 2], this method can better resist rotation, scaling, brightness change and other attacks, but its ability to resist translation, filtering and shearing is still limited. In order to achieve large-scale repetitive image retrieval [4–6], Zhou Zhili et al. also proposed a coverless image steganography based on visual vocabulary bag. This method firstly extracts local features from images and quantifies them as visual words through K-means algorithm. Then, the image and inverse structure index are used for image retrieval. Finally, the secret information is extracted according to the steganography algorithm. However, the main problem of this model is that the retrieval efficiency is very limited when searching for the required image in a large data image database.

Coverless image steganography based on texture synthesis can be further divided into two categories: process-based synthesis algorithms and instance-based synthesis algorithms. The texture synthesis algorithm based on example is the hotspot in the research of texture synthesis algorithm, which generates new texture image by resampling the original image. The new texture image can not only be of any size, but also its appearance is similar to the original image. Lu Hai [2] and Otori [6–9] et al. proposed a pixel-based texture synthesis steganography. The method first encodes the secret information into colorful dot patterns. Then, draws these dot patterns into blanks images; Finally, the method of texture synthesis is used to fill the remaining positions to hide secret information. Wu et al. [10] proposed an image steganography based on patch texture synthesis.

This method synthesizes a new image according to the index table and the original image, so it produces overlapping regions in the synthesis process, and calculates the Mean Square Error (MSE) of the overlapping region and the candidate block. Then, the candidate blocks are sorted by Mean Square Error. Finally, the candidate blocks with the same sequence number as the secret information are combined into the overlap region to hide the secret information. However, the capacity of this algorithm is poor. Inspired by the marble deformation texture synthesis algorithm, Xu [11] proposed a reconfigurable image steganography algorithm based on texture deformation. This method reversibly distorts the original image containing secret information and hides it by synthesizing different marble textures. However, the robustness of the algorithm is limited.

3 Image Information Hiding Without Carrier Based on DenseNet

In 2017, Huang Gao and Liu Zhuang et al. [12] constructed a deep convolutional neural network called DenseNet based on the design idea of the ResNet network, connecting every two layers in the network with a "skip connection". The input of each layer of the network is the union of the outputs of all the previous layers, realizing cross-layer connection, which is different from the previous network where each layer of the network is only connected with the front and rear adjacent layers. Because of this design, the DenseNet network not only solves the problem of gradient dispersion, but also effectively uses the features from the previous layers of convolution, reduces the amount of calculation of each layer of network parameters and shows excellent classification performance. Compared with the previous networks such as AlexNet, InceptionV3, VGG19, and ResNet50, using the high-dimensional features of the DenseNet network not only greatly reduces the network parameters, but also significantly improves the characterization of features.

3.1 Binary Hashing Algorithm Based on DenseNet

The DenseNet network was trained on the ImageNet image set, and then fine-tuned by back propagation on the target data set through migration learning to fine-tune to achieve domain adaptation.

After training the network model required by the target domain, the network model is used to extract and map features. Given a pre-trained DenseNet network, the input image k in the first convolution layer is mapped to d^1 feature maps with dimension $n^1 \times n^1$. In any position (i, j) of feature map, $1 \leq i \leq n^1$, $1 \leq j \leq n^1$, we can extract a space vector $f_{i,j} \in R^{d^1}$ with dimension d^1, which is called depth descriptor on position (i, j). In the first convolution layer of image C, a total of $n^1 \times n^1$ depth descriptors can be extracted. The depth descriptors set of the first convolution layer is $F_c^1 = \{f_{1,1}^1, f_{1,2}^1, \ldots, f_{n^1,n^1}^1\} \in R^{d^1 \times n^1}$, F_c^1 can be used as the feature set of image C, and the generated feature description set is $F = \{F_1^1, F_2^1, \ldots, F_N^1\}$, where N is the number of images. In order to generate a compact global image representation, F is hashed by the algorithm.

The feature activation of fully connected layer introduced by the input image can be regarded as visual features, which can be used to improve the accuracy of image classification and retrieval. However, these features have high dimensions and are not suitable for direct hashing. Therefore, we set a function to learn the image representation of a specific region and a set of similar hashes (or binary codes) at the same time. The final output of classification layer FC10 depends on a set of hidden attributes, and images with similar binary activation will have similar labels. The hash layer *H* is embedded between FC9 and FC10, as shown in Fig. 1. Hash layer *H* is a fully connected layer, which is not only adjusted by the later coding semantic features and FC10 layer, but also learns the rich abstraction of image features from FC9, bridging the intermediate features and advanced semantics. In order to facilitate the training of network model, hash function is designed as continuous function. Therefore, in our design, the neurons in hash layer *H* are activated by sigmoid function, so the activation is approximately {0, 1}, as shown in Eq. 1.

$$[Out^j(H)]^T = [sigmoid(W * F_C^H + b)]^T \tag{1}$$

The initial weight of DenseNet network is designed as the pre-training model of ImageNet, and the weight of hashing layer *H* and FC10 layer is initialized randomly. Under supervised learning, the hash code can be adjusted from local sensitivity hash to a form that better matches the data. This model is capable of learning both the visual representation of a specific domain and the hashing-like function without modifying the large-scale network model. The main function of hash layer *H* is to establish the mapping relationship between the hash layer and the extracted features of the middle layer, so that the hash code corresponds to the features one by one. Compared with the heterogeneous samples, the Hamming distance of the similar samples after passing through the hash

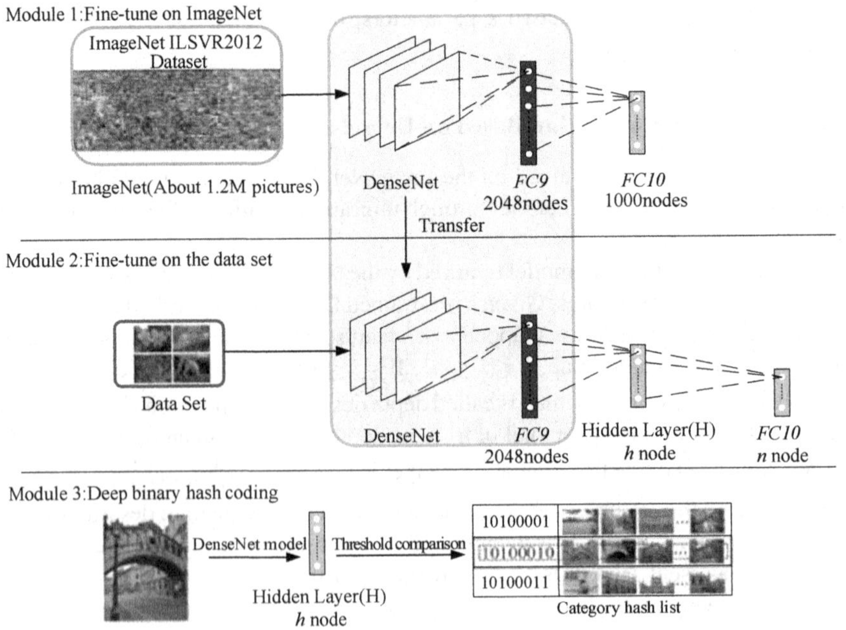

Fig. 1. The hash model based on the feature of DenseNet network.

layer H is relatively close, that is, the Euclidean distance between the intermediate layer features of the similar samples is small. For a given image c, first extract the output of hashing layer H as the depth descriptor of the image in hash layer H, represented by $F_c^H = \{f_{1,1}^H, f_{1,2}^H, ..., f_{n^1,n^1}^H\}$. Secondly, we binarize the depth descriptor of hash layer H through a threshold, and obtain the binary code $H^j(H)$, as shown in Eq. 2, thus obtain the category hash table T_H corresponding to each type of image in the coverless image library. For each bit $j = 1, 2, ..., h$, where h is the number of nodes in the hash layer. The characteristic dimension after passing the hash layer is h. The binary code of output hash layer H is as follows:

$$H^j = \begin{cases} 1 \ Out^j(H) \geq 0.5, \\ 0 \ otherwise. \end{cases} \tag{2}$$

3.2 The Establishment of Inverted Index

The Densenet model is trained to get uniform and compact binary hash features. However, when the hash feature dimension is high and the quantity is large, the efficiency of linear retrieval will be relatively low. Therefore, this paper constructs a quadtree hash inverted index based on the feature that the extracted hash sequence has uniformity and intra class similarity, as shown in Fig. 2.

First, the sender divides the secret information M into h bits of information according to the length of the image hash value, and then retrieves the carrier image corresponding to the information segment in the coverless image database. In fact, the successful retrieval of secret information requires the establishment of a large enough image library to satisfy this mapping relationship, and the mapping between the secret information and the image hash requires an image database of at least 2^h images, which makes the task complicated and difficult to implement. Therefore, in order to solve the problem that the mapping between the secret information and the image hash caused too much data in the coverless image database, we classify each image and correspond with its hash code to form the same hash code of the image. In practical application, when constructing the image database, there are hash codes with different hash numbers of 8 bits, 12 bits, 16 bits, 32 bits and 64 bits for each type of image, so that each type of carrier image can represent up to five hash sequences.

Then, we construct the inverted index of the category hash table, which is divided into the following three steps:

The first step is to number all the images in the image database and assign an *ID* value to each image. Then, after adopting DeepCNNs feature hash encoding for each image, assign the obtained hash value to each type of image.

The second step is to establish a quadtree with 10 layers. Each tree node has four child nodes with values of 0, 1, 2 and 3, respectively representing four different hash values: 00, 01, 10 and 11. The *ID* value of the corresponding image is stored in each leaf node, thus forming an index table sorted by image *ID* and hash value, and each leaf node contains at least one carrier image *ID*.

In the third step, starting from the leftmost side of the quadtree, hash codes are matched in the image database according to the secret information fragments. Since the hash code generated by our hash algorithm has intra-class similarity, the secret information fragments can correspond to multiple images in a class of images, which greatly ensures the difference of the carrier images transmitted.

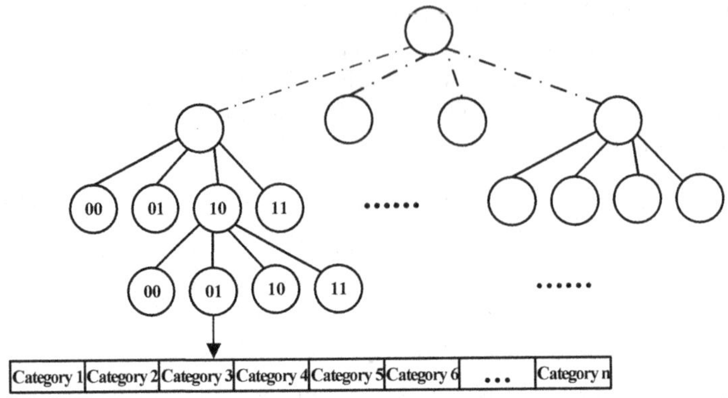

Fig. 2. Image library quadtree index structure.

3.3 Hiding and Extraction of Secret Information

Using the method based on deep convolution feature, coverless information hiding will be realized through the following steps, as shown in Fig. 3. After the sender encrypts the auxiliary information, the deep hash mapping algorithm and the encryption key of the auxiliary information M_k are shared by both parties.

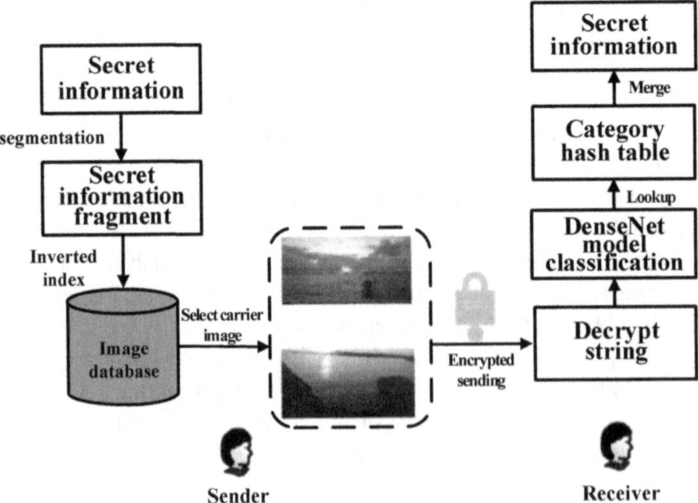

Fig. 3. Secret information hiding and recovery.

The sender will hide the secret information through the following three steps, as shown in Algorithm 1.

The first step is the segmentation of secret information. Since each carrier image hides h-bit secret information in the form of hash value, in the process of steganography, the encrypted secret information M must be divided into t h-bit secret information segments M_t, as shown in Eq. 3. I represents the length of secret information. Considering that the last segment of the secret information M may be less than h bits when it is divided, several bits of 0 are filled at the end of the last segment of the secret information to achieve the h-bit steganography capacity.

$$t = \begin{cases} \frac{I}{h}, & I\%h = 0 \\ \frac{I}{h} + 1, & otherwise \end{cases} \tag{3}$$

The second step is to index the carrier image P_{cover} which maps with the secret information. Through the natural image database $\mathrm{P} = \{\mathrm{P}_1, \mathrm{P}_2, \ldots \mathrm{P}_N\}$ established in the previous step, the quadtree index structure is used to search for the carrier image $\mathrm{Po_i}$ corresponding to each segment of secret information t_i, where $i = 1, 2, \ldots, t$, so that the value of all nodes in the retrieval path is the same as that of the secret information segment, and an image is randomly selected on the leaf node as the carrier image Po_i of this segment of secret information.

The third step is to send the indexed carrier image $P_{cover} = \{P_{O_1}, P_{O_2}, \ldots, P_{O_t}\}$ and the encrypted auxiliary information M_t to the receiver.

The receiver receives all the carrier images $P_{cover} = \{P_{O_1}, P_{O_2}, \ldots, P_{O_t}\}$ in turn and inputs them into the trained DenseNet network for classification. The classification result $Out(P_{O_i})$ corresponds to the category m_i of the carrier image P_{O_i}. Then, the binary sequence H_i^j mapped by the category m_i is obtained by looking up the category hash table T_H. Finally, the sequencing order $ID = \{id_i | i = 1, 2\ldots, t\}$ of each carrier image P_{O_i} is extracted from the auxiliary information M_k through decryption, and successively connect the binary sequence H_i^j mapped by the carrier image P_{O_i}, that is, the secret information M is recovered.

Algorithm 1: Coverless image information hiding algorithm based on deep convolution features

---

Input: Image database $P = \{P_1, P_2, \ldots P_N\}$; Secret message M of length I;
Output: Carrier image set mapped with secret information fragments $\mathrm{P_{cover}} = \{\mathrm{P_{O_1}}, \mathrm{P_{O_2}}, \ldots, \mathrm{P_{O_t}}\}$
1: *for i* =1 *to t do*
2: according to Eq. 3, cut secret message M: $M_t = Cut(M)$:
3: $\mathrm{P_{O_i}}$= Quadtree Index (P, M_i)
4: *end for*
5: Get the selected pictures $\mathrm{P_{cover}} = \{\mathrm{P_{O_1}}, \mathrm{P_{O_2}}, \ldots, \mathrm{P_{O_t}}\}$
6: *return* $\mathrm{P_{cover}}$

---

4 Experimental Results and Analysis

4.1 Data Set

This paper uses the public data sets.

Calded-101 Data Set: This data set contains 101 categories of images, each categories contains approximately 40–800 images, most of which are 50 images/ category, and the size of each image is about 300 × 200 pixels.

Caldot-256 Data Set: This data set contains 257 categories of images, a total of 30,608 images, each category has approximately 80–110 images, and the size of each image is about 250 × 150 pixels.

Cifar-10 Data Set: Each category of this data set contains 6000 32 × 32 color images, and there are altogether 10 categories. During the training, 5000 pieces are randomly selected from each class as the training set, and 1000 pieces are randomly selected as the verification set. During the test, 100 pieces of data from each category are randomly selected as the test set.

4.2 Experimental Analysis

The environment of our experiment was written in Python language under Windows 10 system, using Intel(R) Core (TM) i5-8400 CPU, 16.00 GB RAM and a Nvidia GeForce GTX 1080Ti GPU. We completed this experiment on the deep learning open-source framework TensorFlow.

Capacity Analysis. The capacity of the existing coverless image steganography based on mapping rules is usually determined by the dimension h of H^j. The bigger h is, the larger the capacity is. Accordingly, the number of carrier images N_p required to hide fixed-length secret information is small, as shown in Eq. 4. Theoretically, the H^j dimension of a hash sequence can be arbitrary. However, the increase of hash sequence dimension increases the difficulty of retrieving carrier images and reduces the robustness of the algorithm. Therefore, we analyze and discuss the dimension h of hash sequence.

$$N_p = \frac{I}{h} \tag{4}$$

Where N_p is the number of carrier images transmitting secret information, and I represents the length of secret information.

Selection of Dimension h of Hash Sequence. There are certain rules for the setting of h. We express the category information in an image dataset as $C = \{c_1, c_2, \ldots, c_m\}$, where m is the total number of image categories. As the hash code of image features is generally represented by two numbers, we select 0 and 1 in this paper.

In the hash layer H, at least min_h node, namely min_h-bit features, are required to represent the image feature, which is calculated as shown in Eq. 5 below, that is, to ensure that each different category in the image data set has at least one unique hash feature code.

$$min\_h = log_2 m \tag{5}$$

And the maximum value of h is set to max_h, the maximum value of h should not exceed the number of nodes in the full connection layer of the previous layer of DenseNet network, because the purpose of adding hash layer h is to reduce the dimension of a layer of output characteristics, and use low dimension features to represent the image features of this kind, so as to reduce the retrieval time. Therefore, the value range of h is shown in Eq. 6 below.

$$min\_h \leq h \leq max\_h \tag{6}$$

When h is selected within this range, it will not increase the training burden of the model due to excessive selection, resulting in information redundancy in features and low efficiency of hash coding. Moreover, it will not lead to the inability of the extracted features to express the content of the image and the inability to distinguish various images because the selection is too small. In this paper, different h values are selected to verify the influence of hash feature dimension on classification accuracy, and the results are shown in Table 1.

Table 1. The influence of different hash dimensions to the network accuracy.

Data set	Network name	The dimension h of the hash sequence				
		$h = 8$	$h = 12$	$h = 16$	$h = 32$	$h = 64$
Caltch-101	DenseNet121	37.94%	37.64%	81.24%	72.92%	82.12%
	DenseNet169	36.93%	37.82%	43.54%	62.39%	83.95%
	DenseNet201	51.27%	74.69%	83.36%	91.39%	92.45%
	ResNet50	46.31%	67.55%	79.23%	89.14%	91.74%
Caltch-256	DenseNet121	24.43%	41.06%	58.13%	75.68%	77.69%
	DenseNet169	12.10%	13.18%	16.52%	21.94%	52.39%
	DenseNet201	26.23%	53.57%	70.12%	80.12%	81.34%
	ResNet50	18.93%	31.82%	44.58%	68.26%	74.94%
Cifar-10	DenseNet121	91.13%	88.85%	89.55%	91.42%	91.48%
	DenseNet169	92.64%	92.56%	93.03%	92.93%	92.78%
	DenseNet201	93.15%	93.79%	93.92%	94.08%	94.14%
	ResNet50	90.31%	90.64%	90.80%	91.82%	91.83%

It can be seen from Table 1 that on the caldot-101 data set, when $h = 8$, the hash code of each type of image is greatly different, and the network model is difficult to distinguish the category of each type of image. Therefore, it is difficult to carry out category mapping according to the different hash sequence of each type of image. With the increase of H, the classification effect of DenseNet network is getting better and better, in which the DenseNet201 network shows a good classification performance, and each category of hash code has a strong representational power. Therefore, in this paper, we set the range of h value between 16 and 64, which is different from the algorithms in literature [2, 3, 13], and these algorithms all use a fixed length. When conducting experiments on Cifar-10, the DenseNet network and ResNet50 network have similar classification effect, because each type of image contains up to 5000 images, so the network learns more features of the images.

Experimental results are shown in Table 2. Transmitting the same secret information without considering image segmentation, Hash-SIFT [2] requires the least number of carrier images with the largest capacity. Since the fixed Hash sequence dimension h is 18, the number of image samples required by the algorithm is at least 2^{18} carrier images, which is difficult to achieve in reality. In contrast, the h value of Pixel [13] and BOF_SIFT [3] is only 8, and their capacity is relatively low. As can be seen from the table, the capacity of our method is second only to that of literature [2]. When transmitting secret information of 1B and 10B, the required encrypted images are even less than that of literature [2].

Table 2. The steganographic capacity comparison.

Algorithm	N_p				h
	1B	10B	100B	1KB	
Pixel [13]	1	10	100	1024	8
Hash_SIFT [2]	2	6	46	457	18
BOF_SIFT [3]	1	10	100	1024	8
DenseNet_DWT [6]	2–9	7–81	55–801	548–8193	1–15
The algorithm of this article	1	2–10	50–100	500–1000	8–64

Hash Feature Analysis. After training Caltech-101 data set with DenseNet network, the features of hash layer H can be extracted. According to Eq. 2, the hash features can be binarized to obtain the binary-valued feature of this category of image, in which part of the category features of Caltech-101 data set are shown in Table 3. Each category of graph in the data set can be represented by 16-bit binary hash code, which indicates that the extracted image hash features are compact and have intra class similarity.

Robustness. In the image processing, there will be various operations such as filtering, enhancement, JPEG compression and noise addition, but the content of the image will not be changed. This is to save channel resources in the process of transmission, so the dense carrier will be damaged in the transmission process with high probability. In view of this situation, robustness is an important index to measure the performance of hash algorithm. Strong robustness, low steganography capacity, and those with poor robustness have high steganography capacity, so we need a balance between steganographic capacity and robustness. On the one hand, the steganography capacity of hashing algorithm should be improved to meet the requirement of transmitting secret information. On the other hand, the hash algorithm needs to be robust enough to withstand some normal operations in image processing. Therefore, coverless image information hiding must take into account

Table 3. The binary hash code of images.

images	Categories in the data set	Hash binary Code Characteristics (16 bits)
	27	0111111010010111
	2	1011111011111110
	90	0010001100001001

the damage of carrier image and the non-malicious threat, so the carrier image has certain robustness to the general lossy compression technology. In this paper, the carrier image is rotated, translated and scaled as shown in Table 4. Then the deep neural network DenseNet is used to extract the hash binary sequence to verify the robustness of this algorithm.

Table 4. Noise parameters.

Attack type	Specific parameters
JPEG compression	The quality factor Q is 10%, 30%, 50%, 70%, 90%
Gaussian noise	Mean value $\mu = 0$, variance σ is 0.001, 0.005 and 0.1
Salt and pepper noise	Mean value $\mu = 0$, variance σ is 0.001, 0.005 and 0.1
Speckle noise	Mean value $\mu = 0$, variance σ is 0.01, 0.05 and 0.1
The median filter	Window size 1×1, 3×3, 5×5, respectively with 7×7
Median filtering	Window size 1×1, 3×3, 5×5, respectively with 7×7
Gaussian low-pass filtering	Window size 1×1, 3×3, 5×5, respectively with 7×7
Center attack	The ratio is 20% and 50%
Edge attack	The ratio is 20% and 50%
Rotation	The rotation angle is 10°, 30° and 50°
Scaling	The ratio is 0.3, 0.5, 0.75, 1.5, 3
Gamma correction	The gamma correction coefficient is 0.8

Fig. 4. Partial noise examples.

Table 5. Success rate of recovery under different noise attacks.

Noise attack	Parameter	Accuracy		
		h = 16	h = 32	h = 64
JPEG compression	Q (10)	81.77%	89.09%	89.73%
	Q (30)	83.13%	91.39%	91.56%
	Q (50)	83.66%	90.68%	91.50%
	Q (70)	83.19%	91.39%	92.04%
	Q (90)	83.30%	91.33%	92.27%
Gaussian noise	σ (0.001)	79.53%	87.85%	87.37%
	σ (0.005)	79.59%	87.20%	87.20%
	σ (0.1)	79.12%	86.90%	87.20%
Salt and pepper noise	σ (0.001)	83.19%	91.33%	91.92%
	σ (0.005)	81.95%	90.21%	91.21%
Speckle noise	σ (0.01)	83.24%	90.74%	92.21%
	σ (0.05)	77.99%	85.84%	85.37%
	σ (0.1)	70.38%	77.46%	76.81%
The median filter	(1 × 1)	83.42%	91.45%	92.15%
	(3 × 3)	82.06%	89.56%	91.27%
	(5 × 5)	78.88%	86.08%	89.03%
	(7 × 7)	75.75%	81.89%	85.25%
Median filtering	(1 × 1)	83.42%	91.45%	92.15%
	(3 × 3)	81.95%	89.44%	91.33%
	(5 × 5)	78.23%	86.25%	88.02%

(continued)

Table 5. *(continued)*

Noise attack	Parameter	Accuracy		
		h = 16	h = 32	h = 64
	(7 × 7)	73.92%	80.65%	84.54%
Gaussian low-pass filtering	(1 × 1)	83.42%	91.45%	92.15%
	(3 × 3)	83.19%	91.09%	92.15%
	(5 × 5)	83.19%	91.03%	92.09%
	(7 × 7)	83.19%	91.03%	92.09%
Center attack	1%	80.47%	88.97%	85.60%
	5%	58.64%	62.06%	65.96%
	10%	46.90%	39.53%	49.50%
	20%	27.02%	13.98%	28.32%
Edge attack	10%	82.18%	90.56%	91.45%
	20%	82.12%	90.32%	91.62%
Rotation	10°	76.64%	68.44%	83.95%
	30°	23.66%	25.49%	29.38%
	50°	10.56%	14.51%	15.10%
Translation	(80, 50)	47.79%	52.86%	58.41%
	(160, 100)	10.09%	10.91%	14.81%
	(320, 200)	00.59%	00.41%	00.35%
Zooming	0.3	72.86%	78.82%	76.93%
	0.5	81.77%	88.20%	89.26%
	0.75	83.13%	90.62%	90.97%
	1.5	83.24%	91.21%	92.45%
	3.0	83.36%	91.50%	92.21%
Gamma correction	σ (0.1)	83.19%	91.15%	92.09%

In this paper, we use the 16-bit, 32-bit and 64-bit hash codes trained by DenseNet201 network to conduct robustness experiments on Caltch-101 data set. The test set we used has 1695 pictures. The noise-adding process as shown in Table 4 is carried out respectively, and the noise-adding pictures are shown in Fig. 4. The noisy image is input into the trained DenseNet model, and the classification accuracy is tested. The results are shown in Table 5.

As can be seen from Table 5, the DenseNet201 hash network we trained has good anti-robustness. It is still robust to JPEG compression, Gaussian noise, Speckle noise, the median filter, Median filtering, Gaussian low-pass filtering, Edge attack, Gamma correction and other noises. For the Middle attack, Geometric attacks such as rotation, translation, especially for translation (320,200) and rotation of 50 degrees almost no robustness, this is because the image size of the Caltch-101 data set we used is difficult to meet this type of noise processing. After the noise was added, the image appeared completely black, so that it was impossible to use the network to learn the image characteristics and correctly classify it.

When 1695 test images were set to JPEG compression with quality factors of 10, 30, 50, 70 and 90, the robustness was enhanced with the increase of h for different h values. Especially when $h = 64$ bits, the DenseNet201–64 network we trained still had the accuracy of 92.27%.

Even the DenseNet201-32 network had an accuracy of no less than 86.90% when set to a Gaussian noise with variance σ of 0.001, 0.005, and 0.1 for 1,695 test images.

Table 6. Robustness comparison between ours and literature [2].

Noise	Parameter	Literature [2]	The method of this paper
JPEG compression	Q (10)	58.62%	81.77%
Gaussian noise	σ (0.001)	52.87%	79.53%
Salt and pepper noise	σ (0.001)	86.21%	83.19%
Speckle noise	σ (0.01)	62.07%	83.24%
The median filter	(3 × 3)	77.01%	82.06%
Median filtering	(3 × 3)	87.36%	81.95%
Gaussian low-pass filtering	(3 × 3)	95.40%	83.19%
Center attack	3%	35.63%	83.42%
Edge attack	3%	48.28%	83.42%
Rotation	10°	01.15%	76.64%
Translation	(80, 50)	01.15%	47.79%
Zooming	3.0	97.70%	83.36%

The DenseNet201-64 and DenseNet201-32 networks have a similar accuracy of more than 90% when set with 1695 test images plus variance σ noise of 0.001 and 0.005, respectively.

When setting different window sizes for median filtering, with the increase of window size, the DenseNet201-64 and DenseNet201-32 networks we trained have similar accuracy.

According to the experimental results in Table 6, compared with the traditional feature method based on SIFT [2], the deep convolution neural network can effectively improve the robustness of image hashing. In particular, the deep convolutional neural network still has strong robustness for image rotation and translation operations. In addition, in actual applications, different deep hash network models should be selected according to the specific carrier image.

5 Conclusion

The DenseNet network is trained to learn the category hash sequence of the image, and a quadtree index is constructed with the secret information to realize the mapping steganography of the secret information. Compared with the traditional coverless steganography, it has higher steganography capacity and stronger robustness. Since coverless steganography has the ability of natural anti steganalysis, the algorithm proposed in this paper also has high security. However, when constructing an image database, a large image set and secret information need to be mapped, resulting in high computational overhead.

Acknowledgement. The author would like to thank the support of Central South University of Forestry & Technology and the support of National Science Fund of China.

Funding Statement. This project is supported by the Degree & Postgraduate Education Reform Project of Hunan Province under Grant 2019JGYB154, the Postgraduate Excellent teaching team Project of Hunan Province under Grant [2019]370-133, the National Natural Science Foundation of China under Grant 61772561, the Science Research Projects of Hunan Provincial Education Department under Grant 18A174, the Science Research Projects of Hunan Provincial Education Department under Grant 18C0262 and the Natural Science Foundation of Hunan Province under Grant 2020JJ4141.

References

1. Zhou, Z., Sun, H., Harit, R., Chen, X., Sun, X.: Coverless image steganography without embedding. In: Huang, Z., Sun, X., Luo, J., Wang, J. (eds.) ICCCS 2015. LNCS, vol. 9483, pp. 123–132. Springer, Cham (2015). https://doi.org/10.1007/978-3-319-27051-7_11
2. Zheng, S., Wang, L., Ling, B., Donghui, H.: Coverless information hiding based on robust image hashing. In: Huang, D.-S., Hussain, A., Kyungsook Han, M., Gromiha, M. (eds.) ICIC 2017. LNCS (LNAI), vol. 10363, pp. 536–547. Springer, Cham (2017). https://doi.org/10.1007/978-3-319-63315-2_47
3. Yuan, C., Xia, Z., Sun, X.: Coverless image steganography based on SIFT and BOF. J. Internet Technol. **18**(2), 435–442 (2017)
4. Zhou, Z., Cao, Y., Sun, X.: Coverless information hiding based on bag-of-words model of image. J. Appl. Sci. **34**(5), 527–536 (2016)
5. Deng, Y.: Image Hidden Information Detection for Hugo Steganography Algorithm. Central South University of Forestry and Technology (2014)

6. Liu, Q., Xiang, X., Qin, J., Tan, Y., Luo, Y.: Coverless steganography based on image retrieval of densenet features and DWT sequence mapping. Knowl.-Based Syst. **192**(15), 105375–105389 (2020)
7. Lu, H., Shao, L.: Coverless test paper disguise combined with non-direct transmission and random codebook. J. Appl. Sci. **36**(2), 331–346 (2018)
8. Otori, H., Kuriyama, S.: Data-embeddable texture synthesis. In: Butz, A., Fisher, B., Krüger, A., Olivier, P., Owada, S. (eds.) SG 2007. LNCS, vol. 4569, pp. 146–157. Springer, Heidelberg (2007). https://doi.org/10.1007/978-3-540-73214-3_13
9. Otori, H., Kuriyama, S.: Texture synthesis for mobile data communications. IEEE Comput. Graph. Appl. **29**(6), 74–81 (2009)
10. Wu, K., Wang, C.: Steganography using reversible texture synthesis. EEE Trans. Image Process. **2**(5), 99–110 (2016)
11. Xu, J., et al.: Hidden message in a deformation-based texture. Vis. Comput. **31**(12), 1653–1669 (2014). https://doi.org/10.1007/s00371-014-1045-z
12. Huang, G., Liu, Z., Laurens, V., Weinberger, K.: Densely connected convolutional networks. In: Proceedings of the IEEE Conference on Computer Vision and Pattern Recognition, pp. 2261–2269. IEEE Computer Society, Washington (2017)
13. Chen, X., Sun, H., Tobe, Y., Zhou, Z., Sun, X.: Coverless information hiding method based on the Chinese character encoding. J. Internet Technol. **18**(2), 313–320 (2017)

Data Detection and Recognition

Fusion and Visualization Design of Violence Detection and Geographic Video

Qiming Liang[1], Chuanqi Cheng[2], Yong Li[1,2](✉), Kaikai Yang[1], and Bowei Chen[1,3]

[1] Engineering University of PAP, Xi'an 710086, China
liyong@nudt.edu.cn
[2] Joint Laboratory of Counter-Terrorism Command and Information Engineering, Xi'an 710086, China
[3] Key Laboratory of the Armed Police Force On Network and Information Security, Xi'an 710086, China

Abstract. The fusion of violence detection and geographic video (GeoVideo) helps to strengthen the comprehensive dynamic perception of the objective area and better maintain social security and stability. To address the problem that the surveillance screen is fragmented from the geographic space after the occurrence of an abnormal situation in the surveillance scene by combining the positions of cameras to detect where it occurs, the violence detection and geographic video is fused to implement the visualization design. Firstly, we adopt the action detection algorithm to detect the violent actions in the video, and output the position information of the subject in the image coordinate system; then we map the position information in the image coordinate system to the world coordinate system to realize the mapping of the dynamic information obtained by the deep learning model to the static geographic space; finally, the position information of the subject is automatically marked in the remote sensing image to complete the visualization design. The results show that the fusion and visualization design of violence detection and geographic video can accurately map the location information in the surveillance screen to geographic space, which helps to grasp the global security situation of the surveillance scene.

Keywords: Violence detection · Geospatial mapping · Visualization · Information fusion · GeoVideo

1 Introduction

Violence detection is an important research scenario for action detection, and has broad application prospects in the fields of video content review and intelligent security. Real-time detection of violence through surveillance video helps Police departments, security companies and other functional departments to timely find abnormal situations in the duty area and better maintain social security and stability. GeoVideo is a new way to integrate image space information and geospatial information for information expression [1–3], which can fuse dynamic data information in surveillance video with static geospatial implementation information, and visually map the dynamic information in the real

Z. Cai et al. (Eds.): NCTCS 2021, CCIS 1494, pp. 33–46, 2021.
https://doi.org/10.1007/978-981-16-7443-3_3

world perceived by surveillance video in static geospatial. The combination of violence detection and geographic video, the fusion and visualization of location information and action category information obtained from violence detection with geospatial design can help strengthen the global grasp of surveillance scenes by on-duty security personnel.

According to the way of feature extraction, the methods of action detection include traditional manual feature extraction as well as automatic feature extraction, which are also known as deep learning-based feature extraction method [4–8]. The algorithms SlowFast [9], YOWO [10], and YOWOv2 [11], which are currently effective in action detection, all use deep learning-based feature extraction methods. The literature [12] achieves a simple fusion of action recognition and geospatial information, but the traditional method of manual feature extraction is used in the process of recognizing actions, which has limited effect on the recognition of actions and no visualization design of the fused results. The literature [13] achieves an effective fusion of surveillance images with geospatial, but does not extract any dynamic information from the surveillance video. The literature [14] constructs a geovideo based on pedestrian tracking and realizes the visualization design of dynamic targets in geospatial, mapping the pedestrian trajectory information into a two-dimensional vector map. Previous research has not yet achieved effective fusion of action detection information with geospatial and visualization design, so this paper combines action detection with geovideo based on previous work.

In this paper, we first use YOLO [15] and DeepSort [16] to achieve the detection of behavior subjects, and then use SlowFast network to classify the actions. The information fusion in different spaces is achieved by constructing the intrinsic and extrinsic matrix of the camera to map the detected location information of behavior subject to the geographic space. In this paper, violence detection is combined with geographic video to realize the mapping of the information of violence occurring in the objective area to the two-dimensional remote sensing image map, and a hypermedia map with dynamic perception capability is constructed.

2 Mapping of Image Spatial Information to Geographic Space

There is a specific mapping relationship between the spatial information in the image and the geographic information in the real world, and in order to depict this relationship, we construct the image coordinate system, camera coordinate system and world coordinate system to perform the parameter operation. The image coordinate system is a two-dimensional coordinate system with the upper left point of the image as the origin, the camera coordinate system is a three-dimensional coordinate system with the focus point as the origin and the optical axis as the Z-axis, and the world coordinate system is a three-dimensional coordinate system with the ground plumb line as the Z-axis. For a point $\boldsymbol{p}$ $(u,\ y)$ in the image coordinate system and its corresponding point $P_c\left(X_c\ Y_c\ Z_c\right)$ in the camera coordinate system, the mapping relationship between the two is

$$Z_c\begin{pmatrix} u \\ v \\ 1 \end{pmatrix} = \begin{pmatrix} f_x & 0 & u_0 \\ 0 & f_y & v_0 \\ 0 & 0 & 1 \end{pmatrix}\begin{pmatrix} X_c \\ Y_c \\ Z_c \end{pmatrix} \tag{1}$$

Where (u_0, v_0) are the coordinates of the principal point in the image coordinate system, and f_x, f_y, are the pixel unit values of the focal length in the direction of the two image elements, respectively. The above equation can also be written as

$$\lambda p = KP_c \tag{2}$$

Where λ is the scale factor and K is the intrinsic matrix determined by the intrinsic parameters of the camera. The points $P_c(X_c\ Y_c\ Z_c)$ in the camera coordinate system have specific mapping relationships to the corresponding points $P_w(X_w\ Y_w\ Z_w)$ in the world coordinate system.

$$\begin{pmatrix} X_c \\ Y_c \\ Y_c \end{pmatrix} = R_{3\times3}\begin{pmatrix} X_w \\ Y_w \\ Y_w \end{pmatrix} + t_{3\times1} \tag{3}$$

$$\begin{pmatrix} X_c \\ Y_c \\ Y_c \end{pmatrix} = (R_{3\times3} \mid t_{3\times1})\begin{pmatrix} X_w \\ Y_w \\ Z_w \\ 1 \end{pmatrix} \tag{4}$$

$$P_c = (R_{3\times3} \mid t_{3\times1})\,(P_w \mid 1)^T \tag{5}$$

Where $R_{3\times3}$ is the rotation matrix, $t_{3\times1}$ is the translation matrix, and $(R_{3\times3} \mid t_{3\times1})$ constitutes the extrinsic matrix of the mapping. As a result, the mapping relationship between the point $\boldsymbol{p}$ (u, y) in the image coordinate system and the point $P_w(X_w\ Y_w\ Z_w)$ in the world coordinate system is

$$\lambda\begin{pmatrix} u \\ v \\ 1 \end{pmatrix} = \begin{pmatrix} f_x & 0 & u_0 \\ 0 & f_y & v_0 \\ 0 & 0 & 1 \end{pmatrix}(R_{3\times3} \mid t_{3\times1})\begin{pmatrix} X_w \\ Y_w \\ Z_w \\ 1 \end{pmatrix} \tag{6}$$

In this paper, only the points on the ground are considered in the world coordinate system during the experiment, so for all the points in the world coordinate system, Z_w can be written as 0. Therefore, the Eq. (6) can be further written as:

$$\begin{pmatrix} u \\ v \\ 1 \end{pmatrix} = \frac{1}{\lambda}K\,(R_{3\times2} \mid t_{3\times1})\begin{pmatrix} X_w \\ Y_w \\ 1 \end{pmatrix} = H\begin{pmatrix} X_w \\ Y_w \\ 1 \end{pmatrix} \tag{7}$$

Therefore

$$\begin{pmatrix} X_w \\ Y_w \\ 1 \end{pmatrix} = H^{-1}\begin{pmatrix} u \\ v \\ 1 \end{pmatrix} \tag{8}$$

Where

$$H^{-1} = \left(\frac{1}{\lambda}K\,(R_{3\times2} \mid t_{3\times1})\right)^{-1} \tag{9}$$

From Eq. (9), it can be seen that after obtaining the intrinsic and extrinsic matrix of the camera, the position information in the image coordinate system can be mapped to the world coordinate system to achieve the information mapping from surveillance video to geospatial.

3 Violence Detection and Its Location Information Representation

3.1 SlowFast Action Recognition

Understanding human behavior in video requires not only understanding the static spatial information in a single frame, but also the temporal information contained in the "context". As shown in Fig. 1, the SlowFast network uses parallel Slow and Fast channels to extract spatio-temporal information from video frames at the same time. SlowFast network's Slow channel efficiently extracts spatial information from images by using a 3D convolutional neural network at a lower frame rate, and the Fast channel uses a light-weight 3D convolutional neural network with a higher frame rate to extract the temporal information in consecutive frames, while the information in the Fast channel is fused into the Slow channel to achieve the fusion of spatio-temporal information. The 3D convolutional neural network used in this paper is ResNet50 [17], in which the temporal dimension of the Slow channel is 1/8 of that of the Fast channel, i.e., α is 8, and the dimension of the Slow channel is 8 times that of the Fast channel, i.e., β is 8. Therefore, the Slow channel can process 2 frames per second and the Fast channel can process 16 frames per second in the recognition process. Finally, the output results of the two channels are globally averaged and pooled to achieve the recognition of behavior types through the fully connected layer.

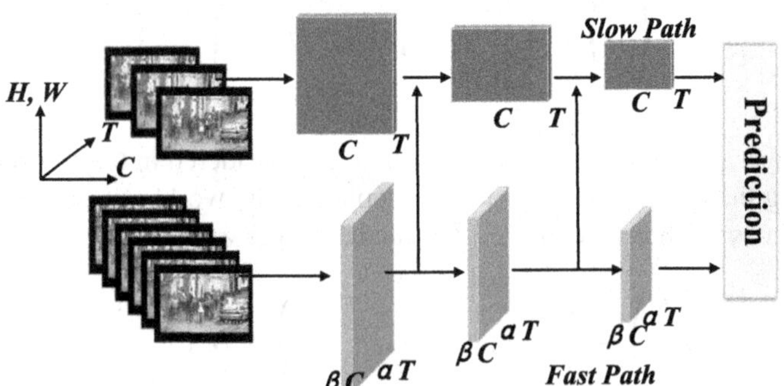

Fig. 1. SlowFast network structure diagram.

3.2 Action Detection

Action recognition is the classification of action categories, and action detection is the marking of the location of the behavior subject in the frame based on the recognition. Action recognition is the basis of action detection, and action detection is an extended expansion of the action recognition task. In order to achieve the action detection, as in Fig. 2, this paper introduces YOLOv3 target detector and DeepSort multi-object tracker on the basis of SlowFast network to detect and track the behavior subject. Specifically, for the input continuous video frames, the background frames are firstly eliminated by differential screening, the YOLOv3 detector is used to achieve the detection of pedestrians, and the coordinates of the target frame of the behavior subject are output, while the DeepSort multi-target tracker is used to distinguish different behavior subjects afterwards. Finally, the behavior subject in the target frame is sent to the SlowFast network to realize the differentiation of behavior categories, and the coordinates of the target frame, the behavior category and the category score are output, and the behavior subjects is marked in the frame to realize the action detection.

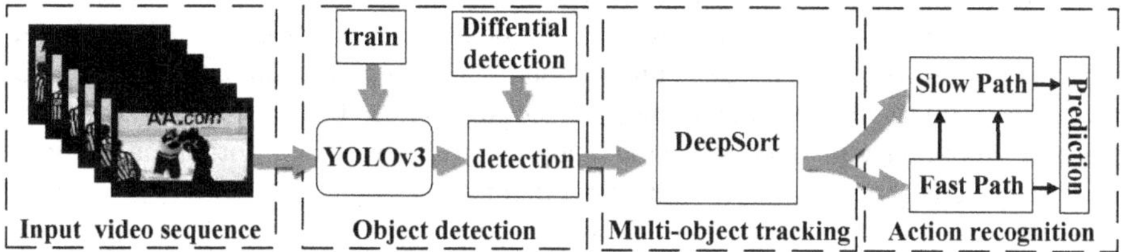

Fig. 2. Flow chart of behavior detection.

3.3 Extraction and Mapping of Behavior Subject Location Information

In order to extract the position information of the behavior subject in the image space, this paper outputs the coordinate information of the target frame detected by the target detector YOLOv3. In order to reflect the real position of the behavior subject in the image space, this paper selects the coordinates of the lower right corner of the target frame as the initial value, and further optimizes the position information by combining with the detected scenes. In this paper, a two-player fight scene is selected for the detection of violent action. For the set scene, the detection of violent action occurs in three cases:

(1) The two detected parties do not commit acts involving violence, and the location information of both is not extracted at this time.

(2) One party of the behavior is detected to have done the act involving violence, and the other party does not do the act involving violence. At this time, the coordinates of the person involved in violence are output, but there is a certain deviation between the coordinates output by the model and the real position of the behavior subject in the frame, and the coordinates need to be calibrated. Suppose the coordinates of the lower right corner of the target frame detected at this time are $p_1\ (u_1,\ v_1)$, and the coordinates of the upper left corner are $p_2\ (u_2,\ v_2)$, then the position of the behavior subject is calibrated as follows:

$$p\left(\frac{u_1 + u_2}{2},\ v_1\right) \tag{10}$$

(3)Both sides of the act are detected to do acts involving violence, i.e., both sides of the act fight with each other. At this point, the model outputs the coordinates of the bounding box of both sides of the fight, assuming that the coordinates of the lower right corner of the target box of behavior subject A are $p_1(u_1, v_1)$, the coordinates of the upper left corner are $p_2(u_2, v_2)$, and the coordinates of the lower right corner of the target box of behavior subject B are $p_3(u_3, v_3)$, the coordinates of the upper left corner are $p_4(u_4, v_4)$, then the position of the behavior subject at this point is uniformly calibrated as:

$$p\left(\frac{u_1 + u_2 + u_3 + u_4}{4}, \frac{v_1 + v_3}{2}\right) \tag{11}$$

After obtaining the position information of the behavior subject in the image coordinate system through the action detection, the position of the behavior subject in the world coordinate system can be obtained through the mapping change from the image space to the geographic space, and then the location of the behavior is marked in the remote sensing image map to realize the mapping of the dynamic information obtained from the surveillance video to the static geographic space.

$$(P_w \mid 1)^T = H^{-1}(P \mid 1)^T \tag{12}$$

Where P_w is the coordinates of the behavior subject in the world coordinate system and **P** is the coordinates of the behavior subject in the corresponding image coordinate system.

4 Experiment

4.1 Acquisition of the Intrinsic and Extrinsic Matrices

In order to obtain the intrinsic matrix of the camera, this paper adopts Zhang Zhengyou's calibration method [18] to take 16 black-and-white checkerboard calibration board photos for calibration. In the experimental process, a **Honor 20** cell phone with 1920 × 1080 pixels is used for photographing, and the side length of the checkerboard grid is 30 mm, the camera calibrator in MATLAB is used for measurement, and the results of the operation are shown in Fig. 3.

From the above figure, it can be seen that the overall average error of the calibration is 0.46 pixels, and the final calculated intrinsic matrix is:

$$K = \begin{pmatrix} 1734.548 & 0 & 957.024 \\ 0 & 1735.024 & 538.878 \\ 0 & 0 & 1 \end{pmatrix} \tag{13}$$

In order to obtain the mapped extrinsic matrix, this paper calibrates a number of points in the world coordinate system of the shooting area to correspond with the pixel points in the image coordinate system. In this paper, we adopt the algorithm of EPNP + iterative optimization [19, 20] commonly used in perspective-n-points (PNP) to measure the mapped extrinsic matrix, and the specific correspondence is shown in Table 1.

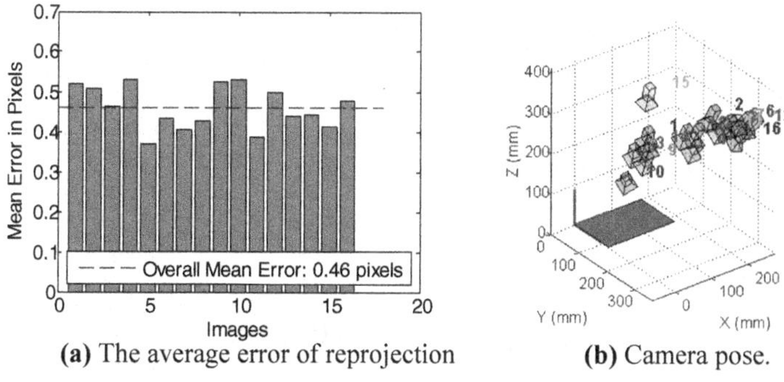

(a) The average error of reprojection (b) Camera pose.

Fig. 3. Calibration results

Table 1. Coordinate mapping relations

World coordinate	Image coordinate
(29713,16224,0)	(521,232)
(30000,20000,0)	(1024,234)
(29730,22194,0)	(1311,221)
(17998,22194,0)	(1151,33)
(15735,22194,0)	(1573,526)

The final result of the calculation is:

$$R_{3\times3} = \begin{pmatrix} 6.47787271 \times 10^{-4} & 0.999896924 & -1.43430209 \times 10^{-2} \\ 0.389417703 & -1.34630372 \times 10^{-2} & -0.920962865 \\ -0.921061036 & -4.98883825 \times 10^{-3} & -0.389386285 \end{pmatrix} \tag{14}$$

$$t_{3\times1} = \left(-19534.65036013 \ -13672.7752463 \ 40571.22851043\right)^T \tag{15}$$

$$\left(R_{3\times2} \mid t_{3\times1}\right) = \begin{pmatrix} 6.47787271 \times 10^{-4} & 0.999896924 & -19534.65036013 \\ 0.389417703 & -1.34630372 \times 10^{-2} & -13672.7752463 \\ -0.921061036 & -4.98883825 \times 10^{-3} & 40571.22851043 \end{pmatrix} \tag{16}$$

$$H^{-1} = \begin{pmatrix} 3.71180827 & 2.44414946 \times 10^{2} & 1.07508255 \times 10^{4} \\ 19.3660027 & 1.08507101 \times 10^{2} & 2.61373067 \times 10^{3} \\ 8.66480005 \times 10^{-5} & 5.56212902 \times 10^{-3} & 1 \end{pmatrix} \tag{17}$$

As in Fig. 4, after obtaining the mapped intrinsic and extrinsic matrices, the single-response matrix transformation of the surveillance video can be realized, converting the surveillance image into a bird's-eye view with real geographic information and realizing the mapping from image space to geographic space.

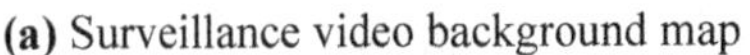

(a) Surveillance video background map

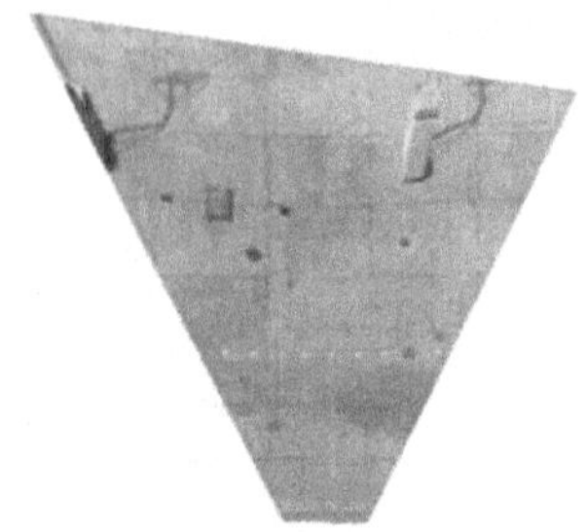

(b) Geospatial mapping of surveillance video

Fig. 4. Geospatial mapping of surveillance video.

4.2 Construction of Action Detection Model

In this paper, the programming language used in the action detection experiment is Python3.7, the deep learning framework used is Pytorch1.5, the operating system is Ubuntu16.04, the CPU is Intel I9-10920X, the GPU is accelerated by CUDA10.2, and two NVIDIA RTX2080super with 8GB of video memory are used for parallel computing. The use of pre-trained models in the experiments can avoid repetitive experiments. For the target detector YOLOv3, this paper uses a model trained on the COCO dataset, for the multi-objective tracker DeepSort this paper uses a model trained on the MOT16 [21] dataset, and for the behavior recognition network SlowFast, this paper uses a model trained on the AVA2.1 [22] dataset. The color of the border is adjusted in the detection process for the violent scenes in a targeted manner, and the red border is used to calibrate the behavior subjects who made fighting actions, and the green border is used to calibrate the rest of the actions, and the specific detection results are shown in Fig. 5.

4.3 Alignment of Geographic Information

In order to obtain the low-altitude remote orthophoto image of the surveillance video area, this paper adopts ***DJI-Inspire 2*** UAV for aerial photography, and the height of the aerial photography is 60 m. As in Fig. 6, the area captured by the surveillance video is in the red border.

In order to achieve the fusion of different spatial layers, this paper carries out field calibration in the surveillance video shooting area, as in Fig. 7(a), a total of 18 groups of control points is calibrated, and the position information of the control points in the world coordinate system is obtained. In this paper, the geospatial mapping map of surveillance video is obtained in Fig. 4(b), which can be used to query and measure geospatial information. As in Fig. 7(b), according to the coordinate information of the calibrated control points, this paper realizes the fusion of Fig. 4(b) and Fig. 6 in SuperMap software, which also completes the alignment of the surveillance video with the low-altitude remote sensing orthophoto map.

(a) Violent scenes (b) Non-violent scenes.

Fig. 5. Action detection results.

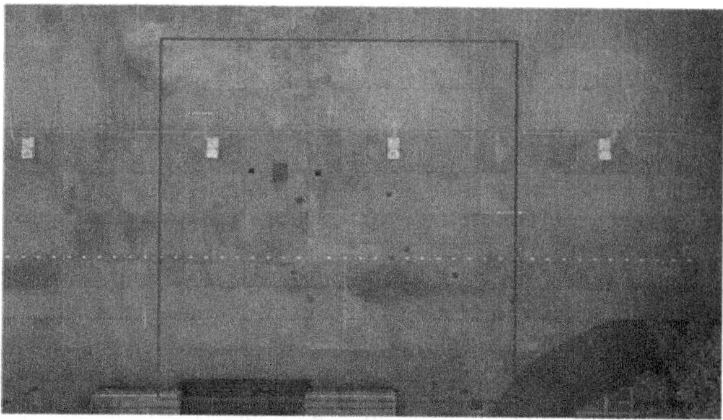

Fig. 6. Low-altitude remote sensing orthophoto image.

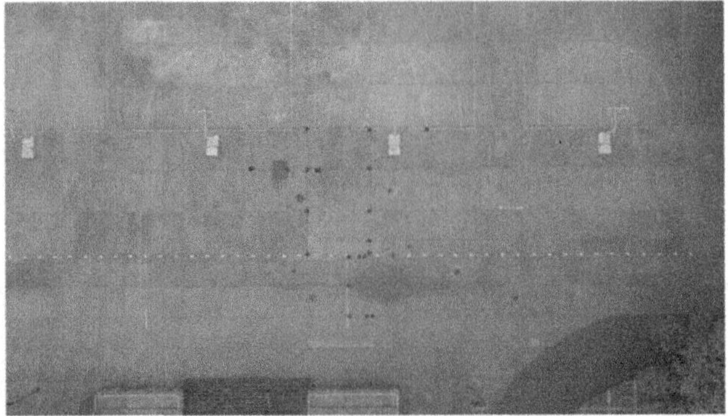

(**a**) Calibration of low-altitude remote sensing orthophoto

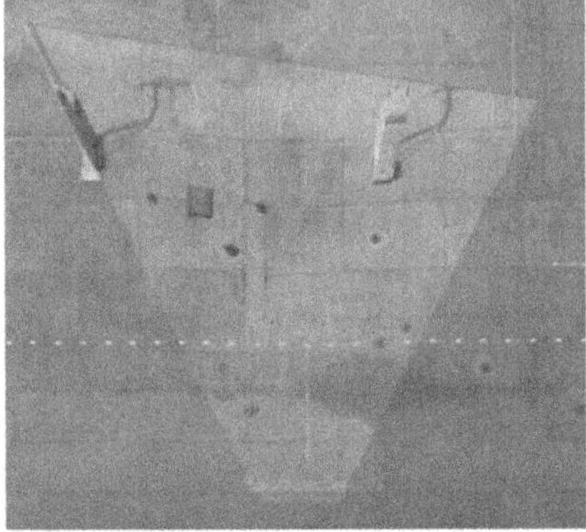

(**b**) Geographic information alignment map

Fig. 7. Geographic information alignment.

The low-altitude remote sensing orthophoto after alignment with the geospatial mapping of surveillance video achieves the fusion of image spatial information and geospatial information in the surveillance video, and the geographic information alignment map obtained after the fusion can truly reflect the location of the behavior subject in the surveillance screen in the real world.

5 Results

5.1 Fusion of Violence Detection and Geospatial Information

The SlowFast network is currently the best performing algorithm in the AVA2.1 dataset, and Table 2 shows the detection results of SlowFast in the experiments. The mean average precision (mAP) of SlowFast in the AVA2.1 dataset reaches 24.2%, and the average precision (AP) of fight/hit, reaches 40.9%, and the frames per second (FPS) processed in this paper for the action detection experiment is 16.43.

Table 2. Action detection results

mAP	AP(fight/hit)	FPS
24.2%	40.9%	16.43

In order to verify the effect of spatial mapping, 14 points are marked in the objective area for mapping transformation. The results of the mapping are shown in Table 3, where the unit of image coordinate system is pixels, and the units of world coordinate system as well as mean square error are millimeters. From the table, it can be seen that the maximum mean square error of the 14 mapped points is 64.761 mm and the minimum is 3.162 mm, and the average mean square error of the final 14 points is 28.271 mm. The mapping results show that the average error is less than 3 cm after mapping the location information of the behavior subject from the video to the geographic space, which can meet the need of judging the location information of the behavior subject in the geographic space.

Table 3. Mapping results

Image coordinates	Marked world coordinates	Mapped world coordinate system	Mean square error (unit: mm)
(679, 78)	(21683, 16202)	(21662, 16230)	24.748
(1183, 70)	(21685, 22190)	(21618, 22200)	47.901
(723, 36)	(17683, 16201)	(17605, 16249)	64.761
(521, 232)	(29731, 16201)	(29709, 16217)	19.235
(1022, 226)	(29731, 20000)	(29750, 20007)	14.317
(1022, 235)	(30000, 20000)	(30004, 20004)	4
(1035, 234)	(30000, 20010)	(30020, 20093)	60.369
(1037, 342)	(32721, 20000)	(32816, 19988)	67.708
(1072, 530)	(35732, 20000)	(35703, 20016)	23.420
(1508, 528)	(35732, 21900)	(35703, 21908)	21.272
(1573, 526)	(35732, 22190)	(35734, 22194)	3.162
(1195, 232)	(30000, 21290)	(30030, 21274)	24.041
(1282, 188)	(28493, 22190)	(28496, 22181)	6.7082
(1236, 231)	(30000, 21590)	(30016, 21578)	14.142
Mean variance on average			28.271

5.2 Spatial Information Fusion Visualization

In this paper, a video of 2 min and 35 s in length containing a two-person fight scene was taken during the experiment, in which the actors adjusted their positions in the objective area during the fight. As shown in Fig. 6, the detection results of five moments are selected for display. The left column shows the results of surveillance video violence detection, in which the location information of the actor in the screen is output during the detection process; the middle column shows the schematic diagram of surveillance video and geospatial fusion, in which the location information obtained by the violence detection model is also mapped into geospatial space after fusion; the right column shows the geospatial information map, in which the location information obtained by the violence detection model can be directly marked in the geospatial space after spatial fusion after transformation. The red dots in the diagram are the locations of the violent actions automatically marked by OpenCV based on the coordinate information output in the left column.

From Fig. 8, it can be seen that the fusion of violence detection and geographic video in this paper can accurately map the information of violence occurring in the objective area to the geographic space and visualize the violence information in the remote sensing image. The fusion of violence detection and geographic video can accurately link the surveillance images with geographic information, which helps the security personnel on duty to have a global control of the security area and help maintain the security and stability of the objective area.

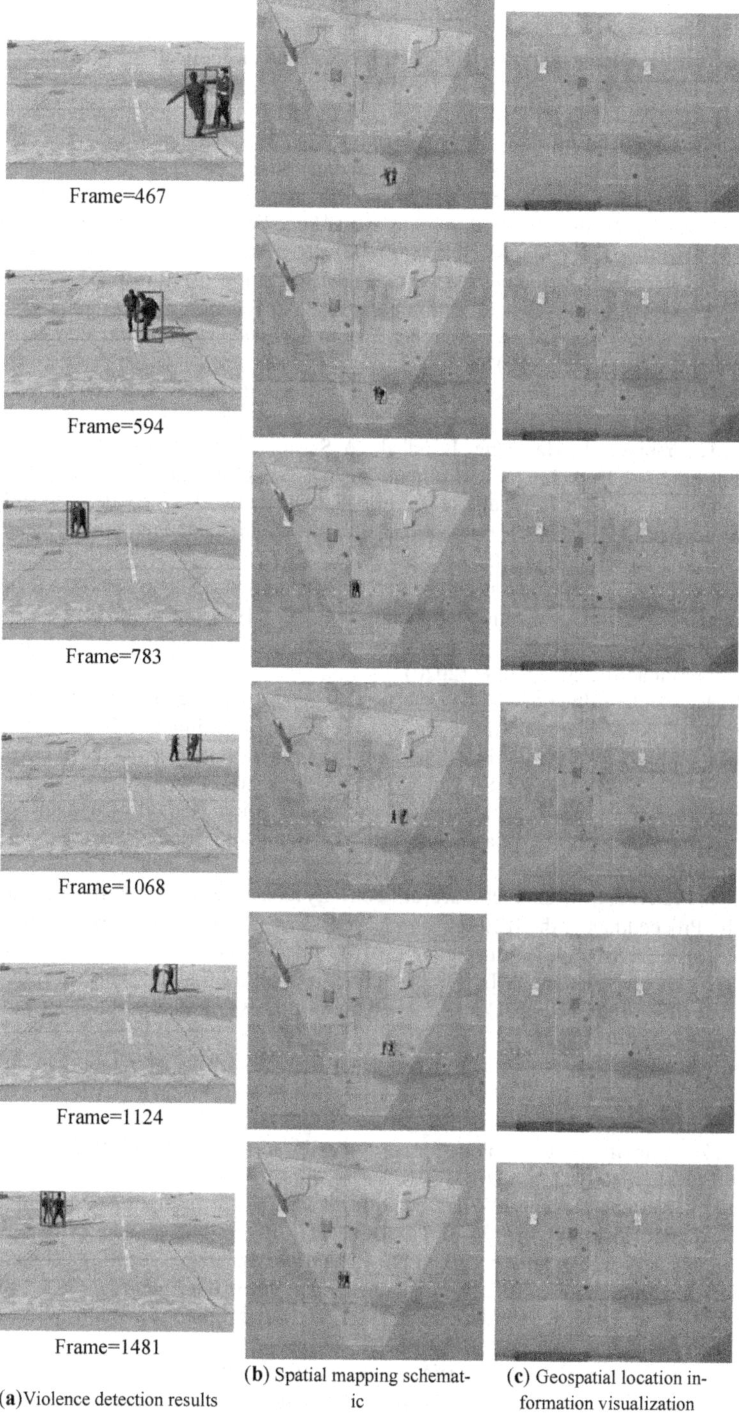

(a) Violence detection results (b) Spatial mapping schematic (c) Geospatial location information visualization

Fig. 8. Mapping visualization results.

References

1. Yun-feng, K.: Research on the GeoVideo data model and its application development. Geogr. Geo-Inf. Sci. **25**(05), 12–16 (2009)
2. Song, H., Liu, X., Lu, G., et al.: Research on enhanced expression of Geographic scene based on Video. Geogr. Geo-Inf. Sci. **28**(05), 6–9+113 (2012)
3. Xie, X., Zhu, Q., Zhang, Y., et al.: Hierarchical semantic model of geovideo. Acta Geodaetica et Cartographica Sinica **44**(5), 555 (2015)
4. Zhao, D., Zhang, J., Guo, C., et al.: A Survey of Video behavior recognition methods based on Deep Learning. Telecommun. Sci. **35**(12), 99–111 (2019)
5. Cheng, S.: Research on feature extraction and recognition of Human behavior in Video sequence. Doctor, University of Electronic Science and Technology, Chengdu China (2020)
6. Zhu, Y., Li, X., Liu, C., et al.: A comprehensive study of deep video action recognition. arXiv preprint arXiv, 2012.06567 (2020)
7. Zhang, S.: Research on the method of human behavior detection and recognition in video sequence. Doctor, Huazhong University of Science and Technology, Wuhan China (2019)
8. Qiang, C., Yibiao, D., Haisheng, L., et al.: A Summary of Human behavior recognition methods based on Deep Learning. Comput. Sci. **47**(04), 85–93 (2020)
9. Feichtenhofer, C., Fan, H., Malik, J., et al.: Slowfast networks for video recognition. In: Proceedings of the IEEE/CVF International Conference on Computer Vision, Seoul, Korea, 27 October–2 November (2019)
10. Kpüklü, O., Wei, X., et al.: You only watch once: a unified CNN architecture for real-time spatiotemporal action localization. arXiv preprint arXiv, 1911.06644 (2019)
11. Mo, S., Tan, X., Xia, J., et al.: Towards improving spatiotemporal action recognition in videos. arXiv preprint arXiv, 2012.08097 (2020)
12. Liu, L.: Research on dynamic Target Detection and behavior recognition based on Geographic constraint scene. Master, Guilin University of Technology, Guilin (2020)
13. Zhang, X., Liu, X., Wang, S.: Mutual mapping between surveillance video and 2D geospatial data. J. Wuhan Univ. (Inf. Sci. Ed.) **40**(08), 1130–1136 (2015)
14. Zhang, X., Hao, X., Li, J., et al.: Fusion and visualization method of dynamic targets in surveillance video with geospatial information. Acta Geodaetica et Cartographica Sinica **48**(11), 1415–1423 (2019)
15. Redmon, J., Divvala, S., Girshick, R., et al.: You only look once: unified, real-time object detection. In: Proceedings of the IEEE Conference on Computer Vision and Pattern Recognition, Las Vegas, USA, 27 June–29 June 2016 (2016)
16. Wojke, N., Bewley, A., Paulus, D.: Simple online and realtime tracking with a deep association metric. In: IEEE International Conference on Image Processing (ICIP), Beijing, China, 17–20 September 2017 (2017)
17. He, K., Zhang, X., Ren, S., et al.: Deep residual learning for image recognition. In: IEEE/CVF Conference on Computer Vision and Pattern Recognition (CVPR), Lag Vegas, USA, 27–29 June 2016. IEEE (2016)
18. Zhang, Z.: A flexible new technique for camera calibration. IEEE Trans. Pattern Anal. Mach. Intell. **22**(11), 1330–1334 (2000)
19. Lepetit, V., Moreno-Noguer, F., Fua, P.: EPnP: an accurate O(n) solution to the PnP problem. Int. J. Comput. Vision **81**(2), 155–166 (2009)
20. Penate-Sanchez, A., Andrade-Cetto, et al.: Exhaustive linearization for robust camera pose and focal length estimation. IEEE Trans. Pattern Anal. Mach. Intell. **35**(10), 2387–2400 (2013)
21. Milan, A., Leal-Taixé, L., Reid, I., et al.: MOT16: a benchmark for multi-object tracking. arXiv preprint arXiv, 1603.00831 (2016)
22. Gu, C., Sun, C., Ross, D.A., et al.: AVA: a video dataset of spatio-temporally localized atomic visual actions. In: Proceedings of the IEEE Conference on Computer Vision and Pattern Recognition, Salt Lake City, 18 June 2017 (2017)

A New RGB-D Gesture Video Dataset and Its Benchmark Evaluations on Light-Weighted Networks

Guojian Xiao, Zhendong Lu, Zhirong Yang, Panji Jin, Kuan Li(✉), and Jianping Yin

Dongguan University of Technology, Dongguan 523808, Guangdong, China
likuan@dgut.edu.cn

Abstract. Video-based gesture recognition plays an important role in the field of human-computer interaction (HCI), and most of the existing video-based gesture recognition works are based on traditional RGB gesture videos. Compared with RGB gesture videos, RGB-D gesture videos contain additional depth information along with each data frame. Such depth information is considered effective to help overcome the impact of illumination and background variations. So far as we know, there are few RGB-D gesture video datasets, which fully consider sufficient illumination and background variations. We believe this missing factor is quite common in daily usage scenarios and will bring non-necessary obstacles to the development of gesture recognition algorithms. Inspired by this observation, this paper uses embedded devices to collect and classify a set of RGB-D gesture videos which retain both color information and depth information, and proposes a new RGB-D gesture video data set named DG-20. Specifically, DG-20 fully considers the changes of illumination and background when capturing data, and provides more realistic RGB-D gesture video data for the future research of RGB-D gesture recognition algorithms. Furthermore, we give out the benchmark evaluations about DG-20 on two representative light-weighted 3D CNN networks. Experimental results show that the depth information encoded within RGB-D gesture videos could effectively improve the classification accuracy when dramatic changes in illumination and background exist.

Keywords: Dynamic gesture recognition · Light-weighted network · RGB-D

1 Introduction

Non-contact human-computer interactions, such as voice control, image control, video control and somatosensory control, have attracted more and more research interests [1, 2] in the field of HCI (Human Computer Interaction). Among them, gesture recognition is an important category of human-computer interaction based on images and videos. Gesture recognition could be subdivided into static gesture recognition and dynamic gesture recognition. Static gesture recognition mainly obtains gesture information through a single image, while dynamic gesture recognition parses gesture information through a set of image sequences (video clips).

Z. Cai et al. (Eds.): NCTCS 2021, CCIS 1494, pp. 47–58, 2021.
https://doi.org/10.1007/978-981-16-7443-3_4

Compared with static gesture images, dynamic gesture videos have stronger expression ability [3] and could encode more information between video frames. In other words, dynamic gestures are more expressive and practical than static gestures. In the field of dynamic gesture recognition, most studies focus on using RGB video. Zhao et al. proposed a gesture recognition algorithm which first utilizes an elliptical skin color model to segment out hand regions, then extracts the feature vector of gesture by fusing HOG features and fingertip features, finally a DAGSVM multi-classification model based on directed acyclic graph is constructed for gesture recognition [4]. In ref [5], the SGM and K-means methods are combined to segment gesture regions, then HOG features and an improved 9ULBP descriptor are fused to extract gesture features. Finally, a SVM classifier is used to do the classification. The above gesture recognition methods based on RGB videos actually utilize the appearance information of each frame in the video. In real-life scenarios, the appearances of the images and videos vary a lot under different illumination conditions and backgrounds/environments. This will definitely pose a big challenge to the design of subsequent classification and recognition algorithms.

Nowadays, depth information acquisition equipment has been miniaturized and portable. It is now realistic to deploy depth-capturable cameras in embedded devices such as mobile phones and control boxes to acquire RGB-D videos. Compared with the traditional three-channel RGB image/video, the RGB-D image/video has four channels composed by three RGB channels and one additional depth information channel. There are some researches on dynamic gesture recognition based on RGB-D images. Li et.al. obtains the initial gesture region by a segmentation algorithm integrating skin color and depth information, and then uses the distance transformation algorithm to obtain the palm position, finally Kalman filter tracking algorithm is used for gesture tracking and dynamic gestures are identified by a decision tree model [6]. A dynamic gesture recognition algorithm based on depth data and the DTW is proposed in ref [7]. The algorithm takes the bone nodes in the center of the shoulder as the reference point, and the distance between the center of the two sections and the middle of the spine as the reference distance. The related bone nodes are normalized and centralized to form the feature vector of dynamic gestures. Finally, DTW algorithm is used for dynamic gesture recognition. In the RGB-D gesture video recognition aspect, Farhood Negin proposed an RGB-D gesture video dataset PRAXIS recorded by Kinect V2, which contains specific gestures suggested by clinicians and recorded from both experts and patients performing the gesture set. The purpose of this dataset is to investigate the potential of static and dynamic upper-body gestures based on the Praxis test and their potential in a medical framework to automatize the test procedures for computer-assisted cognitive assessment of older adults. Based on this RGB-D dataset, they developed a system used by the clinicians for further assessment in decision making processes [8]. Yifan Zhang introduced a new RGB-D dataset named EgoGesture. The dataset is collected by Intel RealSenseSR300 which contains both RGB and depth data. This dataset is proposed to help egocentric (first-person view) gesture recognition algorithm design with sufficient size, variation and reality [9]. Xiujuan Chai presented a large vocabulary sign language recognition system based on the RGB-D video data input which used a novel Grassmann Covariance Matrix (GCM) representation to encode a long-term dynamic of a sign sequence; simultaneously, the discriminative kernel SVM is adopted for the sign classification [10].

Table 1. RGB-D gesture video datasets

Dataset	Introduction
Chalearn LAP IsoGD database [11–13, 18]	It includes 47933 RGB-D gesture videos. Each RGB-D video represents one gesture only, and there are 249 gestures labels performed by 21 different individuals
PRAXIS GESTURE DATASET [8]	64 volunteers, including 29 gesture categories, without specifying the size of the data set
EgoGesture [9]	It contains 2,081 RGB-D videos, 24,161 gesture samples and 2,953,224 frames from 50 distinct subjects
NYU hand pose dataset [14]	2 volunteers, a total of 72757 frames of training data and 8252 frames of test data

We carefully investigated existing RGB-D dynamic gesture datasets, as shown in Table 1. And we found that few real-life RGB-D video datasets existed. It means that most of these data sets don't consider enough about the changes of illumination and background in real-life scenes when collecting and constructing. These variations are common when classify gesture types through portable devices. Therefore, this paper uses embedded devices to collect and construct a new human-computer interaction-oriented RGB-D video data set DG-20 with full consideration of illumination and background variations. Furthermore, two representative light-weighted 3D CNN networks are used for benchmark evaluation of DG-20. In addition, DG-20 is not only limited to the light-weighted network designation, but also expected to provide effective training and reasoning data support for the future RGB-D dynamic gesture recognitions in real-life interactive scenes.

The reminder of the paper is organizing as follows: Sect. 2 presents the design principles of DG-20. In Sect. 3, we focus on the benchmark evaluation of DG-20. Finally, the concluding remarks are given in Sect. 4.

2 Design Principles of DG-20

2.1 Overview of DG-20 Dataset

The proposed DG-20 RGB-D video dataset focuses on the dynamic gesture recognition in real scenes, which contains a total of 4710 gesture segments in 20 categories. The duration of all gesture segments varies from 1.5 s to 2.5 s, with 30 frames of RGB-D images per second, and the size of each RGB-D image is 480 $\times$ 270. The overall description of DG-20 is shown in Table 2.

Four gesture acquisition volunteers demonstrated 20 kinds of actions under different scenes and different illuminations. Detailed information such as the number of videos included in each class, the average number of video frames of each class, and the standard deviation of video length (number of frames per video) [15] of each class are shown

Table 2. Dataset review

Heading level	Example
Type of data	RGB/Depth
Type of file	. NPY
Numbers of video	4710
Average frames of video	70
Average number of each class	47
Numbers of volunteer	4
Numbers of class	20

Table 3. Analysis of dataset

Class	Number of video	Average number of frames	Frame number variance
c	43	70.28	9.59
Circle	48	77.94	10.59
Come	44	70.68	12.98
Come on	49	64.51	11.78
Dislike	49	73.12	10.69
Forbid	49	74.94	11.93
Good	40	58.15	7.36
Grasp1	58	82.64	11.65
Grasp2	42	67.26	8.84
Helpless	47	62.36	8.60
Me	42	67.71	5.94
No	56	75.11	8.41
Non	41	68.93	10.40
Pat	46	65.89	7.42
Please	41	56.63	7.54
Pray	44	70.36	8.43
Pull	51	73.41	11.40
Push	44	65.20	11.43
s	64	79.59	10.05
Wave	44	65.93	6.78

in Table 3. The 20 types are chosen based on massive investigations on existing gesture recognition systems (detailed descriptions could be found on our public website). Furthermore, DG-20 reserves sufficient space for future extension.

2.2 Methods and Principles of Data Collection

Intel® RealSense D455 depth camera is used as the data acquisition device. Volunteers made each action in about 2 s according to the action specification, and ensure that there are certain differences within the same class. Each RGB-D data stream collected is saved to a video clip and annotated manually. The working interface for video capture and annotation is shown in Fig. 1.

Fig. 1. Video acquisition interface.

To fully simulate real-life human-computer interaction scenarios, DG-20 includes multiple illumination conditions, multiple background environments, and different capture distances (distance from person to camera). The main collection principles are: 1) The illumination varies within a certain range; 2) The background is randomly chosen from a background group; 3) The distance between person and the camera varies within a certain range; 4) Only very simple action specifications are given to the volunteer and no requirements about the movement speed/trajectory are given. 5) The volunteers complete the action naturally, and there is no uniform requirement for the length of the video sample. The above five principles are proposed to make the collected RGB-D video dataset conforms to the actual scene of human-computer gesture interaction as much as possible. As far as we know, there is no other RGB-D video datasets that simultaneously meet the above five principles. An example set of the video screenshots is shown in Fig. 2.

2.3 Storage of Dataset

Intel® RealSense™ Depth Cameras D455 output bag files. We transform the bag files to NPY files, which benefits future usage of the data in deep learning framework. In detail, we use the pyrealsense2 library to extract RGB image frames and the depth image frames from the bag files, and add the depth image as the fourth image channel to the original RGB image frame, and perform data enhancement on it. The public download address of this dataset and the evaluation codes is https://github.com/xiaooo-jian/DG-20.

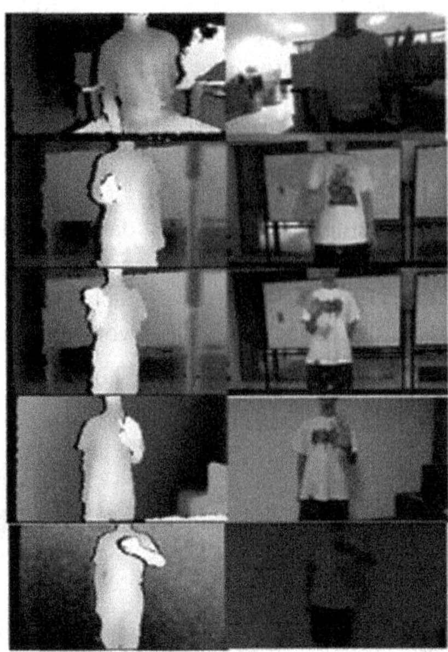

Fig. 2. DG-20 video screenshots, including different illumination conditions and different backgrounds

3 Evaluation

DG-20 is designed to facilitate designing dynamic gesture recognition algorithms for portable devices under real-life scenarios. Therefore, this paper uses two mainstream light-weighted 3D CNN networks (3D MobileNet and 3D ShuffleNet) which are suitable for deployment on embedded devices to carry out benchmark evaluations on DG-20. However, we need to clarify that DG-20 could not only be used in light-weighted neural networks, but also provides essential RGB-D data support for the research of various types of dynamic gesture recognition algorithms.

In terms of data input, this paper intuitively treats depth information as the fourth dimension of video data, and does not distinguish depth information and RGB color information at a higher level. In other words, the RGB video data is a tensor of 3 * N * W * H, and the RGB-D video data can be viewed as a tensor of 4 * N * W * H (3 represents the RGB three-channel data, 4 represents the RGB-D four-channel data, N represents the number of frames in the video, W represents the width of each frame, H represents the height of each frame). In future researches, we will fully consider the relationship between depth information and RGB information, trying to design better data format and better recognition algorithm.

3.1 Introduction of 3D MobileNet and 3D ShuffleNet

3D MobileNet begins with a convolutional layer, followed by 13 MobileNet blocks [16], ending with a linear layer. Table 4 shows the detail architecture of a 3D MobileNet.

Table 4. The architecture of 3D MobileNet

Layer/Stride	Repeat	Output size
Input clip		4* × 32 × 256 × 256
Conv (3 × 3 × 3)/s (1, 2, 2)	1	32 × 16 × 128 × 128
Block/s (2 × 2 × 2)	1	64 × 16 × 64 × 64
Block/s (2 × 2 × 2)	1	128 × 8 × 32 × 32
Block/s (1 × 1 × 1)	1	128 × 8 × 32 × 32
Block/s (2 × 2 × 2)	1	256 × 4 × 16 × 16
Block/s (1 × 1 × 1)	1	256 × 4 × 16 × 16
Block/s (2 × 2 × 2)	1	512 × 2 × 8 × 8
Block/s (1 × 1 × 1)	5	512 × 2 × 8 × 8
Block/s (1 × 1 × 1)	1	1024 × 2 × 8 × 8
Block/s (1 × 1 × 1)	1	1024 × 2 × 8 × 8
AvgPool (1 × 4 × 4)/s (1, 1, 1)	1	1024 × 1 × 1 × 1
Linear (1024)	1	20

Notice that when using data in RGB format, the number of channels (mark in the table by '*') should be 3, instead of 4.

Table 5. The architecture of 3D ShuffleNet

Layer/Stride	Repeat	Output size
Input clip		4* × 32 × 256 × 256
Conv (3 × 3 × 3)/s (1, 2, 2)	1	24 × 32 × 128 × 128
MaxPool (3 × 3 × 3)/s (2, 2, 2)	1	24 × 16 × 64 × 64
Block/s (2 × 2 × 2)	1	240 × 8 × 32 × 32
Block/s (1 × 1 × 1)	3	240 × 8 × 32 × 32
Block/s (2 × 2 × 2)	1	480 × 4 × 16 × 16
Block/s (1 × 1 × 1)	7	480 × 4 × 16 × 16
Block/s (2 × 2 × 2)	1	960 × 2 × 8 × 8
Block/s (1 × 1 × 1)	3	960 × 2 × 8 × 8
Conv (1 × 1 × 1)/s (1, 1, 1)	1	960 × 1 × 1 × 1
AvgPool (1 × 4 × 4)/s (1, 1, 1)	1	960 × 1 × 1 × 1
Linear	1	20

3D ShuffleNet uses two new operations, which are point wise group convolution and channel shuffle. 3D ShuffleNet [17] begins with a convolutional layer, followed by 16

ShuffleNet blocks, and then a convolutional layer and finally ending with a linear layer. Table 5 shows the architecture of 3D-ShuffleNet.

3.2 Experimental Setup

In order to evaluate the actual performances of the above two light-weighted neural networks on DG-20, 3D MobileNet and 3D ShuffleNet are used as classification models, and all RGB-D video streams and RGB video streams (without depth information) in DG-20 are used as training and testing data, trying to demonstrate how the depth information could help overcome the impacts of variations of background and illumination conditions.

Table 6. Experimental environment

Deep Learning framework	PyTorch
Programming language	Python 3.7
Operating system	Ubuntu 18.04.5
CPU	Xeon Silver 4210R
GPU	GeForce RTX 3090
Memory	64G

We randomly divide 4710 video data into training set and test set by a 1: 1 ratio. The optimizer of all the network is Adam, and the initial learning rate is 3e−5. With the iteration of training, the learning rate will gradually decay to ensure that loss decreases smoothly to the optimal solution.

3.3 Benchmark Results on DG-20

3D MobileNet and 3D ShuffleNet [19] are used as classification models and RGB-D video streams and RGB video streams in DG-20 are used as training and testing data, there will be four combinations:

- 3D MobileNet + RGB
- 3D MobileNet + RGB-D
- 3D ShuffleNet + RGB
- 3D ShuffleNet + RGB-D

The detailed benchmark results are elaborated as follows:

1) **Overall evaluation of classification performance**
The results of the overall classification accuracy, classification accuracy precision, the recall value and the f1 score of the four combinations after 50 epochs are shown in Table 7. It can be seen that for both 3D MobileNet and 3D ShuffleNet, the

Table 7. The overall classification results

Metrics	Network			
	3D MobileNet		3D ShuffleNet	
	RGB-D	RGB	RGB-D	RGB
Accuracy %	**91.51**	81.34	**89.78**	69.83
Precision %	**91.81**	82.27	**90.59**	72.39
Recall %	**91.64**	81.82	**90.11**	70.00
f1 score	**0.916**	0.816	**0.902**	0.704

classification performances on RGB-D data are significantly better than those on corresponding RGB data.

Figure 3 shows the dynamic classification accuracy, classification accuracy precision, the recall value and the f1 score of the four combinations corresponding to each epoch. The results show that for both the convergence rate and the absolute value, the two networks based on RGB-D video data all have better performance than the other two networks based on RGB video data.

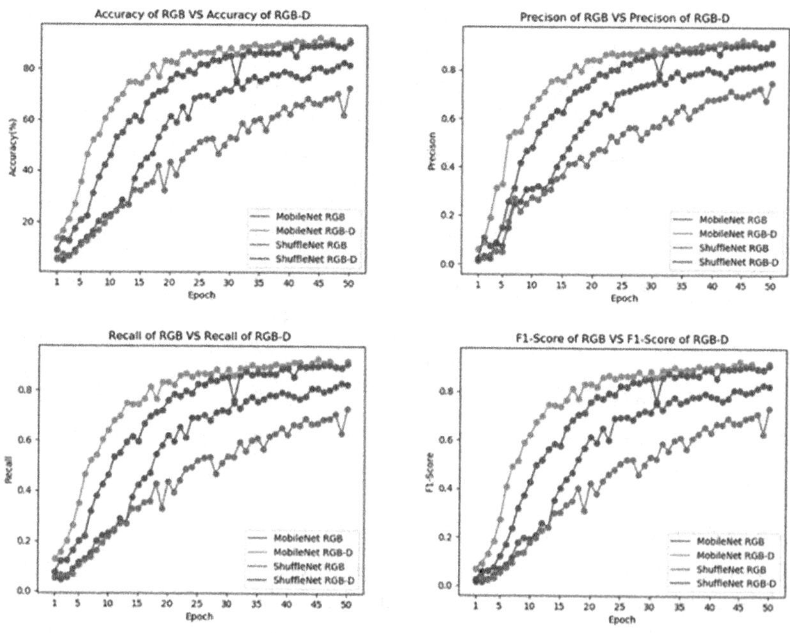

Fig. 3. The curves of accuracy, precision, recall and F1-score

2) **Comparison of classification accuracy**

Table 8 shows the detailed classification accuracy of four combinations for each class. When using 3D MobileNet, except for two gestures "dislike" and "pray", the classification accuracies of RGB-D data exceed those of RGB data. For 3D ShuffleNet, the classification accuracies of RGB-D data exceed those of RGB data for all gesture classes.

Table 8. Classification accuracies for each class

Class	Network			
	3D MobileNet		3D ShuffleNet	
	RGB-D	RGB	RGB-D	RGB
C	**96.3**	80.6	**94.7**	75.1
Come on	**89.8**	78.1	**82.1**	64.1
s	**96.6**	76.5	**95.2**	79.1
Forbid	**98.9**	89.8	**98.4**	91.5
Good	**89.8**	80.6	**91.4**	66.9
Non	**98.8**	82.9	**98.8**	70.3
Dislike	86.9	**87.3**	**82.1**	69.4
Helpless	**97.8**	78.5	**95.2**	75.2
Come	**94.3**	82.8	**91.3**	69.4
No	**85.1**	80.2	**83.3**	66.7
Please	**93.6**	87.2	**95.0**	64.2
Pull	**95.4**	89.3	**98.9**	78.8
Push	**97.7**	84.7	**95.0**	65.7
Me	**88.3**	77.2	**87.3**	69.1
Circle	**89.1**	77.0	**87.4**	71.5
Pat	**89.3**	87.6	**93.2**	65.9
Wave	**88.4**	82.5	**83.4**	71.5
Pray	90.1	**95.8**	**90.3**	81.8
Grasp2	**87.8**	72.0	**89.0**	58.1
Grasp1	**78.9**	65.6	**70.3**	45.8

3) **Analysis of loss function**
The training loss function curves of four combinations are shown in Fig. 4. It could be found that the two networks based on RGB-D data could achieve convergence state faster than the other two networks solely based on RGB data. In other words, more training epochs are needed when training networks with only RGB data.

In summary, under the design principles of DG-20 dataset, dramatic changes in illumination and background will significantly affect the appearance of RGB videos, which poses a challenge to the classification algorithms. The models using RGB-D

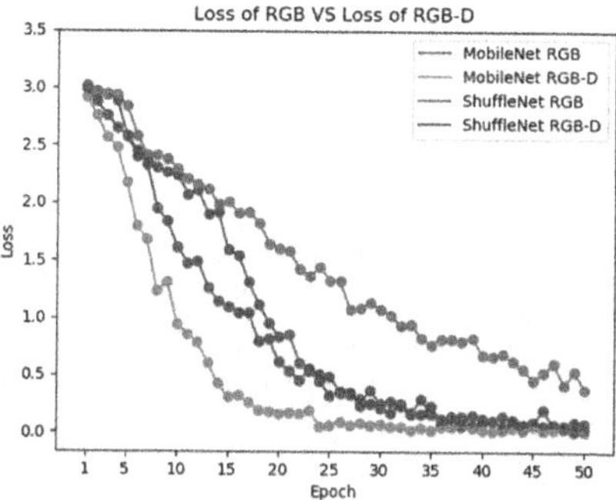

Fig. 4. The loss function curves in RGB-D/RGB data

data with additional depth information achieved better classification results in terms of classification performance, convergence speed and stability of training process. This paper used two typical light-weighted 3D CNN networks to evaluate in the way of channel superposition. Further consideration could be given to how to fully exploit the values of depth information within RGB-D data to achieve better results.

4 Conclusion

In this paper, we build a new RGB-D gesture video dataset named DG-20 which tried to simulate real-life human computer interactive scenes. DG-20 is constructed by dynamic gesture video streams/clips collected by an embedded device, retaining the color information and depth information of the image, and released with complete annotations. DG-20 fully reflects the various conditions of illuminations and backgrounds that may be faced in the real-life gesture based human computer interactions. Benchmark results based on two light-weighted 3D CNN networks show that drastic changes in illumination and background significantly affect the appearance of RGB videos, which in turn seriously reduce classification performances; RGB-D videos can provide resistance to illumination and background changes, which alleviate the impact of those drastic changes on the classification accuracy, as well as other classification metrics. DG-20 can provide effective training and reasoning data support for the development of future RGB-D gesture video recognition algorithms.

In the future, we will focus on two aspects. Firstly, the number of volunteers is not large enough, it will somehow affect the distribution of video samples. We will consider including more people in order to make it closer to the practical scenes. Secondly, the method used in the evaluation section of this paper is to use depth information as the fourth dimension to collage after the three RGB image dimensions. In the future, we will come up with more advanced methods to fully explore the connections and differences between the depth information and the RGB channels.

References

1. Chen, Z.L., Lin, X.L., Chen, J.Y., Huang, Q.Y., Li, C.: Research and application of gesture recognition and rehabilitation system based on computer vision. Comput. Meas. Control **7**, 203–207 (2021)
2. Su, B.Y., Wang, G.J., Zhang, J.: Smart home system based on internet of things and kinect sensor. J. Cent. South Univ. (Sci. Technol.) **44**, 181–184 (2013)
3. Sha, J., Ma, J., Mou, H.J., Hou, J.H.: A review of vision based dynamic hand gestures recognition. Comput. Sci. Appl. **10**, 990–1001 (2020)
4. Zhao, Q.N.: Research on gesture recognition technology based on computer vision. Dalian University of Technology (2020)
5. Zhou, S.: Gesture recognition based on feature fusion: Zhengzhou University (2019)
6. Li, J.M.: 3D hand gesture recognition in RGBD images. Graduate School of National University of Defense Technology (2017)
7. Kang, C.Q.: Hand gesture recognition and application based on RGBD Data. Chang'an University (2017)
8. Negin, F., et al.: PRAXIS: towards automatic cognitive assessment using gesture recognition. Expert Syst. Appl. **106**, 21–35 (2018)
9. Zhang, Y.F., Cao, C., Cheng, J., Lu, H.: EgoGesture: a new dataset and benchmark for egocentric hand gesture recognition. IEEE Trans. Multimed. **20**(5), 1038–1050 (2018)
10. Chai, X.X., Wang, H., Yin, F., Chen, X.: Communication tool for the hard of hearings: a large vocabulary sign language recognition system. In: 2015 International Conference on Affective Computing and Intelligent Interaction (ACII), pp. 781–783 (2015)
11. Lin, F., Wilhelm, C., Martinez, T.: Two-hand global 3D pose estimation using monocular RGB. In: The CVF Winter Conference on Applications of Computer Vision (WACV), pp. 2373–2381 (2021)
12. Wan, J., Li, S.Z., Zhao, Y., Shuai, Z., Escalera, S.: ChaLearn looking at people RGB-D isolated and continuous datasets for gesture recognition. In: 2016 IEEE Conference on Computer Vision and Pattern Recognition Workshops (CVPRW), pp. 761–769 (2016)
13. Yuan, S.H., Jordi, S.R., Taking, L., Kai, L.H., Wen, H.C.: LaRED: a large RGB-D extensible hand gesture dataset. In: Xu, C.S. (ed.) Multimedia Systems Conference, pp. 53–28 (2014)
14. Tompson, J., Stein, M., Lecun, Y., Perlin, K.: Real-Time continuous pose recovery of human hands using convolutional networks. ACM Trans. Graph. **33**, 1–10 (2014)
15. Qin, F.: Real-time dynamic gesture recognition based on deep learning. Zhejiang University (2020)
16. Howard, A.G., et al.: MobileNets: efficient convolutional neural networks for mobile vision applications. arXiv (2017)
17. Zhang, X., Zhou, X., Lin, M., Sun, J.: ShuffleNet: an extremely efficient convolutional neural network for mobile devices. In: 2018 IEEE/CVF Conference on Computer Vision and Pattern Recognition, pp. 6848–6856 (2018)
18. Escalera, S., Baro, X., Escalante, H.J., Guyon, I.: ChaLearn looking at people: a review of events and resources. In: Choe, Y. (ed.) 2017 International Joint Conference on Neural Networks (IJCNN), pp. 1594–1601 (2017)
19. Kopuklu, O., Kose, N., Gunduz, A., Rigoll, G.: Resource efficient 3D convolutional neural networks. In: IEEE/CVF International Conference on Computer Vision Workshop (ICCVW), pp. 1910–1919 (2019)

The High Precision Real-Time Facial Landmark Detection Technique Based on ShufflenetV2

Shulin Lv, Jie Liu, Chunye Gong(✉), Bo Yang, and Xinbiao Gan

National University of Defense Technology, Changsha, China

Abstract. Although in the past few decades, many methods such as heatmap, 3D morphable model (3DMM), and generative adversarial network (GAN), have been used to assist facial landmarks extraction, there is a lack of research on balancing the models' size and accuracy. Therefore, this paper proposes a landmark detection model based on the ShufflenetV2 module and the Wingloss function. The model achieves 86% accuracy on the WFLW extended testing set when its size is only 789.9KB ($\times 0.5$), and its speed can reach 60 FPS on a single Intel i5-8250U CPU. We also use pruning to further compress the model. After pruning, the size of the model is reduced by about 30%, the accuracy is reduced by 4%, and the speed is increased by 17%.

Keywords: Facial landmark detection · ShufflenetV2 · Wingloss · Pruning

1 Introduction

Facial landmark detection, also known as facial landmarks location or face alignment, refers to locating the key areas, including eyebrows, eyes, nose, mouth, and facial contour on a given face. There are three methods for Facial landmark detection. 1. Model-based Active Shape Model (ASM) and active appearance model (AAM) methods. 2. Cascaded shape regression CPR method. 3. Deep learning-based approaches. Among them, the deep learning method performs best. Compared with model-based ASM and AAM methods, the deep learning method has better model robustness in difficult recognition [1, 2]. And compared with the cascade regression CPR method, it is not constrained by the initial shape [3].

In recent years, facial landmarks detection based on deep learning has made great progress. Let's review the development since 2015. In 2015, Wu et al. first explored the features that CNN learned in facial landmarks detection tasks. They used the Mixed Gauss model to cluster the features of different layers. For the first time, they found that CNN used a coarse-to-fine positioning in the task of facial landmarks location, and thus proposed TCNN. TCNN is a network architecture with smaller feature maps and deeper channels as the layer grows, which achieved the best detection results on AFLW, AFW, and 300W datasets at that time [4]. In 2017, Kowalski et al. introduced the characteristic landmarks heatmap into the model. In their proposed DAN network, the input of each stage is the connection of corrected images, feature landmarks heatmaps, and feature maps, and the output is the face shapes. The advantage of DAN is that it can get features

Z. Cai et al. (Eds.): NCTCS 2021, CCIS 1494, pp. 59–71, 2021.
https://doi.org/10.1007/978-981-16-7443-3_5

from the whole image and overcome the problems of pose and initialization [5]. In the same year, Bulat et al. used Generative Adversarial Network (GAN) [6] to improve the performance of the facial landmark detection model in the low-resolution occasion. The Super-FAN proposed by them first located the facial landmarks through the heatmap regression integrated sub-network, and then refined the feature landmarks through the super-resolution processing network based on GAN. Super-FAN made a good visual effect on the low-resolution face image in the real-world dataset (WiderFace) for the first time, which reflected the advantages of joint training of two networks in dealing with the generated images of arbitrary face posture and low-resolution images [7]. In 2018, Wu et al. Introduced edge perception into the model to eliminate the ambiguity of facial landmark location. The LAB model proposed by them was composed of three parts, the edge-aware feature landmarks regression, the edge heatmap regression, and the edge validity discriminant. LAB made use of the advantages of heatmap and GAN, which made the model not only improved the quality of edge heatmap generation but also better coped with the challenges of occlusion. On the datasets 300-W, COFW, and AFLW, the LAB model all broke records at that time [8].

Although the model dealing with Facial landmark detection develops rapidly and is becoming more and more accurate, we can also see that the design of the model is becoming more and more complex, which will inevitably bring the problem of increased model parameters. At present, with the need of transplanting the model on mobile terminals, we need to consider reducing the model's parameters while ensuring accuracy. PFLD proposed in 2019 is a typic Facial landmark detection algorithm for mobile terminals that considers accuracy, speed, and model size at the same time. The algorithm framework of PFLD is composed of two main parts, 1. The main network, which is used to extract features and predict landmarks, is built by the bottleneck block of MobileNetV2 [9] to ensure the model's accuracy and speed. 2. The Auxiliary network, which is used to predict the Euler Angle of face posture, is built to make the predicted feature landmark position more stable and robust. In facial landmarks prediction, PFLD only uses the main network. The $\times 1$ PFLD model has 1.88 NME on the full AFLW dataset at a size of only 12.5 MB, it's acceptable in the mobile case [10].

To meet the requirement of deploying facial landmark detection tasks in the mobile terminal, a lightweight model based on the ShufflenetV2 mobile module is proposed in this paper [11]. Our model can achieve high accuracy on WFLW datasets after simple training. The remain of this paper is structed as follows:

1. Methodology. In this section, first, we explain how to use shufflenetV2 module to build our model. Second, we explain how to choose the loss function. Third, we explain how we express our model.
2. Experiment. In this section, we experiment with the performance of the model and analyze it.
3. Conclusion. In this section, we summarize our work and propose future work.

2 Methodology

2.1 Network Model Design

Because ShufflenetV2 can maintain similar accuracy with fewer parameters than traditional networks, we use ShufflenetV2 to build our regression network of landmark points for the sake of minimizing the model. ShufflenetV2 is a kind of mobile network module proposed by Ningning Ma et al. in 2018. Its design follows four basic principles, 1. To minimize the memory access cost, the number of input channels and the number of output channels should be as equal as possible, 2. To reduce the memory access cost, the number of groups in convolution should be as small as possible, 3. To improve the degree of network parallelism, the network structure should be as simple as possible, 4. To reduce operation consumption, the number of activation and addition operations should be as small as possible. Ningning Ma et al. have compared ShufflenetV2 with ShufflenetV1, MobileNetV2, Xception, and DenseNet on ImageNet2012 classification dataset, and compared with Xception, ShufflenetV1, and MobileNetV2 on Coco target detection dataset. And the results verified ShufflenetV2's fast and accurate performance [11]. The main modules of ShufflenetV2 are shown in Fig. 1. Imitating TCNN, our facial landmark location model follows the principle that the feature graph gets smaller and the channel gets deeper as the hierarchy grows [4].

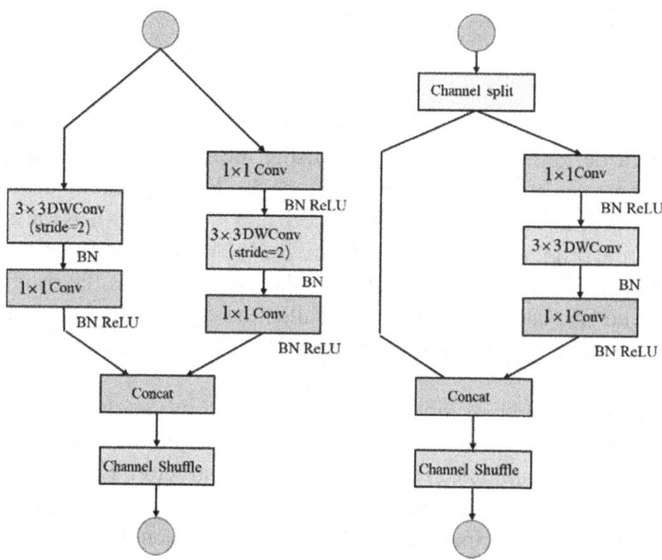

Fig. 1. The ShufflenetV2 module [11]

Our model mainly modifies the network framework proposed in shufflenetV2 paper, but adjusts the input to 112 × 112 pictures, removes the tail structure, and returns the facial landmarks directly from the last stage for the sake of reducing model size. And for the sake of ensuring model accuracy, bias items are added to each level of convolution.

The structure of our model is shown in Table 1, where *c* represents each layer's output channel num, *n* represents the number of duplicates of this layer, and *s* represents the convolution stride.

Table 1. The model structure

Stage	Input	Operator	*C*	*N*	*S*
1	112 × 112 × 3	conv 3 × 3	24	1	2
2	56 × 56 × 24	Shuffleunit	out_1	1	2
	28 × 28 × out_1	Shuffleunit	out_1	3	1
3	28 × 28 × out_1	Shuffleunit	out_2	1	2
	14 × 14 × out_2	Shuffleunit	out_2	7	1
4	14 × 14 × out_2	Shuffleunit	out_3	1	2
	7 × 7 × out_3	Shuffleunit	out_3	3	1
5	7 × 7 × out_3	Avgpool	out_3	1	–
	1 × 1 × out_3	FC	196	1	–
Width	out_1	out_2	out_3		
0.5	48	96	192		
1	116	232	464		

In the model ×0.5 version, because its parameter amount is less than the ×1 version's, its accuracy will be lower. So, we consider using the SENet module to improve the accuracy. The structure of SENet is shown in Fig. 2. Its design is mainly divided into two parts, called Squeeze and Excitation. The Squeeze part is also known as the compression part. Assuming the original characteristic figure is $H \times W \times C$, the function of Squeeze is to compress it to $1 \times 1 \times C$, in which case the 1×1 part has the original $H \times W$ sensing field. The Excitation section is also called the excitation section, in which the squeeze result is predicted by a full connection layer and then is used on the original feature map [12].

For the sake of not adding too many parameters to the model, we only consider adding the SENet layer after the last pointwise convolution layer on the right side of the shufflenetV2 stride-1 module. The changed module structure is shown in Fig. 3. We add SENet layers to different stages of the network to explore the appropriate model structure. Details of the experiment are given in the experiment section of this paper.

2.2 Loss Function Design

PFLD designs a loss function that considers both angle transformation and sample balancing, and it significantly improves model accuracy. However, the same loss function requires an auxiliary network to calculate angles, which will add more parameters to

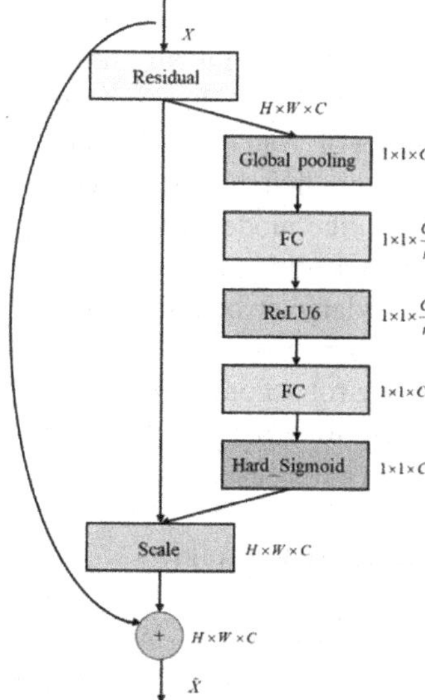

Fig. 2. SENet module [12]

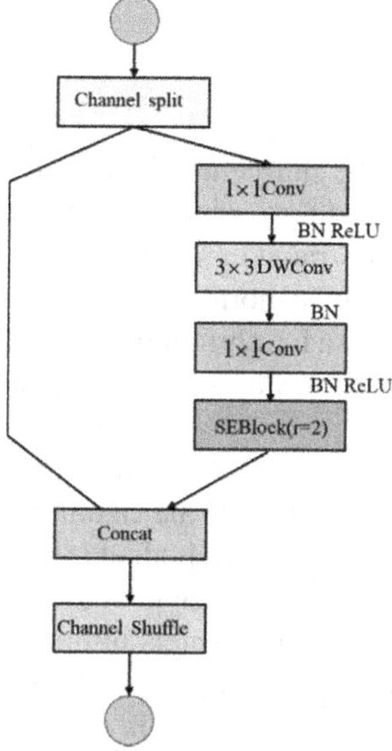

Fig. 3. ShufflenetV2 module with SENet block

the model. Although the model can then be slimmed by removing the auxiliary network, there are additional operations involved. Therefore, we prefer to try a simple loss function that does not require an additional network structure.

To cope with the challenge of facial landmarks localization brought by face angle and expression, we adopted the Wingloss function proposed by Feng et al. (2018) to reduce the wing loss. Traditional facial landmark location models usually use L2 as a loss function. However, Feng et al. found that because the derivative of the L2 loss function is $\frac{dL2(x)}{dx} = x$, when the predicted value differs too much from the true value, a large gradient will occur. Thus, the model will be dragged by landmarks with large errors and deviate from the optimal solution. The way they solved this problem was to use a loss function close to L1 for large errors. Since the derivative of L1 is constant, its performance on outliers is not as sensitive as L2. The application of L1 on large errors can make the model training more robust on outliers. For small errors, they use *lnx*-like functions to enhance their impact. Since the gradient of function *lnx* is $\frac{1}{x}$, the gradient of the function becomes larger when x becomes small. Therefore, the model can be further refined in small errors [13].

The Wingloss function is expressed as follows.

$$wing(x) = \begin{cases} wln(1 + |x|/\varepsilon) & if\ |x| < w \\ |x| - C & otherwise \end{cases} \tag{1}$$

where w is a positive number that limits the range of the non-linear part to the interval $[-w, w]$, ε is the curvature of the constrained non-linear region, and $C = w - wln(1 + |x|/\varepsilon)$.

2.3 Pruning Design

Although our model built with the shufflenetV2 module is small enough, we still consider further compressing the model to achieve faster inference speed and enable the model to migrate to memory-constrained mobile devices. Pruning is a common model compression method. We use both L1 norm pruning and network slimming pruning to compress our model. Firstly, we use L1 norm pruning to change the size of the convolution layer. Secondly, we use network slimming pruning to further remove unimportant channels.

L1 norm pruning reduces the model structure by sorting the L1 norm of each channel in the convolutional layer to reduce the channel with less weight. In this paper, as shown in Fig. 4, the pruning is mainly embodied in the ShufflenetV2. For both types of modules, the pruning is carried out on the right branch. In Fig. 4, the side length of the quadrilateral represents the number of channels in this direction. Because the number of output channels in the first layer, the number of input and output channels in the second layer, and the number of input channels in the third layer reduced after pruning, the right side of Fig. 4 shows a bottleneck shape. Since neither the number of input channels nor the number of output channels of the module can be easily changed, we choose to apply the pruning method to the output channels of the first layer convolution. Because the second layer of the right branch of the ShufflenetV2 module is designed as a separable convolution, the pruning of the first layer will affect both the input and the output channel num of the second layer. And when the output channel of the second layer is changed, the convolution of the third layer will also be affected. Finally, the pruned right branch of the module becomes a bottleneck. Therefore, it can be said that pruning is done on the entire right branch of the module. We set the pruning rate of 0.2, 0.1 and 0.01 respectively for the second, third, and fourth stages of the network, and fine-tune the model after pruning.

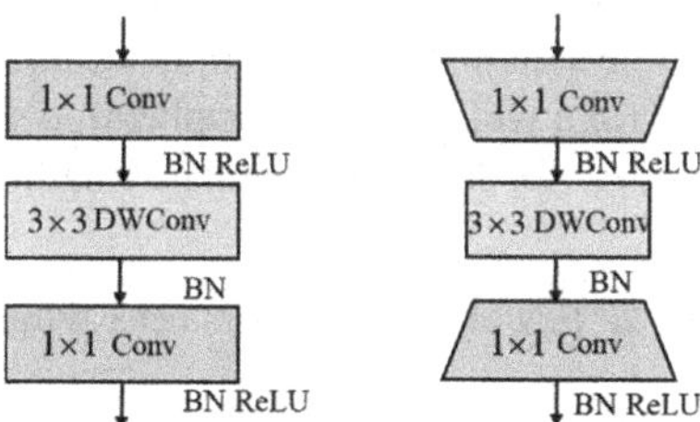

Fig. 4. Pruning scheme (left: the right branch of ShufflenetV2 module, right: the pruned right branch of figShufflenetV2 module)

Network slimming is a channel-level pruning scheme, whose basic idea is joint training weights and an introduced scale factor γ which measures the importance of each channel. Network slimming regularizes the scale factor sparsely and prunes channels according to the channels' scale factor γ. In the implementation of Network slimming pruning, the scale factor is the γ of the BN layer that is next to the convolution layer. By imposing L1 regular constraints on the network BN layer, Network slimming can guide the model to adjust parameters to structural sparseness during training. We can get new networks by pruning out channels whose γ value is less than the threshold [14]. L1-norm pruning is essentially a less flexible hierarchical pruning method. So, after using L1-norm pruning, we further use Network slimming pruning to compress our model.

According to the basic idea of Network Slimming, the loss function of the model is adjusted as

$$L^* = L + \lambda \sum_{\gamma \in \Gamma} g(\gamma) \tag{2}$$

where L is the original loss term, $g(s) = |s|$, and λ is the sparse penalty.

According to the paper of Network slimming, the pruning scheme of network slimming can remove about 80% of the channels of Vgg, Resnet-164, DenseNet-40 networks without significant loss of accuracy [14]. Because of the complexity of our network, in our experiment, we only pruned 50% of the channel for the network. And according to the structural characteristics of ShufflenetV2, we reconstruct a small network to transplant model parameters after fine-tuning step.

3 Experiment

3.1 Environment and Parameter Setting

Our environment and parameter setting are shown in Table 2. In our experiment, we select the WFLW dataset to train and validate the model. WFLW dataset is a 98 facial landmarks dataset, including 10000 images, 7500 for training, and 2500 for testing. Because WFLW includes six attributes of the face, including pose, expression, lighting, makeup, occlusion, and blur, it covers the extreme situation in the real world [8]. It's suitable for measuring the performance of the model. We expand the training set and the testing set to 10 times the original size by rotating, mirroring, and boundary disturbing the image, to better simulate the situation in a real application. Extending the training set can make our model suitable for a wider range of application scenarios while extending the testing set can better validate the landmark detection ability of our model.

Table 2. Environment and parameter setting

Training	Platform	Titan Rtx
	Dataset	WFLW extened training dataset
	Lr	0.0001
	batch_size	128
	weight_decay	5.00E−05
	MultiStepLR	MILESTONES = [15, 40, 170]
Testing	Platform	Intel i5-8250U CPU
	Dataset	WFLW extened testing dataset

3.2 Performance Metrics

Accuracy Indicators

Failure Rate. We use the eye spacing normalization error to measure the error between a face's predicted landmarks and its ground-truth landmarks. To eliminate unreasonable changes caused by facial size discrepancy, we use the ratio of feature landmarks deviation to pupil spacing as the basis for judging the accuracy. When the ratio is less than 0.1, the landmark is considered to be accurately located. The formula is as follows

$$e_i = \frac{\left\| x_i - x_i^g \right\|_2}{d_{IOD}} \tag{3}$$

where x_i is the predicted landmark, x_i^g is the ground-truth landmark, d_{IOD} is the distance between the centers of the eyes. When the mean ratio of all points of a face is less than 0.1, we regard the position of the landmark of this face as correct, otherwise, it is an error. The error rate of the model on the test set is recorded as the failure rate.

Mean Normalization Error. $e = \frac{\sum_{i=1}^{N} \left\| x_{(i)}^e - x_{(i)}^g \right\|_2}{N \times d_{IOD}} \times 100\%.$

CED Curve. CED curve is used to measure the proportion of datasets that have been covered when the NME reaches a certain error rate. It is also an indicator of the robustness of the model.

Model Size
Flops. The Flops means floating-point count, which is used to measure the calculation amount of the model.

Size. We simply use model file size as an intuitive indicator of model size.

Model Speed
fps. fps means the number of images processed by the model per second.

3.3 Training

For the $\times 1$ and $\times 0.5$ model, we trained five models respectively, which correspond to the simplified version without SENet module, the version with SENet module added in model stages 1, 2, and 3, and the version with SENet module used in the whole model. To compare with our model, we also trained the PFLD model under the WFLW dataset. The source code for the PFLD model was derived from the PyTorch version of the code published on GitHub. We trained the PFLD model on the WFLW dataset by following the original parameters provided by its code. The validation result of the model on the WFLW extended testing set (containing 25,000 images) is shown in Table 3. And the CED curve is shown in Fig. 5.

Table 3. The comparison of models on the WFLW extended testing set

Model		failure_rate	Nme	Size	Flops	fps
1	–	10.7%	0.061	3.6 MB	235.43M	37.56
	+2	10.3%	0.060	3.6 MB	235.35M	35.55
	+3	10.0%	0.060	3.9 MB	235.62M	34.18
	+4	9.9%	0.060	4.2 MB	235.75M	36.03
	+all	9.5%	0.059	4.6 MB	235.96M	31.52
0.5	–	14.0%	0.067	789.9 KB	50.31M	60.62
	+2	14.0%	0.067	800.3 KB	50.31M	56.89
	+3	13.5%	0.067	863.5 KB	50.34M	52.91
	+4	13.2%	0.067	905.2 KB	50.37M	56.77
	+all	13.1%	0.066	989.2 KB	50.40M	47.67
	Pruned	18.3%	0.077	574 KB	25.85M	71.35
PFLD 1		23.7%	0.087	7.0 MB	783.46M	35.53

According to the results in Table 3 and Fig. 5, we can conclude that the accuracy of the $\times 1$ model is significantly higher than the $\times 0.5$ model, which is inevitable, because the $\times 1$ model means more parameters and better feature extraction ability. But at the same time, we also know that the $\times 0.5$ model is faster than the $\times 1$ model. Therefore, the

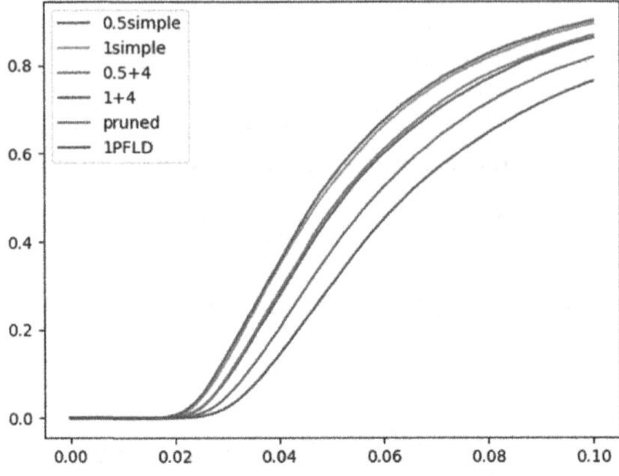

Fig. 5. CED curve

use of the $\times 1$ or $\times 0.5$ model should be judged according to the specific requirements. The function of the SENet module is not as obvious as expected, but when it is used in the fourth stage, we can see that the accuracy of the model can be improved by 1%. The fourth stage of our model does not have many network layers. However, it has many channels. Therefore, we can conclude that SENet is more suitable for layers that have more channels.

We compared our models with the $\times 1$ PFLD model on the WFLW dataset and recorded the results in Table 3 and Fig. 4. First, as shown in Table 3, the failure_rate of our models is lower than that of $\times 1$ PFLD, which means that our models are more accurate. And, as shown in Fig. 5, the curves of our models are above the curve of $\times 1$ PFLD, which means that our model has better robustness. Then, except for the models with SENet modules, our models are faster than $\times 1$ PFLD. For instance, our $\times 0.5$ model is about 70% faster than the PFLD. Finally, the size of our models is smaller than that of $\times 1$ PFLD. In conclusion, our model is superior in accuracy, size, and speed than $\times 1$ PFLD on the WFLW dataset.

3.4 Prunning

In the expected further study, we prefer to use smaller models rather than more accurate ones, so we only pruned the $\times 0.5$ model. Our pruning scheme is divided into two steps, L1 norm pruning and network slimming pruning.

L1 Norm Pruning

In the experiment, we found that if we simply set a uniform pruning rate for all stages of the model, the model's accuracy will be greatly reduced. Therefore, we chose to set different pruning rates for each stage of the model. The final pruning rates were set as 0.2, 0.1, and 0.01, which correspond to the model's second, third and fourth stages respectively. We then transplanted the pruning results to the corresponding small model and finally used 40 epoch training to restore the accuracy. The L1 norm pruning step didn't reduce the model's accuracy.

According to the concept proposed by Liu et al., the effect of training a small model from scratch is the same as that of drawing a small model from a large model [15]. Therefore, we can regard L1 norm pruning as a process to find a suitable model structure. We trained the found model structure and used it for network slimming pruning.

Network Slimming Pruning

The result of using L1 norm pruning is far less than our pursuit of model compression. Our goal is to compress the model to 1/2 of its original size. Liu et al. demonstrated with Vgg, Resnet-164, and Densenet-40 in their experiments, and proposed that network slimming pruning can remove more than 80% of redundant channels [14]. Given the powerful pruning ability of network slimming, we used it to further prune the model obtained from the first pruning step. We first added the parameters of gramma and beta to the BN layer to make it can be trained. Second, we trained the model for 200 rounds to induce the BN layer to be sparse by adding the L1 regularization constraint term of the BN layer's gamma coefficient. Third, we then ranked the importance of the model's overall channels by the weight of the BN layers' gramma parameters to find which channel can be discarded. Then, we pruned 50% channels of the model and refined our model for 40 rounds to restore its accuracy. Finally, we built a smaller model again to transplant the parameters.

When building a small model, considering the particularity of the shufflenetV2 module, we still used the scheme shown in Fig. 4, which means we only changed the right-wing of the shufflenetV2 module. The reconstructed small model is shown in Table 4, where input is the input of each layer, operator is the operation of that layer (we call the Shufflenetv2 block shuffleunit_ after modification), c is the final output channel number of the layer, s is the convolution stride, and m is the output channel num of the middle layer. The performance of our pruned model is shown in Table 3. It can be seen that the size of the model (compared with the model without SENet) is reduced by about 30%, the accuracy is reduced by 4.3%, and speed is improved by 17.7%. Because in our design we didn't move all pruned channels of the model, the model can be further compressed in fact.

4 Conclusion

To solve the problem of deploying the task of facial point detection in the mobile terminal, we proposed a facial point detection model based on the shufflenetV2 module and Wingloss function to balance both the model size and accuracy. Our model achieves 86% accuracy on the WFLW extended testing set when its size is only 789.9 KB ($\times 0.5$). And, to further compress the model, we used the L1 norm pruning and the Network slimming pruning method. Our smallest model is only 574 KB, and it has 81.7% accuracy in WFLW extended testing set. Compared with PFLD, our model is much smaller, more accurate and more robust on the WFLW dataset. Moreover, our model still has the potential to be further compressed.

The model proposed in this paper realizes the pursuit of smaller, faster, and more accurate. However, it still lacks verification in the actual use environment. So, we intend to use more datasets to test the performance of our model in the future. And, in the

Table 4. The pruned model

Stage	Input	Operator	c	s	M
1	112 × 112 × 3	conv 3 × 3	24	2	–
2	56 × 56 × 24	shuffleunit_	24	1	4
	28 × 28 × 48	shuffleunit_	48	1	3
		shuffleunit_	48	1	5
		shuffleunit_	48	1	5
3	28 × 28 × 48	shuffleunit_	48	2	21
	14 × 14 × 96	shuffleunit_	96	1	14
		shuffleunit_	96	1	21
		shuffleunit_	96	1	25
		shuffleunit_	96	1	26
		shuffleunit_	96	1	30
		shuffleunit_	96	1	29
		shuffleunit_	96	1	28
4	14 × 14 × 96	shuffleunit_	192	2	46
	7 × 7 × 192	shuffleunit_	192	1	62
		shuffleunit_	192	1	71
		shuffleunit_	192	1	35
5	7 × 7 × 192	Avgpool	192	1	–
	1 × 1 × 192	FC	196	1	–

further study, we will also consider combining other technologies, such as GAN and 3DMM to enhance the capability of the model.

References

1. Cootes, T.F., Taylor, C.I., Cooper, D.H.: Active shape models-their training and application. Comput. Vis. Image Underst. **61**(1), 38–59 (1995)
2. Cootes, T.F., Edwards, G.J., Taylor, C.J.: Active appearance models. IEEE Trans. Pattern Anal. Mach. Intell. **23**(6), 681–685 (2001)
3. Dollár, P, Welinder, P., Perona, P.: Cascaded pose regression. In: IEEE Computer Society Conference on Computer Vision and Pattern Recognition, CA, San Francisco, vol. 1, pp. 1078–1085 (2010)
4. Wu, Y., Hassner, T., Kim, K.: Facial landmark detection with tweaked convolutional neural networks. IEEE Trans. Pattern Anal. Mach. Intell. **40**(12), 3067–3074 (2017)
5. Kowalski, M., Naruniec, J., Trzcinski, T.: Deep alignment network: a convolutional neural network for robust face alignment. In: IEEE Conference on Computer Vision and Pattern Recognition Workshops, pp. 2160–7516. IEEE, Honolulu (2017)

6. Goodfellow, I.J., Pouget-Abadie, J., Mirza, M.: Generative adversarial networks. Adv. Neural Inf. Process. Syst. **3**, 2672–2680 (2014)
7. Bulat, A., Tzimiropoulos, G.: Super-FAN: integrated facial landmark localization and super-resolution of real-world low resolution faces in arbitrary poses with GANs. In: IEEE Conference on Computer Vision and Pattern Recognition, pp. 109–117. IEEE, Salt Lake City (2018)
8. Wu, W., Qian, C., Yang, S.: Look at boundary: a boundary-aware face alignment algorithm. In: IEEE/CVF Conference on Computer Vision and Pattern Recognition. IEEE, Salt Lake City (2018)
9. Sandler, M., Howard, A., Zhu, M.: MobileNetV2: inverted residuals and linear bottlenecks. In: IEEE/CVF Conference on Computer Vision and Pattern Recognition. IEEE, Salt Lake City (2018)
10. Guo, X., Li, S., Yu, J.: PFLD: a practical facial landmark detector. arXiv (2019)
11. Ma, N., Zhang, X., Zheng, H.-T., Sun, J.: ShuffleNet V2: practical guidelines for efficient CNN architecture design. In: Ferrari, V., Hebert, M., Sminchisescu, C., Weiss, Y. (eds.) Computer Vision – ECCV 2018. LNCS, vol. 11218, pp. 122–138. Springer, Cham (2018). https://doi.org/10.1007/978-3-030-01264-9_8
12. Iandola, F.N., Han, S., Moskewicz, M.W.: SqueezeNet: AlexNet-level accuracy with 50x fewer parameters and <0.5MB model size. In: International Conference on Learning Representations, Berkeley (2017)
13. Feng, Z.H., Kittler, J., Awais, M.: Wing loss for robust facial landmark localisation with convolutional neural networks. In: IEEE/CVF Conference on Computer Vision and Pattern Recognition, pp. 2235–2245. IEEE, Salt Lake City (2018)
14. Zhuang, L., Li, J., Shen, Z.: Learning efficient convolutional networks through network slimming. In: IEEE International Conference on Computer Vision, vol. 1, pp. 2755–2763. IEEE, Venice (2017)
15. Zhuang, L., Sun, M.., Zhou, T.: Rethinking the value of network pruning. In: International Conference on Learning Representations, New Orleans (2019)

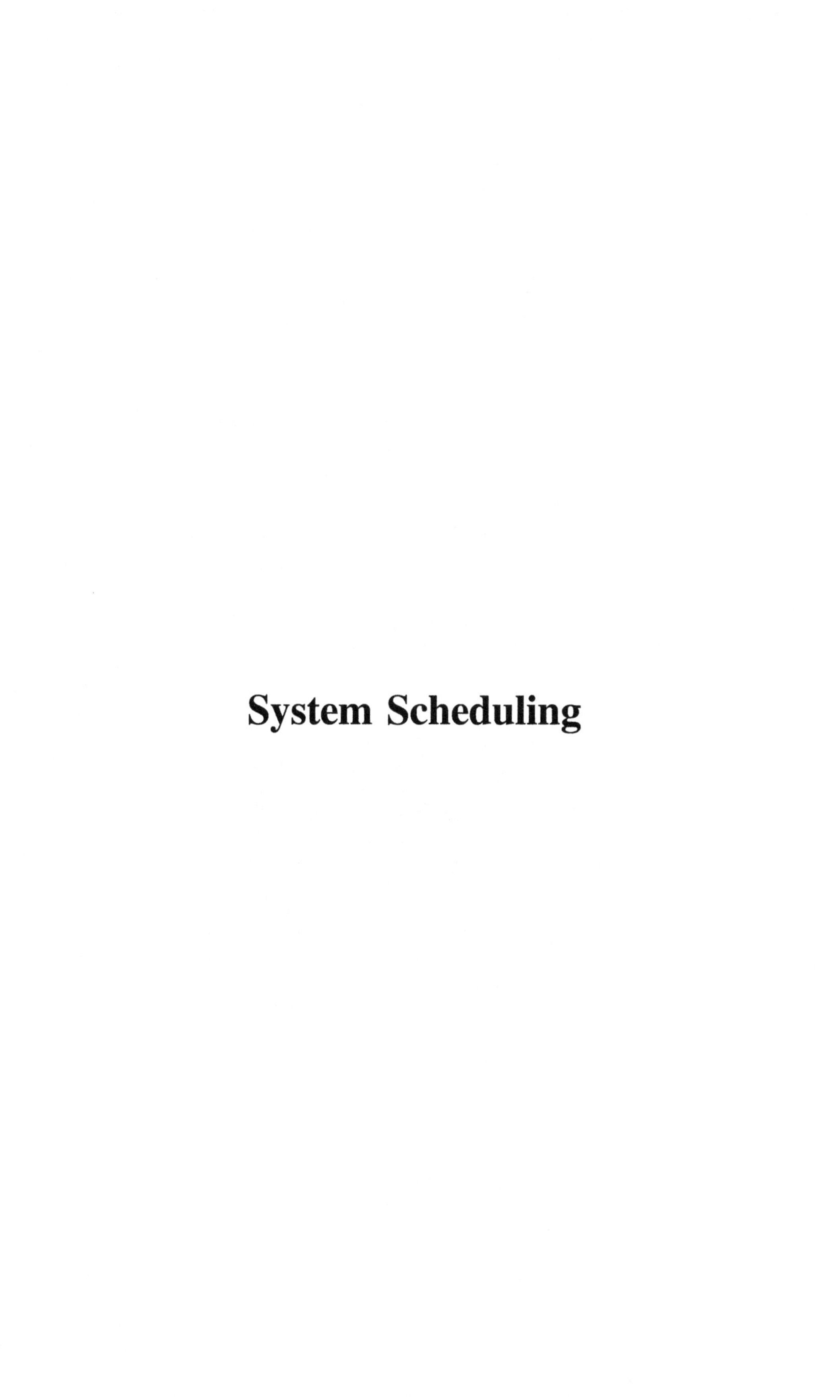

System Scheduling

Computation Tree Logic Model Checking over Possibilistic Decision Processes Under Finite-Memory Scheduler

Wuniu Liu, Qing He, and Yongming Li(✉)

School of Computer Science, Shaanxi Normal University, Xi'an, Shaanxi, China
{liuwuniu,heqing,liyongm}@snnu.edu.cn

Abstract. Possibilistic model checking has been studied extensively, but the nondeterministic actions contained in the system are absent in previous possibilistic model checking. In order to add this nondeterminism to the model, we introduce the notion of generalized possibilistic decision processes (GPDP, in short) in this paper. We propose the scheduler to solve the nondeterminism of actions. We study the model checking under finite-memory scheduler, i.e., giving a GPDP, a finite-memory scheduler and a generalized possibilistic computation tree logic (GPoCTL) formula, compute its possibility under this scheduler. What's more, a method based on Entropy-weight TOPSIS is given to select the optimal schedulers from all given schedulers over possibility and necessity measures.

Keywords: Possibilistic decision processes · Generalized possibilistic computation tree logic · Finite-memory schedulers · Optimal schedulers · Model checking

1 Introduction

Model checking [1,3] is a formal automated verification technique. It has been widely used in actual systems. Classical model checking is applicable to Boolean systems, but actual systems are often in some uncertain environments. If use classical Boolean logic to build the such system, then such uncertain information can not be expressed. In order to embed uncertainty into the model, some quantitative model checking methods are proposed, including probabilistic model checking [1], possibilistic model checking[12–17,19], etc., techniques.

In the previous possibilistic model checking, the possibilistic transition serves to quantify the possibilistic outcomes. Although generalized possibilistic computation tree logic (GPoCTL) [16] is more expressive than possibilistic computation tree logic (PoCTL) [15], it does not take nondeterministic actions into account. In process of designing actual systems, we usually encounter the model of a nondeterministic system in which each state may has be multiple possibilistic distributions to transfer to other states. Such nondeterministic information is absent in generalized possibilistic Kripke structures (GPKS) [16].

Z. Cai et al. (Eds.): NCTCS 2021, CCIS 1494, pp. 75–88, 2021.
https://doi.org/10.1007/978-981-16-7443-3_6

For example, assume that there is a new virus, we have few knowledge about this virus. Only two feasible drugs can be given based on experience and then treatment plans can be made to treat. Doctors make two treatments α and β. The treatment α recommends only using the α drug. The treatment β recommends a combination of the two drugs which depending on the physical status of patients. What are the possibilities that the patient will eventually recover under these two treatments? Therefore, it is necessary to embed such nondeterministic into systems to model checking under given schedulers. We call this multi-possibility distribution actions. The GPKS embedded in nondeterministic actions is called the generalized possibilistic decision process (GPDP). More importantly, we need to obtain the optimal schedulers. We study the optimal scheduler for a GPoCTL formula based on possibility measures and necessity measures. A preliminary work on model checking based on GPDP is studied in this paper.

The content of this paper is arranged as follows. Section 2 gives an introduction of generalized possibility theory and generalized possibilistic Kripke structures defined in [16]. In Sect. 3, we give the definition of GPDP and schedulers. In Sect. 4, we introduce the syntaxes and semantics of GPoCTL with schedulers. Section 5, we study the model checking for GPoCTL formulas with schedulers under finite-memory schedulers. In Sect. 6, we give a method based on Entropy-weight TOPSIS to select a optimal scheduler in all given schedulers. A patient's example is given in Sect. 7 and this paper ends with conclusions.

2 Preliminaries

Possibility theory is an uncertainty theory devoted to the handling of incomplete information and provides an alternative to probability theory, which use a pair of dual set-functions, i.e., possibility and necessity measures, instead of only one measure in probability theory. Zadeh first introduced possibility theory in 1978 as an extension of fuzzy sets and logic [22,23]. Dubois and Prade made a further study in [6,7,9–11].

For simplicity, assume that the universe of discourse U is a nonempty set, and assume that all subsets are measurable. A possibility measure is a function Π from the powerset 2^U to $[0,1]$ such that:

(1) $\Pi(\emptyset) = 0$, (2) $\Pi(U) = 1$, (3) $\Pi(\bigcup E_i) = \bigvee \Pi(E_i)$ for any subset family $\{E_i\}$ of the universe set U, where we use $\bigvee_{i\in I} a_i$ to denote the supremum or the least upper bound of the family of real numbers $\{a_i\}_{i\in I}$; dually, we use $\bigwedge_{i\in I} a_i$ to denote the infimum or the largest lower bound of the family of real numbers $\{a_i\}_{i\in I}$.

If Π only satisfies the conditions (1) and (3), then we call Π a generalized possibility measure [16].

It follows that the generalized possibility measure on a nonempty set is determined by its actions on singletons:

$$\Pi(E) = \bigvee_{x\in E} \Pi(\{x\}). \tag{1}$$

The function $\pi : U \to [0,1]$ defined by $\pi(x) = \Pi(\{x\})$ is called the possibility distribution of Π, and the measure Π is uniquely defined by Eq. (1), i.e., Π is uniquely defined by the possibility distribution π.

Possibility theory uses two concepts: the possibility and the necessity of the event [5,8]. For any set E, the necessity measure N is defined by

$$N(E) = 1 - \Pi(U - E). \tag{2}$$

A necessity measure is a function N from the powerset 2^U to $[0,1]$ such that:

(1) $N(\emptyset) = 0$, (2)$N(U) = 1$, and (3)$\bigcap E_i = \bigwedge N(E_i)$ for any subset family $\{E_i\}$ of the universe set U.

If N only satisfies the conditions (2) and (3), then we call N a generalized necessity measure.

We will use generalized possibility measures and generalized necessity measures to model checking and to determine optimal scheduler in this paper.

3 Generalized Possibilistic Decision Processes

Definition 1. *A Generalized possibilistic decision processes (GPDP) is a six tuple $M = (S, Act, P, I, AP, L)$, where*

(1) S is a countable set of states;
(2) Act is a set of actions;
(3) $P : S \times Act \times S \to [0,1]$ is the possibilistic transition function such that for all states $s \in S$, there exist $\alpha \in Act$ and $t \in S$ satisfying $P(s,\alpha,t) > 0$;
(4) $I : S \to [0,1]$ is initial distribution such that $I(s) > 0$ for some state s;
(5) AP is a set of atomic propositions;
(6) $L : S \times AP \to [0,1]$ is a possibilistic labeling function, which is the same as in Definition of GPKS in [16].

Reasoning about possibilities of sets of paths of a GPDP relies on the resolution of nondeterminism. This resolution is performed by the *scheduler* (c.f. [1]).

Definition 2 *(Scheduler). Let $M = (S, Act, P, I, AP, L)$ be a finite GPDP, a scheduler for M is a function $\mathfrak{S} : S^+ \to Act$ such that $\mathfrak{S}(s_0 s_1 \cdots s_n) \in Act(s_n)$ for all $s_0 s_1 \cdots s_n \in S^+$. Here, S^+ denotes the set of finite nonempty strings of S.*

The path $\pi = s_0 \xrightarrow{\alpha_1} s_1 \xrightarrow{\alpha_2} s_2 \xrightarrow{\alpha_3} \cdots$ is called a $\mathfrak{S}$-Path if $\alpha_i = \mathfrak{S}(s_0 \cdots s_{i-1})$ for all $i > 0$. For convenience, we write $\pi = s_0\alpha_1 s_1 \alpha_2 s_2 \alpha_3 \cdots \in \mathfrak{S}$-Paths.

Definition 3 *(Memoryless Scheduler). Let M be a GPDP with state space S, a scheduler $\mathfrak{S}$ is memoryless if and only if for each state sequence $s_0 s_1 \cdots s_n$ and $t_0 t_1 \cdots t_m \in S^+$ with $s_n = t_m$: $\mathfrak{S}(s_0 s_1 \cdots s_n) = \mathfrak{S}(t_0 t_1 \cdots t_m)$.*

We simply write $\mathfrak{S}(s_n)$ instead of $\mathfrak{S}(s_0 s_1 \cdots s_n)$ if scheduler $\mathfrak{S}$ is memoryless.

Memoryless schedulers are somehow extreme as they simply select one action per state while ignoring all others. A variant of memoryless schedulers are so called finite-memory schedulers. The behavior of a finite-memory scheduler is described by a deterministic finite automaton (DFA). The selection of the action to be performed in the GPDP M depends on the current state of M and the current state (called mode) of the scheduler, i.e., the DFA.

Definition 4 *(Finite-Memory Scheduler). Let M be a GPDP with state space S and action set Act, a finite-memory scheduler $\mathfrak{S}$ is a tuple $\mathfrak{S} = (Q, act, \Delta, start)$ where*

(1) Q is a finite set of modes;
(2) $\Delta : Q \times S \rightarrow Q$ is the transition function;
(3) $act : Q \times S \rightarrow Act$ is a function that selects an action $act(q, s) \in Act(s)$ for any mode $q \in Q$ and a state s;
(4) $start : S \rightarrow Q$ is a function that selects a starting mode q_0 for state s of M.

The finite-memory schedulers are related to the notion of a scheduler, see Definition 2. A finite-memory scheduler $\mathfrak{S} = (Q, act, \Delta, start)$ is identified with the function $\mathfrak{S}' : Paths_{fin} \rightarrow Act$. For the starting state s_0, let $\mathfrak{S}' = act(start(s_0), s_0)$ and $\mathfrak{S}'(\hat{\pi}_n) = act(q_n, s_n)$, where $q_0 = start(s_0)$ and $q_{i+1} = \Delta(q_i, s_i)$ for $0 \leqslant i \leqslant n$.

4 Generalized Possibilistic Computation Tree Logic with Schedulers

This section introduces the quantitative GPoCTL with schedulers to describe the properties in a finite GPDP. The main difference with the setting for GPoCTL is that the possibilistic operator $Po_{\mathfrak{S}}(\cdot)$ is under a scheduler $\mathfrak{S}$. Thus, $Po_{\mathfrak{S}}(\varphi)$ asserts that the possibility of the $\mathfrak{S}$-*Paths* satisfies the path formula φ.

Definition 5 *(Syntax). GPoCTL state formulas with schedulers over the set AP of atomic propositions are formed according to the following grammar:*

$$\Phi ::= r \mid a \mid \Phi_1 \wedge \Phi_2 \mid \neg\Phi \mid Po_{\mathfrak{S}}(\varphi)$$

where $r \in [0, 1]$, $a \in AP$, φ is a PoCTL path formula and $\mathfrak{S}$ a scheduler.

PoCTL path formulas are formed according to the following grammar:

$$\varphi ::= \bigcirc\Phi \mid \Phi_1 \sqcup \Phi_2 \mid \Phi_1 \sqcup^{\leqslant n} \Phi_2 \mid \Box\Phi$$

where Φ, Φ_1 and Φ_2 are state formulas, and $n \in \mathbb{N}$

Definition 6 *(Semantics). Let $M = (S, Act, P, I, AP, L)$ be a GPDP, $s \in S$ be a state, Φ, Ψ be GPoCTL state formulas, and φ be a GPoCTL path formula. For state formulas r, a, $\Phi_1 \wedge \Phi_2$, $\neg\Phi$, theirs semantics, regardless of schedulers, is a* *fuzzy set* $\|\Phi\| : S \to [0,1]$ *(here,* $\|\Phi\|$ *denotes the possibility of state formula* Φ*), which is defined recursively as follows, for any* $s \in S$ *and* $r \in [0,1]$*:*

$$\|r\|(s) = r \tag{3}$$

$$\|a\|(s) = L(s,a) \tag{4}$$

$$\|\Phi \wedge \Psi\|(s) = \|\Phi\|(s) \wedge \|\Psi\|(s) \tag{5}$$

$$\|\neg\Phi\|(s) = 1 - \|\Phi\|(s) \tag{6}$$

For $Po_{\mathfrak{S}}(\varphi)$*, its semantics depend on the scheduler* $\mathfrak{S}$*, i.e.,*

$$\|Po_{\mathfrak{S}}(\varphi)\|(s) = Po_{\mathfrak{S}}(s \models \varphi). \tag{7}$$

Let fuzzy set $\|\varphi\|_{\mathfrak{S}}$*:* $\mathfrak{S}$*-Paths(M)* $\to [0,1]$*, which is defined recursively for* $\pi = s_0\mathfrak{S}(\hat{\pi}_0)s_1\mathfrak{S}(\hat{\pi}_1)s_2\cdots$ *as follows:*

$$\|\bigcirc\Phi\|_{\mathfrak{S}}(\pi) = P(s_0, \mathfrak{S}(\hat{\pi}_0), s_1) \wedge \|\Phi\|(s_1),$$

$$\|\Diamond\Phi\|_{\mathfrak{S}}(\pi) = \bigvee_{j=0}^{\infty} \bigwedge_{k \leqslant j} P(s_{k-1}, \mathfrak{S}(\hat{\pi}_{k-1}), s_k) \wedge \|\Phi\|(s_j),$$

$$\|\Phi \sqcup \Psi\|_{\mathfrak{S}}(\pi) = \|\Psi\|(s_0) \vee \bigvee_{j>0} ((\|\Phi\|(s_0) \wedge \bigwedge_{k<j} P(s_{k-1}, \mathfrak{S}(\hat{\pi}_{k-1}), s_k) \wedge \|\Phi\|(s_k)) \wedge P(s_{k-1}, \mathfrak{S}(\hat{\pi}_{k-1}), s_j) \wedge \|\Psi\|(s_j)),$$

$$\|\Phi \sqcup^{\leqslant n} \Psi\|_{\mathfrak{S}}(\pi) = \|\Psi\|(s_0) \vee \bigvee_{0<j\leqslant n} ((\|\Phi\|(s_0) \wedge \bigwedge_{k<j} P(s_{k-1}, \mathfrak{S}(\hat{\pi}_{k-1}), s_k) \wedge \|\Phi\|(s_k)) \wedge P(s_{j-1}, \mathfrak{S}(\hat{\pi}_{j-1}), s_j) \wedge \|\Psi\|(s_j)),$$

$$\|\Box\Phi\|_{\mathfrak{S}}(\pi) = \bigwedge_{i=0}^{\infty} \bigwedge_{j=0}^{i-1} P(s_j, \mathfrak{S}(\hat{\pi}_j), s_{j+1}) \wedge \|\Phi\|(s_i).$$

where path formula $\Diamond\Phi$ *(eventually) is defined by* $\Diamond\Phi = true \sqcup \Phi$*. Similarly, for step-bounded eventually, we have* $\Diamond^{\leqslant n}\Phi = true \sqcup^{\leqslant n} \Phi$*.*

$Po_{\mathfrak{S}}(s \models \varphi)$ *is defined as follows:*

$$Po_{\mathfrak{S}}(s \models \varphi) = \bigvee_{\pi \in \mathfrak{S}\text{-}Paths(M)} Po^{M_s}(\pi) \wedge \|\varphi\|_{\mathfrak{S}}(\pi). \tag{8}$$

$Po_{\mathfrak{S}}(s \models \varphi)$ *denotes the largest possibility of the* $\mathfrak{S}$*-Paths starting at* s *satisfying the formula* φ*, where* $M_s = (S, Act, P, \{s\}, AP, L)$ *with only one single initial state* s*.*

5 Model Checking of GPoCTL Under Finite-Memory Schedulers

Since a scheduler resolves the nondeterministic actions in GPDP and only possibilistic transitions left, it can induces a GPKS to model checking. For a given finite GPDP M, a finite-memory scheduler $\mathfrak{S}$, a state s in M, and a GPoCTL state formula Φ, compute the value $\|\Phi\|_{\mathfrak{S}}(s)$ under this scheduler.

5.1 Model Checking Under Finite-Memory Schedulers

Finite-memory schedulers enjoy the property that the GPKS $M_{\mathfrak{S}}$ can be identified with a GPKS where the states are just pairs $\langle s, q\rangle$ where s is a state in the GPDP and q is a mode of finite-memory schedulers $\mathfrak{S}$. Formal definition as follows:

Definition 7 (Product of GPDP and Finite-memory Scheduler). *For a finite GPDP $M = (S, Act, P, I, AP, L)$ and a finite memory scheduler $\mathfrak{S}$ denoted by a DFA $A = (Q, act, \Delta, start)$, the product $M \otimes A$ is an GPKS $M_{\mathfrak{S}} = (S \times Q, P_{\mathfrak{S}}, I_{\mathfrak{S}}, AP, L_{\mathfrak{S}})$, where*

(1) State space is $S \times Q$;
(2) $P_{\mathfrak{S}}(\langle s, q\rangle, \langle t, p\rangle) = P_{\mathfrak{S}}(s, act(q, s), t)$;
(3) $I_{\mathfrak{S}}(\langle s, q\rangle) = I(s)$;
(4) $L_{\mathfrak{S}}(\langle s, q\rangle, a) = L(s, a)$ for $a \in AP$.

The possibilistic transition function $P_{\mathfrak{S}}$ can also be represented by a fuzzy matrix. This fuzzy matrix is also written as $P_{\mathfrak{S}}$, i.e.,

$$P_{\mathfrak{S}} = (P_{\mathfrak{S}}(\langle s, q\rangle, \langle t, p\rangle))_{\langle s,q\rangle, \langle t,p\rangle \in S\times Q}$$

The paths in $M_{\mathfrak{S}}$ is defined as follows

$$\pi^+ = \langle s_0, q_0\rangle \to \langle s_1, q_1\rangle \to \langle s_2, q_2\rangle \to \cdots$$

Since S and Q are finite sets, then $S \times Q$ is finite. Therefore the induced GPKS $M_{\mathfrak{S}}$ is finite.

Example 1. Consider a GPDP in Fig. 1. This GPDP is deterministic apart from s where a nondeterministic choice between actions α and β exists. For a finite-memory scheduler $\mathfrak{S}$ that selectd between α and β alternately. Note that this scheduler starting with α on visiting s. The precise definition of the finite-memory scheduler $\mathfrak{S} = (Q, act, \Delta, start)$ is depicted in the Fig. 2. It has two modes: in the first mode only α can be selected, while in the other mode only β can be selected. The scheduler switches mode whenever visiting s. Formally,

(1) $Q = \{q_\alpha, q_\beta\}$;
(2) $act(q_\alpha, s) = \alpha$, $act(q_\beta, s) = \beta$, $act(q_\alpha, t) = act(q_\beta, t) = \alpha$;
(3) $\Delta(q_\alpha, s) = q_\beta$, $\Delta(q_\beta, s) = q_\beta$, $\Delta(q_\alpha, t) = q_\alpha$, $\Delta(q_\beta, t) = q_\beta$;
(4) $start(s) = q_\alpha$ for all $s \in S$.

We can obtain a GPKS $M_{\mathfrak{S}}$ with state space $S \times Q$, where $M_{\mathfrak{S}} = M \otimes A_{\mathfrak{S}}$, see Fig. 3

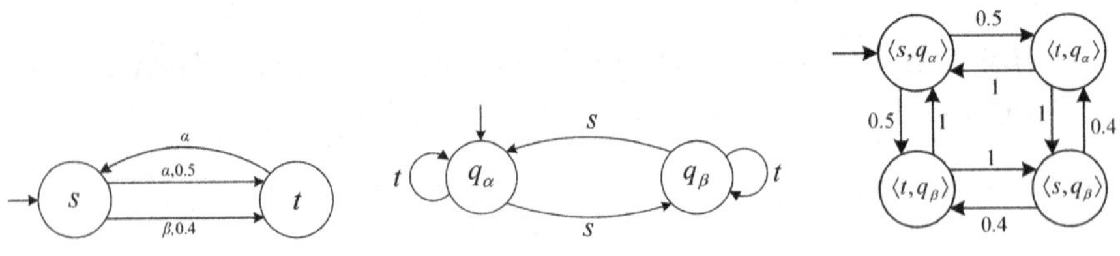

Fig. 1. GPDP **Fig. 2.** DFA $A_{\mathfrak{S}}$ **Fig. 3.** GPKS $M_{\mathfrak{S}}$

We next study the model checking of GPoCTL under finite-memory schedulers.

Theorem 1. *For a GPDP M, a finite-memory scheduler $A_{\mathfrak{S}}$ and a state formula $\Phi = Po_{\mathfrak{S}}(\bigcirc\Psi)$, then*

$$Po_{\mathfrak{S}}^{M}(s \models \bigcirc\Psi) = Po^{M\otimes A_{\mathfrak{S}}}(\langle s, q\rangle \models \bigcirc\Psi). \tag{9}$$

where $q = start(s)$.

Proof. Let $s = s_0, q_0 = start(s_0)$, then

$$\begin{aligned}
& Po_{\mathfrak{S}}^{M}(s_0 \models \bigcirc\Psi) \\
= & \bigvee_{\pi\in\mathfrak{S}\text{-}Paths(s_0)} Po_{\mathfrak{S}}(\pi) \wedge \|\bigcirc\Psi\|_{\mathfrak{S}}(\pi) \\
= & \bigvee_{\pi=s_0\mathfrak{S}(s_0)s_1\mathfrak{S}(ss_1)s_2\cdots\in\mathfrak{S}\text{-}Paths(s_0)} P(s_0, \mathfrak{S}(s_0), s_1) \wedge \|\Psi\|(s_1) \wedge P(s_1, \mathfrak{S}(ss_1), s_2) \wedge \cdots \\
= & \bigvee_{s_0,s_1\cdots\in S} P(s_0, act(start(s_0), s_0), s_1) \wedge \|\Psi\|(s_1) \wedge P(s_1, act(\Delta(start(s_0), s_0), \\
& s_1), s_2) \wedge \cdots \\
= & \bigvee_{s_0,s_1\cdots\in S} \bigvee_{\substack{q_1,q_2\cdots\in Q \\ q_{i+1}=\Delta(q_i,s_i)}} P(s_0, act(q_0, s_0), s_1) \wedge \|\Psi\|(s_1) \wedge P(s_1, act(q_1, s_1)), s_2) \wedge \cdots \\
= & \bigvee_{\pi^+=\langle s_0,q_0\rangle\cdots\in Paths^{M\otimes A_{\mathfrak{S}}}(\langle s_0,q_0\rangle)} P(\langle s_0, q_0\rangle, \langle s_1, q_1\rangle) \wedge \|\Psi\|(\langle s_1, q_1\rangle) \wedge P(\langle s_1, q_1\rangle, \\
& \langle s_2, q_2\rangle) \wedge \cdots \\
= & Po^{M\otimes A_{\mathfrak{S}}}(\langle s_0, q_0\rangle \models \bigcirc\Psi)
\end{aligned}$$

According to [16], we have

Corollary 1. *For a GPKS $M \otimes A_{\mathfrak{S}}$ and a formula $\Phi = Po_{\mathfrak{S}}(\bigcirc\Psi)$, we have*

$$Po^{M\otimes A_{\mathfrak{S}}}(\langle s, q\rangle \models \bigcirc\Psi) = P \circ D_{\Psi} \circ r_p(\langle s, q\rangle), \tag{10}$$

where P is the possibilistic transition matrix of GPKS $M \otimes A_{\mathfrak{S}}$, the definitions of D_{Ψ} and r_p are the same as in [16].

Theorem 2. *For a GPDP M, a finite-memory scheduler $A_{\mathfrak{S}}$ and a state formula $\Phi = Po_{\mathfrak{S}}(\Psi_1 \sqcup^{\leqslant n} \Psi_2)$, then*

$$Po_{\mathfrak{S}}^{M}(s \models \Psi_1 \sqcup^{\leqslant n} \Psi_2) = Po^{M\otimes A_{\mathfrak{S}}}(\langle s, q\rangle \models \Psi_1 \sqcup^{\leqslant n} \Psi_2).$$

where $q = start(s)$.

Proof. *Let* $s = s_0, q_0 = start(s_0)$, *then*

$$
\begin{aligned}
& Po_{\mathfrak{S}}^{M}(s_0 \models \Psi_1 \sqcup^{\leqslant n} \Psi_2) \\
= & \bigvee_{\pi \in \mathfrak{S}\text{-}Paths(s_0)} Po_{\mathfrak{S}}(\pi) \wedge \|\Psi_1 \sqcup^{\leqslant n} \Psi_2\|_{\mathfrak{S}}(\pi) \\
= & \bigvee_{\pi \in \mathfrak{S}\text{-}Paths(s_0)} P(s_0, \mathfrak{S}(s_0), s_1) \wedge \cdots \wedge (\|\Psi_2\|(s_0) \vee \bigvee_{0<j\leqslant n} ((\|\Psi_1\|(s_0) \wedge \bigwedge_{k<j} \\
& P(s_{k-1}, \mathfrak{S}(\hat{\pi}_{k-1}), s_k) \wedge \|\Psi_1\|(s_k)) \wedge P(s_{j-1}, \mathfrak{S}(\hat{\pi}_{j-1}), s_j) \wedge \|\Psi_2\|(s_j))) \\
= & \bigvee_{\pi = s_0 s_1 \cdots \in Paths(s_0)} \bigvee_{\substack{q_1, q_2 \cdots \in Q \\ q_{i+1} = \Delta(q_i, s_i)}} P(s_0, act(q_0, s_0), s_1) \wedge \cdots \wedge (\|\Psi_2\|(s_0) \vee \\
& \bigvee_{0<j\leqslant n} ((\|\Psi_1\|(s_0) \wedge \bigwedge_{k<j} P(s_{k-1}, act(q_{k-1}, s_{k-1}), s_k) \wedge \|\Psi_1\|(s_k)) \wedge \\
& P(s_{j-1}, act(q_{j-1}, s_{j-1}), s_j) \wedge \|\Psi_2\|(s_j))) \\
= & \bigvee_{\pi^+ = \langle s_0, q_0\rangle \cdots \in Paths^{M \otimes A_{\mathfrak{S}}}(\langle s_0, q_0\rangle)} P(\langle s_0, q_0\rangle, \langle s_1, q_1\rangle) \wedge \cdots \wedge \|\Psi_2\|(\langle s_0, q_0\rangle) \vee \\
& \bigvee_{0<j\leqslant n} ((\|\Psi_1\|(\langle s_0, q_0\rangle) \wedge \bigwedge_{k<j} P(\langle s_{k-1}, q_{k-1}\rangle, \langle s_k, q_k\rangle) \wedge \|\Psi_1\|(\langle s_k, q_k\rangle)) \\
& \wedge P(\langle s_{j-1}, q_{j-1}\rangle, \langle s_j, q_j\rangle) \wedge \|\Psi_2\|(\langle s_j, q_j\rangle))) \\
= & Po^{M \otimes A_{\mathfrak{S}}}(\langle s_0, q_0\rangle \models \Psi_1 \sqcup^{\leqslant n} \Psi_2)
\end{aligned}
$$

Corollary 2. *For a GPKS* $M \otimes A_{\mathfrak{S}}$ *and a formula* $\Phi = Po_{\mathfrak{S}}(\Psi_1 \sqcup^{\leqslant n} \Psi_2)$, *we have*

$$Po^{M \otimes A_{\mathfrak{S}}}(\langle s, q\rangle \models \Psi_1 \sqcup^{\leqslant n} \Psi_2) = \bigvee_{i=0}^{n} (D_{\Psi_1} \circ P)^i \circ D_{\Psi_2} \circ r_p(\langle s, q\rangle),$$

where P *is the possibilistic transition matrix of GPKS* $M \otimes A_{\mathfrak{S}}$.

Let $N = |S \times Q|$, for any $n \geqslant N$, we have

$$Po^{M \otimes A_{\mathfrak{S}}}(\langle s, q\rangle \models \Psi_1 \sqcup^{\leqslant n} \Psi_2) = (D_{\Psi_1} \circ P)^* \circ D_{\Psi_2} \circ r_p(\langle s, q\rangle),$$

By the definition of $\Psi_1 \sqcup \Psi_2$, we have

$$Po^{M \otimes A_{\mathfrak{S}}}(\langle s, q\rangle \models \Psi_1 \sqcup \Psi_2) = \lim_{n \to \infty} \|Po^{M \otimes A_{\mathfrak{S}}}(\Psi_1 \sqcup^{\leqslant n} \Psi_2)\|(\langle s, q\rangle),$$

it follows that

$$Po^{M \otimes A_{\mathfrak{S}}}(\langle s, q\rangle \models \Psi_1 \sqcup \Psi_2) = (D_{\Psi_1} \circ P)^* \circ D_{\Psi_2} \circ r_p(\langle s, q\rangle), \tag{11}$$

where $q = start(s)$.

Theorem 3. *For a GPDP* M, *a finite-memory scheduler* $A_{\mathfrak{S}}$ *and a state formula* $\Phi = Po_{\mathfrak{S}}(\Box\Psi)$, *then*

$$Po_{\mathfrak{S}}^{M}(s \models \Box\Psi) = Po^{M \otimes A_{\mathfrak{S}}}(\langle s, q_0\rangle \models \Box\Psi). \tag{12}$$

Proof. Let $s = s_0, q_0 = start(s_0)$, then

$$\begin{aligned}
&Po^M_{\mathfrak{S}}(s_0 \models \Box\Psi) \\
= &\bigvee_{\pi\in\mathfrak{S}\text{-}Paths(s_0)} Po_{\mathfrak{S}}(\pi) \wedge \|\Box\Psi\|_{\mathfrak{S}}(\pi) \\
= &\bigvee_{\pi=s_0\alpha_1 s_1\cdots\in\mathfrak{S}\text{-}Paths(s)} \bigwedge_{j=0}^{\infty} P(s_j, \mathfrak{S}(\hat{\pi}_j), s_{j+1}) \wedge \bigwedge_{j=0}^{\infty} \|\Psi\|(s_j) \\
= &\bigvee_{s_1,s_2\cdots\in S} \bigwedge_{j=0}^{\infty} P(s_0, act(start(s_0), s_0), s_1) \wedge P(s_1, act(\Delta(start(s_0), s_0), \\
&s_1), s_2) \wedge \cdots \wedge \bigwedge_{j=0}^{\infty} \|\Psi\|(s_j) \\
= &\bigvee_{s_1,s_2\cdots\in S} \bigvee_{\substack{q_1,q_2\cdots\in Q \\ q_{i+1}=\Delta(q_i,s_i)}} \bigwedge_{j=0}^{\infty} P(s_0, act(q_0, s_0), s_1) \wedge P(s_1, act(q_1, s_1), s_2) \\
&\wedge \cdots \wedge \bigwedge_{j=0}^{\infty} \|\Psi\|(s_j) \\
= &\bigvee_{\pi^+=\langle s_0,q_0\rangle\cdots\in Paths^{M\otimes A_{\mathfrak{S}}}(\langle s_0,q_0\rangle)} \bigwedge_{j=0}^{\infty} P(\langle s_j, q_j\rangle, \langle s_{j+1}, q_{j+1}\rangle) \wedge \bigwedge_{j=0}^{\infty} \|\Psi\|(s_j) \\
= &Po^{M\otimes A_{\mathfrak{S}}}(\langle s_0, q_0\rangle \models \Box\Psi)
\end{aligned}$$

Corollary 3. *Let* $x = (Po^{M\otimes A_{\mathfrak{S}}}(\langle s,q\rangle \models \Box\Psi))_{\langle s,q\rangle\in S\times Q}$, *then* x *is the greatest fixpoint of follows function.*

$$f(x) = \|\Psi\| \wedge P \circ x \tag{13}$$

where P *is possibilistic transition matrix of GPKS* $M \otimes A_{\mathfrak{S}}$. *The proof is similar to proof of fixpoint in [16] and thus is omitted here.*

In the same way, for the model checking based on necessity measures, we have following equations.

$$Ne_{\mathfrak{S}}(s \models \bigcirc\Psi) = 1 - Po_{\mathfrak{S}}(s \models \bigcirc\neg\Psi); \tag{14}$$

$$\begin{aligned} Ne_{\mathfrak{S}}(s \models \Psi_1 \sqcup \Psi_2) = (1 - Po_{\mathfrak{S}}(s \models \neg\Psi_2 \sqcup (\neg\Psi_1 \wedge \neg\Psi_2)))\wedge \\ (1 - Po_{\mathfrak{S}}(s \models \Box\neg\Psi_2)); \end{aligned} \tag{15}$$

$$\begin{aligned} Ne_{\mathfrak{S}}(s \models \Psi_1 \sqcup^{\leqslant n} \Psi_2) = (1 - Po_{\mathfrak{S}}(s \models \neg\Psi_2 \sqcup^{\leqslant n} (\neg\Psi_1 \wedge \neg\Psi_2)))\wedge \\ (1 - Po_{\mathfrak{S}}(s \models \Box^{\leqslant n}\neg\Psi_2)); \end{aligned} \tag{16}$$

$$Ne_{\mathfrak{S}}(s \models \Box\Psi) = 1 - Po_{\mathfrak{S}}(s \models \Diamond\neg\Psi); \tag{17}$$

$$Ne_{\mathfrak{S}}(s \models \Diamond\Psi) = 1 - Po_{\mathfrak{S}}(s \models \Box\neg\Psi). \tag{18}$$

5.2 Model Checking Under Memoryless Schedulers

Memoryless scheduler can be considered as finite-memory scheduler with just a single mode. That is, the GPKS $M_{\mathfrak{S}}$ induced by the memoryless scheduler can be view as a finite GPKS with state space S. Hence $|S \times Q| = |S|$. For a memoryless scheduler, we can obtain a induced GPKS with state space S.

Definition 8. *For a memoryless scheduler $\mathfrak{S}$, its possibilistic transition matrix can be defined as $P'_{\mathfrak{S}}$ such that*

$$P'_{\mathfrak{S}}(s,t) = P(s, \mathfrak{S}(s), t) \tag{19}$$

for any $s, t \in S$.

Theorem 4. *Let M be a finite GPDP, $\mathfrak{S}$ a memoryless scheduler and φ a GPoCTL path formula, $M'_{\mathfrak{S}}$ a GPKS with possibilistic transition matrix $P'_{\mathfrak{S}}$, then we have*

$$Po^M_{\mathfrak{S}}(s \models \varphi) = Po^{M'_{\mathfrak{S}}}(s \models \varphi). \tag{20}$$

The proof is obvious and is omitted here.

The corresponding algorithm of model checking as follows:

Algorithm 1: model checking based on finite-memory schedulers

Input: GPDP M, GPoCTL formula Φ, finite-memory scheduler $A_{\mathfrak{S}}$
Output: $\|\Phi\|_{\mathfrak{S}}(s)$
$M_{\mathfrak{S}} \leftarrow M \otimes A_{\mathfrak{S}}$; `// product the GPKS` $M_{\mathfrak{S}}$
Procedure GPoCTLCheck($\Phi, M_{\mathfrak{S}}$); `// this algorithm see[16]`
return $\|\Phi\|_{\mathfrak{S}}(s)$

The model checking under finite-memory schedulers is induced by the deterministic finite automata into a finite GPKS with state $S \times Q$, then we have following theorem about time complexity of model checking according to [16]. The proof can be found in [16] and is omitted here.

Theorem 5. *For a finite GPDP M and a GPoCTL with schedulers formula Φ, the model checking based on finite-memory schedulers can be determined in $O(size(M) \times ploy(|S \times Q|) \times |\Phi|)$. For $\Box\Phi$, it is can be determined in $O(|S \times Q|^3)$. Specially, the model checking under memoryless schedulers can be determined in $O(size(M) \times ploy(|S|) \times |\Phi|)$, where $|\Phi|$ denotes the length of formula Φ [16].*

6 Optimal Scheduler Based on Entropy-Weight TOPSIS

The optimal scheduler is to choose a scheduler that have optimal decisions between the all given schedulers. The selection of optimal scheduler in GPDP mainly depends on two factors: possibility measures and necessity measures. For example, the scheduler with the maximal possibility is may not be the optimal scheduler, since its necessity measures may be low, which leads to less feasibility of such scheduler. In the actual decision systems, the greater the measure change, the more useful decision information can be reflected. Decisions generally depends on widely varying measures. We need to assign weight to each measure in making decisions.

A simple example, for a formula φ, assuming that all given schedulers have the same necessity measures, thus making decisions that which scheduler is selected depend on possibility measures rather than necessity measures. Therefore, in order to determine which schedulers is optimal, we define d the decision factor function such that $d : \mathfrak{S} \to [0,1]$. Intuitively, the decision factor represents the distance between the current scheduler and the optimal scheduler. The larger or smaller the decision factor of a scheduler, the closer this scheduler is to the optimal scheduler.

We provide a method for selection of optimal scheduler based on Entropy-weight TOPSIS [21], see Algorithm 2. The weights of each measure can be obtained by method of Entropy-weight, the rank for distance (priority for schedulers) between a current scheduler and the optimal scheduler can be calculated by TOPSIS. Finally, an example is given to illustrate the optimal scheduler model checking algorithm.

7 Illustrative Example

We consider the patient's example studied in [2,4,18,20] to illustrate the applications of optimal scheduler based on Entropy-weight TOPSIS and a little revision is adopted for our purpose. Assuming that there exists a new virus, doctors don't have enough knowledge and experience about the virus, so they can't make powerful treatment. In the end, they provide eight feasible drugs. Writing such eight drugs as α_i for $1 \leqslant i \leqslant 8$ respectively. Doctors want to choose the best treatment from these eight treatments, that is, choosing a scheduler such that its possibility and necessity measure as large as possible. We use GPDP to model the treatment process. The doctor describes the physical status of patients in three states: *good*, *poor* and *bad*. States can be described by using crisp set over atomic proposition. For convenience, let $AP = S = \{good, poor, bad\}$ and each edge in the model represents the possibility distributions of eight drugs.

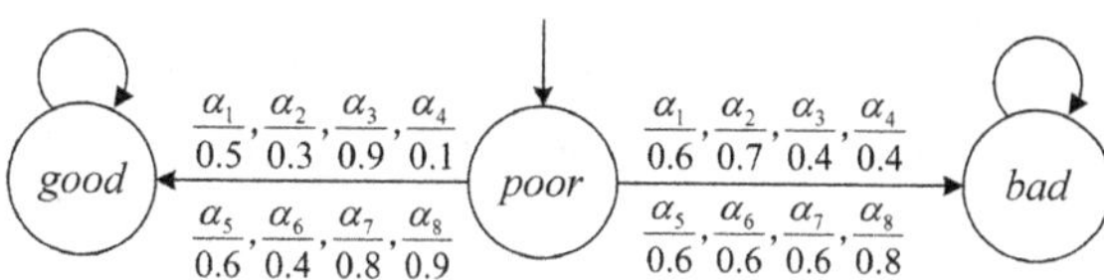

Fig. 4. patient's model

The property that a patient finally recovery from poor physical status can be described by a GPoCTL formula, i.e., $Po_{\mathfrak{S}}(poor \models \Diamond good)$. Intuitively, when selecting the optimal scheduler from these eight schedulers, the change of the

Algorithm 2: Calculate d based on Entropy-weight TOPSIS

Input: $Po_{\mathfrak{S}_i}(s \models \varphi)$ and $Ne_{\mathfrak{S}_i}(s \models \varphi)$
Output: $d[i]$ and $DNe_{\mathfrak{S}_i}(s \models \varphi)$

$n \leftarrow |\mathfrak{S}_i|$; `// The number of given schedulers is assigned to` n
Matrix $x[n][2]$, $p[n][2]$, $z[n][2]$, $z^*[n][2]$
Row $d[2]$, $w[2]$, $z^{*+}[n]$, $z^{*-}[n]$, $D^+[n]$, $D^-[n]$, $C[n]$; `// Define matrix and array`
for $i = 1, 2, \cdots, n$ **do**
  $x[i][1] \leftarrow Po_{\mathfrak{S}_i}(s \models \varphi)$
  $x[i][2] \leftarrow Ne_{\mathfrak{S}_i}(s \models \varphi)$; `// Construct original measure matrix`
for $i = 1, 2, \cdots, n$ **do**
  for $j = 1, 2$ **do**
    $p[i][j] \leftarrow x[i][j] / \sum_{i=1}^{n} x[i][j]$; `// Calculate the ratio of each measure`
for $j = 1, 2$ **do**
  $u[j] \leftarrow 1 + 1/\ln n \cdot \sum_{t=1}^{n} p[t][j] \ln p[t][j]$; `// Calculate the information utility value`
  $w[j] \leftarrow u[j]/u[1] + u[2]$; `// Determine the weights for each measures`
for $i = 1, 2, \cdots, n$ **do**
  for $j = 1, 2$ **do**
    $z[i][j] \leftarrow x[i][j] / \sqrt{\sum_{t=1}^{n} x[t][j]^2}$; `// Construct normalized matrix`
    $z^*[i][j] \leftarrow z[i][j] \cdot w[j]$; `// Construct matrix with weights`
for $i = 1, 2, \cdots, n$ **do**
  $z^{*+}[i] \leftarrow z[i][1] \vee z[i][2]$; `// The optimal solution`
  $z^{*-}[i] \leftarrow z[i][1] \wedge z[i][2]$; `// The worst solution`
  $D^+[i] \leftarrow \sqrt{\sum_{t=1}^{2} (z^*[i][t] - z^{*+}[t])^2}$; `// Calculate the optimal distance`
  $D^-[i] \leftarrow \sqrt{\sum_{t=1}^{2} (z^*[i][t] - z^{*-}[t])^2}$; `// Calculate the worst distance`
  $d[i] \leftarrow D^-[i] / (D^+[i] + D^-[i])$; `// Calculate the relative distance`
return $d[i]$; `// Return decision factors for any schedulers`

possibility measures is larger than its necessity measures, so when selecting the optimal scheduler, the possibility measures will reflect more information utility in making decisions and thus its weight should be greater. Specifically, for $\varphi = \Diamond good$, we can obtain the weight of possibiity measures is 0.61 and necessity measures 0.39 by parameter w in Algorithm 2. The final calculation results are shown in Table 1.

By the results of calculation, it can be found that although the possibility measures for $\mathfrak{S}_4$ is the largest in a given schedulers, its priority is lower than $\mathfrak{S}_8$. The reason may be that the possibility measure of $\mathfrak{S}_4$ is not much different from possibility measure of $\mathfrak{S}_8$, but the former's necessity measure is smaller and thus affects the priority of $\mathfrak{S}_4$. After determining the weights for each measure, the model checker finally determines $\mathfrak{S}_8$ as the optimal scheduler. In addition,

Table 1. The results based on entropy TOPSIS

Schedulers	$\mathfrak{S}_1$	$\mathfrak{S}_2$	$\mathfrak{S}_3$	$\mathfrak{S}_4$	$\mathfrak{S}_5$	$\mathfrak{S}_6$	$\mathfrak{S}_7$	$\mathfrak{S}_8$
$Po_{\mathfrak{S}}$	0.5	0.3	0.9	1	0.6	0.4	0.8	0.9
$Ne_{\mathfrak{S}}$	0.4	0.3	0.6	0.6	0.4	0.4	0.6	0.8
d	0.27	0	0.79	0.85	0.39	0.15	0.69	0.87
Priority	6	8	3	2	5	7	4	1

if the necessity measures of the two schedulers are the same, the model checker will choose a scheduler with a larger possibility such as the priority of $\mathfrak{S}_5$ is higher than $\mathfrak{S}_6$. If the possibility measures of the two schedulers are the same, the model checker will choose the scheduler with larger necessity such as the priority of $\mathfrak{S}_8$ is higher than $\mathfrak{S}_3$.

8 Conclusions

We have studied the model checking based on possibilistic decision process under finite-memory schedulers in this paper. The behavior of finite-memory schedulers can be described by a deterministic finite automaton (DFA) and thus we can induce a GPDP to be an finite GPKS by a finite-memory scheduler. The model checking of computation tree logic based on GPKS has been completely studied in [16]. Furthermore, we study the model checking under memoryless schedulers and the time complexity analysis of possibilistic decision process under finite-memory schedulers are presented. Finally, a method based on Entropy-weight TOPSIS is given to select a optimal scheduler.

Further work is required to calculate the maximum or minimal possibility and corresponding optimal schedulers when ranged over all schedulers.

Acknowledgment. This work was partially supported by National Science Foundation of China (Grant Nos: 12071271,11671244) and the Fundamental Research Funds For the Central Universities (Grant No: 2020CSLY016). Useful suggestions given by Junmei Wang, Dr. Na Chen and Dr. Xianfeng Yu are also acknowledged.

References

1. Baier, C., Katoen, J.P.: Principles of Model Checking. The MIT press, Cambridge (2008)
2. Cao, Y., Ying, M.: Observability and decentralized control of fuzzy discrete-event systems. IEEE Trans. Fuzzy Syst. **14**(2), 202–216 (2006)
3. Clarke, E., Grumberg, O., Peled, D.: Model Checking. Massachusetts, London, UK, Cambridge (1999)
4. Deng, W., Qiu, D.: Bifuzzy discrete event systems and their supervisory control theory. IEEE Trans. Fuzzy Syst. **23**(6), 2107–2121 (2015)
5. Drakopoulos, J.A.: Probabilities, possibilities, and fuzzy sets. Fuzzy Sets Syst. **75**(1), 1–15 (1995)

6. Dubois, D.: Possibility theory and statistical reasoning. Comput. Stat. Data Anal. **51**(1), 47–69 (2006)
7. Dubois, D., Prade, H.: Possibility theory, probability theory and multiple-valued logics: a clarification. Ann. Math. Artif. Intell. **32**(1–4), 35–66 (2001)
8. Dubois, D., Prade, H.: Possibility theory. Scholarpedia **2**(10), 2074 (2007)
9. Dubois, D., Prade, H.: Possibility theory and its applications: where do we stand? In: Kacprzyk, J., Pedrycz, W. (eds.) Springer Handbook of Computational Intelligence, pp. 31–60. Springer, Heidelberg (2015). https://doi.org/10.1007/978-3-662-43505-2_3
10. Dubois, D., Dupin de Saint-Cyr, F., Prade, H.: Update postulates without inertia. In: Froidevaux, C., Kohlas, J. (eds.) ECSQARU 1995. LNCS, vol. 946, pp. 162–170. Springer, Heidelberg (1995). https://doi.org/10.1007/3-540-60112-0_19
11. Dubois, D., de Saintcyr, F.D., Prade, H.: Updating, transition constraints and possibilistic Markov chains. In: Bouchon-Meunier, B., Yager, R.R., Zadeh, L.A. (eds.) IPMU 1994. LNCS, vol. 945, pp. 261–272. Springer, Heidelberg (1995). https://doi.org/10.1007/BFb0035959
12. Li, Y.: Quantitative model checking of linear-time properties based on generalized possibility measures. Fuzzy Sets Syst. **320**, 17–39 (2017)
13. Li, Y., Lei, L., Li, S.: Computation tree logic model checking based on multi-valued possibility measures. Inf. Sci. **485**, 87–113 (2019)
14. Li, Y., Li, L.: Model checking of linear-time properties based on possibility measure. IEEE Trans. Fuzzy Syst. **21**(5), 842–854 (2013)
15. Li, Y., Li, Y., Ma, Z.: Computation tree logic model checking based on possibility measures. Fuzzy Sets Syst. **262**, 44–59 (2015)
16. Li, Y., Ma, Z.: Quantitative computation tree logic model checking based on generalized possibility measures. IEEE Trans. Fuzzy Syst. **23**(6), 2034–2047 (2015)
17. Li, Y., Wei, J.: Possibilistic fuzzy linear temporal logic and its model checking. IEEE Trans. Fuzzy Syst. **29**(7), 1899–1913 (2021)
18. Lin, F., Ying, H.: Modeling and control of fuzzy discrete event systems. IEEE Trans. Syst. Man Cybern. Part B (Cybern.) **32**(4), 408–415 (2002)
19. Pan, H., Li, Y., Cao, Y., Ma, Z.: Model checking fuzzy computation tree logic. Fuzzy Sets Syst. **262**, 60–77 (2015)
20. Qiu, D.: Supervisory control of fuzzy discrete event systems: a formal approach. IEEE Trans. Syst. Man Cybern. Part B (Cybern.) **35**(1), 72–88 (2005)
21. Yoon, K.P., Hwang, C.L.: Multiple Attribute Decision Making: An Introduction. Sage publications, Thousand Oaks (1995)
22. Zadeh, L.A.: Fuzzy sets. Inf. Control **8**(3), 338–353 (1965)
23. Zadeh, L.A.: Fuzzy sets as a basis for a theory of possibility. Fuzzy Sets Syst. **1**(1), 3–28 (1978)

A Survey of Real-Time Scheduling on Multiprocessor Systems

Zhenyu Sun, Mengying Guo, and Xingwu Liu(✉)

Institute of Computing Technology, Beijing, China
{sunzhenyu,liuxingwu}@ict.ac.cn

Abstract. Real-time system scheduling draws a lot of attention in the past half-century. In this survey, we give a general introduction to real-time scheduling on multiprocessor systems. Basic concepts, terms, and definitions are explained. We describe a series of classic results published several decades ago that still have a wide impact on academia today, and also novel and inspiring results in recent years. These results cover global, partition, and hybrid scheduling approaches. Lately, more and more works focus on scheduling special task models like AVR tasks, MC tasks, and so on, which will also be introduced in this survey. We discuss research directions that are potentially promising in real-time scheduling on multiprocessor systems to conclude this survey.

Keywords: Real-time system · Scheduling algorithm · Multiprocessor · Performance

1 Introduction

Real-time systems are widely studied and implemented in the past few decades. From electronic engineering, aircraft engineering to communication engineering, and many other areas, clients release repeatable requests that demand low response time, and sometimes, the inter-release time between requests is unpredictable. To meet this kind of demand, real-time system developers need to make an effort at both the hardware and software levels.

At the software level, a series of approaches have been proposed and draw attention from the 1960s till today. At the beginning stage of research on real-time scheduling, researchers put more effort into uniprocessor scheduling, since the uniprocessor platform was more widely developed. However, the progress on the uniprocessor plat-forms encountered the bottleneck, eventually. Purely increasing clock speeds does not increase performance, since the current architecture cannot deal with excessive power consumption and heat dissipation. Under this circumstance, both industry and academia put their effort into multiprocessor platforms. In the first decade of the 21st century, commercial multiprocessors chips were released, which drew much more attention to researches on real-time scheduling on multiprocessor platforms.

Researches on multiprocessor platforms have a long history. In the groundbreaking paper [1], researchers proposed systemic fundamental theoretical results on the feasibility of task systems under multiprocessor platforms. This work, with several other works,

Z. Cai et al. (Eds.): NCTCS 2021, CCIS 1494, pp. 89–118, 2021.
https://doi.org/10.1007/978-981-16-7443-3_7

made researchers realize that scheduling under multiprocessor platforms is much harder than that under uniprocessor platforms. It is worth mentioning the "Dhall effect" in [2], which showed that in some specific task systems, the low utilization task keeps unschedulable under global scheduling, no matter how many processors are provided. From the "Dhall effect", researchers saw the characters of both global and partition scheduling. In the cases showing the "Dhall effect", partition scheduling is always superior to global scheduling. While later [3] showed that the primary reason for the "Dhall effect" comes from high utilization tasks in the system, instead of global scheduling manner.

These works told researchers that scheduling under multiprocessor platforms is not as trivial as transplanting uniprocessor scheduling algorithms into multiprocessor platforms with task migrating (i.e., global scheduling). Global scheduling and partition scheduling became two basic branches in multiprocessor scheduling. Besides these two typical approaches, hybrid approaches [4, 5], which combine characters from both global scheduling and partition scheduling, are proposed in recent years. These approaches usually outperform traditional approaches for specific task systems, which is proved by both empirical and theoretical evidence.

Besides discussing global/partition scheduling manner or even hybrid approaches, another trend of research on scheduling algorithms is to deal with special task models. Basic task models can be seen as a set of tasks that can only be executed sequentially. While for the DAG task model [6], tasks have inner parallelism that can be exploited under multiprocessor platforms. In addition, Mixed-Criticality (MC) task model [7] allows the scheduler to assign different criticality levels to different tasks, which brings challenges to scheduling. We will introduce several typical kinds of special task models in the latter sections.

In this survey, we systematically introduce basic concepts and terms in real-time scheduling, and a series of results in multiprocessor scheduling, including classic results in the past half-century, and also popular results in the last decade. This survey is organized as follows. Section 2 introduces basic concepts and notations in real-time scheduling. Section 3 introduces several approaches to evaluate scheduling algorithms, for example, the speedup factor. Section 4 introduces classic results of global/partition scheduling on sequential tasks (basic task model). Section 5 embraces typical results of hybrid approaches like federated scheduling. Section 6 describes several kinds of special task models and some results on these models from recent years. We conclude this survey in Sect. 7.

2 Basic Concepts and Notations

In this section, we introduce basic definitions and terms in real-time scheduling. These definitions are widely used in many branches in real-time system scheduling researches. Notice that much more terms are embraced only in specific topics in real-time scheduling. We defer the introduction of these terms to later sections where those researches are introduced.

2.1 Task and Job

A typical configuration of scheduling problems comprises two parts: a task system of n tasks and a group of m processors. Each task constantly releases jobs that are executed on processors. Every job released by the same task follows some common properties and needs a certain amount of processor time to finish execution while not violating time constraints. Each task perhaps corresponds to a piece of code that will be called by the system every once in a while, and each job corresponds to a single calling. The running time of a single calling may be a variate determined by a specific environment during runtime. Therefore, for analyzing use, we usually consider the worst-case execution time of a job.

In the general task model, a task system is a set $\tau = \{\tau_1, \tau_2, \ldots, \tau_n\}$, and each task τ_i is represented by a tuple $\tau_i = (C_i, D_i, T_i)$, where C_i is the Worst-Case Execution Time (WCET) of each job released by τ_i, D_i denote the relative deadline of τ_i. In the hard-real time scheduling, the job τ_{ij} released by task τ_i at time instant r_i must finish execution by the time instant $r_i + D_i$ (the latter one usually called absolute deadline). T_i is the minimum inter-release time between any continuous jobs corresponding to the same task. In addition, we define *utilization* of task τ_i as $u_i = \frac{C_i}{T_i}$, and *density* of task τ_i as $\delta_i = \frac{C_i}{\min\{T_i, D_i\}}$.

A real-time scheduling algorithm should decide how to assign jobs to processors and decide the execution order of jobs in the same processor, to guarantee all jobs not violating their time constraints. The major topic, in real-time system scheduling, is to propose different scheduling algorithms under different circumstances and prove their effectiveness in theoretical and empirical aspects.

2.2 Hard Real-Time and Soft Real-Time

In the terms of time constraints, scheduling can be categorized as hard real-time scheduling [8] and soft real-time scheduling [9]. In hard real-time scheduling, a correct schedule should make sure that each job finishes execution before its absolute deadline. While in soft real-time scheduling, jobs are allowed to break the deadline, but the execution time after absolute deadline should be bounded. Note the response time R_i of a job released by τ_i as the length of time interval from being released to finish execution. In hard real-time scheduling, $R_i - D_i$ (usually called t*ardiness*) should be non-positive, while in soft real-time scheduling, the tardiness should have a positive upper bound.

2.3 Periodic and Sporadic

From the perspective of minimum inter-release time T_i, a task system can be classified as a periodic task system or a sporadic task system. In the periodic task system [10], each task $\tau_i = (C_i, D_i, T_i)$ releases a job every exact T_i units of time. In a sporadic task system [11], each task releases a job at least every T_i units of time.

It is clear to see that in periodic task systems, the behavior of the tasks will be easier to predict. Therefore, results in periodic task systems are much more than in sporadic task systems.

2.4 Constrained, Implicit and Arbitrary Deadline

For any task τ_i, period T_i and deadline D_i decide most of the behavior of the task, hence lead to the difficulty of correctly scheduling. Based on the relation of T and D from all the tasks, a task system τ can be categorized into the following types:

- Constrained-deadline: $D_i \leq T_i$, for all task s$\tau_i \in \tau$
- Implicit-deadline: $D_i = T_i$, for all tasks $\tau_i \in \tau$
- Arbitrary-deadline: D_i and T_i are independent for all tasks $\tau_i \in \tau$.

Among these types, the task systems with an implicit deadline are the most widely analyzed, since it gives the most information about the task systems.

2.5 Fixed Job Priority, Fixed Task Priority and Dynamic Priority

The behavior of scheduling algorithms can be seen as a process that assigning priorities to tasks so that every task can execute on processors based on priorities. According to the priority assigning policy, the scheduling algorithms can be classified into the following types.

Fixed task priority: before the arrival of any job, the algorithm assigns a fixed priority to each task based on the parameters already given by this task. All jobs released by this task will inherit its priority to compete for processors. The priority assignment will remain unchanged.

Deadline Monotonic (DM) [12–16] and Rate Monotonic (RM) [17–22] are two typical scheduling algorithms based on fixed task priority policy. These two algorithms have different intuitions. DM algorithm assigns a higher priority to the task that has a shorter relative deadline D_i. On the contrary, the RM algorithm focuses on the period of each task. A task with a shorter period will release jobs more frequently, and hence will be assigned higher priority by the RM algorithm.

Fixed job priority: unlike fixed task priority policy, in fixed-job priority policy [23–25], each job will be assigned priority individually once it is released. Therefore, the jobs from the same task will probably get different priorities. One of the classic algorithms based on this policy is Earliest Deadline First (EDF) algorithm [1]. At the arrival of any job τ_{ij} from any task τ_i, the EDF algorithm will check its absolute deadline $d = a_{ij} + D_i$, where a_{ij} is the arrival time instant of job τ_{ij}. The job with an earlier absolute deadline will be assigned a higher priority.

Dynamic priority: in the dynamic priority policy, each job will have a priority that varies with time. For example, consider an algorithm assigning priorities to jobs based on their waiting time, that is, the longer time a ready job has waited for processors, the higher priority this job will have.

For now, we have introduced several classic scheduling algorithms: EDF, DM, and RM. These are the foundation of many scheduling algorithms.

In [26], researchers proposed a two-level scheduling framework that logically divides a given task set into two sets: higher-priority task set *HP* and lower-priority task set *LP*. The framework schedules *HP* by the implicit-deadline optimal algorithms (such as ER-Fair [27], U-EDF [28], QPS [29]) and LP by the heuristic algorithms (such as EDZL

[30], FPZL [31], LLF [32]). This work also considered incorporating the idea of fluid scheduling into the framework, which brings significant schedulability improvement. Experiments showed the effectiveness of this framework by finding a series of task systems that cannot be guaranteed schedulable by classic scheduling algorithms but can be guaranteed schedulable by the proposed framework, especially for task systems with heavy tasks (the task with $\Sigma_{\tau_i \in \tau}\left(\frac{C_i}{D_i}\right) > m$).

Former works had shown that optimization problems in real-time scheduling can be formed as Integer Linear Programming (ILP), wherein most of the cases, task priority assignment will be part of variables, and the WCRT (worst-case response time) will be considered as constraints or objective function. This configuration aims to find the optimal priority assignment to get minimum response time.

Though a string of advanced techniques has been incorporated into ILP solvers like CPLEX, the solver still can't handle large-scale cases. [33] proposed several problem-specific observations, which will be used to generate a framework that is much more efficient. For example, though it has been shown that the calculation of WCRT is NP-hard, while in practice, the calculation is fairly efficient in many cases [34]. The general ILP solver does not consider this observation. This paper also proposed an efficient algorithm that calculates the maximum virtual deadline that just leads the task system unschedulable. The framework combines these two observations with a classic ILP solver. Experiments showed that this framework runs 1000 times faster than traditional solvers, without loss of optimality.

2.6 Preemptive and Non-preemptive

Since different tasks or jobs will have different priorities, a natural question arises: should scheduling algorithms allow the higher-priority jobs to preempt lower-priority jobs during execution?

Scheduling algorithms can be divided into three categories by the decision on the question above:

Preemptive: at any time, an executing lower-priority job can be preempted by a higher-priority job. The higher-priority job will get the processor and execute until it finishes or gets preempted by a much higher-priority job. The lower-priority job that is preempted will be suspended until enough idle processors are provided. In a preemptive manner, the lower-priority job will probably wait for a very long time to finish when higher-priority jobs keep arriving and preempting the lower-priority jobs.

Non-preemptive: once a job begins execution, it cannot be preempted until it finishes and releases processors. In a non-preemptive manner, the higher-priority job that arrives later will probably wait for a long time since the earlier-arrived lower-priority jobs have occupied all the processors already.

Cooperative: a job only can be preempted by a higher-priority job in one or some subintervals of its execution time. The cooperative manner is the combination of preemptive and non-preemptive. [35] proposed Fixed-Priority with Deferred preemption Scheduling (FPDS). In FPDS, each job will set a "non-preemptive interval", during which any other job cannot preempt the current job, hence delaying the preemption. Essentially, the job in a non-preemptive interval has the highest priority. FPDS absorbs the concept of both *preemptive* and *non-preemptive* scheduling since if we set the length of the non-preemptive interval of task τ_i to 0, FPDS degrades into "preemptive", and if the length is set to C_i, FPDS degrades into "non-preemptive".

In [35], researchers considered two questions: *a.* given task system and their priority assignment, how to decide the length of the non-preemptive interval of each task? *b.* given task system, how to assign each task's priority while deciding its length of non-preemptive interval? To address these two questions, this paper firstly calculates the minimum length of the non-preemptive interval of taskτ_i, which is $F(i) = \max_g\{F(i, g)\}$, where g represents every job released in the concerning interval, and

$$F(i, g) = \max\big(C_i - S_{i,g}, 1\big)$$

$$S_{i,g} = \max_{t \in P_{i,g}} \big\{S_{i,g}(t) | C_i - S_{i,g}(t) \leq gT_i + D_i - t \wedge S_{i,g}(t) \geq 0\big\}.$$

Note $P_{i,g}$ the start time of legal non-preemptive interval of job g, we have

$$P_{i,g} = \big(\forall_{j \in hp(i)} \{hT_j - 1\} \in [gT_i, gT_i + D - 1]\big) \cup \{gT_i + D_i - 1\},$$

where *hp*(*i*) is the task subset containing all the tasks whose non-preemptive interval has been calculated and that have higher priority than τ_i.

The procedure above determines the minimum length of the non-preemptive interval of every task, which achieves a trade-off. On the one hand, this guarantees the lower-priority job being schedulable, and gives higher-priority job enough time interval to preempt, making it easier to schedule higher-priority job.

For question *a*, [35] proposed FNR (Final Non-preemptive Region) algorithm, that considers each job from low priority task to high priority and calculates their non-preemptive interval, then schedules the task system.

For question *b*, [35] proposed FNR-PA (Final Non-preemptive Region with Priority Assignment), which for every task that not be assigned priority, try to assign each possible priority from lowest to highest and calculate the corresponding length of the minimum non-preemptive interval. If the algorithm gets a legal non-preemptive interval for the current task under current priority assigning, then set this configuration fixed. Repeat this procedure until every task gets its priority and non-preemptive interval.

This paper proved that if the above algorithm successfully generates an assignment for the task system in the ordering described above, then the task system is deemed schedulable. In addition, the optimality of these two algorithms is also proven (the definition of *optimality* will be given in Sect. 3), that is, for any given task system τ, if each task gets a legal priority assignment and a non-preemptive interval that makes τ schedulable, then the algorithms above are guaranteed to calculate it correctly.

2.7 Schedulable and Feasible

Given a task system $\tau = \{\tau_1, \tau_2, \tau_3, \ldots, \tau_n\}$, considering the cases that the arrival time of the first job released by each task can be varied and inter-release time of continuous jobs can be varied in sporadic case. In these cases, τ can generate multiple job sequences during runtime.

A task system τ is *schedulable* on algorithm $\mathcal{A}$, if $\mathcal{A}$ can generate a legal schedule on τ.

A task system τ is *feasible*, if and only if an algorithm exists that can schedule any job sequence generated by τ.

Schedulable and feasible are two important concepts describing the performance of scheduling algorithms. Specifically, to properly describe the performance of an algorithm $\mathcal{A}$, we should discuss how many different task systems it can schedule and the amount of resource it needs (e.g., number of processors, speed of processors).

For typical configuration we have some basic results about feasibility:

$$U \leq m \begin{cases} \Leftrightarrow \textit{feasible}, \quad \textit{implicit deadline}\,[1] \\ \Leftarrow \textit{feasible}, \; \textit{constrained or arbitrary deadline} \end{cases},$$

and for constrained or arbitrary deadline task system, it suffices to be feasible if

$$\textit{load}(\tau) \leq m.$$

2.8 Algorithm and Schedulability Test

As mentioned above, one measurement to the effectiveness of a scheduling algorithm $\mathcal{A}$ is the range of task systems that are schedulable by $\mathcal{A}$. *Schedulability test* is a concept based on this perspective.

For a given scheduling algorithm $\mathcal{A}$, a *sufficient* schedulability test gives a sufficient condition, any task system that satisfies this condition is deemed schedulable. Correspondingly, a *necessary* schedulability test gives a necessary condition for any task system that is deemed schedulable. If a schedulability test is both sufficient and necessary, it is called an *exact* test.

[36] and [37] proposed K2Q and K2U, which are two powerful and applicable schedulability analysis frameworks that apply to a wide selection of real-time task models. The general concept behind this framework is to test only a subset of time points in running time for verifying the schedulability. Specifically, the frameworks test k points under any fixed-priority scheduling when checking the schedulability of the task with the k-th highest priority in the system, while only partial information of $k-1$ higher-priority tasks is required.

To accomplish this, [36] defined LRTO (Last Release Time Ordering) which is the ordering of $k-1$ tasks that has higher priority than the current task τ_k in the time window of interest. LRTO is used for formulating the test with simple and linear arithmetic based on the complete ordering.

In some cases, this (worst case) ordering can be easily obtained, but in most cases not. This paper yet tells us that finding the worst-case ordering is not a hard problem, which just requires sorting $k-1$ higher-priority tasks under a simple criterion.

The main results in the K2Q framework are as follows:

(*Schedulability test*) This framework obtains a k-points schedulability test under a given last release time ordering π of the $k-1$ higher-priority tasks. For fixed-priority scheduling policy, to test its schedulability, it suffices to verify the existence of t_j with $j = 1, 2, ..., k$ such that $0 \leq t_1 \leq t_2 \leq \cdots \leq t_{k-1} \leq t_k$ and

$$C_k + \sum_{i=1}^{k-1} \alpha_i t_i U_i + \sum_{i=1}^{j-1} \beta_i C_i \leq t_j,$$

where $C_k > 0$, for $i = 1, 2, ..., k-1$, $\alpha_i > 0$, $U_i > 0$, $C_i \geq 0$, and $\beta_i > 0$ depend on the setting of the task models and task τ_i.

(*Response time analysis*) This framework proposes a k-point last-release response time analysis under a fixed-priority scheduling policy. Given the last release time ordering π of the $k-1$ higher-priority tasks, the response time of k-th highest priority task is obtained by finding the maximum

$$t_k = C_k + \sum_{i=1}^{k-1} \alpha_i t_i U_i + \sum_{i=1}^{k-1} \beta_i C_i,$$

with $0 \leq t_1 \leq t_2 \leq \cdots \leq t_{k-1} \leq t_k$ and

$$C_k + \sum_{i=1}^{k-1} \alpha_i t_i U_i + \sum_{i=1}^{j-1} \beta_i C_i > t_j, \forall j = 1, 2, \ldots, k-1,$$

where

$$C_k > 0, \text{ for } i = 1, 2, \ldots, k-1, \ \alpha_i > 0, \ U_i > 0, \ C_i \geq 0, \text{ and } \beta_i > 0.$$

are dependent upon the setting of the task models and task τ_i. α_i and β_i can be decided by other simple criteria.

Based on the exact configuration of the task model (constrained/implicit deadline, DAG/Self-suspend task, uniprocessor/multiprocessor, and so on) it may come up with different α_i and β_i. In general, this is a quadratic-form framework to generate schedulability test and response time analysis.

Chen et al. also proposed another framework named K2U, which is based on the same general idea with K2Q, to generate a new and improved schedulability test compared with K2Q. The differences between K2Q and K2U are: when considering task τ_k, K2Q needs the $k-1$ higher-priority tasks' utilizations and execution times, while K2U only needs their utilizations; K2Q generates quadratic-form schedulability condition while K2U obtains the hyperbolic form.

2.9 Demand Bound Function

For a processor, demand bound $h(t)$ is denoted as the maximum amount of work that may be assigned to the current processor in the time interval $[0, t)$, that is,

$$DBF(t) = \sum_{i=1}^{n} \max\left(0, \left\lceil \frac{t - D_i}{T_i} \right\rceil + 1\right) C_i.$$

The load function $h(t)$ [38] is defined as the maximum amount of work that may be assigned to a processor in unit-time, given task system τ:

$$load(\tau) = \max_{t>0}\left(\frac{DBF(t)}{t}\right).$$

These two functions give quantitative description workload bound from the perspective of processors, hence are widely used in the analysis of scheduling algorithms.

3 Measurement

Essentially, the scheduling algorithm is an approximation algorithm since the algorithm is always given partial information about the scheduling problem. So basically, the way to evaluate a scheduling algorithm is to compare its performance with optimal performance. Here, the concept of optimal performance stands for the performance in ideal circumstances, like providing an infinite number of processors or full knowledge of tasks' behavior (also called clairvoyance). Based on the above idea, several tools can measure the effectiveness of scheduling algorithms sensibly.

3.1 Utilization Bound

Given a task system $\tau = \{\tau_1, \tau_2, \ldots, \tau_n\}$, denote $U = \Sigma_{i=1}^{n} u_i$ as utilization of τ, where u_i is the utilization of task τ_i.

For a given algorithm $\mathcal{A}$, the worst-case utilization bound is the least possible utilization for a task system that guarantees to be schedulable under $\mathcal{A}$. According to this definition, if an algorithm $\mathcal{A}$ has utilization bound $U_{\mathcal{A}}$, then for any arbitrarily small ϵ, there exists a task system with utilization $U_{\mathcal{A}} + \epsilon$ that not schedulable under algorithm $\mathcal{A}$, while any task system with utilization no more than $U_{\mathcal{A}}$ is schedulable under $\mathcal{A}$. Utilization bound gives a sufficient condition for schedulability of algorithm, so it is a sufficient yet not necessary test.

3.2 Dominance, Equivalence and Incomparable

Under most circumstances, we want to compare the performance between two actual scheduling algorithms under the same condition (number and speed of processors, the behavior of task system, etc.). A trivial approach to this is to find which algorithm can schedule more task systems than the other one.

Given two scheduling algorithms $\mathcal{A}$ and $\mathcal{B}$, $\mathcal{A}$ *dominate* $\mathcal{B}$ if any task system that is schedulable under $\mathcal{B}$ is also schedulable under $\mathcal{A}$. The check of schedulability in the definition above can be achieved by tests of the corresponding algorithms.

If "$\mathcal{A}$ dominate $\mathcal{B}$" and "$\mathcal{B}$ dominate $\mathcal{A}$" hold for the same time, we say $\mathcal{A}$ is *equivalent* to $\mathcal{B}$. The equivalence between two algorithms indicates that they have equal performance in the perspective of "number of schedulable task systems".

If a task system is schedulable under algorithm $\mathcal{A}$ while not schedulable under $\mathcal{B}$, and vice versa, then we say these two algorithms are *incomparable.*

If there exists a scheduling algorithm, for any feasible task system, that always generates a legal schedule, then we call this algorithm is *optimal*, named OPT. Clearly, OPT can schedule most of the task systems, hence dominate all other algorithms. This OPT stands for the ideal case.

For the clairvoyance environment, [39] proposed an $O(N^3)$ optimal algorithm that generates an optimal schedule for any periodic task system, where N is the number of jobs. Later works showed that optimal algorithms under most of the cases also require clairvoyance. For example, [40] proved that the optimal online algorithm for sporadic task systems with constrained and arbitrary deadlines does not exist since it requires clairvoyance.

Luckily, several algorithms for periodic task systems with implicit deadlines are shown to be optimal, like the Proportionate Fair algorithm [41] based on fluid scheduling. Here, fluid scheduling is an idea that divides processor time into slots and decides the schedule in each slot separately.

The general idea of Pfair (Proportionate fair) is that in each slot, the algorithm assigns resource (processor capacity) to each task proportionally so that the total execution time for task τ_i will be $[\alpha u_i]$, where α is some factor and $[\cdot]$ is integral function since execution time must be an integer. [41] proved that Pfair has utilization bound $U_{Pfair} = m$, which implies the optimality of Pfair. However, this method is not practical due to its large overheads coming from the design that fluid scheduling divide runtime into many small pieces.

3.3 Speedup Factor

As the discussion above, a normal way to evaluate a scheduling algorithm is to compare its performance with optimal performance. The result of comparing is usually formulated as a ratio, also called a competitive ratio.

Note $\mathcal{S}$ as the set containing all the task systems that schedulable under OPT with unit-speed processors (i.e., feasible), if an algorithm $\mathcal{A}$ can schedule a task system τ in $\mathcal{S}$ under processors with the speed of at most $f(\tau)$ units, then we call the algorithm has speedup factor (also called resource augmentation bound) $f(\tau)$ on τ. It is easy to see that for any $\tau, f(\tau) \geq 1. f(\tau) = 1$ stands for the behavior of OPT algorithm. Based on this definition, algorithm $\mathcal{A}$ may admit different speedup factors on different task systems. To clarify, we define the speedup factor $f_{\mathcal{A}}$ considering the worst-case of all the possible task systems, i.e., $f_{\mathcal{A}} = \max_{\forall \tau \in S} f(\tau)$.

Calculating the speedup factor of an algorithm requires considering all possible instances and comparing it with the ideal case to find the worst-case. However, the number of instances is infinite, so the calculation is intractable. In practice, researchers always focus on the bound of the speedup factor. For example, in the partition-EDF algorithm, the lower bound is 1.5 (in [42]), and the current upper bound is 1.556 (in [43]).

3.4 Capacity Augmentation Bound

[44] proposed a new measurement for algorithm on DAG task, called capacity augmentation bound. DAG task is a special task model whose job is in form of a Directed Acyclic Graph, so the job can be executed in parallel. An algorithm $\mathcal{A}$ has capacity augmentation bound b on task system τ, if (1) it has utilization bound b; (2) for each DAG task $\tau_i \in \tau$, its critical path length $L_i \leq \frac{D_i}{b}$.

Capacity augmentation bound is a stronger condition than utilization bound and speedup factor. In other words, the fact that an algorithm has a capacity augmentation bound b indicates: (1) speedup factor is b; (2) utilization bound is at most b.

3.5 Approximation Ratio

Instead of comparing the requirement for the speed of processors, the approximation ratio focuses on comparing the number of processors required by two algorithms under the same circumstances. For a task system τ, note $N_O(\tau)$ as the number of processors needed by OPT, and $N_{\mathcal{A}}$ as the number of processors needed by $\mathcal{A}$, define the approximation ratio of $\mathcal{A}$ as $r_{\mathcal{A}} = \lim_{N_O \to \infty} \left(\max_{\forall \tau} \frac{N_{\mathcal{A}}(\tau)}{N_O(\tau)} \right)$. Like the speedup factor, for any algorithm, we have $r \geq 1$. $r = 1$ stands for the performance of OPT algorithm.

3.6 Empirical Methods

All the measurements discussed above evaluate performance from an analytical way, and mostly in the worst-case. Practice indicates that the calculation for these measurements always requires tricks, and only hold in theoretical aspect. Specifically, the actual execution process of a job (e.g., a piece of code) is made up of multiple stages, not only being assigning processors. This process will lead to overheads that are hard to predict.

From a practical aspect, to compare among algorithms, researchers can generate actual task systems for scheduling (or simulate the execution of algorithms), and compare the ratio of schedulable tasks in the whole set of the task system. The ratio used here is called the acceptance ratio. This is a numerical method that is easy to use. Similarly, one can measure the response time of different algorithms on the same task systems to evaluate algorithms from a different aspect.

The most important issue in this approach is to generate task systems that are no-bias. In other words, the generated task system should not be easier to schedule for any of the compared algorithms. In addition, a stable algorithm that can generate task systems based on given parameters (the WCET C, period T, deadline D, etc.) is also required, so that researchers can longitudinally discuss the change of performance with different parameters of task systems.

[45] proposed LITMUS^{RT}, a real-time Linux-based test platform for empirically evaluating real-time scheduling algorithms under multiprocessor. The original version of LITMUS^{RT} is modified from Linux 2.6.9 and can only be run on an SMP (Symmetric Multi-Processor) with 4 identical Intel(R) Xeon processors, with 2 GB of main memory. This platform can execute several classic scheduling algorithms in a real-time environment, which not only check and compare the function of algorithms but also embrace real overheads (context switching, task migrating, etc.).

This original version has two main drawbacks. First, it only runs on SMP including 4 processors. Generalization work is not obtained in this version. Second, many features were not implemented in this system, such as synchronization and variable workload. This system keeps updating till today, and the current version of LITMUS^{RT} was presented in [46].

4 Scheduling on Sequential Task System

In this section, we will focus on some basic results on multiprocessor scheduling. Notice that in this part, we do not concern about special task models, but only provide results on sequential task models. Partition scheduling is an approach that assigning each task to a specific processor (this procedure is called *partition*), so all the jobs generated by the same task will run on the same processor, and not cause the overheads from migration.

Finding a good partition strategy is tricky. The first step is to define what a "good" partition strategy looks like. In general, a good partition to tasks makes the best use of limited processor capacity. To accomplish this, we consider each processor as a bin with unit capacity, and each task with a specific utilization as an item with a certain size, then the partition problem can be seen as a bin-packing problem. Furthermore, many bin-packing strategies can be transformed into partition strategies, such as First-Fit, Best-Fit, Next-Fit [47], and Worst-Fit. These strategies have been thoroughly analyzed from the aspect of bin-packing in the past few decades, which gives a solid theoretical foundation to partition strategies. However, we should notice that the analogy between partitioning and bin-packing indicates the former problem is NP-hard, which leads to the complexity of the partition problem.

Partitioning approach opens a way to apply many classic uniprocessor scheduling algorithms into multiprocessor scheduling. After partition, each processor can apply EDF, RM, DM, or other classic uniprocessor algorithms to serve the corresponding task subset in a specific task ordering.

In general, the partitioning approach mainly comprises three parts:

- Bin-packing heuristics, such as First-Fit, Best-Fit, Next-Fit, and Worst-Fit.
- Uniprocessor scheduling algorithms, such as EDF, RM, and DM.
- Task ordering, i.e., the ordering in which each task is considered into partition, such as DU (decreasing utilization) and ID (increasing deadline).

In the rest of this section, we will roughly introduce the major results in partition scheduling, especially the results on numerical measurements, such as approximation ratio, speedup factor, and so on.

4.1 Implicit Deadline

Many works were proposed in the last several decades that about the approximation ratio of algorithms with different partitioning heuristics. One of the classic results is RMMatching [48] algorithm based on RM, which has an approximation ratio of $3/2$. In addition, [49] proposed the RMST algorithm, which is used on small tasks with a utilization of less than $1/2$. This paper also showed that RMST has an approximation ratio of $1/(1 - u_{max})$, where u_{max} is the maximum utilization through all the tasks. This result reveals deep relation between the statistics u_{max} and approximation ratio.

Other results also showed that u_{max} is related with the utilization bound. In [49], researchers proved that RMST has a utilization bound of $(m - 2)(1 - u_{max}) + 1 - \ln 2$. Another important result [50] showed the lowest and highest utilization bound can be achieved by any EDF-based partition algorithm, that is, the lower bound is $U_{LB} = m - (m - 1)u_{max}$, and the upper bound is $U_{UB} = \frac{\lfloor 1/u_{max} \rfloor m+1}{\lfloor 1/u_{max} \rfloor +1}$.

4.2 Constrained and Arbitrary Deadline

For task systems with constrained deadlines, [51] proposed the EDF-FFID algorithm and thoroughly studied it in later works. EDF-FFID is an EDF-based partition algorithm combined with first-fit partitioning and ordering of increasing deadline. This paper proposed a sufficient schedulability test, that is,

$$m \geq \frac{2load(\tau) - \delta_{max}}{1 - \delta_{max}},$$

where δ_{max} is the maximum density of the task systems with constrained deadlines.

For the case of the arbitrary deadline, the sufficient test is, the task system is schedulable if the following holds:

$$m \geq \frac{load(\tau) - \delta_{max}}{1 - \delta_{max}} + \frac{U_\tau - u_{max}}{1 - u_{max}}.$$

Note that both of the tests involve statistics like u_{max} and δ_{max}. [52, 53] further proved that this algorithm has a speedup factor (upper bound) of $3 - 1/m$ for task systems with constrained deadlines and $4 - 2/m$ with arbitrary deadlines.

The partitioned-EDF scheduling with constrained deadlines draws more attention later. In [42], researchers improved the upper bound of speedup factor to $2.6322 - 1/m$, and derives the asymptotic lower bound of 2.5. The latest result is in [43], where the upper bound was improved to $2.5556 - 1/m$. The novelty of this work was finding the proper transformation of the task system to estimate the workload while keeping the concerned properties unchanged.

5 Hybrid Approaches

In this part, we discuss hybrid scheduling that combines the char-acter of global scheduling and partition scheduling. Recently, the most famous and efficient hybrid approach is federated scheduling. [44] systematically studied federated scheduling on DAG tasks, and several other works about variants of federated scheduling have been proposed since then.

5.1 Federated Scheduling

[44] proposed federated scheduling on DAG tasks under multi-processors. As mentioned before, a DAG task generates jobs formed as a directed acyclic graph. Based on this structure, the DAG job can be executed in an intra-parallelism manner where nodes from the same DAG job may be executed on different processors at the same time. Therefore, there possibly exists task τ_i whose utilization $u_i = \frac{C_i}{T_i} \geq 1$. In federated scheduling, this kind of task is called the *heavy* task. Instead, the task with utilization $u_i < 1$ is called the *light* task.

For each heavy task τ_i, federated scheduling assigns m_i dedicated processors, where m_i is determined by parameters of τ_i,

$$m_i = \left\lceil \frac{C_i - L_i}{D_i - L_i} \right\rceil,$$

where L_i is the critical path length of τ_i's DAG. After assigning dedicated processors to every heavy task, the light tasks share the remaining processors. This paper proved that the idle processors are always enough for light tasks.

This approach schedules heavy tasks in a partitioned manner, while light tasks in a global manner, therefore it is called federated scheduling.

For theoretical analysis, [44] defined canonical form, which is a transformed structure of the DAG task while keeping some key features for analytical use. For a light task, its canonical form is a chain, each node of which has a workload ϵ; for a heavy task, its canonical form is characterized by a chain following a star. In the canonical form of heavy task, the job will be executed in the highest degree of parallelism and then in sequence. The canonical form keeps C, D, and T the same as the original task form, it represents the worst-case during scheduling where maximum workload occurs in unit time.

[44] showed the effectiveness of federated scheduling with implicit deadlines, in the sense that its capacity augmentation bound is 2 (asymptotically tight, when $m \to \infty$). Interestingly, this result is independent of specific algorithms used on light tasks. This paper also showed the capacity augmentation bound for the Global-EDF algorithm is 2.618 (asymptotically tight, when $m \to \infty$), and for Global-RM is 3.732.

Several works focus on federated scheduling after [44]. [54] proved the performance of federated scheduling on sporadic DAG tasks with constraint deadline in the sense that the speedup factor is $3 - 1/m$. In addition, [55] proved that federated scheduling has no constant speedup factor on DAG tasks with constraint deadlines. However, [56] proved that the speedup factor of federated scheduling with arbitrary deadlines has an upper bound $3 + 2\sqrt{2}$.

The results above show that federated scheduling does have great performance. However, several details worth discussing: is it the best option that separating heavy and light tasks based on whether utilization is more than 1 or not? Instead, can we modify threshold 1 as any other value? In addition, is it optimal that assigning $m_i = \lceil \frac{C_i - L_i}{D_i - L_i} \rceil$ tasks to heavy tasks? Several works mentioned next will partially answer these questions.

5.2 Semi-federated Scheduling

Semi-federated scheduling was firstly proposed in [57]. This paper promotes a problem about original federated scheduling, where it assigns $m = \lceil \frac{C-L}{D-L} \rceil$ processors for heavy tasks. Note the number of processors is rounded up, which may lead to waste. To be specific, one heavy task needs $\frac{C-L}{D-L} = x + \epsilon, x \in Z, \epsilon \in [0, 1)$ processors, but the algorithm assigns $x + 1$ processors. In an extreme case, where $x = 1, \epsilon \to 0$, this will cause 100% of redundancy. To address this problem, [57] proposed semi-federated scheduling, whose improvement is it only assigns x processors to each heavy task. The remaining workload of each heavy task will be scheduled together with light tasks on shared processors.

Intuitively, semi-federated scheduling saves about 1 processor of redundancy for each heavy task. In the theoretical aspect, this paper does not give the competitive ratio but derives the upper bound of the response time $R_i \leq \frac{C_i + \lambda L_i}{S_m}$ of task τ_i, where λ and S_m are dependent on the speed of processors.

[57] also showed the performance of semi-federated scheduling using the empirical methods. The experiment implemented semi-federated scheduling in two ways and compared them with federated scheduling and other classic algorithms. In the technical aspect, the experiment had a novelty that is generated tasks with $T = \left(L + \frac{C}{0.4*mU}\right) * (1 + 0.25\Gamma(2, 1))$, where $\Gamma(\cdot, \cdot)$ is Γ-distribution. It had been shown that the task system with this configure will keep the workload balance with other task parameters.

5.3 Reservation-Based Federated Scheduling

[56] proposed reservation-based scheduling on the DAG task system. Just like semi-federated scheduling, it is also a decomposition-based strategy. For each task, reservation-based scheduling generates several reservation servers, which is essentially a special kind of sequential task. The scheduler assigns processors to servers, instead of original tasks. Therefore, at the beginning of runtime, scheduler generates servers based on tasks, and during runtime, scheduler attaches task with servers and then schedule servers in federated scheduling strategy. [56] proposed and proved a test that if the conservation server set is schedulable, then the original task system is also schedulable. This test indicates that the decomposition strategy makes sense.

Reservation-based scheduling is a novel approach since it essentially transforms DAG tasks into sequential tasks. It is reasonable to say that scheduling on sequential tasks will reduce the overheads induced by parallel execution, like migration.

[58] proposed a far simpler approach to establish empirically near-optimal schedulability, which combines three well-known techniques (reservations, semi-partitioned, and period transformation) with some novel task-placement heuristics. Intuitively, this work intended to show that pragmatically (not theoretically for sure) global scheduling is not required for independent, implicit-deadline, sporadic/periodic tasks.

Firstly, this paper defines *schedulable utilization*, that is, an algorithm empirically achieves a *schedulable utilization* of $X\,\%$ if all (tested) workloads with condition

$$\frac{U(\tau)}{m} \leq \frac{X}{100}$$

are schedulable.

Generally, the scheduler works as follows: the top-level scheduler (like EDF) doesn't serve on tasks, instead, it serves the reservations. First, the scheduler runs a two-phase partition process: phase one, tasks are assigned on reservations based on some bin-packing heuristics (like FFD or WFD, i.e., First Fit Utilization Decreasing or Worst Fit Decreasing), and skip any task that couldn't find feasible assignment; In phase two, apply task-split to all the remaining tasks that fail to pass phase one. The split method applied, called $C = D$, converts one original task into two small ones, one of which has equivalent $C_i^{'}$ and $D_i^{'}$ (hence the name of "$C = D$"). The other subtask is the "residue" of the first one, which means, its deadline $D_i^{''} = T_i - D_i^{'}$. After splitting, assign subtasks into reservations with flipped order (the one with property "$C = D$" will be activated later). Second, the top-level scheduler service those reservations among processors. When a reservation underruns its WCET, the scheduler will reclaim the slack to other depleted reservations. Examples showed that this tweak will reduce the migrations.

In conclusion, this work proposed a semi-partition scheduling policy combined with several effective heuristics.

In the above parts, we have introduced federated scheduling and its typical variants, which together indicate that federated strategy is a novel and efficient hybrid approach. It keeps drawing much attention from researchers until today. In Sect. 6, we will further introduce federated scheduling algorithms on MC tasks and other special task models.

6 Scheduling on Special Task Models

For the purpose that applying real-time scheduling into more complex cases, studies about scheduling on special task models are becoming a central topic in real-time scheduling. These special task models are defined based on practical characters and raise different additional constraints to scheduling. In this part, we will introduce several typical task models that draw much attention in recent years and show key results around them.

6.1 Gang Task Model

[59] studied scheduling of sporadic gang task systems under GEDF and derive two sufficient utilization-based schedulability tests. The weaker one is, a hard-real-time sporadic gang task set is schedulable under GEDF if the following condition holds for every task τ_i:

$$U_\tau \leq (m+1) \times \left(1 - \frac{u_i}{m_i}\right) + 2u_i - m_i,$$

where U_τ is the sum of the utilization of all the tasks in task set τ, and m_i is the parallelism degree of task τ_i. The parallelism degree of a gang task τ_i is the number of processors that each τ_i's job needs for execution at the same time.

The schedulability test above is based on a fairly trivial observation, that is, if a gang task τ_i releases a job but it didn't get execution during an interval, then the number of idle processors at any time in that interval is at most $m_i - 1$, otherwise leading a contradiction.

However, this is also a pessimistic observation, since one can safely argue that the number of idle processors during that interval may be much smaller than $m_i - 1$. This paper proposed an optimization approach to dig into this idea and derives a much tighter sufficient schedulability test: a hard-real-time sporadic gang task set is schedulable under GEDF if the following condition holds for every task τ_i:

$$U_\tau \leq (m - \Delta_i) \times \left(1 - \frac{u_i}{m_i}\right) + u_i,$$

where Δ_i is the maximum possible number of idle processors during the non-execution interval mentioned above for task τ_i, which is passively estimated as $m_i - 1$ in the first test. This paper provides a poly-time algorithm based on dynamic programming to calculate Δ_i more precisely.

6.2 DAG Task Model

[60] proposed decomposition strategy on DAG using GEDF algorithm, that is, a DAG task is transformed into a set of independent sporadic tasks. To achieve this elegant decomposition, this paper focuses on finding structure characteristic value. The challenge here is that it is unrealistic to enumerate all possible decompositions for a DAG, so finding a good decomposition quickly becomes a challenge.

Previous work showed that a decomposed task set τ is schedulable under G-EDF if

$$l_{\Sigma} \leq m - (m-1)\delta_{max}$$

where m is the number of processors, l_{Σ} is the sum of load from all the tasks, δ_{max} is the maximum density of all the vertices in τ.

Therefore, the goal is to find a good decomposition strategy that minimizes l_{Σ} and δ_{max} (these two varies when strategies change), so increase the chance of decomposed task set be schedulable.

First of all, for each task τ_i, the algorithm separates the window $[0, L_i]$ (assuming the task is released at time 0) into small segments by ready time instant of each vertex of τ_i, and assign the laxity $D_i - L_i$ into each segment. Second, assign each vertex into segments to make the load and density of every segment as balancing as possible.

Note the length of a segment s as $e(s)$, and the workload assigned into s as $c(s)$, the segment with property $\frac{c(s)}{e(s)} \leq C_i/L_i$ as the *heavy segment*, and the *light segment* otherwise. All the heavy segments form the set $\mathcal{H}$, and all the light segments form the set $\mathcal{L}$.

Derivation shows that to make the segment as balanced as possible (that is, improving the possibility of schedulability), one can minimize the factor $\Omega_i = \frac{C_i^{\mathcal{K}}}{C_i} + \frac{L_i^{\mathcal{L}}}{L_i}$, where $C_i^{\mathcal{K}}$ is the workload of $\mathcal{K}$ and $L_i^{\mathcal{L}}$ is the length of the segment set $\mathcal{L}$. Name Ω_i as the structure characteristic value.

The procedure to assign jobs into segments while getting the minimum Ω_i is: consider each segment in time order, assign jobs into the segment and try the best to keep the segment "light". If at some point, assigning the current job will lead to a heavy segment anyway, then assign it arbitrarily. It is proved that this procedure will get a correct (i.e., schedulable) assignment.

Later work showed that this decomposition method combining with Global EDF has the resource augmentation bound ranging $[2 - 1/m, 4 - 2/m)$.

[61] worked on the analysis for schedulability of DAG tasks in a partitioned, non-preemptive manner. The proposed analysis has two parts. First, it transforms each original DAG task into a group of non-preemptive self-suspending tasks. The self-suspending tasks from the same group will execute on the same processor. Second, it provides a fine-grained analysis for such non-preemptive self-suspending tasks that executing on a single processor, which is so far the best analysis under the same environment. To be specific, it provides a much tighter (lower) upper bound of the response time of the self-suspending tasks. However, the analysis did not provide an explicit and simple expression for response time, instead, it provides an algorithm for calculating it.

[62] proposed a novel scheduling technique to better exploit hardware parallelism of DAG tasks. This technique has two components, that is, the Lazy-Cpath policy and

a DAG-specific executing/non-executing interval-based analysis technique. The Lazy-Cpath policy aims to generate an execution order of all the ready jobs from the same DAG, hence when applying GEDF later, it can mostly get away with the precedence constraints in DAG.

Based on the scheduling technique above, this paper yielded an efficient utilization-based schedulability test. Specifically, a hard-real-time DAG task system τ is schedulable under GEDF with Lazy-Cpath policy if for each task $\tau_i \in \tau$,

$$\sum\nolimits_{i=1}^{n} \eta_i \leq m - (m-1) \times \sigma_k,$$

where σ_k is the sum of the utilization of subtasks on the critical path of task τ_k, and η_i is an upper bound of the average workload of task τ_i in a defined busy window, which is based on the executing/non-execution interval-based analysis technique mentioned above. The η_i is formally defined in Lemma 10 in [62].

[63] studied single periodic DAG running on multiprocessor system which involves identical cores. This work proposed Concurrent Provider and Consumer (CPC) model to exploit node parallelism and independence to reduce the overhead. The basic idea of the CPC model is to divide the critical path of this DAG into sub-paths. During execution, for each sub-path, the node from the critical path is executed on one core and its corresponding non-critical nodes are executed in parallel on other cores. The execution of the next sub-path is delayed until the current sub-path is finished. Based on this idea, the CPC model orders the nodes in DAG in a specific way and achieves a new response time bound.

6.3 AVR Task Model

AVR (Adaptive Variable Rate) task model was firstly proposed in [64], which is a task with multiple WCETs and periods. The general idea of this model comes from the physical engine. In the classic engine structure, once the rods rotate a circle, the piston will work for once. This motion implies a simple trade-off: when rods rotate slowly, the piston will work in low frequency but each rotation will release a larger work since more fuel is transformed into energy; when the rods rotate quickly, the piston will work in high frequency but generate smaller work each time. The traditional periodical task model is not suitable for modeling this system because it will lead to pessimistic scheduling by overestimating the workload. Therefore, the AVR task is defined to model this process. In the AVR task model, a new parameter angular speed ω is considered. When ω is larger, the task will release smaller jobs (i.e., with low C_i) more frequently (i.e., with smaller T_i); when ω is smaller, the task will release larger jobs less frequently (i.e., with larger C_i but larger T_i too).

Most recently, the most interesting topic about the AVR task model is: in what mode (i.e., the speed mode of ω) the task system will generate maximum workload in the considered time interval? Once we get enough knowledge about the bound of workload, we will have the foundation to research on schedulability of AVR task systems. The basic trade-off described above indicates that calculating the maximum workload is not a trivial question.

In the seminal work [64], the researchers studied the task system including only one AVR task and several regular tasks. In this work, the scheduler assigned the highest priority to the only AVR task, then apply the RM algorithm to the whole system. [65] extended the research of this task system by giving a sufficient schedulability test and speedup bound.

The above two pieces of research have two drawbacks, (1) they only focused on a special kind of task system where one AVR task share processors with several regular tasks; (2) they assumed that the acceleration between releasing of two consecutive jobs keeps static. These drawbacks indicated the results mentioned above are not applicable in the regular AVR model. However, [65] proposed a novel idea, that is, instead of focusing on the angular speed at the arrival of each job, one can focus on shortening the time between arrivals of two consecutive jobs to get the maximum workload. This idea influences the following work that working on the general AVR task system.

We will use the specific definition of the AVR task given in [66]. For simplicity, the range of speed $\omega \in [\omega_{min}, \omega_{max}]$ is divided into small intervals (modes), each mode corresponds to fixed-job size. Specifically, an AVR task system is represented as

$$\mathcal{M} = \left\{\left(C_m, \left[\omega_m, \omega_{m+1}\right)\right) | m = 1, 2, 3, \ldots, M, \ \omega_1 = \omega_{min}, \omega_{M+1} = \omega_{max}\right\},$$

which include M mode, each mode associates with a speed range $\left[\omega_m, \omega_{m+1}\right)$ and jobs size C_m.

Since this model is designed to model actual physic process, the angular speed ω is a continuous variable, which is controlled by angular acceleration $\alpha \in [\alpha_{min}, \alpha_{max}]$, with assumption $\alpha_{min} = -\alpha_{max}$. The motion can be described as following:

$$\omega_{(t)} = \dot{\theta} = \frac{d\theta}{dt}$$

$$\alpha_{(t)} = \dot{\omega} = \frac{d\omega}{dt}$$

If a motion starts with speed ω_0, and constant acceleration α, the end speed after i radians is

$$\Omega_i(\omega_0, \alpha) = \sqrt{\omega_0^2 + 2i\alpha}.$$

Intuitively, once the rod starts from mode m_i, indicating the initial speed in (ω_i, ω_{i+1}), after rotating one single round, the end speed will lie in a range which is easy to be calculated. The possible mode at the end is also easy to find based on end speed.

[66] proposed DRT model (Digraph Real-Time) to represent the mode transformation. The DRT is a directed graph $G(V, E)$, where $|V| = M$, each node represents a mode, each edge $\forall (u, v) \in E$, $u, v \in V$ represents that it is possible mode u transforms to mode v after a motion. Edge (u, v) is assigned weight $p(u, v)$, which is the minimum inter-time from mode u to mode v. The value of $p(u, v)$ can be derived from basic parameters. The main contribution of this paper is using the DRT model to derive the optimal speed function $\omega(t)$ with time t. When angular speed follows this function, the system will generate maximum workload, hence answer the question proposed above.

[67] proposed a different view for the AVR task. In this paper, the author proposed a basic observation: the shorter the time between two adjacent types of mode, the more work this system will generate. Based on this observation, the author argues that it is not necessary to calculate $\omega(t)$ mentioned above precisely. Instead, a valid speed sequence $\Omega = \{\omega_1, \omega_2, \ldots, \omega_k\}$, where continuous ω_i and ω_{i+1} represents adjacent modes, is enough. Generally, this sequence stands for a series of legal mode transformations, and the system releases a job at each ω_i. Therefore, the sequence Ω corresponds to a workload during a time interval, noted as $W(\Omega)$.

Now the target is to find an optimal speed sequence Ω^* that generates the maximum amount of work $W(\Omega^*)$. [67] applies knapsack to solve this problem. Calculating an optimal sequence is a multi-stage decision, with each stage stands for choosing a mode. Like the idea in [66], the possible mode following the current mode is clear, which applies a specific selection range (bound) in a multi-stage process. In the context of the knapsack problem, the size of each item (i.e., job) is the minimum time gap with the next possible jobs, the value of each item is the workload of the corresponding job, and the target is getting the subset of items (jobs) with maximum value (workload) and not overload the capacity (total amount of time). This is a typical BPCKP (Bounded Precedence Constraint Knapsack Problem) that can be solved by classic dynamic programming. The result showed the estimation of workload using BPCKP can be tighter than or equal with the method in [66], and more importantly, the solving process is much faster since it can be solved using dynamic programming.

This paper also derived some properties which the optimal sequences have by introducing a concept called *dominance sequence set*, where the optimal sequence must belong to. By calculating the dominance sequence set, one can reduce the search space for optimal sequences to solve BPKCP more efficiently.

6.4 Task System with Affinity Masks

In multiprocessor systems, the affinity mask is a property attached with programs (or specific pieces of code) indicating that this program must execute on designated processors. At the system level, the affinity mask for a specific task can be represented as a 0–1 vector of length m, where the i-th digit is 1 means this task can be executed on i-th processor, and 0 otherwise. Scheduling on tasks with affinity masks is now becoming one of the hot topics in real-time scheduling, including algorithms, schedulability tests, complexity, and so on.

The affinity masks on the whole task system can be represented by an affinity graph (which is also a bipartite graph) $G = (X, Y)$, where X and Y stand for tasks and processors, respectively. An edge $e = (x_i, y_j)$ exists if and only if task τ_i is allowed to be executed on processor j. Note $\alpha_i = \{j | (x_i, y_j) \in E(G)\}$, i.e., α_i is the subset of processors that task τ_i can execute on.

Affinity masks on task systems can be divided into three classes:

- Acyclic: the corresponding bipartite graph is acyclic.
- Hierarchical: $\forall i, j, \alpha_i \cap \alpha_j = \varnothing\, or\, \alpha_i \subset \alpha_j\, or\, \alpha_j \subset \alpha_i$, i.e., the affinity relation of every task can be represented as a hierarchical structure.
- Arbitrary: no additional properties on affinity masks.

[68] proposed a semi-partitioned scheduler AM-Red, which is an optimal scheduler for task systems with arbitrary affinity masks. The novelty of this scheduler is adding a source s and a sink t to the affinity graph. s has weighted edges with all the vertex in X, and so as v with all the vertex in Y. The derivation of the algorithm is based on reducing to network flow problem on this resulted network. Here the reduction means simplifying the structure of the affinity graph to reduce the complexity and overheads while keeping the feasibility. After reduction, the schedule will have at most $m - 1$ migrating tasks and at most $2m - 2$ migrations.

At the beginning of scheduling, AM-Red has an offline phase during which the algorithm decides whether or not each task can migrate during execution based on given parameters. That is, some tasks can execute on several processors based on their affinity masks but some tasks cannot. Instead, these tasks can only choose one processor to execute on. That is why AM-Red is a semi-partitioned scheduler.

This algorithm works in both SRT (soft real-time) and HRT (hard real-time) environments. In the SRT environment, the scheduler is given a super parameter $|F|$ which is the length of the considered time window and also the upper bound of tardiness. AM-Red is guaranteed to be optimal can provides a trade-off: the larger $|F|$ means larger tardiness but less migration, hence fewer overheads; the smaller $|F|$ means smaller tardiness but more migration, hence larger overheads. In the HRT environment, AM-Red is also guaranteed to be optimal if the parameter $|F|$ divided the periods of all the tasks.

In [69], researchers focus on the variant of EDF under arbitrary processor affinities (APA), which is called *Strong APA* EDF. In their prior work [70], they proved that *Strong APA* EDF is SRT-optimal, which means it guarantees bounded tardiness for any task system not over-utilizing multiprocessor platform. However, the SRT-optimality of a practical version of APA EDF remains open, which is called SCHED_DEADLINE (SD) scheduler under Linux. In [69], researchers disproved the SRT-optimal of SD scheduler based on the fact that SD scheduler treats affinities as a secondary issue for practical reasons.

6.5 Mixed-Criticality Task Model

Like the AVR task model, the MC (Mixed-Criticality) task model is also one of the hot topics in real-time scheduling. MC task model considers the criticality of tasks and assuming that jobs released by the same task may have different criticality during runtime. The job in low criticality may transform to high criticality during execution and immediately ask for more processor capacity, and the scheduler should deal with this sudden request and is allowed to drop other low criticality jobs to focus on high criticality jobs.

The general scene indicating mixed-criticality can be exampled as following: a program consists of several modules, one of which is controlling the key section of the system. The developer implements two versions of the key module, for low criticality and high criticality respectively. Each version has different pieces of code, hence a different amount of workload during execution. When it comes to the key module, the program will choose the specific one version based on the current context. This is decided by the program so the scheduler probably will not know this ahead.

The basic MC gang task model is defined as follows. An MC task system is $\tau = \{\tau_1, \tau_2, \ldots, \tau_n\}$, each task τ_i is represented as $\tau_i = \left(m_i, \chi_i, c_i^{LO}, c_i^{HI}, T_i, D_i\right)$, where

- m_i is the number of processors needed for execution, which follows the behavior of Gang tasks.
- $\chi_i \in \{LO, HI\}$ stands for two possible criticality levels, *LO* stands for low criticality and *HI* stands for high criticality.
- c_i^{LO} is the workload for each processor of task τ_i in LO-criticality, while c_i^{HI} is of HI-criticality.
- T_i is the period of task τ_i, and D_i is the deadline of τ_i.

Note τ_{HI} the subset of all the *HI*-tasks (i.e., τ_i with $\chi_i = HI$), and τ_{LO} the subset of all the *LO*-tasks.

For task τ_i with $\chi_i = HI$, it starts with *LO*-criticality. If the job is not finished after receiving c_i^{LO} of workload, then it automatically switches to *HI*-criticality with workload of c_i^{HI}, but keeps period and deadline as the same. At this time, to meet the time constraint of *HI*-jobs, the scheduler is allowed to drop other *LO*-jobs. Note that the *HI*-jobs switch to *HI*-criticality randomly, i.e., not all *HI*-jobs are guaranteed to turn to *HI*-criticality during execution.

[71] proposed GEDF-VD (Global EDF with Virtual Deadline) algorithm for the MC gang model with the implicit deadlines. The novelty of this algorithm is to set a virtual deadline (that is less than the original deadline) on each HI-task (and HI-job released by it). At the beginning of execution, the algorithm schedules HI-tasks with virtual deadlines, if this job switches to HI-criticality during execution, the algorithm will schedule this job with the original deadline. The virtual deadline is noted as $\widetilde{D_i} = xD_i, x \in (0, 1)$, where x is calculated by the algorithm at the beginning. Clearly, the virtual deadline is less than the original deadline. The idea behind this design is (1) setting a tighter deadline for each HI-job to save processor capacity for HI-mode later; (2) tighter deadline gives HI-job higher priority since the scheduler applies GEDF algorithm.

GEDF-VD designs a preprocessing phase. At the beginning of scheduling, the algorithm checks if each HI-task will finish execution with the original deadline in the worst-case (i.e. release WCET workload). If so, the scheduler will not assign a virtual deadline to it; otherwise, assign a virtual deadline where the factor x follows: $\forall x \in [A, B]$, where

$$A = \max\{A_1, A_2\};$$

$$A_1 = \max_{i:\tau_i \in \tau_{LO}} \left\{ \frac{U_{HI}^{LO}}{M - \Delta_i - U_{LO}^{LO}} \right\}$$

$$A_2 = \max_{i:\tau_i \in \tau} \left\{ \frac{m_i U_{HI}^{LO} + u_i^{LO}(M - \Delta_i - m_i)}{m_i\left(M - \Delta_i - U_{LO}^{LO}\right)} \right\}$$

$$B = \min_{i:\tau_i \in \tau_{HI}} \left\{ 1 - \frac{m_i U_{HI}^{HI} + u_i^{HI}(M - \Delta_i - m_i)}{m_i(M - \Delta_i)} \right\}$$

The parameters mentioned above are given or can be calculated at the beginning. For example, U_{HI}^{LO} is the utilization of a subset of all HI-tasks at LO-mode, and Δ_i is the maximum number of idle processors during the time interval when the ready job of τ_i is not executing because it is not assigned enough processors, which is also computable at the beginning.

[71] also proposed sufficient schedulability test for the GEDF-VD algorithm, that is, an MC task system is schedulable under the GEDF-VD algorithm if both

$$U_{LO}^{LO} < m - \max_{\mathrm{i}}\{\Delta_i\}$$

$$A \leq B$$

hold, where m is the number of processors and A, B is mention above.

Notice that the schedulable here is MC-schedulable. That is, the scheduler only needs to guarantee the schedulability of HI-jobs when it comes to HI-mode, but all the jobs when all the jobs are in LO-mode. This paper also gives theoretical results that GEDF has a speedup bound of 2 on the Non-MC gang task system, and GEDF-VD has a speedup bound of $\sqrt{5} + 1$ on the MC gang task system.

In addition to traditional sporadic MC tasks, [72] studies federated scheduling on the MC DAG task systems. Each vertex of the DAG represents a sequential job. The edges in the DAG represent the precedence between jobs (vertices). The criticality shows at two levels: (1) each vertex v in a DAG has two WCET parameters, $c^{LO}(v)$, $c^{HI}(v)$, estimating the workload of the current vertex in LO-criticality and HI-criticality respectively. (2) Certain vertices of DAG are labeled as HI-criticality at the beginning, and their predecessor vertices (immediate and transitive) will also be automatically labeled as HI-criticality. All the remaining vertices are labeled as LO-criticality.

The key points of the algorithm proposed for semi-partition federated scheduling are the following:

- Calculate the number of dedicated processors for each heavy task. Through binary search, one can find the minimum number of processors that make sure it is feasible for the current task.
- Generate schedule table $\mathrm{S}_{\mathrm{i}}^{\mathrm{HI}}$ and $\mathrm{S}_{\mathrm{i}}^{\mathrm{LO}}$ for each heavy task, which is used to indicate the ordering of jobs' execution, using list scheduling.
- For each light MC DAG task, map it into a sporadic sequential task so it turns to dual-criticality Liu & Layland tasks model, then run partition scheduling on the remaining processors.

This paper proved the correctness of the above algorithm. The main argument is that each HI job will receive at least as much execution in S_i^{LO} as in S_i^{HI}. Therefore, when the transition occurs from S_i^{LO} to S_i^{HI} (which means a job has been executed beyond its LO-criticality execution time without asserting completion), each HI-job is guaranteed to receive enough execution before the deadline.

The author in [72] also provided the thought that this algorithm can be simply applied to multi-criticality case that has more than two criticality levels. However, this will lead to a large number of switches among schedule tables and hence exorbitant overhead.

[73] focused on the primary difficulty of scheduling on MC task, which is assuring enough processing capacity when the system changes to the HI-Criticality mode. To address this issue, this paper proposed a sufficient condition to guarantee a correct schedule from LO-mode to HI-mode. Define that $\psi_i^{\chi}(t_1, t_2)$ is the total execution time allocated to task τ_i in the mode χ during the time interval $[t_1, t_2]$. The sufficient condition that guarantees an MC-correct schedule is,

$$\psi_i^{LO}\left(r_{i,k}, t\right) < C_i(LO) \Rightarrow$$
$$\psi_i^{LO}\left(r_{i,k}, t\right) \geq \psi_i^{HI}\left(r_{i,k}, t\right).$$

The main idea behind this property is that a task in LO-mode should be allocated more processing capacity than in the HI-mode.

Based on this property, this paper proposed a general heuristic for MC-DAG scheduling: first calculate the scheduling table for HI mode and check its correctness, then calculate the scheduling table for LO-mode while assuring the property above and check correctness in LO-mode.

The typical MC task model has a property that the exact execution time of a HI-job will only be revealed during actual execution. In other words, the scheduler won't foresee the mode transition (from LO to HI), but only wait until it happens at any time.

To extend this model, [74] considered a different semi-clairvoyant MC model, whereupon the arrival of a job the scheduler will know whether the current job will complete or not within LO-criticality WCET, i.e., which mode this job will be in.

Note γ_i as the actual running time (workload) of a job of task τ_i, and c_i^L as the WCET of the task τ_i in LO-mode, c_i^H as the WCET in the HI-mode.

Semi-clairvoyance means that when a new job of task τ_i arrives, the scheduler will simply know the answer to "$\gamma_i <= c_i^L$ or not?".

A more idealistic assumption is clairvoyance, where when a new job of task τ_i arrives, the scheduler will know the exact value of γ_i, so scheduler will get much more information than under semi-clairvoyance circumstance. This assumption makes sense from a pragmatic perspective. In some cases, the developer will provide several versions of a job for different circumstances (i.e., LO-criticality or HI-criticality). The system will choose a version of this job based on the circumstances when the job is released. Therefore, the scheduler will know the exact WCET of the current job immediately.

[74] proposed a theoretic framework for scheduling MC task under the semi-clairvoyance circumstance, and get several pretty fundamental results:

- Any semi-clairvoyant scheduling algorithm will have a speedup factor lower bound 3/2;
- An optimal semi-clairvoyant scheduling algorithm called LPSC is proposed in this paper. That is, under the semi-clairvoyance circumstance, if an MC task set is schedulable by any semi-clairvoyant algorithm, then it is schedulable by LPSC;
- LPSC has speedup bound of 3/2. Combing with the first result, this result showed that 3/2 is a tight bound for any semi-clairvoyance algorithm.

Not only this paper opened a journey of exploring semi-clairvoyant scheduling of MC tasks, it also made a very impressive contribution. However, many problems keep open in the semi-clairvoyant scheduling of MC tasks. First, [74] only analyzed dual-criticality cases using linear programming, but it is not clear how to apply the same technique to the multi-criticality cases. Second, the algorithm proposed by [74] has remarkable theoretical significance, but not practical. Therefore, the design of an efficient and easy-to-implement algorithm for semi-clairvoyance scheduling remains open.

6.6 Task System with Parallelization Options

[75] studied a new parallel task model with parallelization options. Here, parallelization options mean the number of threads the scheduler can create for each task for parallel execution. Parallelization options range from 1 to m, where 1 means sequential execution, and m means this task uses all the processors for execution.

A basic trade-off lies behind this option. More parallelization threads will reduce execution time for each thread (note that execution time of each thread from the same task may be varied) but increase the total execution time, because of the parallelization overheads (such as threads communication). On the other hand, increasing the parallelization option for a task may interfere with the parallel execution for other tasks and may cause performance degradation of the whole system. Therefore, it is tricky to assign an optimal parallelization option for every task while guaranteeing the schedulability for the task system.

The definition of the parallelization-free task is as follows. Consider a sporadic priority-based task set of n tasks denoted by Γ as $\Gamma = \{\tau_1, \tau_2, \ldots, \tau_n\}$, each task is represented by a tuple $\tau_k = (T_k, D_k, E_k)$, the definition of T_k and D_k remain the same as typical task model, while E_k is the thread execution time table according to the parallelization options O_k of task τ_k, i.e., for every possible assignment of O_k, E_k gives the execution time of each of O_k threads need. The l-th thread of task τ_k is $\tau_k^l(O_k)$, with WCET $e_k^l(O_k)$. In addition, the total amount of execution of O_k threads are denoted by

$$C_k(O_k) = \Sigma_{l=1}^{O_k} e_k^l(O_k).$$

This paper proposed a polynomial-time algorithm to generate optimal parallelization options assignment so that GEDF can be applied to the scheduling of the threads. The main idea behind this algorithm is, when increasing the parallelization option of a task, its execution time becomes shorter, hence its *tolerance* for threads from other tasks gets larger. However, its interference to threads from other tasks gets larger, too. This is a trade-off that needs to be considered among the entire task set. The proposed algorithm starts from no-parallelization ($O_k = 1$ for all the tasks τ_k) and iteratively increases each task's parallelization option until its *tolerance* becomes larger than *interference*.

[75] proved the optimality of this algorithm by embracing an existing interference-based schedulability analysis called BCL, which tests whether a task can meet a deadline even if it receives maximum interference from higher-priority jobs.

6.7 Resource-Oriented Task System

[76] studied partitioned scheduling on multiprocessors but with *resource sharing*, that is, tasks system may have critical sections, for which different tasks may have to compete

to get ready for execution. The general policy proposed in this paper can be depicted as follows:

- Each shared resource will be assigned to one processor, hence the critical section for this shared resource from any task will be executed on this designated processor.
- Each non-critical section of a task will also be executed on the designated processors, which will differ from the ones with the critical sections.

This policy regards execution with the shared resource as the top priority so the response time of the critical section will be as short as possible.

7 Conclusions

Real-time scheduling keeps as a hot topic in theoretic computer sciences in the past few decades. Till today, researchers have proposed a huge amount of works that form fundamental of real-time systems. Many algorithms in these works have been widely implemented in the industry.

Recently, more and more works focus on two topics of real-time system scheduling: hybrid scheduling approaches and scheduling on special task models. These may still be promising research directions in the future since many questions still open, such as the competitive ratio and the fact that many potential approaches for scheduling on AVR or MC task model have not been studied yet. Results that may be obtained in the future in these topics may help us get more fundamental knowledge about real-time scheduling and have better exploitation of the capacity of multiprocessors.

References

1. Liu, C.L., Layland, J.W.: Scheduling algorithms for multiprogramming in a hard-real-time environment. J. ACM (JACM) **20**(1), 46–61 (1973)
2. Dhall, S.K., Liu, C.L.: On a real-time scheduling problem. Oper. Res. **26**(1), 127–140 (1978)
3. Phillips, C.A., Stein, C., Torng, E.: Optimal time-critical scheduling via resource augmentation. In: Proceedings of the Twenty-Ninth Annual ACM Symposium on Theory of Computing, pp.140–149 (1997). https://doi.org/10.1145/258533.258570
4. Li, J., Chen, J.J., Agrawal, K.: Analysis of federated and global scheduling for parallel real-time tasks. In: Proceedings of 2014 26th Euromicro Conference on Real-Time Systems, Spain, pp. 85–96. IEEE (2014)
5. Ueter, N., Von Der Brüggen, G., Chen, J.J., et al.: Reservation-based federated scheduling for parallel real-time tasks. In: Proceedings of the 2018 IEEE Real-Time Systems Symposium, USA, pp. 482–494. IEEE (2018)
6. Baruah, S.K., Bonifaci, V., Marchetti-Spaccamela, A., Stougie, L., Wiese, A.: A generalized parallel task model for recurrent real-time processes. In: Proceedings of the IEEE Real-Time Systems Symposium, Puerto Rico, pp. 63–72. IEEE (2012)
7. Baruah, S., Bonifaci, V., D'Angelo, G., Marchetti-Spaccamela, A., Ster, S., Stougie, L.: Mixed-criticality scheduling of sporadic task systems. In: Demetrescu, C., Halldórsson, M.M. (eds.) ESA 2011. LNCS, vol. 6942, pp. 555–566. Springer, Heidelberg (2011). https://doi.org/10.1007/978-3-642-23719-5_47

8. Davis, R.I., Burns, A.: A survey of hard real-time scheduling for multiprocessor systems. ACM Comput. Surv. (CSUR) **43**(4), 1–44 (2013)
9. Devi, U.M.: Soft real-time scheduling on multiprocessors (2006)
10. Serafini, P., Ukovich, W.: A mathematical model for periodic scheduling problems. SIAM J. Discret. Math. **2**(4), 550–581 (1989)
11. Jeffay, K., Stanat, D.F., Martel, C.U.: On non-preemptive scheduling of periodic and sporadic tasks. In: Proceedings of the IEEE Real-Time Systems Symposium, USA, pp. 129–139. IEEE (1991)
12. Audsley, N.C., Burns, A., Richardson, M.F., et al.: Hard real-time scheduling: the deadline-monotonic approach. IFAC Proc. Vol. **24**(2), 127–132 (1991)
13. Audsley, N.C., Burns, A., Wellings, A.J.: Deadline monotonic scheduling theory and application. Control. Eng. Pract. **1**(1), 71–78 (1991)
14. Baker, T.P.: Multiprocessor EDF and deadline monotonic schedulability analysis. In: Proceeding of the 24th IEEE Real-Time Systems Symposium, Mexico, pp. 120–129. IEEE (2003)
15. Baruah, S., Fisher, N.: Global deadline-monotonic scheduling of arbitrary-deadline sporadic task systems. In: Tovar, E., Tsigas, P., Fouchal, H. (eds.) OPODIS 2007. LNCS, vol. 4878, pp. 204–216. Springer, Heidelberg (2007). https://doi.org/10.1007/978-3-540-77096-1_15
16. Baruah, S., Goossens, J.: Deadline monotonic scheduling on uniform multiprocessors. In: Baker, T.P., Bui, A., Tixeuil, S. (eds.) OPODIS 2008. LNCS, vol. 5401, pp. 89–104. Springer, Heidelberg (2008). https://doi.org/10.1007/978-3-540-92221-6_8
17. Sha, L., Rajkumar, R., Sathaye, S.S.: Generalized rate-monotonic scheduling theory: a framework for developing real-time systems. Proc. IEEE **82**(1), 68–82 (1991)
18. Lehoczky, J., Sha, L., Ding, Y.: The rate monotonic scheduling algorithm: exact characterization and average case behavior. In: Proceeding of the IEEE Real-Time Systems Symposium, USA, pp. 166–171. IEEE (1989)
19. Atlas, A., Bestavros, A.: Statistical rate monotonic scheduling. In: Proceedings of the 19th IEEE Real-Time Systems Symposium, Spain, pp. 123–132. IEEE (1998)
20. Sha, L., Rajkumar, R., Sathaye, S.S.: Generalized rate-monotonic scheduling theory: a framework for developing real-time systems. Proc. IEEE **82**(1), 68–82 (1994)
21. Warren, C.: Rate monotonic scheduling. IEEE Micro **11**(3), 34–38 (1991)
22. Santos, J., Orozco, J.: Rate monotonic scheduling in hard real-time systems. Inf. Process. Lett. **48**(1), 39–45 (1991)
23. Audsley, N.C., Burns, A., Davis, R.I., et al.: Fixed priority pre-emptive scheduling: an historical perspective. Real-Time Syst. **8**(2), 173–198 (1995)
24. Lehoczky, J.P.: Fixed priority scheduling of periodic task sets with arbitrary deadlines. In: Proceeding of the 11th Real-Time Systems Symposium, USA, pp. 201–209. IEEE (1990)
25. Lehoczky, J.P., Ramos-Thuel, S.: An optimal algorithm for scheduling soft-aperiodic tasks in fixed-priority preemptive systems. In: Proceedings of the IEEE Real-Time Systems Symposium, USA, pp. 110–123. IEEE (1992)
26. Baek, H., Chwa, H.S., Lee, J.: Beyond implicit-deadline optimality: a multiprocessor scheduling framework for constrained-deadline tasks. In: Proceeding of 2017 IEEE Real-Time Systems Symposium, France, pp. 331–342. IEEE (2017)
27. Anderson, J.H., Srinivasan, A.: Early-release fair scheduling. In: Proceeding of the 12th Euromicro Conference on Real-Time Systems, Sweden, pp. 35–43. IEEE (2000)
28. Nelissen, G., Berten, V., Nelis, V., Goossens, J., Milojevic, D.: U-EDF: an unfair but optimal multiprocessor scheduling algorithm for sporadic tasks. In: Proceeding of the Euromicro Conference on Real-Time Systems, Italy, pp. 13–23. IEEE (2012)
29. Massa, E., Lima, G., Regnier, P., Levin, G., Brandt, S.: Quasi-partitioned scheduling: optimality and adaptation in multiprocessor real time systems. Real-Time Syst. **52**(5), 566–597 (2016)

30. Cirinei, M., Baker, T.P.: EDZL scheduling analysis. In: Proceeding of the Euromicro Conference on Real-Time Systems, Italy, pp. 9–18. IEEE (2007)
31. Davis, R.I., Burns, A.: FPZL schedulability analysis. In: Proceeding of the 17th IEEE Real-Time and Embedded Technology and Applications Symposium, USA. IEEE (2011)
32. Lee, J., Easwaran, A., Shin, I.: LLF schedulability analysis on multiprocessor platforms. In: Proceeding of the IEEE Real-Time Systems Symposium, USA, pp. 25–36. IEEE (2010)
33. Zhao, Y., Zeng, H.: The virtual deadline based optimization algorithm for priority assignment in fixed-priority scheduling. In: Proceeding of the 2017 IEEE Real-Time Systems Symposium (RTSS), France, pp. 116–127. IEEE (2017)
34. Davis, R., Zabos, A., Burns, A.: Efficient exact schedulability tests for fixed priority real-time systems. IEEE Trans. Comput. **57**(9), 1261–1276 (2008)
35. Davis, R.I., Bertogna, M.: Optimal fixed priority scheduling with deferred pre-emption. In: Proceeding of the 2012 IEEE 33rd Real-Time Systems Symposium, PR, pp. 39–50. IEEE (2012)
36. Chen, J.J., Huang, W.H., Liu, C.: k2U: a general framework from k-point effective schedulability analysis to utilization-based tests. In: Proceeding of the 2015 IEEE Real-Time Systems Symposium, USA, pp. 107–118. IEEE (2015)
37. Chen, J.J., Huang, W.H., Liu, C.: k2Q: a quadratic-form response time and schedulability analysis framework for utilization-based analysis. In: Proceeding of the 2016 IEEE Real-Time Systems Symposium, Portugal, pp. 351–362. IEEE (2016)
38. Baruah, S.K., Mok, A.K., Rosier, L.E.: Preemptively scheduling hard-real-time sporadic tasks on one processor. In: Proceeding of the 11th Real-Time Systems Symposium, USA, pp. 182–190. IEEE (1990)
39. Horn, W.A.: Some simple scheduling algorithms. Naval Res. Logist. Q. **21**, 177–185 (1974)
40. Fisher, N., Baruah, S.: The global feasibility and schedulability of general task models on multiprocessor platforms. In: Proceeding of the 19th Euromicro Conference on Real-Time Systems, Italy, pp. 51–60. IEEE (2007)
41. Baruah, S.K., Cohen, N.K., Plaxton, C.G., et al.: Proportionate progress: a notion of fairness in resource allocation. Algorithmica **15**(6), 600–625 (1996). https://doi.org/10.1007/BF01940883
42. Chen, J.J., Chakraborty, S.: Resource augmentation bounds for approximate demand bound functions. In: Proceeding of the Real-Time Systems Symposium, Austria, pp. 272–281. IEEE (2011)
43. Han, X., Zhao, L., Guo, Z., et al.: An improved speedup factor for sporadic tasks with constrained deadlines under dynamic priority scheduling. In: Proceeding of the 2018 IEEE Real-Time Systems Symposium, USA, pp. 447–455. IEEE (2018)
44. Li, J., Saifullah, A., Agrawal, K.: Capacity augmentation bound of federated scheduling for parallel DAG tasks (2014)
45. Calandrino, J.M., Leontyev, H., Block, A.: LITMUS^{RT}: a testbed for empirically comparing real-time multiprocessor schedulers. In: Proceeding of the 2006 27th IEEE International Real-Time Systems Symposium (RTSS 2006), Rio de Janeiro, pp. 111–126. IEEE (2006)
46. Brandenburg, B.B., Anderson, J.H.: On the implementation of global real-time schedulers. In: Proceeding of the 2009 30th IEEE Real-Time Systems Symposium, USA, pp. 214–224. IEEE (2009)
47. Bays, C.: A comparison of next-fit, first-fit, and best-fit. Commun. ACM **20**(3), 191–192 (1977)
48. Rothvoss T.: On the computational complexity of periodic scheduling. Ph.D. thesis, EPFL (2009)
49. Burchard, A., Liebeherr, J., Oh, Y.: New strategies for assigning real-time tasks to multiprocessor systems. IEEE Trans. Comput. **44**(12), 1429–1442 (1995)

50. López, J.M., García, M., Diaz, J.L.: Worst-case utilization bound for EDF scheduling on real-time multiprocessor systems. In: Proceeding of the 12th Euromicro Conference on Real-Time Systems, Sweden, pp. 25–33. IEEE (2000)
51. Baruah, S., Fisher, N.: The partitioned multiprocessor scheduling of sporadic task systems. In: Proceeding of the 26th IEEE International Real-Time Systems Symposium, USA, p. 329. IEEE (2005)
52. Baruah, S., Fisher, N.: The partitioned multiprocessor scheduling of deadline-constrained sporadic task systems. IEEE Trans. Comput. **55**(7), 918–923 (2006)
53. Baruah, S.K., Fisher, N.W.: The partitioned dynamic-priority scheduling of sporadic task systems. Real-Time Syst. **36**(3), 199–226 (2007)
54. Baruah, S.: The federated scheduling of systems of conditional sporadic DAG tasks. In: Proceeding of the 2015 International Conference on Embedded Software (EMSOFT), The Netherlands, pp. 1–10. IEEE (2015)
55. Chen, J.-J.: Federated scheduling admits no constant speedup factors for constrained-deadline DAG task systems. Real-Time Syst. **52**(6), 833–838 (2016). https://doi.org/10.1007/s11241-016-9255-2
56. Ueter, N., Von Der Brüggen, G., Chen, J.J.: Reservation-based federated scheduling for parallel real-time tasks. In: Proceeding of the 2018 IEEE Real-Time Systems Symposium (RTSS), USA, pp. 482–494. IEEE (2018)
57. Jiang, X., Guan, N, Long, X.: Semi-federated scheduling of parallel real-time tasks on multiprocessors. In: Proceeding the 2017 IEEE Real-Time Systems Symposium (RTSS), pp. 80–91 (2017)
58. Brandenburg, B.B., Gül, M.: Global scheduling not required: simple, near-optimal multiprocessor real-time scheduling with semi-partitioned reservations. In: Proceeding of the 2016 IEEE Real-Time Systems Symposium (RTSS), Portugal, pp. 99–110. IEEE (2016)
59. Dong, Z., Liu, C.: Analysis techniques for supporting hard real-time sporadic gang task systems. Real-Time Syst. **55**(3), 641–666 (2018). https://doi.org/10.1007/s11241-018-9318-7
60. Jiang, X., Long, X., Guan, N., et al.: On the decomposition-based global edf scheduling of parallel real-time tasks. In: Proceeding of the 2016 IEEE Real-Time Systems Symposium (RTSS), Portugal, pp. 237–246. IEEE (2016)
61. Casini, D., Biondi, A., Nelissen, G., et al.: Partitioned fixed-priority scheduling of parallel tasks without preemptions. In: Proceeding of the 2018 IEEE Real-Time Systems Symposium (RTSS), USA, pp. 421–433. IEEE (2018)
62. Dong, Z., Liu, C.: An efficient utilization-based test for scheduling hard real-time sporadic DAG task systems on multiprocessors. In: Proceeding of the 2019 IEEE Real-Time Systems Symposium (RTSS), China, pp. 181–193. IEEE (2019)
63. Zhao, S., Dai, X., Bate, I.: DAG scheduling and analysis on multiprocessor systems: exploitation of parallelism and dependency. In: Proceeding of the IEEE Real-Time Systems Symposium, USA, pp. 128–140. IEEE (2020)
64. Kim, J., Lakshmanan, K., Rajkumar, R.: Rhythmic tasks: a new task model with continually varying periods for cyber-physical systems. In: Proceeding of the 2012 IEEE/ACM Third International Conference on Cyber-Physical Systems, China, pp. 55–64. IEEE (2012)
65. Guo, Z., Baruah, S.K.: Uniprocessor EDF scheduling of AVR task systems. In: Proceeding of the ACM/IEEE Sixth International Conference on Cyber-Physical Systems, USA, pp.159–168. IEEE (2015)
66. Mohaqeqi, M., Abdullah, J., Ekberg, P.: Refinement of workload models for engine controllers by state space partitioning. In: Proceeding of the 29th Euromicro Conference on Real-Time Systems (ECRTS 2017), Croatia. IEEE (2017)
67. Bijinemula, S.K., Willcock, A., Chantem, T.: An efficient knapsack-based approach for calculating the worst-case demand of AVR tasks. In: Proceeding of the 2018 IEEE Real-Time Systems Symposium, USA, pp. 384–395. IEEE (2018)

68. Voronov, S., Anderson, J.H.: An optimal semi-partitioned scheduler assuming arbitrary affinity masks. In: Proceeding of the IEEE Real-Time Systems Symposium (RTSS), USA, pp. 408–420. IEEE (2018)
69. Tang, S., Anderson, J.H.: Towards practical multiprocessor EDF with affinities. In: Proceeding of the 41st IEEE Real-Time Systems Symposium, USA, pp. 89–101. IEEE (2020)
70. Tang, S., Voronov, S., Anderson, J.H.: GEDF tardiness: open problems involving uniform multiprocessors and affinity masks resolved. In: Leibniz International Proceedings in Informatics, p. 133 (2019)
71. Ahmed Bhuiyan, A., Yang, K., Arefin, S., et al.: Mixed-criticality multicore scheduling of real-time gang task systems. In: Proceeding of the 2019 IEEE Real-Time Systems Symposium, China, pp. 469–480. IEEE (2019)
72. Baruah, S.: The federated scheduling of systems of mixed-criticality sporadic DAG tasks. In: Proceeding of the 2016 IEEE Real-Time Systems Symposium, Portugal, pp. 227–236. IEEE (2016)
73. Medina, R., Borde, E., Pautet, L.: Scheduling multi-periodic mixed-criticality dags on multi-core architectures. In: Proceeding of the 2018 IEEE Real-Time Systems Symposium, USA, pp. 254–264. IEEE (2018)
74. Agrawal, K., Baruah, S., Burns, A.: Semi-clairvoyance in mixed-criticality scheduling. In: Proceeding of the 2019 IEEE Real-Time Systems Symposium (RTSS), China, pp. 458–468. IEEE (2019)
75. Cho, Y., Kim, D.H., Park, D.: Conditionally optimal task parallelization for global EDF on multi-core systems. In: Proceeding of the 2019 IEEE Real-Time Systems Symposium (RTSS), China, pp. 194–206. IEEE (2019)
76. Huang, P., Giannopoulou, G., Ahmed, R.: An isolation scheduling model for multicores. In: Proceeding of the 2015 IEEE Real-Time Systems Symposium, USA, pp. 141–152. IEEE (2015)

Encryption Traceability Scheme Based on SGX and Blockchain

Yunong Dai[1,2](✉) and Baixiang Liu[1,2]

[1] School of Computer Science, Fudan University, Shanghai 200433, China
18210240067@fudan.edu.cn
[2] Shanghai Engineering Research Center of Blockchain, Shanghai 200433, China

Abstract. Blockchain has the characteristics of decentralization, difficult to tamper with and traceability. The traceability system based on blockchain solves the problems of insufficient transparency in the process of information processing and non-traceability of processing information. However, excessive information transparency will cause data information leakage, and the limitations of smart contracts used to process transactions on the blockchain make the physical information under the blockchain inconsistent with the information on the blockchain. In view of the above two problems, this paper provides an encryption traceability method based on SGX (Software Guard Extensions) and blockchain, which executes complex contracts in the trusted execution environment under blockchain, and encrypts the contract output results. In this way, inconsistency between information on the chain and information off the chain and transparency of blockchain information can be solved. The analysis results show that this method has the characteristics of non-transparent ledger storage, processing information traceability and decentralization to a certain extent, and can solve the problems of data leakage of the traditional blockchain-based traceability system and the inconsistency between the information on the blockchain and the physical information.

Keywords: SGX · BlockChain · Traceability system

1 Introduction

As the underlying implementation technology of Bitcoin [1], blockchain is decentralized, traceable and difficult to tamper with. The initial blockchain applications are dominated by cryptocurrencies, but such applications have limitations, and the economic characteristics of cryptocurrencies are vulnerable to malicious speculation by the financial community. The current research direction is more inclined to other application fields with blockchain as the underlying technology. Traceability is a common application scenario of blockchain, which relies on the tamper-hard and traceable characteristics of blockchain to achieve traceability. But traditional blockchain smart contracts [2] have difficulty securely supporting operations involving keys and contracts with complex logic. The traceability application system generally involves multiple users, and the data on the blockchain is stored on each node in the form of a transparent ledger. For some applications involving personal privacy data, data security cannot be guaranteed.

Z. Cai et al. (Eds.): NCTCS 2021, CCIS 1494, pp. 119–132, 2021.
https://doi.org/10.1007/978-981-16-7443-3_8

At present, the research on traceability method based on blockchain technology, on the one hand, expands the application of blockchain traceability technology in subdivision scenarios, and the specific schemes and strategies are much the same; On the other hand, it attaches importance to the imtamability of data and ignores the security of private data. Privacy security is the foundation and important issue of blockchain and the traceability system based on blockchain.

Trusted computing [3] is one of the solutions to blockchain privacy issues. The Trusted Execution Environment (TEE) of the computer is used for data operation, and a large number of complex verification logic is moved to the Trusted Execution Environment of the chain for operation. The calculation results are encrypted first, and the Execution credentials of the Trusted Environment are broadcast to the block chain network for verification. The verified results are stored on the chain. TEE has made many achievements in related studies combined with blockchain. For example, Zhang [4] and others used SGX (a specific implementation product of TEE) to solve the problem of energy waste caused by POW (Proof of Work) in Bitcoin. The Ekiden [5] platform uses SGX to execute off-chain "contracts" on the Bitcoin system in combination with the protocols it sets. Its prototype system achieves 600 times higher throughput, 400/1 latency and 1000/1 execution cost than the Ethereum main network. The FastKitten [6] Smart Contract Execution framework is also designed based on SGX to execute off-chain "contracts" on cryptocurrencies that do not support smart contracts. FastKitten is more focused on the efficiency of off-chain contracts than the Ekiden platform. Pointed out that the implementation of "contract" under the chain of the underlying block chain should include at least three security properties "active" and "consistency" and "invariance, and gives its run on the currency system of the test cases and operation performance, the experiment result says the execution efficiency of this method has the characteristics of lower cost and high execution efficiency. In April 2020, Ant Financial services in the summit ACM SIGMOD 20 published a paper [7], and announced the world's first commercially available on-chain privacy protection technology officially open, and external BaaS (Blockchain as a Service, Blockchain service), The paper also uses trusted computing to address privacy issues, enabling smart contracts to be securely executed off-chain and providing users with optional data encryption capabilities.

The existing blockchain-based traceability system [8–10] focuses more on the design of specific businesses and does not analyze the data leakage problems existing in such systems. In the paper [11], hierarchical keys are used to control the permissions of personnel in the supply chain system, and the availability of data is determined according to the permissions. However, this method does not solve the problem of transparent ledger storage of blockchain.

Combined with the research and ideas of other scholars, this paper proposes an encryption traceability method based on SGX and blockchain to solve the problems of data leakage and inconsistency between on-chain information and off-chain information in the traceability system based on blockchain.

The innovative points of this method are as follows:

1. Use the trusted execution environment SGX to execute smart contracts off-chain and encrypt the contract results, and store the encrypted data information on the blockchain to solve the problem of transparent ledger of the blockchain.

2. Use the trusted execution environment SGX to execute business contracts with complex logic off the chain, ensuring the strong consistency between the information on the chain and the information off the chain.

2 Preliminaries

2.1 Blockchain

As the underlying supporting technology of Bitcoin, blockchain is essentially a decentralized distributed database. All full nodes in the blockchain network jointly maintain a block as a unit of chain-like database, using computer cryptography to generate key pairs for each user, users generally take the public key hash as their account address to participate in the network, using consensus algorithm to complete data consistency between nodes. Blocks recognized by the consensus algorithm will record data information in plain text and then be added to the blockchain to become new blocks. Blocks are linked by hash values, and the database grows in chains as more blocks are added. Since all blocks are formed based on the hash of the previous block, the creation of each new block is also an acknowledgement of the authenticity of the previous block. The concept diagram of the blockchain head is shown in Fig. 1.

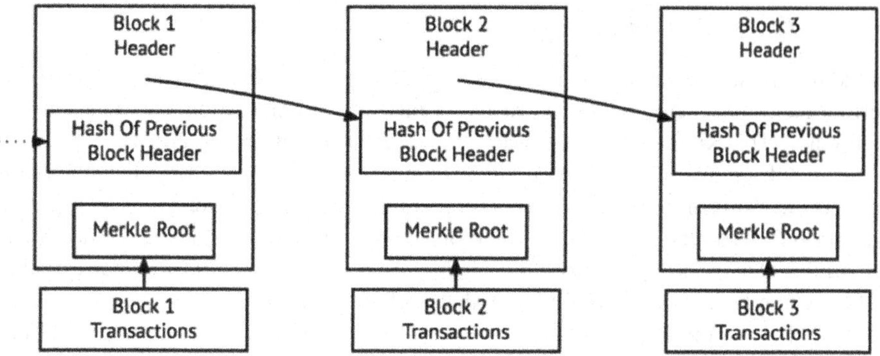

Fig. 1. Blockchain data structure

The block body of the blockchain stores all transaction data of the block at this height. Bitcoin stores transactions with MerkleTree [12] number structure, which is featured by the ability to quickly locate whether a certain transaction is in the block without traversal of all transactions.

This data structure distinguishes blockchain from traditional distributed databases that are hard to tamper with and traceable. However, in order to support the verification of transaction information by multiple nodes, transaction information must be stored in plain text, which makes the data insecure.

2.2 Traceability System Based on Blockchain

The traditional traceability system adopts the centralized storage mode, which records the historical processing records and processing process of data in the database. However, in this storage mode, the central server is vulnerable to internal or external attacks, single node failure and data tampering. The traceability system based on blockchain can effectively solve the above problems, and its distributed storage mode, special block structure and hash algorithm ensure the security of block data.

The traceability system based on blockchain has the following characteristics:

1. Decentralized storage. Distributed storage can effectively prevent data corruption caused by single-node breakdown.
2. Data information can be traced and difficult to tamper with. The chained storage structure of the blockchain ensures that data is hard to tamper with and traceable.
3. Transparent storage. As all nodes in the blockchain network need to agree on the data before storage, data information is transmitted and stored between nodes in the form of plaintext.
4. Support simple smart contracts. Smart contracts based on blockchain have integrity and programmability, but due to the performance constraints of blockchain, they cannot support smart contracts with complex logic.

2.3 Off-Chain Contract

In the traditional blockchain network, for the execution result of a smart contract, the verifier needs to repeat the whole process in the local simulation once to determine its legitimacy. This kind of smart contract On the chain is called "on-chain" contract. In contrast, "off-chain" contracts place a large number of logical operations down the chain, and then determine the results Add proof materials to the chain, other nodes on the chain only need to verify the legitimacy of their proof materials to complete the verification of the results. One of the key points of off-chain is to ensure that the contract code executed Off the chain is correct and provides evidence of its correctness.

SGX [13] is a product launched by Intel corporation in 2013. SGX is divided into Enclave and non-enclave parts internally. SGX can guarantee the confidentiality and integrity of Enclave part of data, and the code programming languages of Enclave part are Turing complete C and C++ languages. Intel also officially provides SGX encryption library based on OpenSSL implementation. This basic condition enables developers to implement encryption, digital signature and complex logic contract code programming in SGX.

3 The Project Design

3.1 Analysis of the Traceability System Scheme Based on Blockchain

The design architecture of the traditional blockchain-based traceability system is shown in Fig. 2. The design has the following problems.

1. On-chain data information and on-chain contract information are stored in plain text, which is easy to cause data leakage.
2. The on-chain contract information is inconsistent with the off-chain physical information. Intelligent contracts in the chain of processing the information A backwardness to downstream contract B for processing, due to the block after the success of the chain in the network intelligent contract once deployed will exist permanent chain network (unless the blocks disappear), so after the contract is called B will be executed, but physical may be due to some reason and no progress to B, This creates the problem of data inconsistency between the on-chain information and the physical information.
3. It is not easy to operate the on-chain contract involving keys, resulting in weak correlation between on-chain information and off-chain information. Since the on-chain contract may exist on any node in the blockchain network after deployment, if the on-chain contract directly performs the encryption processing operation, the encryption key is easy to be stolen, which leads to the signature of data information needs to be carried out in the off-chain untrusted environment. However, this processing method has serious vulnerabilities. The signer can completely sign fake data information to upload, resulting in inconsistency between the information on the chain and the information off the chain.

3.2 Encryption Traceability Scheme Based on SGX and Blockchain

In view of the above problems in the traceability system, the solution of this scheme is as follows:

1. The data information is encrypted and stored on the block chain. SGX is used to provide access control.
2. Data inconsistency caused by parallel processing of data information and physical information. This scheme designs the following data structure, in which contract B generates ciphertext_{AB} to physical information goods_{AB}, so that the processing can proceed to the next step, which ensures the consistency of on-chain data and off-chain data.
3. In order to solve the problem that the on-chain contract is not suitable for the operation related to keys, this paper uses the off-chain contract based on SGX, and the contract content is written into SGX after multi-party negotiation. Due to the confidentiality and integrity characteristics of SGX, can offer intelligent contract execution environment, similar to block chain perform signature and encryption operations on the environment. It is difficult to reveal the key information, at the same time, the environment can provide a verifiable SGX signatures, the rest of the nodes only need to verify the legitimacy of the SGX signature and it is not a duplicate data can complete consensus.

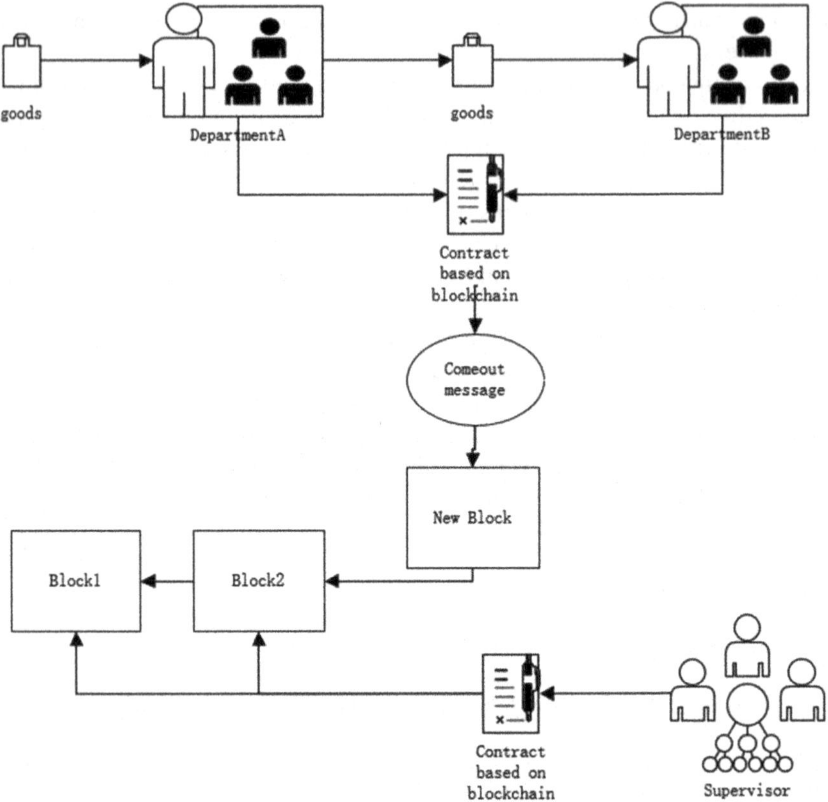

Fig. 2. Traceability system architecture based on blockchain

The Project Design. The overall architecture of this solution is shown in Fig. 3. The traceability system generally has multiple departments, and each department may have different participants. The information circulating in the entire system consists of physical goods, message and ciphertext. Goods and message should ensure the final consistency. In addition, the traceability system has a supervisor who does not interfere in the business process but can supervise the process.

The initial links of this scheme are divided into contractual links, key distribution links and traceability rights distribution links.

Contractual Links. The agreement of the contract shall be negotiated by the parties and the contract shall be executed in full accordance with the content of the contract. The contract content of this scheme is made by offline agreement of multiple parties, but the contract is deployed in the form of code to SGX of each node, and SGX guarantees the integrity and confidentiality of the smart contract.

Key Distribution. Generally speaking, the regulator in the traceability system is a trusted third party, and the CA center in this scheme is also acted by the regulator. When participating in the process agreed by the contract, the regulator assigns keys with

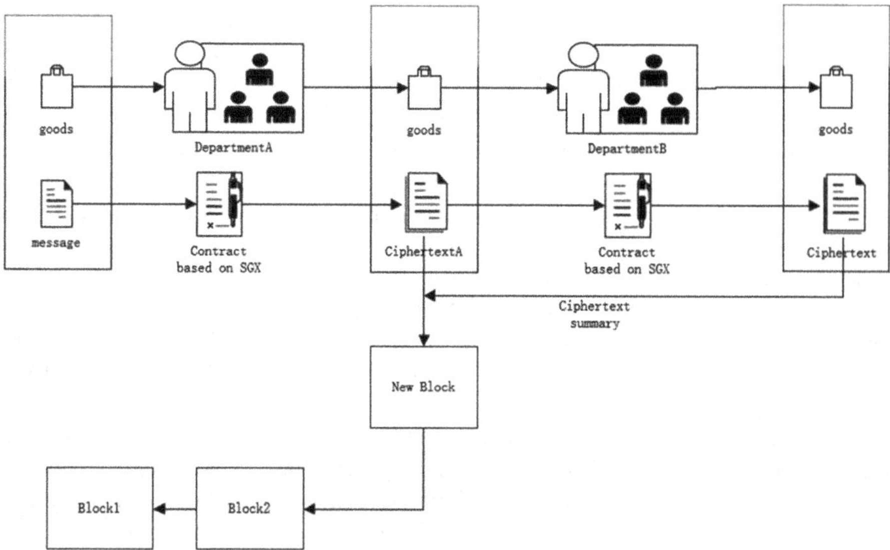

Fig. 3. Solution architecture

different permissions to different departments according to their different processing processes. For example, Pk_i and SK_i are available. Pk_i is the public key, SK_i is the private key, and I means the department.

Traceability Authority Allocation. The supervisor can set the corresponding level of authority for each processing link according to the need of authority. $level_i \in level, i \in \{1, 2, 3, \ldots n\}$ where I represents the level of the department that can be viewed by the permission level. For example, if I is 3, it means that the processing information of the three departments on the final product Goods can be viewed.

The specific operation process of this scheme is as follows:

1. The physical goods and their data information message are first processed by Department A. After receiving the goods, Department A processes the message to get $message_A$. $message_A$ and the signature result $signature_A$, are processed by the contract which be deployed in SGX (after decryptAndVerify, sign, encryptAndCreate algorithm in turn) to get the encryption result, $ciphertext_A$. The $ciphertext_A$ is broadcast to the blockchain, and after the consensus is passed (because of the uniqueness of physical goods, there is no double flower problem in this link), it is added to the block. The physical goods are added with a $ciphertext_A$ and become $goods_A$ to continue on to the next department B.
2. The physical $goods_A$ arrives at Department B, and Department B continues to process according to step 1. Finally, the encrypted data information $ciphertext_{AB}$ is recorded in the block and the physical $goods_{AB}$ is transferred to the next department.
3. Repeat the preceding steps until all departments complete the processing.
4. The contract of the regulatory department has a comprehensive access interface, and the decryptAndSearch algorithm can be used to check the ciphertext of the encrypted

information of each department. The purpose of supervision is to check whether the ciphertext matches the corresponding physical goods information.

Off-Chain Contract Scheme Based on SGX. Traditional intelligent contract although based on block chain can ensure deployment is invoked after a big probability ensure correct implementation process and the results are correct, but the execution of this contract is transparent, the results need to block all nodes in the local chain network simulation run to verify, contract execution efficiency is poor, the problems of slow consensus and safety is not high.

The smart contract scheme based on SGX proposed in this scheme ensures that smart contracts are difficult to be tampered with after being successfully deployed through the confidentiality and integrity of SGX. The confidentiality of SGX ensures that the execution process of the contract is carried out in a "black box", so the execution cost is low. SGX supports operations involving keys, and the execution process is difficult to be detected by outsiders. At the same time, the execution results are encrypted and output, ensuring that the data information is stored in ciphertext in areas outside the Enclave.

Smart contract solutions are generally written as programs and deployed to SGX after a multi-party offline agreement. The SGX-based smart contract scheme of this scheme is generally agreed as follows:

1. Assign different keys based on different permissions of departments to implement permission control.
2. Digital signature and encryption operations are performed in SGX.
3. The smart contract performs symmetric encryption for the processed signature information signature and the original information message. The encryption key is theoretically distributed by the regulatory department and stored in SGX. The ciphertext is broadcast to the rest of the nodes and stored in the block after consensus.

The smart contract of this scheme contains the following four basic algorithms.

Algorithm 1: Sign Algorithm

Require:
    Ciphertext
    SK: privateKey
Procedure:

```
1: get key from enclave
2: signature, message, preCiphertext = decrypt(cryptograph, key)
3: if goods != message
       return false
4: signature = algorithm(message, SK)
5: return signature
```

Algorithm 2: encryptAndCreate Algorithm

Require:

preCiphertext
signature
message

Procedure:

get key from enclave
secret = $encrypt(signature, message, key)$
ciphertext = $new\ Ciphertext(secret, preCiphertext)$
return ciphertext

Algorithm 3: decryptAndSearch Algorithm

Require:

ciphertext
level
res :result initial value

Procedure:

get key from enclave
if level==0 return res
level—;
signature, message, preCiphertext = $decrypt(ciphertext, key)$
res.add(message)
decryptAndSearch(preCiphertext,level,res)
return res

Algorithm 4: decryptAndVerify Algorithm

Require:

ciphertext
Pk
goods

Procedure:

get key from enclave
get secret from goods
message1, signature1 = $decrypt(secret_1, key)$
signature, message, preCiphertext = $decrypt(ciphertext, key)$
if message1 != message return false
if signature1 !=signature return false
return $signVerify(Pk, signature)$

In this scheme, the physical goods are associated with the corresponding ciphertext of the ciphertext information, and the contract decryption and verification algorithm will judge the ciphertext information on the Goods and the ciphertext information obtained from the blockchain network, so that the physical goods have a strong correlation with the ciphertext information.

Blockchain-Based Data Storage. The underlying blockchain data structure of Bitcoin is divided into head and body. The body uses merkleTree to compress and store information, and uses the collision resistance of the hash algorithm to generate the final hash result as the unique identifier of the body. The blockchain storage structure of this scheme is roughly designed as follows:

Ciphertext Structure:

Variable name	Type	Describe
secret	String	Encrypted result of message signature
preCiphertext	String	Previous ciphertext

Head Structure:

Variable name	Type	Describe
height	int	Block's height
hash	String	Block's hash
preHash	String	preBlock's hash
timestamp	long	Block generation timestamp

Body Structure:

Variable name	Type	Describe
height	Int	Block's height
hash	String	Root hash
criphertextTree	Tree<>	A MerkleTree of transactions

The storage relationship between body and ciphertext is a one-to-many relationship, and the preCiphertex in the structure of ciphertext is the last information of the ciphertext information.

When the regulatory department performs traceability query, the smart contract in SGX can view the process information of the physical object in the system according to the authority of the regulatory personnel and the ciphertext information on the physical goods. Since the execution process of smart contract is executed in SGX, it is difficult for the outside world to snoop on the execution process. The tracer can only obtain the range of results agreed by the smart contract to achieve the effect of encrypted tracer.

Table 1. Function analysis table of the scheme

Functional indicators	Literature [8]	Literature [9]	Literature [10]	This plan
Information integrity	✓	✓	✓	✓
Information traceability	✓	✓	✓	✓
Complex contract	✗	✗	✗	✓
Encrypted storage	✗	✗	✗	✓

4 Performance Evaluation of the Scheme

4.1 Solution Function Analysis

By the above Table 1, two results can be seen that the solutions compared to the other three, in addition to meet the requirements of the basic function of traceability system, the scheme is on the way to store encrypted storage, this scheme can prevent leakage data is abnormal and support for complex logical contract, can be done in the contract for the encryption of data operation and business operations.

4.2 Scheme Performance Analysis

In this paper, the performance data of this scheme are verified by the control experiment method. Information about the prototype and reference systems is as follows in Table 2.

Table 2. Experimental environment

	Reference system	Prototype system
OS	Ubuntu18.04.2	Ubuntu18.04.2
SGX	null	Linux 2.3.1 for Ubantu18.04
Consensus algorithm	Raft	Raft
Encryption algorithm	AES	AES
CPU	Intel I7	Intel I7

The test data information size is 2048 bits, the test method is to take the AES method call time t_1, and the return encrypted data time t_2, the difference between the two is $t = t_2 - t_1$, the unit is milliseconds, the data of the 10 experiment results are shown in Table 3.

According to the analysis of experimental results, the introduction of the SGX module causes the encryption time of the prototype system to be about 10% slower than that of the control system, regardless of the time-consuming data transmission. Since the contract results of the off-chain contract do not require the other nodes to simulate and execute locally during the consensus, the time-consuming consensus of the two systems will also be different.

Table 3. Encryption time of two systems

Index	Prototype system	Reference system
1	101	85
2	104	90
3	100	88
4	98	90
5	97	89
6	102	88
7	110	89
8	104	90
9	100	95
10	90	80
AVE	100.6	88.4

This experiment uses the Raft [14] consensus algorithm and the consensus strategy is for all nodes to reach a consensus. Assuming that the number of nodes participating in the consensus is n, the time for each node i to execute the smart contract on the chain locally is T_i, $i \in n$. The time to execute the smart contract in SGX is T_p ($T_p = 0.9T$), and the time to complete data verification in SGX is T_v. Regardless of the data transmission time in the network, the theoretical time To complete the consensus of the prototype system is:

$$T_o = T_p + n \times T_v \tag{1}$$

Comparing the time for the system to complete the consensus T_c:

$$max\{T_1 ... T_n\} \leq T_c \leq \sum\nolimits_{i=1}^{n} T_i \tag{2}$$

The consensus time consumption of the test prototype system and the control system when the number of nodes is 1, 3, 5, and 10 respectively (the consensus strategy is that all nodes reach an agreement), and the unit is milliseconds. The test results are shown in Table 4 below.

According to the analysis of the experimental results, the consensus time of the prototype system is not affected by the number of nodes, while the consensus time of the control system is positively correlated with the number of nodes, and the experimental results are basically consistent with the theoretical analysis results.

In conclusion, although the efficiency of encryption, decryption and digital signature execution in this scheme has a time loss of 10%, in terms of consensus verification, with the increase of the number of nodes, this scheme has a significant performance improvement.

Table 4. Consensus time of the two systems

Number of nodes	Prototype system	Reference system
1	890	872
3	912	2689
5	931	3532
10	1041	9210
20	1201	18293

4.3 Solution Security Analysis

The security proof of this scheme is analyzed from three aspects: anti-conspiracy attack, forged signature and stored result.

A Conspiracy Attack Produced by Cooperation Between Upper and Lower Departments. In this scheme, the physical object and data information are bound. When the physical object is processed by different departments, its data information will be recorded through the off-chain contract. Due to the integrity and confidentiality of the off-chain contract based on SGX, it is difficult for the attacker to change the contract code to forge data information different from the real thing, thus cutting off the cooperation between the upper and lower departments and reducing the success rate of the conspiracy attack.

The Cheater Forged the Signature Result. This scheme uses the symmetric encryption algorithm AES [15] to encrypt data. As the security of AES algorithm is verified by proof, the security risk is the safe preservation of the encryption key. In this scheme, key access and storage are carried out in SGX. SGX has the sealed storage feature, which makes the data stored can only be accessed by the corresponding enclave code, and other areas can only access the ciphertext form of the data. This makes it difficult for an attacker to create a legitimate cipher text.

The Cheater Falsifies the Stored Results. In this scheme, data storage is distributed, and each node will store a complete copy of the data. In order to achieve the attack purpose, the attacker must breach at least 51% of the nodes, tamper with the data information stored by the nodes and forge legitimate ciphertext information. With the increase of the number of nodes and blocks, the success rate of 51% attack will become smaller and smaller, so it is difficult for the attacker to forge the storage results recognized by the whole network.

5 Conclusion

This paper analyzes the privacy security problems existing in the traceability system based on blockchain, and proposes an encryption traceability scheme based on SGX and blockchain. The plan compared to traditional data have to maintain chain and chain data information under the eventual consistency, chain information stored encrypted and the advantage of support complex logic smart contracts, to solve the problem existing in the application system based on block chain privacy problems bring new train of thought, which can support complex intelligent features block chain and maintenance contract, It can also solve the issue of blockchain privacy and security. The next step is to implement the application system in specific scenarios according to the scheme, and gradually optimize the scheme details.

References

1. Nakamoto, S.: Bitcoin: a peer-to-peer electronic cash system (2009)
2. Szabo, N.: Formalizing and securing relationships on public networks. First Monday **2**(9), (1997)
3. Feng, D., Qin, Y., Wang, D., Chu, X.: Research trusted on computer technology. Comput. Res. Dev. **48**(08), 1332–1349 (2011)
4. Zhang, F., Eyal, I., Escriva, R., et al.: Blockchains. In: 26th USENIX Security 2017, pp. 1427–1444 (2017)
5. Cheng, R., Zhang, F., Kos, J., et al.: Ekiden: a platform for confidentiality-preserving, trustworthy, and performant smart contract execution (2018)
6. Das, P., Eckey, L., Frassetto, T., et al.: Fastkitten: practical smart contracts on bitcoin. In: 28th USENIX Security Symposium (USENIX Security 2019), pp. 801–818 (2019)
7. Yan, Y., Wei, C., Guo, X., et al.: Confidentiality support over financial grade consortium blockchain. In: Proceedings of the 2020 ACM SIGMOD International Conference on Management of Data, pp. 2227–2240 (2020)
8. Luo, C.: Research on the traceability system of agricultural products based on blockchain technology. Chengdu University (2021)
9. Li, M., Wang, D., Zeng, X., Bai, Q., Sun, Y.: Design of food safety traceability system based on blockchain. Food Sci. **40**(03), 279–285 (2019)
10. Yu, Z., Guo, C., Xie, Y., Xue, D.: Research on anti-counterfeiting traceability system of medicine based on blockchain. Comput. Eng. Appl. **56**(03), 35–41 (2020)
11. Lu, Y., Wen, J.: Supply chain control and traceability scheme based on Bitcoin technology. Comput. Eng. **44**(12), 85–93+101 (2018)
12. Huang, G., Zou, Y., Xu, Y.: Research on performance of Merkle tree in blockchain. Comput. Syst. Appl. **29**(09), 237–243 (2020)
13. Intel SGX technology, 22 January 2021. https://software.intel.com/en-us/node/708990
14. Ongaro, D., Ousterhout, J.: In search of an understandable consensus algorithm. USENIX Association (2014)
15. He, M., Lin, H.: AES algorithm principle and its realization. Comput. Appl. Res. **12**, 61–63 (2002)

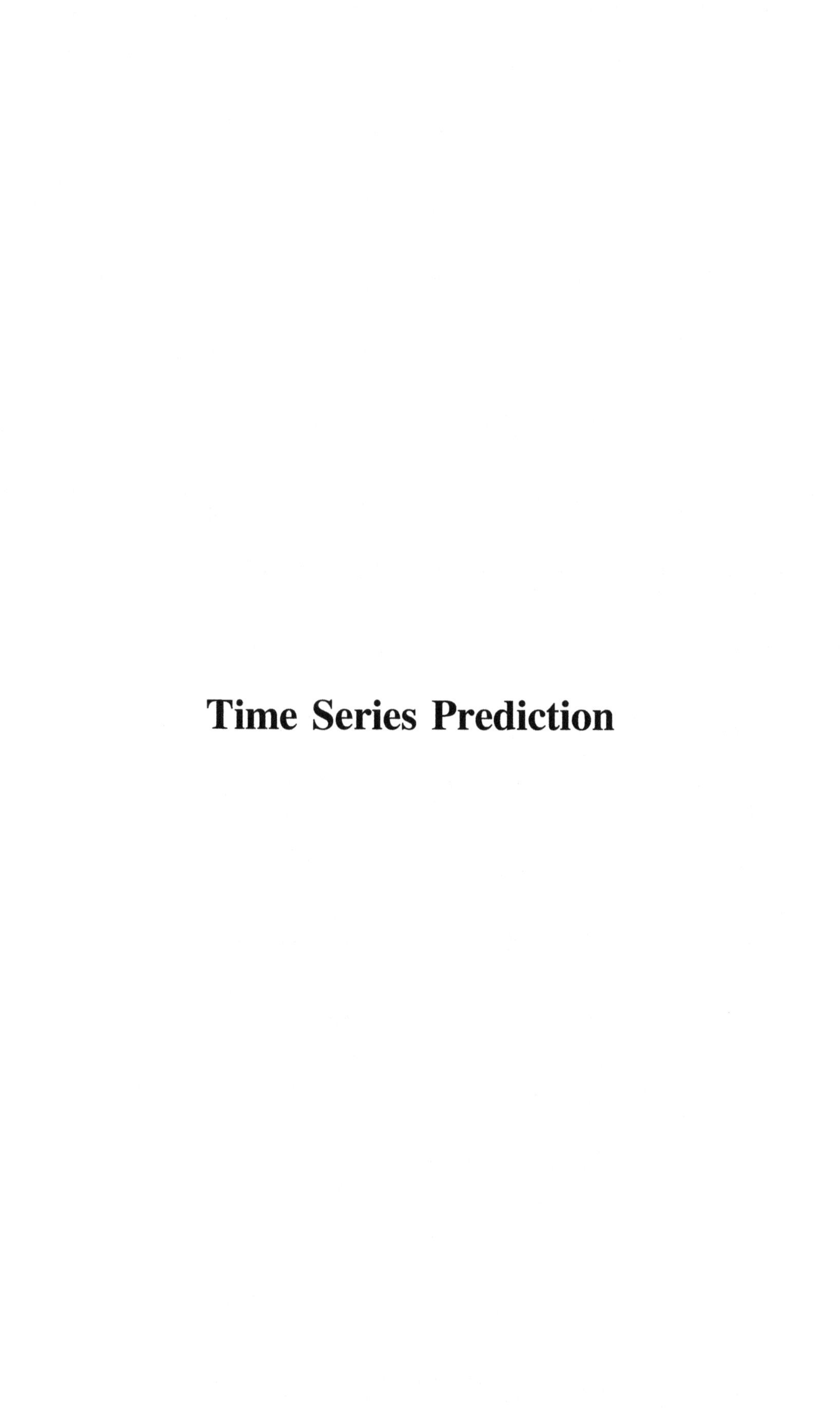

Time Series Prediction

A Load Forecasting Method of Power Grid Host Based on SARIMA-GRU Model

Chen Zheng[1], Yuzhou Wu[1], Zhigang Chen[1(✉)], Kun Wang[2], and Lizhong Zhang[2]

[1] School of Computer Science and Engineering, Central South University, Changsha 410008, China
czg@csu.edu.cn

[2] State Grid Ningxia Electric Power Co. Ltd., Information and Telecommunication Branch, Yinchuan 753000, China

Abstract. With the continuous development of intelligent power grid, how to boost the prediction ability of the future operating mode of information equipment and set the dynamic provision for prediction intervals to adapt to the changes of data are huge challenges for the grid IT operation and maintenance. To solve these problems, this paper proposes a combined time series forecasting model (SARIMA-GRU) based on the traditional Seasonal ARIMA model (SARIMA) and the GRU model in Deep learning, which is the error-fitting model by using the error auto-regressive method to compensate for the prediction result. In order to establish the threshold interval in line with the actual production demand, SARIMA-GRU applies the statistical method and K-nearest neighbor algorithm for global preprocessing, and then divides the non-stationary series into three main components of model: trends, seasonality, and residual terms. By using the corresponding model components to predict, we achieve higher prediction accuracy under the normal operation state. On a real-world power grid dataset, we demonstrate more significant performance improvements over the traditional model ARIMA, SARIMA and combination model, like ARIMA-SVM, and showcase three actual threshold intervals.

Keywords: Time series · Load forecasting · SARIMA · Error compensation · GRU

1 Introduction

With the improvement of people's living standards, the business scale of electric power companies is increasing, and the current level of system operation and

This work is supported by the National Natural Science Foundation of China (Grant No. 71633006) and Intelligent software and hardware system of medical process assistant and its application belong to "2030 Innovation Megaprojects" (to be fully launched by 2020) - New Generation Artificial Intelligence (Project no. 2020AAA0109605).

Z. Cai et al. (Eds.): NCTCS 2021, CCIS 1494, pp. 135–153, 2021.
https://doi.org/10.1007/978-981-16-7443-3_9

maintenance is difficult to support changing business scenarios and problems. To improve the efficiency of operation and maintenance, many experts and scholars have begun to devote themselves to the research of intelligent operation and maintenance of electric power enterprises [1]. One of the key issues is the intelligent monitoring of information equipment. Today is times of highly relying on the Internet, the safe operation of information equipment is related to the normal operation of enterprises and determines whether enterprises can effectively reduce costs and improve efficiency [2]. Up to now operation and maintenance personnel generally monitor host resources through the monitoring program in the system, collect information on the occupation of resources such as memory and CPU, understand the current system operation status, and handle exceptions in time.

In recent years, experts and scholars at home and abroad have carried out extensive research and put forward some effective forecasting schemes in terms of host load forecasting. In 2000, the paper [3] evaluated the predictive effect of the linear model in the host load and finally proved that the AR(16) model is sufficient for host prediction and the cost is small. Subsequently, on its basis, the paper [4] proposed a weighted and improved AR model, which optimizes the prediction performance by weighting the solved parameters, while retaining the advantages of simple autoregressive model modeling and low consumption. The paper [5] applied the ARIMA model to the load forecasting of the storage system, realized short-term early warning and forecasting, and proved that the ARIMA model has strong applicability in load forecasting. The paper [6] combines the ARIMA model with the classification and regression tree [7] (CART), and uses the weighted least square method [8] and boundary judgment [9] to optimize, and makes up for the inability of the autoregressive model through the combination of models. The defect of fitting nonlinear information greatly improves the prediction accuracy. These methods reflect the process of continuous improvement, integration, and innovation of autoregressive prediction models with the development of the times.

Although these prediction algorithms can improve the accuracy of prediction, they also have some shortcomings. On the one hand, these models did not consider the impact of the seasonality of the time series. On the other hand, the fusion-innovated models only used machine learning to fit the prediction residuals without considering their autocorrelation. As a branch of machine learning, deep learning has been widely used in medical [10], power [11], finance [12] and other fields. To this end, this article considers the introduction of error compensation methods to study the linear relationship between residual historical data and forecast data. For example, in the paper [13], based on the multi-step prediction, the RBF neural network uses the historical prediction error to correct the prediction value at the future time, which not only solves the error accumulation problem but also improves the prediction accuracy. On the other hand, the paper [14] Residual Recurrent Neural Network (R2N2) regards the traditional AR model as the initial predictor and uses RNN to estimate the residual. From its experimental conclusions, it can be seen that the compensation for the residual can be greatly improved The accuracy of time series forecasting. These two methods provide research ideas for this article.

Therefore, we proposed a prediction model (SARIMA-GRU) applying complex network error compensation technology on this basis. In the prediction of dissolved oxygen, GRU is proved to have better performance than other neural network models [15]. First, a Seasonal ARIMA model (SARIMA) is established, which decomposes the time series periodically and then separately predicts. The period forecast uses the dissociated period fluctuation value, and the trend forecast uses the ARIMA model. For the prediction error of the SARIMA model, this paper adopts the method of error autoregressive prediction to analyze the correlation between historical error and future error. The final seasonality component, ARIMA trend prediction component, and error compensation prediction component are integrated to obtain the prediction result.

The main contributions of our paper are as follows: 1) We propose an effective time series prediction model—SARIMA-GRU. Extensive experiments on real-world time-series datasets of power grid enterprises show the effectiveness of the model. 2) We design an error compensation module of GRU to solve the problem that the traditional model can not deal with the nonlinear relationship of time series and modify the error of the prediction model to improve the performance of long-distance prediction. Experiments show that the GRU error compensation technology improves the prediction performance and generalization ability of the model. 3) We generate a 95% dynamic threshold interval through the established model, which meets the real-time requirements of the industrial production environment. It can effectively monitor the abnormal fluctuations in business peak, timely inform the operation and maintenance personnel to solve problems, and improve the operation and maintenance efficiency.

2 Methods and Models

Let there be a unique entity Y in a given time series dataset - such as Memory Load in server. The univariate time-series is associated with key operation index $y_t \in \mathbb{R}$ at each time-step $t \in [0, T]$. We divide time-dependent input features into three parts $\widetilde{y}_{0:t}$ which is time series representing long-distance trend information after removing seasonality, $\Omega_{t_0:t_0+\tau}$ which is the seasonal change produced by cycle extraction method, and $x_{t-k:t}$ which are unknown nonlinear factor beforehand. t_0 is the index of seasonal components with seasonal corresponding relation to time t. In short, when the seasonality is Day, t_0 and t are at the same time.

In many scenarios, the predicted confidence interval is very useful for abnormal alarm by giving the probability of the target appearing in a certain interval. When truth data exceeds this interval, it means that the abnormal event with minimal probability has occurred. The confidence interval is calculated by the predicted value $\hat{y}$ based on the confidence theory. Each forecast takes the form below:

$$\hat{y}_{t,\tau} = f_w\left(\tau, \tilde{y}_{0:t}, \Omega_{t_0:t_0+\tau}, x_{t-k:t}\right) \tag{1}$$

where $\hat{y}_{t,\tau}$ is the predicted sample of the τ-step-ahead forecast at time t, and $f_w(.)$ is our prediction model.

2.1 SARIMA

ARIMA [16] (Auto-Regressive Integrated Moving Average) model is a forecasting method based on time series. The main idea of the ARIMA model is to eliminate the local level or trend of the sequence through the difference method, and then apply the differentiated sequence to the ARMA model to realize the prediction of non-stationary time series. The modeling formula of ARIMA is as follows:

$$\tilde{y}_t = \mu + \sum_{i=1}^{p} \gamma_i y_{t-i} + \sum_{i=1}^{q} \theta_i e_{t-i} \tag{2}$$

$\tilde{y}_t$ from the formula represents the value of the current time series X at the time t after the difference, μ represents the constant value; p and q represents the order of the AR and MA models respectively; e represents the error value; γ_i represents the autocorrelation coefficient; θ_i represents the correlation coefficient [17].

On this basis, the SARIMA (Seasonal Auto-Regressive Integrated Moving Average) considers the influence of cyclical factors and refers to a model for predicting cyclical time series. To eliminate the seasonal fluctuation factors in the time series, methods such as STL [18] (Seasonal and Trend decomposition using Loess) are generally used for trend dissociation and prediction [19]. The change seasonality is represented by s. The modeling formula of the product SARIMA model with seasonality s is as follows:

$$\Phi_p(L)A_P\left(L^s\right)\left(\Delta^d \Delta_s^D \tilde{y}_t\right) = \Theta_q(L)B_Q\left(L^s\right)e_t \tag{3}$$

where $\Phi_p(L)$, $A_P\left(L^s\right)$, $\Theta_q(L)$, $B_Q\left(L^s\right)$ are respectively expressed as:

$$\begin{cases} \Phi_p(L) = \left(1 - \phi_1 L - \phi_2 L^2 - \ldots - \phi_p L^p\right) \\ A_P\left(L^s\right) = \left(1 - \alpha_1 L^s - \alpha_2 L^{2s} - \ldots - \alpha_P L^{P_s}\right) \\ \Theta_q(L) = \left(1 + \theta_1 L + \theta_2 L^2 + \ldots + \theta_q L^q\right) \\ B_Q\left(L^s\right) = \left(1 + \beta_1 L^s + \beta_2 L^{2s} + \ldots + \beta_Q L^{Q_s}\right) \end{cases} \tag{4}$$

In the Eq. 4, the predicted value of the modeling sequence is $\tilde{y}_t$, Δ^d and Δ_s^D are the d-order difference of the non-seasonality part and the D-order difference of the seasonal part respectively; e_t represents the error value and obeys the normal distribution; $\Phi_p(L)$ and $A_P\left(L^s\right)$ are the autoregressive polynomials of the non-seasonality part and the seasonal part respectively. ϕ_p indicates the autocorrelation coefficient of the lagging p-order polynomial, and the same applies to α_P; while $\Theta_q(L)$ and $B_Q\left(L^s\right)$ represents the moving average polynomial of the non-seasonality part and the seasonality part, and θ_q represents the correlation coefficient of the lagging q-order polynomial, and the same applies to β_Q. The final model can be expressed as SARIMA(p, d, q)(P, D, Q)s.

SARIMA's modeling process includes the following parts: data preprocessing, seasonality test, stationarity test, difference, BIC criterion [20] order determination, modeling parameters, and residual test. Among them, seasonal inspection is the top priority of SARIMA modeling. The seasonality s is obtained through the observation method of the time series diagram. As shown in Fig. 1, the abscissa is 24 h in a day, and the line segments of different colors represent the load value changes on different days. Trend, observation found that there are two obvious crest curves from 9 to 18, that is, there is an obvious trend of seasonal changes. This paper adopts the ADF test [21], and the experimental data meets the stationarity requirement after the first-order difference.

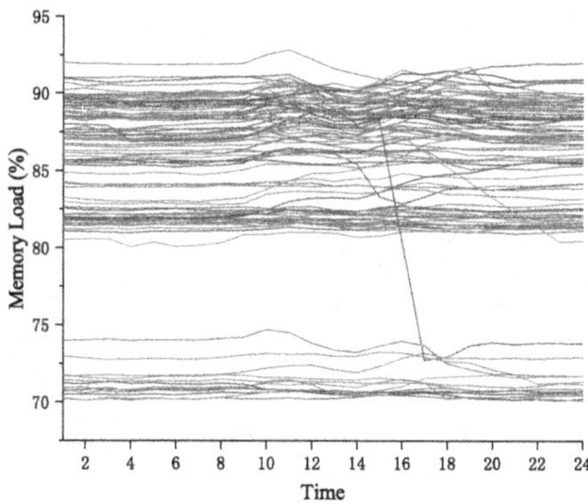

Fig. 1. Daily seasonal diagram of Memory Load time series. The daily Memory Load curve shows the seasonal change rule in one day, for example, two peaks at 10:00 to 12:00 and around 16:00.

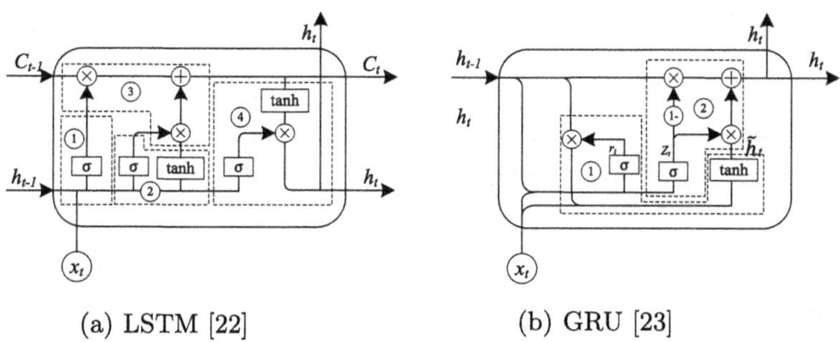

Fig. 2. LSTM and GRU neural network unit. (a): LSTM unit structure, 1, 2, 3, 4 respectively refers to forgetting gate, input gate, update gate, and output gate. (b): In GRU unit structure, 1 and 2 refer to reset gate and update gate respectively.

2.2 GRU

GRU network, also known as gating cycle unit, is a variant of long-term and short-term memory network (LSTM [24]), mainly to solve the problem of high computational complexity in training LSTM network. These problems will cause the feature input LSTM, training time is too long.

The reason why GRU works better is that it reduces the two information flows that run through all units in LSTM to one, and also reduces the number of gating mechanisms. The model structure of GRU and LSTM units is shown in Fig. 2. The complexity of the calculation formula adopted by GRU in the cycle unit is also greatly reduced.

In Fig. 2, LSTM has two information flows to and to, while GRU only has a straight-arrow flow. The specific structure of the GRU unit is described the formulas as follows:

$$r_t = \sigma\left(W_r \cdot [h_{t-1}, x_t] + b_r\right) \tag{5}$$

$$\tilde{h}_t = \tanh\left(W_{\tilde{h}} \cdot [r_t * h_{t-1}, x_t] + b_{\tilde{h}}\right) \tag{6}$$

$$z_t = \sigma\left(W_z \cdot [h_{t-1}, x_t] + b_z\right) \tag{7}$$

$$h_t = (1 - z_t) * h_{t-1} + z_t * \tilde{h}_t \tag{8}$$

$$\tilde{x}_t = \sigma\left(W_o \cdot h_t + b_o\right) \tag{9}$$

where σ is the sigmoid activation function in the neural network. In summary, GRU realizes a time-series data processing model with long and short-term memory through its internal gate control mechanism and model loop structure. W_r, $W_{\tilde{h}}$, W_z, W_o are weight parameters, and b_r, $b_{\tilde{h}}$, b_z, b_o are the bias parameters.

Usually, GRU's update gate is simpler than LSTM's, but the effect is similar. GRU allows SARIMA-GRU to deal with nonlinear components in residuals. The modeling parameters of the GRU model are shown in Table 1. The GRU takes in a primary input x produced by SARIMA intra-sample prediction:

$$x_{t,\tau} = \text{GRU}\left(x_{t-k:t}\right) \tag{10}$$

2.3 SARIMA-GRU

The ARIMA model is widely used in equipment state prediction. It processes non-stationary data through a different method, mines the functional relationship between historical data and predicted data, realizes data prediction, and infers confidence intervals. However, when traditional ARIMA performs multi-step forecasting, there is a phenomenon of error accumulation, which is difficult to meet the forecast accuracy requirements. For this reason, this paper proposes the SARIMA-GRU model. Through STL decomposition, the SARIMA model is established, and then the error compensation analysis is performed on it, and the GRU neural network is trained with the error data. After the training is completed, use the existing historical error data to predict the future error. Finally, the predicted value of the SARIMA model and the error compensation value of the GRU are combined to obtain the predicted value of the index value in the next 12 h.

The modeling process of the SARIMA-GRU model is shown in Fig. 3. First perform data preprocessing, after deleting irrelevant index items, take the hourly average of the memory value as the index value for that hour. Then according to the data missing status, the KNN interpolation method is used to complete the data.

Table 1. GRU model hyperparameter

	Description
SARIMA samples	[2047, 2071, 2095, 2119, 2143, 2167, 2191]
Prediction steps (output size)	[1, 3, 6, 9, 12, 15]
Lag	336
Feature number	[288, 300]
GRU hidden size	[128, 256]
GRU num layer	[1, 2]
GRU learning rate	$1e^{-2}$
Epochs	3000
Optimizer	Adam
Patient	[10, 50, 100]
Adaptive learning rate parameter	300

2.4 Seasonal Decomposition Algorithm

Seasonal decomposition is the core step in SARIMA modeling. There are usually some specific patterns in time series data, so it can effectively improve the accuracy of prediction to get several relatively independent components by some decomposition method, and then carry out prediction according to the characteristics of different components. STL decomposition is a common method in time series decomposition. The method based on loess can decompose time series into trend component, seasonality component, and remainder. The basic principle of loess is as follows:

If t is the current time, for the current time series observation value x_t, the forward and backward intercept length of the observation value is d, the weight function f is used to calculate the data, and the output is the fitting value of the current point. When all observation points are calculated, the line of fitting points is the generated loess curve. The weight function formula is Eq. 11:

$$f(u) = \begin{cases} \left(1-u^2\right)^2 & 0 \leq u < 1 \\ 0 & u > 1 \end{cases} \tag{11}$$

where u is the abscissa of the observed value after unitization, and the calculation method is as follows:

$$u = \frac{|t_i - t|}{d} \tag{12}$$

After the weights of each observation point and its adjacent points d are obtained, the Loess output is obtained by weighted calculation.

The specific STL decomposition algorithm mainly has two steps: outer loop and inner loop. The outer loop is responsible for adjusting the robustness weight of loess, while the inner loop calculates the trend component and seasonal component. The specific implementation is shown in Fig. 4.

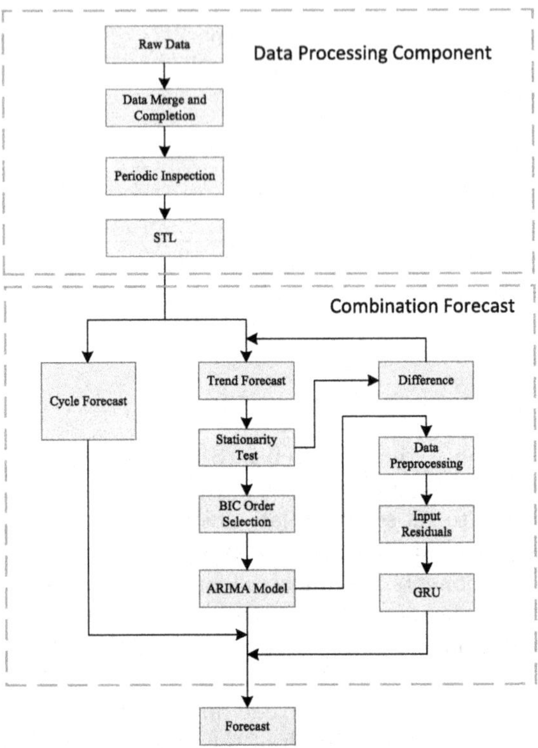

Fig. 3. SARIMA-GRU model. Above: Data Processing Component. By analyzing the statistical properties of the original data, the KNN interpolation method, STL (seasonal and trend decomposition using loess) [18] decomposition algorithm are selected to extract different features of time series. Below: Combination Forecasting. After receiving the dissociated time series, it is predicted separately in the combination model, and the error is extracted from the trend prediction. After feature processing, GRU is used for autoregressive error prediction.

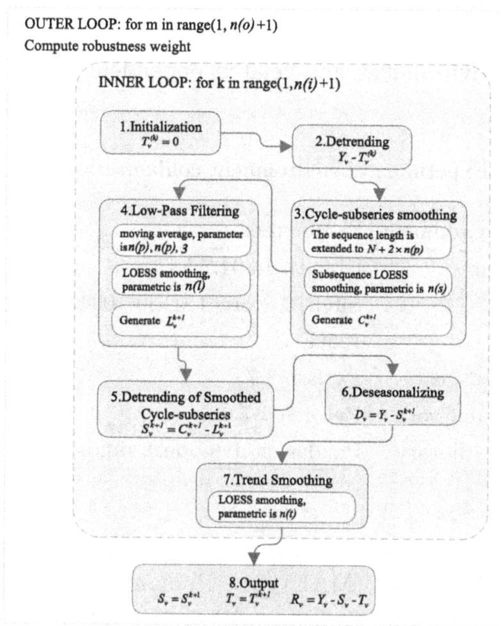

Fig. 4. STL algorithm.

3 Experiment and Analysis

3.1 Datasets

The dataset is the status information data collected on a host server of Ningxia power grid company from March to the end of May 2020. To protect the data privacy information, the IP address, AREA_CODE, CI_ID, and other information of the host server are deleted. There are 25265 records in the original data, some of which are missing, and the missing rate is about 3%. There are 13 fields and 2 effective fields excluding sensitive information, which are "DATA_DT" and "Memory Load", the former is the string corresponding to month, year, day, hour, minute and second, for example, "20200301000500" means that the current recording time is 00:05:00 on March 1, 2020; the latter represents the time series observation value that can be studied in the paper, which means the utilization rate of computer system memory, and is one of the common indicators reflecting the change of server performance. The sampling interval of the original dataset is 5 min. The experiment starts from the original data set and selects the data set with time intervals 1 h as the training test set. This paper takes 6:00 on May 25, 2020 as the dividing line between the training set and the test set.

3.2 Experimental Setup

The experimental environment and related dependency libraries are shown in Table 2.

Table 2. Experimental environment configuration parameters.

Experimental environment	Parameters
Operating system	Ubuntu 16.04.7 LTS
CPU	Intel(R) Core(TM) i9-10940X CPU @ 3.30 GHz
GPU	125G
Programing language	Python 3.7
Deep learning framework	Pytorch 1.7.0
Main dependency library	Pandas, statsmodels, pmdarima

The evaluation metrics of this paper are root mean square error (RMSE) [25] and mean absolute error (MAE) [26]. Root mean square error (RMSE) is sensitive to the maximum or minimum error in a group of prediction results, which can reflect the precision and overall deviation of prediction. The smaller the RMSE value is, the more accurate the model prediction is. MAE is the average of the absolute value of the error between the observed value and the real value, which is a linear evaluation index. MAE can better reflect the actual situation of the error. The specific calculation formula is as follows:

$$RMSE = \sqrt{\frac{1}{\mathcal{T}}\sum_{i=1}^{\mathcal{T}}(y_{\mathcal{T}} - \hat{y}_{\mathcal{T}})^2} \tag{13}$$

$$MAE = \frac{1}{\mathcal{T}}\sum_{i=1}^{\mathcal{T}}|y_{\mathcal{T}} - \hat{y}_{\mathcal{T}}| \tag{14}$$

3.3 Experimental Preprocessing

Time Interval Selection. Generally speaking, the interval selection of time series data follows the following criteria: collect data at fixed intervals and record them in chronological order, so as not to be unable to evaluate the time-related patterns in the data; select regular time intervals (such as once a day or once a week), and ensure that the time intervals conform to the expected patterns, such as estimating the existence of monthly patterns in time series data, It is necessary to collect data at the same time every month to ensure that the amount of data is sufficient for the evaluation experiment. In this study, the sampling interval of the original data set is 5 min. Considering the actual situation of the application scenario, the data fluctuates little in 1 h, so the time interval is set as 1 h, that is, the average of every 12 observations. The data before and after selection is shown in Fig. 5.

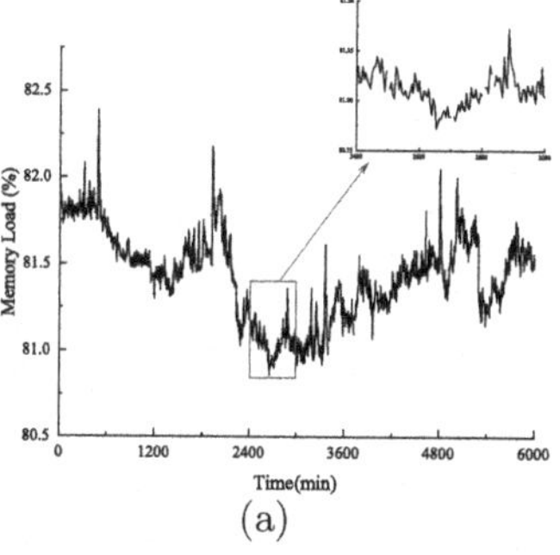

(a)

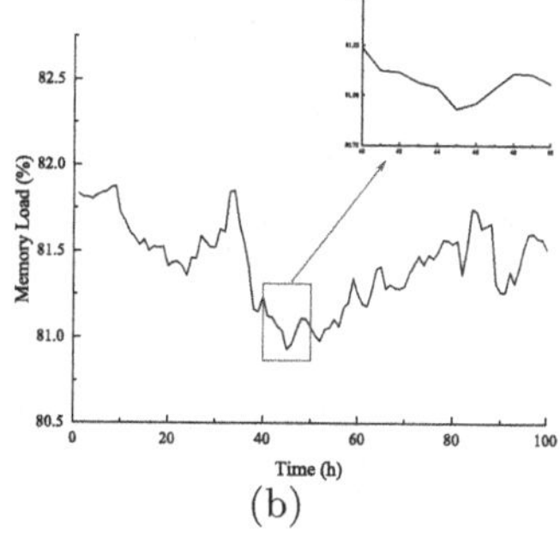

(b)

Fig. 5. Comparison before and after time interval selection. (a) for the original data of the first 100 h, the enlarged image is 40 h to 50 h. It can be found that interval selection has the effect of partially eliminating abnormal noise when considering the actual demand. (b) the processed data of the first 100 h and the enlarged image is also the data of 40 h to 50 h.

Hyperparameter Settings. STL decomposition algorithm is mainly composed of two-loop mechanisms with six adjustment parameters. It is the number of observation points in a seasonality. A subsequence is a time series composed of the same position in each seasonality. For example, when studying the daily seasonal pattern, there are 24 subsequences. When there are no outliers in the general time series data, it does not need robust estimation and can be set, and the value is generally 1 or 2, which satisfies the convergence. Is the smoothing parameter of the low-pass filter, and takes the minimum odd number greater than. It is a seasonal smoothing parameter, which is used to smooth seasonal subsequences. It is usually set to an odd number greater than 7. The selection of trend smoothing parameters is often limited by decomposition, so it is best to set smaller parameters. According to the above criteria, the parameters of this paper are selected as Table 3.

Table 3. STL parameters.

Parameter item	Value
$n(p)$	[24, 168]
$n(i)$	2
$n(o)$	0
$n(l)$	[25, 169]
$n(s)$	9
$n(t)$	25

3.4 Experimental Results

Figure 6 shows the comparison results of the evaluation indexes of the three models in seven prediction periods. Specifically, it refers to the forecast from 7:00 to 18:00 every day from May 25, 2020, to May 31, 2020. Figure 6(a) and Fig. 6(b) show the comparison of RMSE and MAE indicators respectively. SARIMA-GRU model takes the average value of the three prediction results. As shown in the figure, the prediction effect of the three models is better on the 25th, 26th, and 27th, and the worst on the 29th. The observation data shows that the Memory Load changes greatly on the 29th, which leads to a decrease in prediction accuracy. Comparing the RMSE and MAE of the three models, it is found that the SARIMA-GRU model has a great improvement on the 25th, 27th, 28th, and 29th, but no improvement on the 26th, 30th, and 31st. Our improved model may not improve the ARIMA model which has a better prediction effect. The other reason is that the optimal super parameters of the error compensation model used in the prediction interval are 25 days. Therefore, the performance of the model is better and the prediction of the model is more stable in the period closer to the 25th, while the prediction effect is poor in the period far away from the 25th. Finally, figure C shows the running time of each model. Because the automatic mechanism of auto ARIMA applied in this paper cancels the artificial order determination process of ARIMA, the running time of ARIMA and SARIMA models is greatly reduced. At the same time, the SARIMA (SARIMA-GRU) of the proposed error compensation mechanism does not exceed the actual demand in time and is within 2 min.

The images shown in Fig. 7 are the absolute error variation of the three models on the 25th, 27th and 29th. It can be seen from (a), (b) and (c) that compared with the former two models, SARIMA-GRU has better stability and can well reduce the great deviation in multi-step prediction. However, the error compensation mechanism also has defects. When the Memory Load increases or decreases continuously in the future, the prediction performance will not be improved effectively. However, this feature is more conducive to the establishment of dynamic threshold interval, and robust prediction may be more sensitive to anomalies.

As shown in Table 4, we can find that the traditional ARIMA model is difficult to adapt to the situation of multi-step prediction. With the increase of the number of prediction steps, the prediction error begins to increase sharply. In the prediction of the 25th, 29th, and 31st, ARIMA shows such characteristics. In contrast, the error reduction effect of our model is the best when the number of prediction steps is large, and the best prediction effect is achieved in 9 steps, 12 steps, 15 steps on the 25th and 3 steps, 6 steps, 9 steps, 12 steps on the 29th. On the 31st, the ARIMA model's prediction accuracy in all prediction steps was higher than that of other models. The reason is that there was a fluctuation of about 1% before 3steps, which was opposite to the seasonal change. Therefore, the linear ARIMA prediction just caught this change. However, this situation is only a few cases. The prediction of our model on this day is also very close to the prediction effect of ARIMA, and the prediction performance is bet-

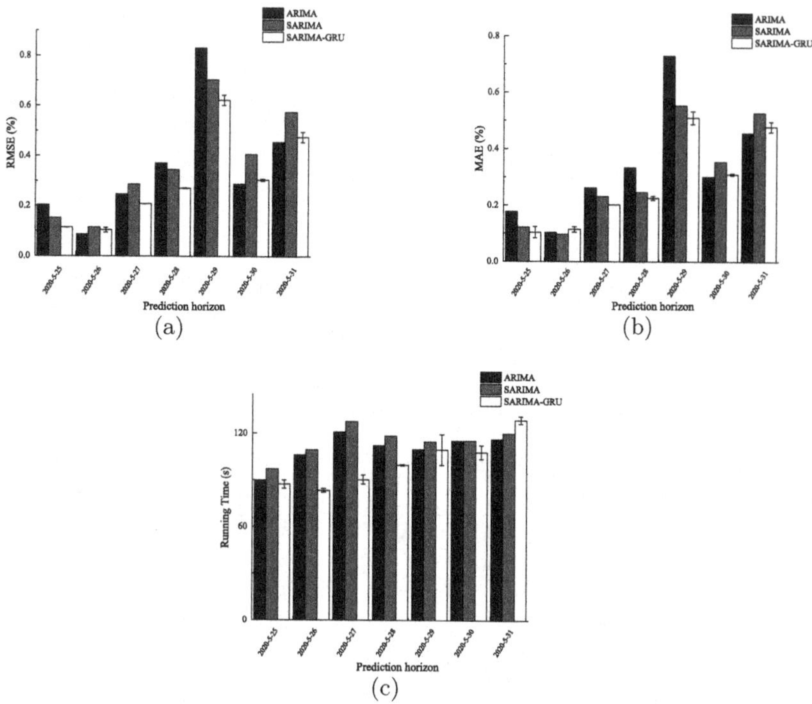

Fig. 6. Prediction metrics of Memory Load in different time t, and τ is 12. The abscissa of (a), (b), and (c) are different forecast dates of the test set. Blue represents the ARIMA model, which uses the integrated automatic ARIMA framework, so the runtime is greatly reduced. Red, blue and white is ARIMA, SARIMA and our proposed model respectively. (Color figure online)

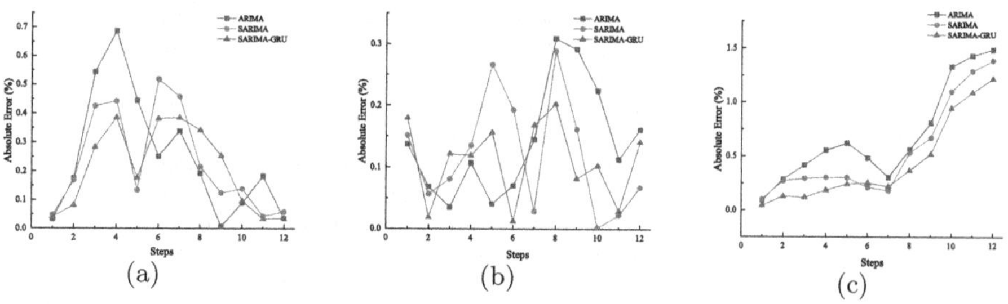

Fig. 7. Absolute prediction error variation. (a), (b) and (c) is the forecast absolute error change of the next 12 h on May 25, May 27, and May 29 respectively. The black line is the ARIMA forecast result, the red line is the SARIMA forecast result, and the blue line is the SARIMA-GRU model. (Color figure online)

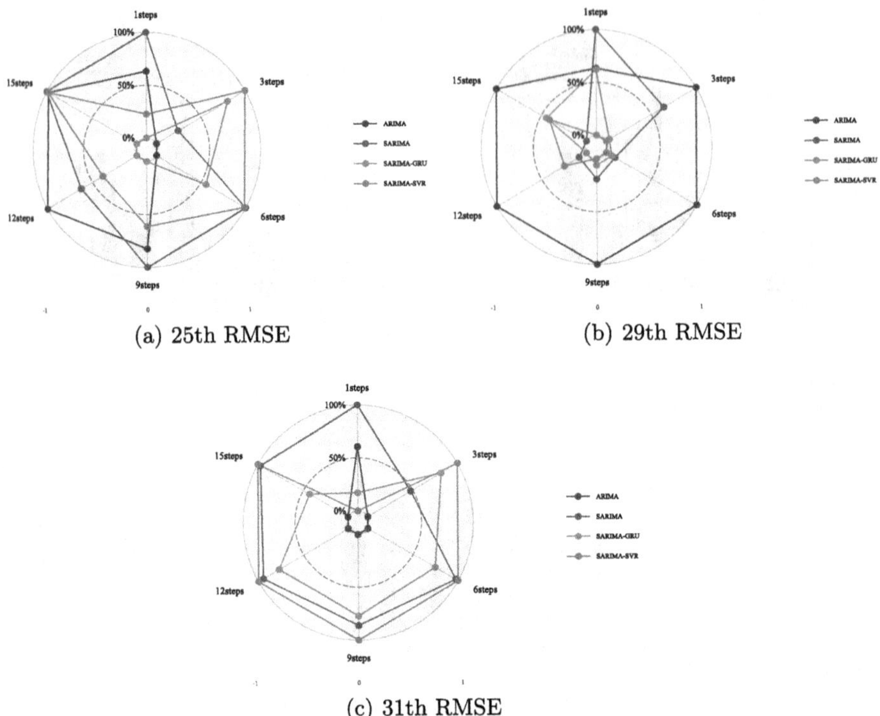

(a) 25th RMSE

(b) 29th RMSE

(c) 31th RMSE

Fig. 8. RMSE error ratio radar. (a), (b) and (c) is the forecasting performance of different τ-step-ahead on May 25, May 29, and May 31 respectively. The diagram is on the right side of the radar, showing the meaning of each curve.

Table 4. Comparison of indicators of different models

Model	Date	MAE_1	MAE_3	MAE_6	MAE_9	MAE_12	MAE_15
ARIMA	25th	0.1375	**0.0805**	**0.0767**	0.1339	0.1420	0.1495
	29th	0.0894	0.2634	0.4072	0.4572	0.6970	0.8553
	31th	**0.0490**	**0.1457**	**0.2786**	**0.3490**	**0.3841**	**0.4319**
SARIMA	25th	0.1517	0.0965	0.1474	0.1516	0.1214	0.1401
	29th	0.1011	0.2218	0.2470	0.3182	0.5528	0.7454
	31th	0.0616	0.1856	0.4374	0.4867	0.5270	0.5407
SARIMA-SVR	25th	0.1220	0.1301	0.1432	0.1384	0.1240	0.1474
	29th	0.0691	0.1288	0.2159	**0.2885**	0.5500	0.7524
	31th	0.0296	0.2249	0.4439	0.5091	0.5356	0.5438
SARIMA-GRU	25th	**0.1132**	0.1093	0.1058	**0.1049**	**0.1074**	**0.1200**
	29th	**0.0890**	**0.1344**	**0.2276**	0.3056	**0.5101**	0.7654
	31th	0.0351	0.2089	0.3994	0.4703	0.4993	0.4803

ter than SARIMA and SARIMA-SVR. We can get a more intuitive conclusion from Fig. 8. SARIMA-GRU, the model represented by the green line segment, performed better on the 25th and 29th, second only to ARIMA model on the 31st. At the same time, we found that our model can achieve higher prediction accuracy in the long-term prediction, indicating that error compensation can improve the accuracy and stability of long-distance prediction.

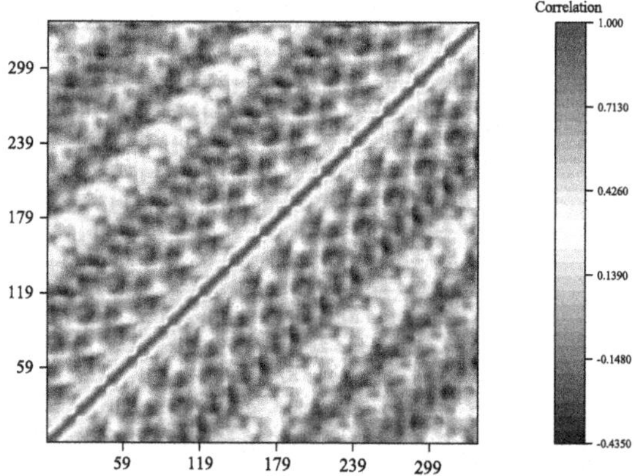

Fig. 9. Absolute prediction error variation. The abscissa and ordinate are the measurement values of the cross-correlation between the current predicted label (The mean value of the label vector in the training set) and its lagged lag order observations, and the measurement function is the Pearson correlation coefficient. The red area represents the autocorrelation of 1, and the white area represents no correlation, and the value is 0. (Color figure online)

Figure 9 shows the error auto-correlation, and the measurement sample is the error generated by the SARIMA model in sampling prediction. By establishing the error auto- regressive matrix between the average value of the label and its 336 order lag, the measurement distance function is the person correlation coefficient. The red line in the figure represents the degree of correlation between each column and itself, so the value is 1. Blue represents negative correlation and white represents no correlation. Therefore, the regular blue bar in the graph indicates that there is a potential correlation in the error sequence, which is autocorrelation.

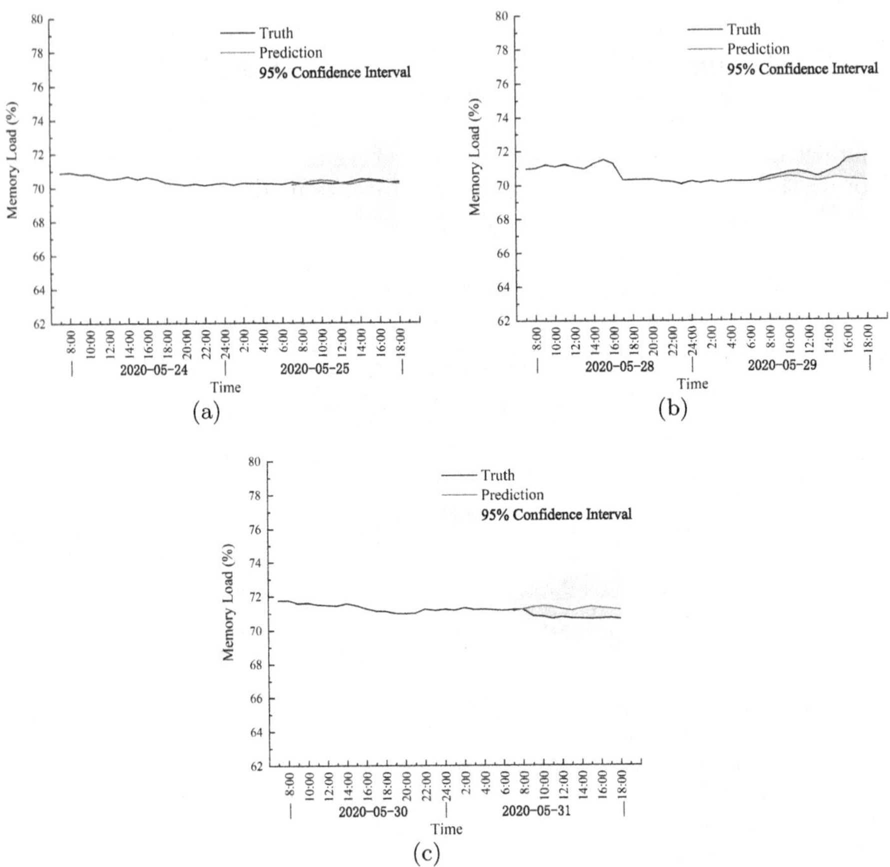

Fig. 10. Absolute prediction error variation. (a) is the 95% dynamic threshold range generated by the forecast results on May 25, the current data fluctuates gently. While (b) is the 95% dynamic threshold range generated by the forecast results on May 29, the current Memory Load shows an upward growth trend but does not exceed the threshold range. (C) is the 95% dynamic threshold range generated by the forecast results on May 31, the current Memory Load shows a downward growth trend, But in addition to a small fluctuation around 8 o'clock, there is no exception.

In addition to the comparison of the prediction performance of the models, this paper also uses the prediction results of the SARIMA-GRU model to generate the dynamic threshold range of Memory Load. As shown in Fig. 10, the prediction and dynamic threshold setting on the 25th, 29th, and 31st are shown respectively. In this paper, the confidence theory is used to generate the shadow interval, which indicates that there is a 95% probability that the index value of the future forecast period will be in this region. First of all, from the comparison between the real value and the predicted value, the model can accurately predict the fluctuation of Memory Load from 7:00 to 18:00 in the daytime business peak. Secondly, when the 95% confidence interval is used as the threshold interval, it can be found that the normal index value fluctuation is within the threshold interval, and the alarm will not be triggered. When the actual Memory Load exceeds the range, it indicates that a memory exception event with a probability of 5% has occurred, and the system informs the operation and maintenance personnel to check the operation status of the equipment. This method, which uses the historical data of server memory to predict and estimate the dynamic threshold of equipment operation index, can improve the predictive ability of equipment failure, fully enhance the initiative of operation and maintenance monitoring and fault repair, and improve the operation and maintenance efficiency.

4 Conclusion

This paper draws on the widely used forecasting models in the field of time series forecasting and cutting-edge algorithm technology in the field of error compensation and proposes a power grid host load forecasting model based on GRU error compensation—SARIMA-GRU model. After comprehensively analyzing the volatility and periodicity of power grid host load data, a SARIMA model is established to separately predict the time series trend and seasonality, and then the GRU error compensation model is used to perform autoregressive analysis on the SARIMA prediction error. In the experimental data, the Memory Load data is taken as an example to verify the accuracy and effectiveness of the model proposed in this paper in the power grid operation and maintenance scenario. The future research work of this paper is as follows:

1) Forecast index items. It is worth noting that the predictive index item in this article is the host Memory Load data. The commonly used equipment operating status indicators in the industry also includes CPU load data. The next step can be to consider multivariate time series forecasting to improve the stability and accuracy of the forecasting model.
2) Real-time. The smart grid is built on an integrated, high-speed two-way network, which requires operation and maintenance personnel to be able to discover and even predict problems promptly. Therefore, we need to reduce the computational consumption of the prediction model and increase the calculation speed while ensuring prediction accuracy.
3) Automation. The power operation and maintenance system is gradually developing towards high integration and high intelligence. The advanced automation system can retrieve historical data and information in real-time, establish an information analysis platform, and prevent unknown risks. In the future, advanced equipment monitoring technology, information decision-making technology, and intelligent dispatching technology will play a huge role in the field of smart grids.

References

1. Zhengguo, G., Yunsheng, L., Peng, W., Tingting, L., Wei, L.: Research and practice on informatization construction of electric power design enterprises. Eng. Technol. (Citation Version) **10**, 211 (2016)
2. Bagdadee, A.H., Zhang, L.: Smart grid: a brief assessment of the smart grid technologies for modern power system. J. Eng. Technol. **8**(1), 122–142 (2019)
3. Dinda, P.A., O'Hallaron, D.R.: Host load prediction using linear models. Clust. Comput. **3**(4), 265–280 (2000)
4. Zonghua, Z., Haiquan, Z., Chi, W., Xinzheng, N.: Load prediction based on an improved AR model with weighting. Comput. Measur. Control **24**(3), 248–251 (2016)
5. Gang, L., Wenjing, W.: Storage load forecasting research based on time series. Intell. Comput. Appl. **8**(3), 188–190 (2018)
6. Wang, D., Huang, L., Chang, J., Mei, K., Niu, X.: Load forecasting model based on ARIMA and CART. J. Shenzhen Univ. (Sci. Eng.) **36**(3), 245–251 (2019)
7. Bin, Z.B.: A load balancing predication algorithm of CART and KNN. J. Beijing Univ. Posts Telecommun. **A1**, 93–97 (2017)
8. Yi, R., Yu, J., Wu, B., Gong, Y.: An improved DV-HOP algorithm based on weighted hyperbolic positioning. Fire Control Command Control **41**(12), 96–100 (2016)
9. Qian, Z.L.: Two improvements on CART decision tree and its application. Comput. Eng. Des. **36**(5), 1209–1213 (2015)
10. Wu, Y., Shen, K., Chen, Z., Wu, J.: Automatic measurement of fetal cavum septum pellucidum from ultrasound images using deep attention network. In: 2020 IEEE International Conference on Image Processing (ICIP), pp. 2511–2515 (2020). https://doi.org/10.1109/ICIP40778.2020.9191002
11. Gasparin, A., Lukovic, S., Alippi, C.: Deep learning for time series forecasting: the electric load case (2019)
12. Choi, H.K.: Stock price correlation coefficient prediction with ARIMA-LSTM hybrid model (2018)
13. Han, P., Wang, D., Wang, F.: Multi-step-ahead prediction of wind speed time series based on error compensation. Comput. Simul. **31**(2), 206–209 (2014)
14. Goel, H., Melnyk, I., Banerjee, A.: R2N2: residual recurrent neural networks for multivariate time series forecasting (2017)
15. Pavithra, M., Saruladha, K., Sathyabama, K.: GRU based deep learning model for prognosis prediction of disease progression. In: 2019 3rd International Conference on Computing Methodologies and Communication (ICCMC), pp. 840–844 (2019). https://doi.org/10.1109/ICCMC.2019.8819830
16. Box, G.E., Jenkins, G.M., Reinsel, G.C., Ljung, G.M.: Time Series Analysis: Forecasting and Control. Wiley, New York (2015)
17. Lu, J., Du, J., Cao, M., Fan, X.: Carbon emissions trading price prediction using the ARIMA-SVM model. J. Xi'an Univ. Sci. Technol. **40**(3), 542–548 (2020)
18. Cleveland, R.B., Cleveland, W.S., McRae, J.E., Terpenning, I.: STL: a seasonal-trend decomposition. J. Off. Stat. **6**(1), 3–73 (1990)
19. Tang, X., Deng, G.: Improvement of ARMA model based on Gevers-Wouters algorithm. Stat. Decis. **2**, 19–23 (2018)
20. Zhu, H., Yuan, Z., Yu, K.: Continuous blood pressure prediction based on the hybrid model of ARIMA and SVM. J. Hangzhou Normal Univ. (Nat. Sci. Ed.) **17**(5), 555–560 (2018)

21. Li, X., Sang, Y., Xie, P., Gu, H.: A method for testing the stationarity of stochastic hydrological process based on discrete wavelet. Syst. Eng. Theory Pract. **38**(7), 1897–1904 (2018)
22. Fischer, T., Krauss, C.: Deep learning with long short-term memory networks for financial market predictions. Eur. J. Oper. Res. **270**(2), 654–669 (2018)
23. Che, Z., Purushotham, S., Cho, K., Sontag, D., Liu, Y.: Recurrent neural networks for multivariate time series with missing values. Sci. Rep. **8**(1), 1–12 (2018)
24. Zhao, Z., Chen, W., Wu, X., Chen, P.C., Liu, J.: LSTM network: a deep learning approach for short-term traffic forecast. IET Intell. Transp. Syst. **11**(2), 68–75 (2017)
25. Tang, M., Lei, X., Long, Y., Tan, Q., Zhang, Z.: Water level forecasting in middle route of the south-to-north water diversion project (MRP) based on long short-term memory (LSTM). China Rural Water Hydropower (10), 189–193 (2020)
26. Ma, Z., Leung, J.Y.: Integration of deep learning and data analytics for SAGD temperature and production analysis. Comput. Geosci. **24**(3), 1239–1255 (2020). https://doi.org/10.1007/s10596-020-09940-x

DWAFE: Achieve Accurate AIOps Fault Early Warning

Yuan Tan[1], Jinsong Gui[1], Kun Wang[2], and Zhigang Chen[1(✉)]

[1] School of Computer Science, Central South University, Changsha 410008, Hunan, China
czg@csu.edu.cn

[2] State Grid Ningxia Electric Power Co., Ltd. Information and Telecommunication Branc, Yinchuan 753000, China

Abstract. Traditional information equipment's operating status perception and fault alarms mainly rely on manual and traditional automated operation and maintenance, which have disadvantages such as high cost, low efficiency, and high false alarm rate. In order to achieve accurate fault warning,this paper proposes a dynamic threshold setting mechanism, which can calculate the dynamic threshold interval under the given confidence level based on the prediction results. In order to get the accurate prediction results, the Discrete Wavelet Transform (DWT)-Autoregressive Integrated Moving Average (ARIMA)-Exponentially Weighted Firefly Algorithm(EWFA)-Extreme Learning Machine (ELM) composite model called DWAFE for short is proposed. In this model, the original time series is divided into several subsequences by discrete wavelet transform, and ARIMA model and ELM optimized by EWFA are used for processing according to different stationarity. Finally, the prediction results of each subsequence are integrated by inverse wavelet transform. In addition, we also propose the Exponential Weighted Firefly Algorithm, which greatly improves the optimization performance and convergence speed of the firefly algorithm. Experiments on the core router data of Ningxia electric power company show that this method achieves better performance than Bi-LSTM, GRU and other benchmark models, and can achieve accurate and efficient information equipment fault early warning, thus greatly reducing the human and material costs of enterprises.

Keywords: Time series prediction · Wavelet transform · Dynamic threshold · Firefly algorithm · ELM

1 Introduction

Artificial Intelligence for IT Operations (AIOps) is a research field that has risen rapidly in recent years. Real-time perception of the operating status of information equipment and accurate early warning of equipment failures are the key objects of AIOps research. The key of accurate warning is to accurately predict the change trend of Key Performance Indicator (KPI) of equipment, so as to prejudge the operation status of equipment in the future. The farther the prediction time is and the more accurate the prediction result is, the more likely the enterprise will take the initiative to make accurate and efficient operation

Z. Cai et al. (Eds.): NCTCS 2021, CCIS 1494, pp. 154–173, 2021.
https://doi.org/10.1007/978-981-16-7443-3_10

and maintenance response in the face of emergency operation and maintenance events, so as to reduce or avoid the possible asset loss and casualties caused by unknown failures. This kind of prediction usually adopts the data format of time series. Therefore, time series prediction plays an increasingly important role in many fields, such as finance [1], energy [2], medicine [3] and astronomy [4].

Due to the complex working environment of the information room and the differences in the information equipment of many different manufacturers, the current static threshold monitoring methods of information equipment are not accurate enough, and they are not enough to cope with the significant high-frequency changes in the monitoring indicators caused by business peak and low fluctuations. If the threshold is set too high, the indicator overload cannot be monitored, and if the threshold is set too low, it will not be able to counter the frequent false alarms of the normal high-load operating state during the business peak period. Therefore, the use of static thresholds brings many problems to operation and maintenance personnel, which greatly affects their work efficiency and the alarm accuracy of the monitoring system. This article attempts to accurately perceive the operating status of the equipment and dynamically set the healthy operating threshold of the equipment to make the operation and maintenance work more in line with the requirements of refinement, intelligence, and efficiency.

The setting of dynamic threshold mainly relies on time series forecasting, and the Autoregressive Integrated Moving Average model (ARIMA) [5] is one of the most important and widely used models in time series forecasting models. In [6], the improved ARIMA model was used to capture the time correlation and probability distribution of wind speed time series data. In [7], ARIMA is applied to network traffic data to predict the risk of DOS and DDoS attacks on servers in the future. ARIMA model is popular because of its statistical characteristics and the famous Box-Jenkins method [8]. But ARIMA model assumes that there is linear correlation structure between time series, so the fitting of nonlinear data is always unsatisfactory. For nonlinear data, neural network is a common choice [9]. Extreme learning machine (ELM) network is favored by many researchers in recent years because of its better fitting ability and faster training speed. In [10], ELM is used to construct a high-performance big data analysis tool. In [11], a hierarchical learning framework based on ELM is proposed, which not only retains the advantages of ELM, but also gets more compact and meaningful feature representation. Traditional ELM mainly focuses on supervised, semi supervised and unsupervised learning in a single domain. Literature [12] Studies ELM with cross domain learning ability, and proposes domain adaptive extreme learning machine (DAELM). This model can compensate drift through a limited number of labeled data in the target domain. Most of the above researches use integrated methods to improve the performance of ELM, but they all have the defects of insufficient stability caused by random initialization parameters.

Based on the above research, the contributions of this paper are as follows:

1) In order to overcome the shortcomings of the traditional operation and maintenance mode, this paper proposes a dynamic threshold setting mechanism, which can give the dynamic threshold interval under the specified confidence level according to the prediction results of the model, and provide strong support for accurate early warning of equipment failure;

2) Inspired by the Adam algorithm and the RMSprop algorithm, this article improves the Firefly algorithm and proposes the Exponentially Weighted Firefly Algorithm (EWFA), which not only obtains better optimization performance than the Firefly algorithm, but also greatly improves the convergence speed;
3) In order to give accurate prediction results, this paper proposes the DWAFE model for the lack of stability of the ELM model and the limitation of the ARIMA model for nonlinear data. By using the EWFA algorithm to overcome the shortcomings of ELM and using discrete wavelet transform to integrate the ARIMA model and the ELM model, higher prediction accuracy and better robust performance than the existing benchmark model are obtained.

The rest of this paper is organized as follows: The second section introduces the system model, which mainly includes the EWFA-ELM model, DWAFE model and dynamic threshold setting mechanism. In the third section, we introduce the pre-work of the experiment, such as data set description, data cleaning and modeling process. The fourth section shows the experimental results and comparative analysis. The fifth section summarizes this article and makes an outlook.

2 System Model

2.1 Autoregressive Integrated Moving Average (ARIMA) Model

In the ARIMA model, the future value of a variable is defined as a linear function of several past observations and random errors [13], that is, the analyzed time series can be expressed by:

$$\begin{aligned} y_t = \theta_0 + \phi_1 y_{t-1} + \cdots + \phi_p y_{t-p} + \varepsilon_t \\ - \theta_1 \varepsilon_{t-1} - \theta_2 \varepsilon_{t-2} - \cdots - \theta_q \varepsilon_{t-q} \end{aligned} \quad (1)$$

where: y_t and ε_t are the actual value and the random error value at time t respectively. The random error is usually the distribution with the mean value of zero and the variance of σ^2. $\phi_i(i = 1, 2, \ldots, p)$ and $\theta_j(j = 0, 1, 2, \ldots, q)$ are the model parameters, p and q are the order of the model. The key to build ARIMA model is to determine the appropriate model order (p, q).In particular, when q = 0, ARIMA model is simplified to p-order AR model, while when p = 0, ARIMA model is simplified to q-order MA model.

The process of building ARIMA model [14] mainly includes three steps: model identification, parameter estimation and diagnostic examination.

1. Model recognition. By matching the empirical autocorrelation pattern with the theoretical autocorrelation pattern, one or more models are identified for a given time series. The autocorrelation function and partial autocorrelation function of sample data are used to identify the order of ARIMA model.
2. Parameter estimation. The parameters are estimated by nonlinear optimization to minimize the fitting error of the model.
3. Diagnostic examination. Diagnostic statistics and residual plots were used to test the fit of the temporarily accepted model to historical data. If the model is not sufficient, a new test model is selected to continue parameter estimation and model validation.

The above modeling process is usually repeated several times until a satisfactory model is selected.

2.2 Discrete Wavelet Transform (DWT)

Compared with the traditional decomposition method, DWT can track the time evolution of different scales in a sequence [15], so that the results can more accurately reflect the multiple characteristics of network traffic in multiple time scales.

The key of DWT is to determine the wavelet function and decomposition level. For the former, the choice can be made according to the comparative experiment. After selecting the appropriate wavelet function, discrete wavelet transform can be carried out.

Given the wavelet function ψ(t) and decomposition level j, the operation of discrete wavelet transform for time series is given by:

$$W_f(j,k) = \int_{-\infty}^{+\infty} f(t)\psi_{j,k}^{*}(t)dt \tag{2}$$

Among them:

$$\psi_{j,k}(t) = a_0^{-j/2}\psi(a_0^{-j}t - b_0 k) \tag{3}$$

In Eqs. (2) and (3), the integer k is the time shift factor, $\psi^{*}(t)$ is the complex conjugate, and $W_f(j,k)$ is the discrete wavelet coefficient of the j-th layer. a_0 and b_0 are constants, usually designated as $a_0 = 2$, $b_0 = 1$, formula (3) can be written as:

$$\psi_{j,k}(t) = 2^{-j/2}\psi(2^{-j}t - k) \tag{4}$$

Each transformation operation corresponding to formula (4) is: half-subband filtering and double down sampling. The result of each transformation is a low frequency sequence and a high frequency sequence. Iteratively transform the low-frequency sequence until the low-frequency sequence meets the requirements of residual test.Then the number of transform is the final decomposition level.

2.3 ELM Model Optimized by Exponentially Weighted Firefly Algorithm (EWFA-ELM)

Extreme Learning Machine (ELM) is a single hidden layer feedforward neural network model, which can be applied to classification and regression problems [16]. Compared with the traditional gradient based learning algorithm, it not only has faster learning speed and higher generalization performance, but also avoids many difficulties faced by the gradient based learning method, such as stop criterion, learning rate, learning time and local extremum [17]. The biggest disadvantage of ELM is that the input weights and deviations are randomly selected, so the robustness of the model is poor, which is also a common problem of parameter random initialization in ANNs. In previous studies, the idea of ELM integration was proposed, that is, to improve the generalization ability of ELM by training a limited number of ELMs and taking the average output of all ELM networks as the final output [18]. However, this method can not guarantee the accuracy of each prediction, and its robustness is also worrying.

Based on the above situation, this paper attempts to find a way to maintain the advantages of ELM and improve its stability. After many comparative studies, the Firefly Algorithm is selected to optimize ELM model.

Algorithm 1: EWFA algorithm

Input: Number of firefly N, threshold τ, MaxGeneration K,DataSet X,Labels Y

Output: EWFA-ELM model

1.**Let** n_hidden=64, n_features=X.shape[1], $s_1 = 0.9, s_2 = 0.999$;

2.**Comput** $biases = random\ (n\_hidden)$

$weights = random\ (n\_features,\ n\_hidden)$

$weights\ {*}{=}\ 3.0\ /\ n\_features{**}0.5$

3.**Implement** K iterations

3.1 For i=1 to N

Build ELM by biases[i] and weights[i];

Compute Lights[i]= Loss ($\hat{Y}$, Y);

Record the LightsBest;

3.2 If $LightsBest > \tau$

Return after Create an ELM by w_{best} and b_{best};

3.3 Move firefly

For i= to N

r= Euclidean distance between $[w,b]_i$ and $[w,b]_{best}$

$\alpha = s_1\alpha + (1 - s_1){*}0.97^t$

$[w,b]_i^{'} = s_2[w,b]_i + (1-s_2){*}(\beta e^{-\gamma r^2}([w,b]_i - [w,b]_j) + \alpha rand())^2$

$[w,b]_i^{'} = \dfrac{[w,b]_i^{'}}{1-s_2^t}$

3.4 If K iterations are reached

Then return after create an ELM by w_{best} and b_{best};

4. **End**;

Firefly Algorithm is an algorithm proposed by Yang [19], which is mainly used to solve various parameter selection [20] and model optimization problems [21]. However, the original Firefly Algorithm uses a fixed step size factor. If it is set too much, the firefly will oscillate around the optimal solution repeatedly. If it is set too small, the firefly will move slowly, so its convergence time is usually long or even unable to converge. In order to improve the firefly algorithm, this paper designs an iterative attenuation step factor and performs an exponentially weighted average of the overall moving distance. In addition, this paper also considers deviation correction to improve the problem of large initial errors, and early termination to accelerate convergence and prevent overfitting.

The design inspiration of this algorithm benefits from the Adam algorithm [22] and RMSprop algorithm [23] in gradient optimization algorithm.

Specifically, in the firefly algorithm used in this paper, the position of each firefly represents a feasible solution of ELM parameters (weights and bias), and the brightness of the firefly represents the fitness of the firefly position, which is obtained by the loss function of ELM. Among firefly individuals, each firefly will fly toward the individual with higher brightness to search for a better position. The attraction of each firefly to other fireflies is directly proportional to the brightness and inversely proportional to the distance. The pseudo code of the algorithm is as Algorithm 1.

The operation flow of Firefly Algorithm is shown in Fig. 1. It can be seen from Fig. 1, the algorithm simulates the behavior of fireflies in nature, finds out the brightest firefly position through repeated iterative search, and finally outputs the optimal parameters for training ELM model. Therefore, the process of using Firefly Algorithm to optimize ELM is as follows:

1) Initialization. Set the number of fireflies to N, and initialize the position of each firefly randomly. Set the absorption coefficient of medium to light as $\gamma = 1$, initial step size $\alpha = .03$ and initial attraction $\beta_0 = 1.0$, and the attraction formula is as follows:

$$\beta(r) = (\beta_{\max} - \beta_{\min})e^{-\gamma r^2} + \beta_{\min} \tag{5}$$

where $\beta_{\min} = 0.2$, $\beta_{\max} = 1$, Eq. (5) can ensure that the minimum attraction between any two fireflies is 0.2 and the maximum attraction is 1.0.

2) Calculate the fitness value of each firefly. R2 is used as fitness, and its calculation formula is as follows:

$$R^2 = 1 - \frac{\sum_i (\hat{y}^{(i)} - y^{(i)})^2}{\sum_i (\bar{y} - y^{(i)})^2} \tag{6}$$

where $\hat{y}^{(i)}$ is the predicted value, $y^{(i)}$ is the real value. The closer the value of is to 1, the greater the brightness of the firefly is. The closer the R^2 is to 1, the brighter the firefly is.

3) Move. Each firefly flies to all fireflies whose brightness is higher than its own, and its position changes as follows:

$$[w, b]_i' = s_2[w, b]_i + (1 - s_2) * (\beta_0 e^{-\gamma r^2}([w, b]_i - [w, b]_j) + \alpha * rand())^2 \tag{7}$$

$$[w, b]_i' = \frac{[w, b]_i'}{1 - s_2^t} \tag{8}$$

In the formula, $[w, b]_j$ represents the position of the firefly whose brightness is higher than that of the i-th individual, and r represents the Euclidean distance between the i-th firefly and the j-th firefly. rand() is a random disturbance and α is the step size factor of the disturbance. Generally, the value of rand() is the uniform distribution within the range of $[-0.5, 0.5]$ or the standard normal distribution of U (0, 1), and α is a decimal between [0, 1]. In order to increase the convergence of the algorithm, we make the step size iteratively decay, then the step size calculation formula of the t-th generation is:

$$\alpha = s_1\alpha + (1 - s_1) * 0.97^t \tag{9}$$

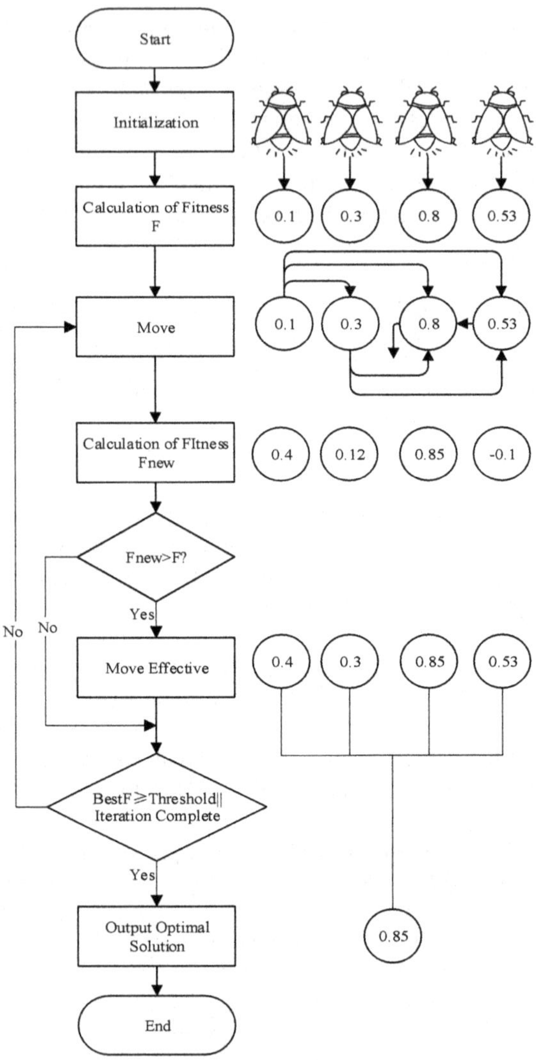

Fig. 1. Flow chart of firefly algorithm

The brightest individual does not move to other fireflies, but updates its position according to formula (10).

$$[w, b]_i' = [w, b]_i + \alpha * rand(-0.5, 0.5) \tag{10}$$

4) Calculate the fitness value of the firefly's new position after moving. If the position is better than the position before the move, the move will take effect, otherwise the firefly will stay where it is.
5) In order to prevent the optimized model from overfitting, a fitness threshold is set in the algorithm. After each iteration is completed, the current optimal fitness is recorded. If the value is not less than the threshold or the algorithm reaches the maximum number of iterations, the searched optimal parameters will be output, otherwise it will skip to step 2 for the next iteration.
6) The ELM model is constructed by using the optimal parameters of Exponentially Weighted Firefly Algorithm.

2.4 DWAFE Model

In the above models, ARIMA is suitable for dealing with time series with linear structure, but the prediction of nonlinear data is not satisfactory; EWFA-ELM model has better fitting effect and higher prediction accuracy for nonlinear data, but its robustness is not as good as ARIMA model in dealing with relatively easy fitting linear data. Therefore, this paper uses discrete wavelet transform to combine the advantages of the two, and the flow of DWAFE model is shown in Fig. 2.

There are two roles in DWAFE model: data manager and model manager. The data manager is responsible for receiving the input data and preprocessing the data. The preprocessing process includes two stages: data cleaning and discrete wavelet transform. The available data set is obtained through data cleaning, and the original data is decomposed into a set of detail sequences and a trend sequence through discrete wavelet transform.

After the data manager completes the processing, the model manager checks the stationarity of all subsequences and creates the model. For stationary series, use the AIC and BIC rules to determine the order before creating the ARIMA model; for non-stationary series, use the Exponentially Weighted Firefly Algorithm to find the best parameters before constructing the ELM model. Finally, the predicted values of each model are combined into the final result as the output of the DWAFE model by using inverse discrete wavelet transform.

2.5 Dynamic Threshold Setting Mechanism

The traditional static threshold depends on the experience of maintenance personnel. The threshold line of each monitoring index item is set artificially. Once it is lower (or higher) than the threshold, an alarm event will be triggered. In the complex real scene, the index data often presents different amplitude fluctuations in each period, and a single and fixed threshold is difficult to adapt to the complex data changes. Then came the early warning mechanism of year-on-year and month-on-month fluc tuations, that is, the threshold is adjusted at a fixed frequency following the reference value[24]. Practice shows that this kind of early warning does not have the ability to fully adapt to changes, needs manual regular maintenance, and the accuracy of early warning is difficult to guarantee [25].

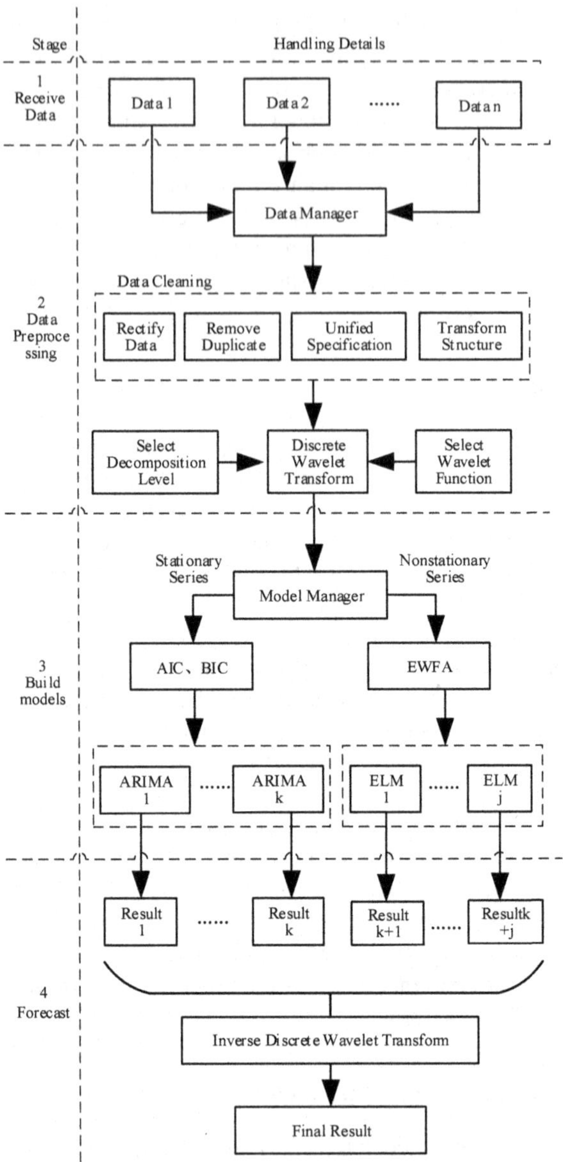

Fig. 2. Flow chart of DWAFE model

In the current industry, dynamic threshold method is mostly used for fault early warning, that is, the threshold range will be adjusted automatically with different scenarios. In order to give the dynamic threshold range, this paper first predicts the value of the index term in the future period through the DWAFE model, and then designs a dynamic threshold setting mechanism, which refers to the confidence interval and the Naive prediction method, and fully considers the impact of the prediction step size on the threshold range. The calculation is shown in formula (11).

$$TR = \hat{y} \pm k\sqrt{\frac{1}{N}\sum_{i=1}^{N}(x_i - u)^2 \times \sqrt{h}} \tag{11}$$

where TR is the dynamic threshold range, n is the total number of samples, Represents the i-th sample, u represents the mean value of the sample, h represents the number of prediction steps, k represents the confidence multiplier. The value of the multiplier is obtained according to the selected confidence level, and its corresponding relationship is shown in Table 1.

Table 1. Confidence multiplier value table

Confidence	Value
80	1.28
85	1.44
90	1.64
95	1.96
96	2.05
97	2.17
98	2.33
99	2.58

3 Experiment

3.1 Dataset Description

The data set used in this experiment comes from the received traffic data of a core router of Ningxia electric power company. The time span is (2020.02.01 00:00:00, 2020.04.30 23:55:00), and the sampling frequency is 5 min. In this experiment, 17280 pieces of data in the first two months were used as training data to iteratively predict the value of the next day. The data timing diagram is shown in Fig. 3.

The autocorrelation analysis of the whole data is shown in Fig. 4. It can be seen from Fig. 4 that there are periods in days, months and quarters in the data, and the period in days is the most significant.

3.2 Data Cleaning

Data cleaning includes four steps: data error correction, deletion of duplicate items, unification of specifications and transformation construction. In the data error correction stage, because the actual scene may have a sudden increase or decrease in network traffic, sample outliers are retained. In the delete duplicate phase, delete duplicate data and attribute columns. In the unified specification stage, all data are uniformly retained with two decimal places and the data is standardized to a normal distribution. In the transformation construction phase, the traffic data in CSV format is transformed into Series objects. After the above cleaning process, the final available data set can be obtained.

3.3 Modeling Process

The environment used in this experiment is shown in Table 2.

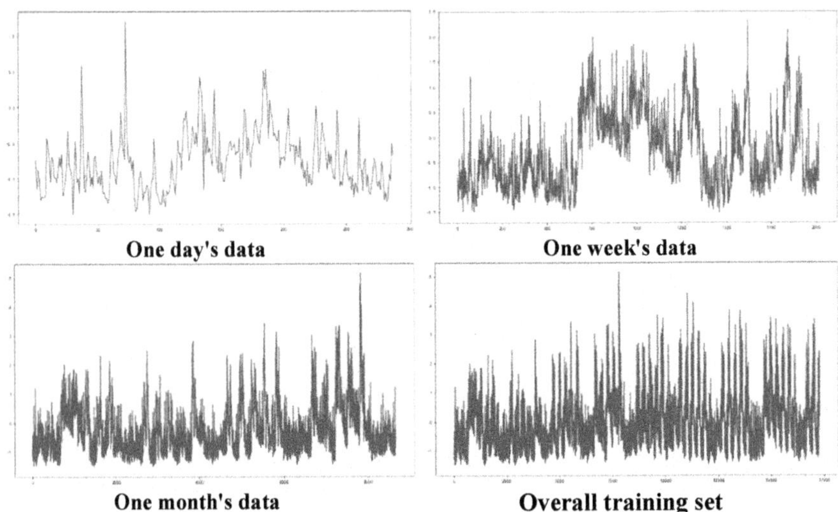

Fig. 3. Data timing diagram. The data of one day, one week, one month and the overall training set are shown respectively.

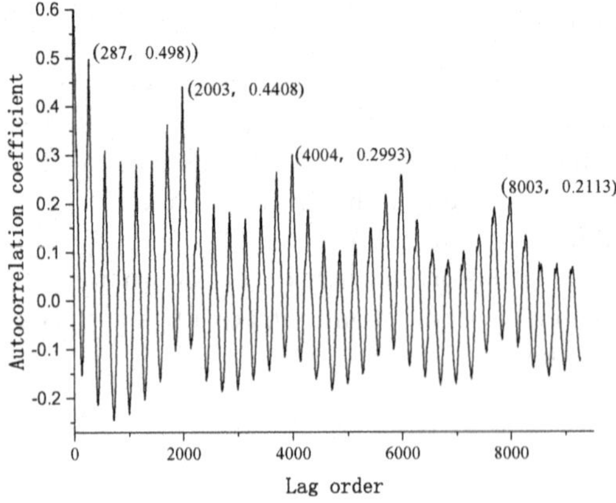

Fig. 4. Data autocorrelation analysis graph

Table 2. Experimental environment

Computing resource	Intel(R) Core(TM) i9-10940X CPU @ 3.30 GHz NVIDIA GeForce RTX3090 * 2 16G Running memory, 512G SSD
Operating environment	Tensorflow2.0, Python2.7.15
Dependency library	Numpy, Pandas, Pywt, Statsmodels, Sklearn

Firstly, the commonly used wavelet functions are compared, and db1 is chosen as the wavelet basis function to decompose the data in four levels. The results are shown in Fig. 5.

When Fig. 5 is sorted from top to bottom, the top layer is the original signal, the images of the second to fifth layers correspond to the high frequency coefficients of the first to the fourth discrete wavelet transform, and the bottom layer is the low frequency coefficients after the fourth discrete wavelet transform. Through ADF test, it is concluded that 2, 3, 6 are stationary series, 4, 5 are non-stationary series.

For stationary series, after the model order is determined according to AIC and BIC criteria, the smaller value is selected as the result of order determination and ARIMA model is constructed; for non-stationary series, EWFA algorithm is used to find out the optimal parameters and then ELM model is constructed. Finally, the prediction results of each model are integrated into the output value of the DWAFE model through inverse wavelet transform.

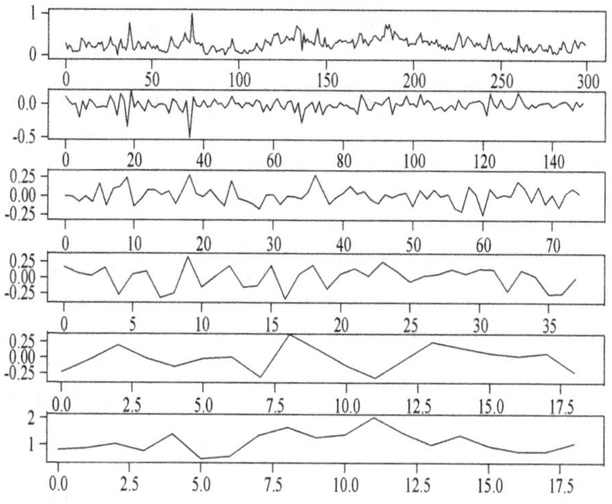

Fig. 5. Wavelet transform result graph

For stationary series, after the model order is determined according to AIC and BIC criteria, the smaller value is selected as the result of order determination and ARIMA model is constructed; for non-stationary series, EWFA algorithm is used to find out the optimal parameters and then ELM model is constructed. Finally, the prediction results of each model are integrated into the output value of the DWAFE model through inverse wavelet transform.

4 Experimental Results and Analysis

In this experiment R2, MAPE, 10%ACC, 15%ACC and 20%ACC were used as evaluation indexes. Among them:

$$MAPE = \frac{100\%}{n} \sum_{i=1}^{n} \left| \frac{\hat{y}_i - y_i}{y_i} \right| \tag{12}$$

$$R^2 = 1 - \frac{\sum_i (\hat{y}_i - y_i)^2}{\sum_i (\overline{y}_i - y_i)^2} \tag{13}$$

$$20\%ACC = 1 - \frac{1}{n} count(\frac{|\hat{y} - y|}{y} > \frac{20}{100}) \tag{14}$$

$$15\%ACC = 1 - \frac{1}{n} count(\frac{|\hat{y} - y|}{y} > \frac{15}{100}) \tag{15}$$

$$10\%ACC = 1 - \frac{1}{n} count(\frac{|\hat{y} - y|}{y} > \frac{10}{100}) \tag{16}$$

where $\hat{y}$ is the predicted value, y is the true value, n is the number of samples, and $count(A > B)$ is the number of samples satisfying the condition $A > B$.

4.1 Comparison Between FA-ELM and EWFA-ELM

In order to explore the improvement effect of Exponential Weighting on Firefly Algorithm, ELM is optimized by FA and EWFA respectively, and ten comparative experiments are carried out.

It can be seen from Table 3 and 4 that the average R2 of EWFA-ELM is 0.591, which is 0.961 higher than that of FA-ELM, indicating that its fitting ability is better. The average MAPE of EWFA-ELM is 0.0904, which is 0.0728 higher than that of FA-ELM, and the 10% ACC, 15% ACC and 20% ACC values of EWFA-ELM are significantly higher than that of FA-ELM, indicating that its prediction accuracy has been greatly improved. The MAPE of EWFA-ELM is stable in the range of (0.0978, 0.0882), which proves that EWFA-ELM can overcome the disadvantage of poor stability of ELM.

In terms of optimization efficiency, the original Firefly Algorithm needs an average of 37 iterations in 162.2 s to find the optimal parameters, while the Exponentially Weighted Firefly Algorithm only needs 23 iterations in 98.6 s, which greatly improves the number and time of iterations required for convergence.

Figure 6 shows the state of the Exponential Weighted Firefly Algorithm iterating 5, 10, 15 times and final state. Each point in the figure represents the position of each firefly

Table 3. Summary table of ten experiments of FA-ELM

	Max	Min	Average
R2	−0.109	−0.989	−0.37
MAPE	0.2092	0.1	0.163
Time	188 s	122 s	162.2 s
Iterations	42	29	37
20%ACC	0.666	0.5	0.5
15%ACC	0.5	0.333	0.466
10%ACC	0.417	0.333	0.366

Table 4. Summary table of ten experiments of EWFA-ELM

	Max	Min	Average
R2	0.6062	0.5669	0.591
MAPE	0.0978	0.0882	0.0904
Time	107 s	91 s	98.6
Iterations	24	22	23
20%ACC	1	0.833	0.916
15%ACC	0.833	0.666	0.75
10%ACC	0.75	0.583	0.666

in the solution space. It can be seen from Fig. 6 that after each iteration, all fireflies will move towards the position with higher brightness to find the better parameter solution.

Through exponential weighting, the algorithm eliminates the fluctuation of the original firefly algorithm on the brightness axis, and indicates a faster optimization path for firefly. Because of the deviation correction, the algorithm can run well in the initial state. In addition, through the strategy of early stopping, the algorithm can effectively suppress the over fitting of the model.

To sum up, compared with the original ELM, the improved EWFA-ELM has obvious advantages in all indicators, and achieves 100% accuracy at most in 20% ACC indicators, which shows that the optimization effect of Exponential Weighted Firefly Algorithm is significant.

4.2 Comparison Between DWAFE and Base Models

In order to explore the performance of DWAFE model, ARIMA model, Bi-LSTM model, GRU model and DWAFE model are used for comparative experiments.

It can be seen from Fig. 7, 8, 9 and 10 that among the four comparison models, the fitting effect of DWAFE is the best, and the 12 predicted points are within the range of 15% ACC; the fitting effect of ARIMA model is the worst, and its predicted value fluctuates slightly and is close to a straight line; the effect of GRU and Bi-LSTM is close, second only to DWAFE model.

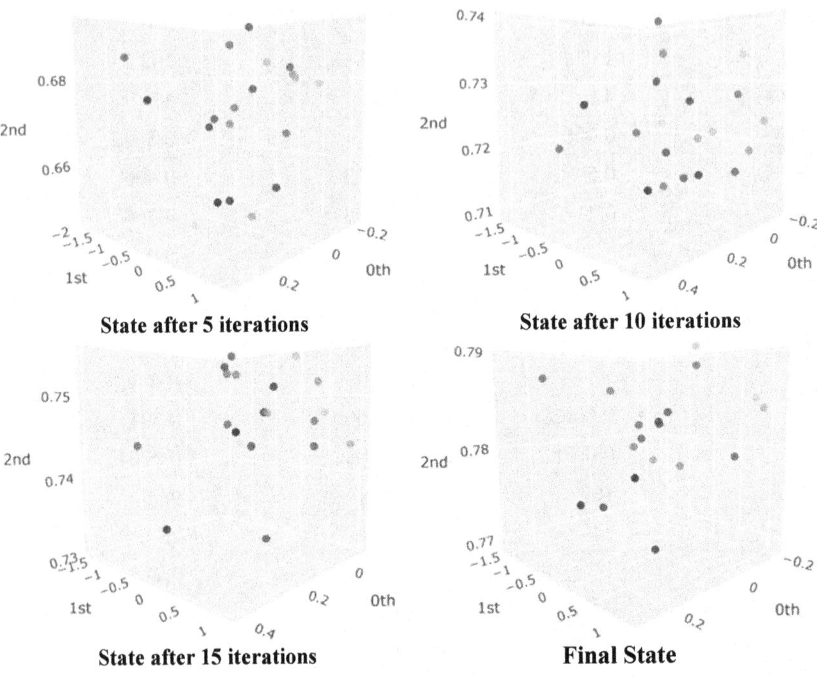

Fig. 6. Iterative optimization graph of exponential weighted firefly algorithm. In this experiment, 20 fireflies are constructed, and each point in the graph represents the position of each firefly in the solution space. The 0th coordinate is the parameter b, the 1th coordinate is the parameter w, and the 2th coordinate is the firefly brightness.

From Table 5 we can know that the R2 value of ARIMA model is the smallest among the four models compared, which indicates that there is a nonlinear structure in the data, resulting in the model can not be well fitted; the R2 value of DWAFE is the closest to 1, which indicates that the model can well adapt to the data and make the best fitting effect. The average absolute percentage error of DWAFE is 7.6%, which is higher than 12.4% of ARIMA.

It can be seen from Fig. 11 and Fig. 12 that Bi-LSTM and GRU have similar performance in terms of various indicators, lying between ARIMA and DWAFE. In addition, according to Fig. 10, with the increase of prediction steps, the prediction error of DWAFE fluctuates less, which indicates that the model has good generalization ability, can well learn the trend and detail changes of training samples, and can accurately predict the future development of data according to historical experience.

Finally, the threshold range is calculated by the sample mean and predicted values. Select the 95% confidence level to get the dynamic threshold interval, as shown in Fig. 13.

Table 5. Comparison results of DWAFE, GRU, Bi-LSTM, ARIMA

	ARIMA	Bi-LSTM	GRU	DWAFE
R2_score	0.161	0.591	0.573	0.623
MAPE	0.124	0.09	0.086	0.076
20%ACC	0.75	0.916	0.916	0.983
15%ACC	0.666	0.75	0.866	0.866
10%ACC	0.5	0.666	0.65	0.7

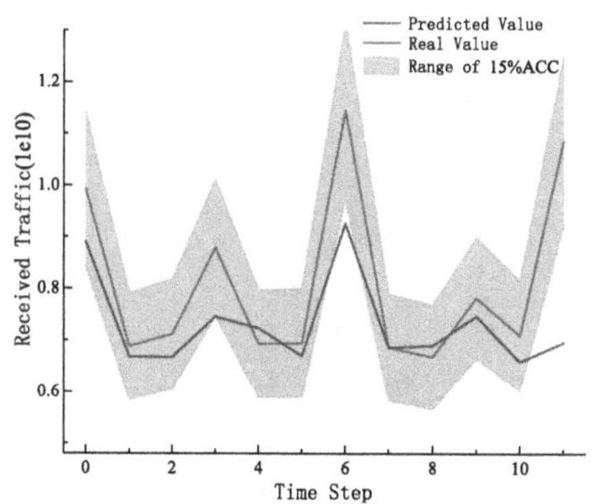

Fig. 7. Bi-LSTM prediction result graph

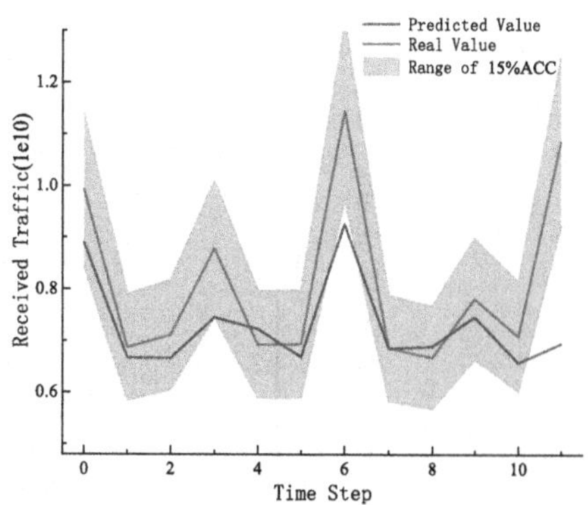

Fig. 8. ARIMA prediction result graph

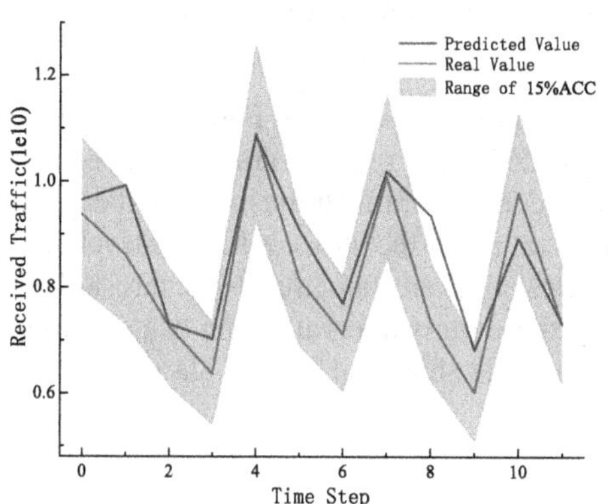

Fig. 9. GRU prediction result graph

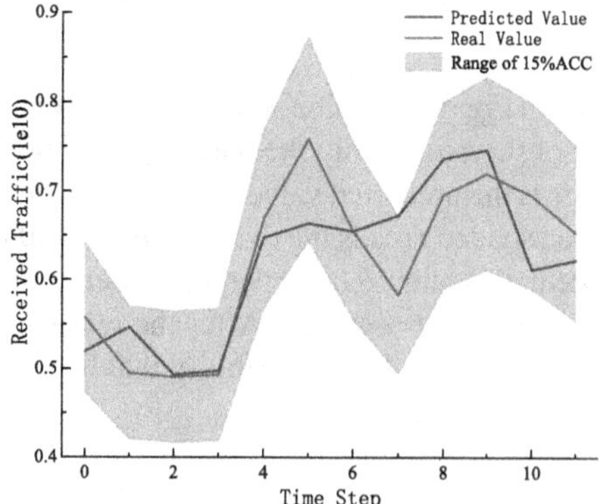

Fig. 10. DWAFE model prediction result graph

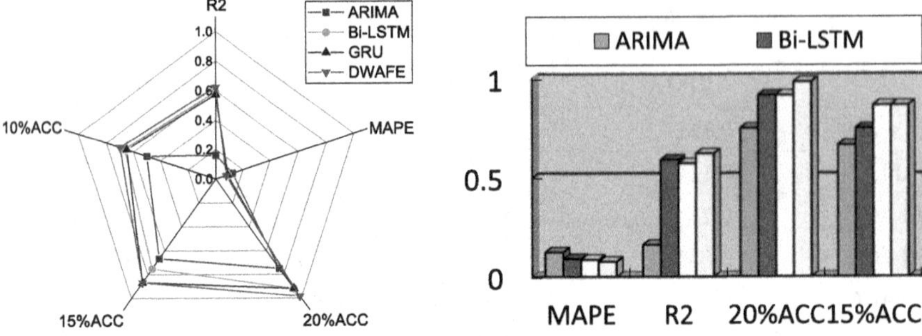

Fig. 11. Model data comparison radar chart **Fig. 12.** Comparison histogram of each mode

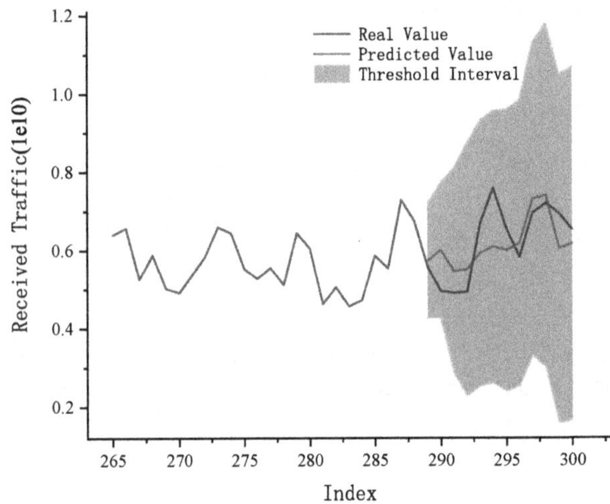

Fig. 13. The dynamic threshold interval graph of the predicted value of the DWAFE model

In Fig. 13, the blue solid line is the real value of the received flow. For the convenience of observation, only the data with an index of (265, 300) range is drawn. The red solid line is the predicted value, which describes the receiving traffic trend in the next day. The blue shaded area is the dynamic threshold interval under the 95% confidence level of the predicted value. The upper and lower boundaries of the area are used as the threshold for triggering the warning. After the real value exceeds this interval, it can be determined that there is a 95% probability that the equipment is abnormal, and an alarm should be issued immediately.

5 Conclusion and Prospect

This paper proposes a dynamic threshold setting mechanism, which can calculate a reasonable dynamic threshold range according to the predicted value. In order to obtain accurate prediction values, we built the DWAFE model based on DWT, ARIMA and

EWFA-ELM. Then compared with benchmark models such as ARIMA, Bi-LSTM, GRU, etc., the conclusions drawn from the experimental results are as follows:

1) The improved EWFA algorithm based on the ideas of exponential weighting, deviation correction, and early stopping can search for better parameter solutions than the FA algorithm, and it is also significantly better than the FA algorithm in the number of iterations and iteration time required for optimization.
2) The EWFA-ELM model optimized by Exponential Weighted Firefly Algorithm is superior to the FA-ELM model in all indexes, and overcomes the disadvantage of poor stability of the original ELM model. After this problem is solved, ELM can be more stable and reliable applied in various fields.
3) The proposed DWAFE model is superior to Bi-LSTM model and GRU model in accuracy and robustness, and significantly superior to ARIMA model in fitting ability and generalization ability.
4) The dynamic threshold setting mechanism proposed in this paper can calculate a more accurate dynamic threshold interval based on the prediction result, and then apply it to equipment operating status perception and fault early warning. Compared with the traditional threshold setting method, this mechanism can adapt to the changes of the real scene and automatically adjust the threshold interval, which has great practical significance.

The current research can predict the data of the next day more accurately, so the next work can use more cutting-edge technologies (such as TDA, Transformer, etc.) to explore methods with longer prediction time and higher prediction accuracy, so as to realize more effective real-time perception of equipment status and early warning of equipment failure.

Acknowledgements. This work was supported in part by the Major Program of the National Natural Science Foundation of China (71633006); Research on Key Technologies and Application of Multi-dimensional Perception of Medical Behavior (2020AAA0109600).

References

1. Navon, A., Keller, Y.: Financial time series prediction using deep learning (2017)
2. Marino, D.L., Amarasinghe, K., Manic, M.: Building energy load forecasting using deep neural networks. In: IECON 2016 - 42nd Annual Conference of the IEEE Industrial Electronics Society, Florence, pp. 7046–7051 (2016). https://doi.org/10.1109/IECON.2016.7793413
3. Kouchaki, S., Sanei, S., Arbon, E.L., Dijk, D.: Tensor based singular spectrum analysis for automatic scoring of sleep EEG. IEEE Trans. Neural Syst. Rehabil. Eng. **23**(1), 1–9 (2015). https://doi.org/10.1109/TNSRE.2014.2329557
4. Ma, R., Boubrahimi, S.F., Hamdi, S.M., Angryk, R.A.: Solar flare prediction using multivariate time series decision trees. In: 2017 IEEE International Conference on Big Data (Big Data), Boston, MA, pp. 2569–2578 (2017). https://doi.org/10.1109/BigData.2017.8258216
5. Calheiros, R.N., Masoumi, E., Ranjan, R., Buyya, R.: Workload prediction using ARIMA Model and its impact on cloud applications' QoS. IEEE Trans. Cloud Comput. **3**(4), 449–458 (2015). https://doi.org/10.1109/TCC.2014.2350475

6. Yunus, K., Thiringer, T., Chen, P.: ARIMA-based frequency-decomposed modeling of wind speed time series. IEEE Trans. Power Syst. **31**(4), 2546–2556 (2016). https://doi.org/10.1109/TPWRS.2015.2468586
7. Tabatabaie Nezhad, S.M., Nazari, M., Gharavol, E.A.: A novel DoS and DDoS attacks detection algorithm using ARIMA time series model and chaotic system in computer networks. IEEE Commun. Lett. **20**(4), 700–703 (2016). https://doi.org/10.1109/LCOMM.2016.2517622
8. Box, G.E.P., Jenkins, G.: Time Series Analysis, Forecasting and Control. Holden-Day, San Francisco (1970)
9. Wu, Y., Shen, K., Chen, Z., Wu, J.: Automatic measurement of fetal cavum septum pellucidum from ultrasound images using deep attention network. In: 2020 IEEE International Conference on Image Processing (ICIP), Abu Dhabi, United Arab Emirates, pp. 2511–2515 (2020). https://doi.org/10.1109/ICIP40778.2020.9191002
10. Akusok, A., Björk, K., Miche, Y., Lendasse, A.: High-performance extreme learning machines: a complete toolbox for big data applications. IEEE Access **3**, 1011–1025 (2015). https://doi.org/10.1109/ACCESS.2015.2450498
11. Tang, J., Deng, C., Huang, G.: Extreme learning machine for multilayer perceptron. IEEE Trans. Neural Netw. Learn. Syst. **27**(4), 809–821 (2016). https://doi.org/10.1109/TNNLS.2015.2424995
12. Zhang, L., Zhang, D.: Domain adaptation extreme learning machines for drift compensation in E-nose systems. IEEE Trans. Instrum. Meas. **64**(7), 1790–1801 (July 2015). https://doi.org/10.1109/TIM.2014.2367775
13. Colak, I., Yesilbudak, M., Genc, N., Bayindir, R.: Multi-period prediction of solar radiation using ARMA and ARIMA models. In: 2015 IEEE 14th International Conference on Machine Learning and Applications (ICMLA), Miami, FL, pp. 1045–1049 (2015). https://doi.org/10.1109/ICMLA.2015.33
14. Amini, M.H., Karabasoglu, O., Ilić, M.D., Boroojeni, K.G., Iyengar, S.S.: ARIMA-based demand forecasting method considering probabilistic model of electric vehicles' parking lots. In: 2015 IEEE Power & Energy Society General Meeting, Denver, CO, pp. 1–5 (2015). https://doi.org/10.1109/PESGM.2015.7286050
15. Duan, F., Dai, L., Chang, W., Chen, Z., Zhu, C., Li, W.: sEMG-based identification of hand motion commands using wavelet neural network combined With discrete wavelet transform. IEEE Trans. Industr. Electron. **63**(3), 1923–1934 (2016). https://doi.org/10.1109/TIE.2015.2497212
16. Javed, K., Gouriveau, R., Zerhouni, N.: A new multivariate approach for prognostics based on extreme learning machine and fuzzy clustering. IEEE Trans. Cybern. **45**(12), 2626–2639 (2015). https://doi.org/10.1109/TCYB.2014.2378056
17. Tang, J., Deng, C., Huang, G., Zhao, B.: Compressed-domain ship detection on spaceborne optical image using deep neural network and extreme learning machine. IEEE Trans. Geosci. Remote Sens. **53**(3), 1174–1185 (2015). https://doi.org/10.1109/TGRS.2014.2335751
18. Zhou, H., Huang, G., Lin, Z., Wang, H., Soh, Y.C.: Stacked extreme learning machines. IEEE Trans. Cybern. **45**(9), 2013–2025 (2015). https://doi.org/10.1109/TCYB.2014.2363492
19. Yang, X.-S.: Firefly algorithm. In: Nature-Inspired Metaheuristic Algorithms, pp. 79–90 (2008)
20. Su, H., Yong, B., Du, Q.: Hyperspectral band selection using improved firefly algorithm. IEEE Geosci. Remote Sens. Lett. **13**(1), 68–72 (2016). https://doi.org/10.1109/LGRS.2015.2497085
21. Su, H., Cai, Y., Du, Q.: Firefly-algorithm-inspired framework with band selection and extreme learning machine for hyperspectral image classification. IEEE J. Sel. Top. Appl. Earth Observ. Remote Sens. **10**(1), 309–320 (2017). https://doi.org/10.1109/JSTARS.2016.2591004

22. Zhang, Z.: Improved Adam optimizer for deep neural networks. In: 2018 IEEE/ACM 26th International Symposium on Quality of Service (IWQoS), Banff, AB, Canada, pp. 1–2 (2018). https://doi.org/10.1109/IWQoS.2018.8624183
23. Zou, F., Shen, L., Jie, Z., Zhang, W., Liu, W.: A sufficient condition for convergences of Adam and RMSProp. In: 2019 IEEE/CVF Conference on Computer Vision and Pattern Recognition (CVPR), Long Beach, CA, USA, pp. 11119–11127 (2019). https://doi.org/10.1109/CVPR.2019.01138
24. Razum, D., et al.: Optimal threshold selection for threshold-based fall detection algorithms with multiple features. In: 2018 41st International Convention on Information and Communication Technology, Electronics and Microelectronics (MIPRO). IEEE (2018)
25. Shen, X., et al.: Dynamic threshold based target signal cooperative extraction method for high frequency electromagnetic environment measurement. In: 2017 3rd IEEE International Conference on Control Science and Systems Engineering (ICCSSE). IEEE (2017)

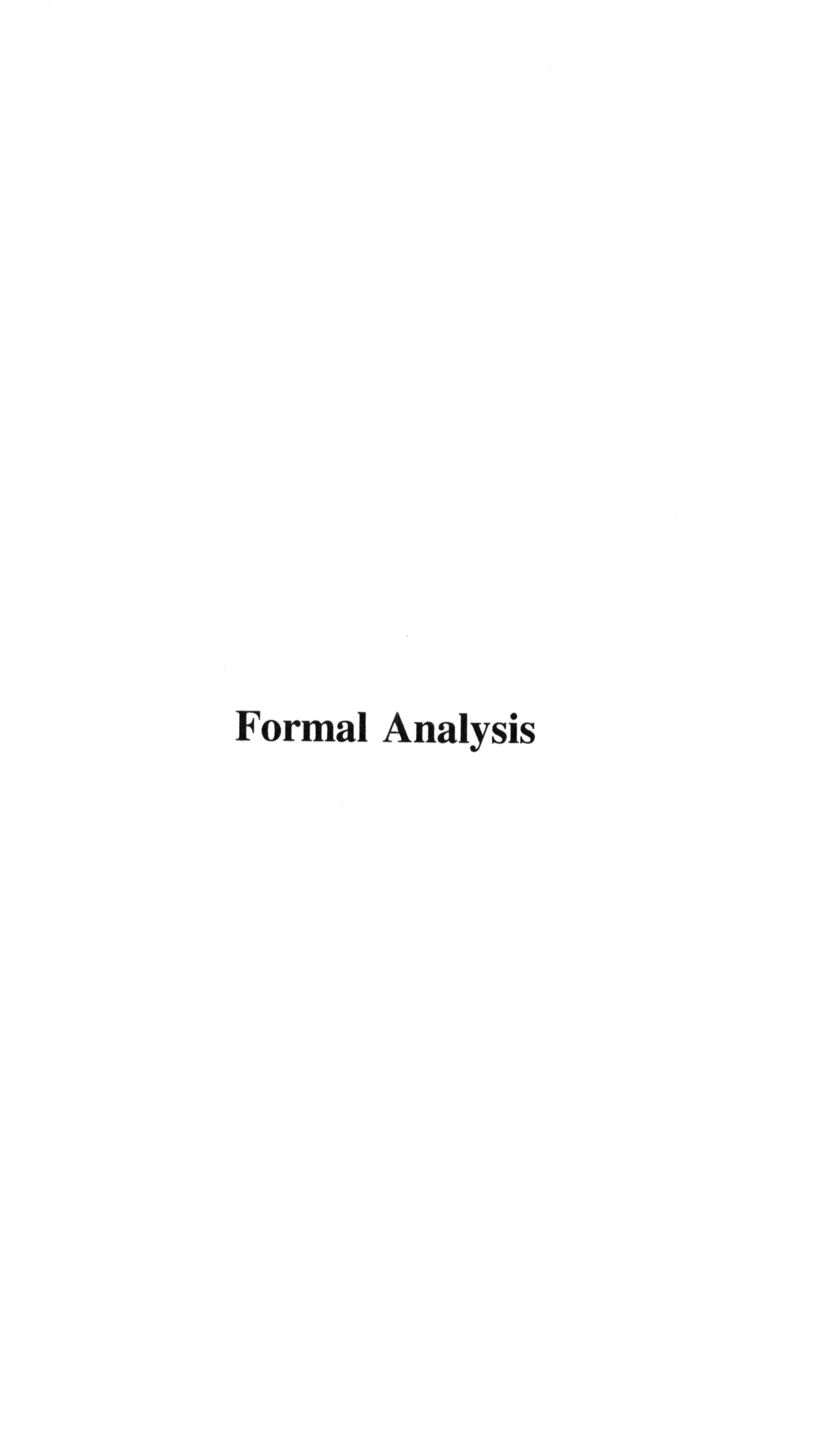

Formal Analysis

The Distribution of Edge-Frequencies Computed with Frequency Quadrilaterals for Traveling Salesman Problem

Yong Wang[1(✉)] and Ruobing Shen[2]

[1] Tarim University, Alar 843300, Xinjiang, China
yongwang@ncepu.edu.cn
[2] Hyundai Mobis Technical Center Europe, Frankfurt 65936, Germany
jeffer_shen@hotmail.com

Abstract. We study the edge-frequencies computed with frequency quadrilaterals for traveling salesman problem. The edge-frequency of an edge in the optimal Hamiltonian cycle is generally much higher than that of a common edge. In this paper, we present the log-beta distribution for all edge-frequencies computed with frequency quadrilaterals in K_n. Moreover, we will show that the edge-frequencies of edges in the optimal Hamiltonian cycle conform to an approximate Dirac delta function. Based on the two distributions, we can cut the edges according to a certain given frequency threshold. In addition, one can estimate the percentage of the eliminated edges according to the log-beta distribution. The experiments are done for the benchmark traveling salesman problem instances. The experimental results verify the two distributions. It also illustrates that enlarging the distances of the eliminated edges will accelerate the algorithms for resolving TSP.

Keywords: Traveling salesman problem · Log-beta distribution · Dirac delta distribution · Frequency quadrilateral

1 Introduction

We consider the symmetrical traveling salesman problem (TSP). That is, we are given a complete graph K_n on the vertex set $\{1, 2, \ldots, n\}$ such that there is a distance function d such that for any two vertices $x, y \in \{1, 2, \ldots, n\}$ and $x \neq y$, $d(x, y) = d(y, x) \geq 0$ is the distance between x and y. The goal is to find an optimal Hamiltonian cycle (OHC) with respect to these distances. That is, we want to explore a permutation $\sigma = (\sigma_1 \ldots \sigma_n)$ of vertices $1, \ldots, n$ such that $\sigma_1 = 1$ and the total distance $d(\sigma) := d(\sigma_n, 1) + \sum_{i=1}^{n-1} d(\sigma_i, \sigma_{i+1})$ is as small as possible. TSP has been extensively studied to find the special classes of graphs where the polynomial-time algorithms exist for either finding an exact solution, that is, finding the OHC, or finding an approximate solution which is

This study was supported by the Fundamental Research Funds for the Central Universities (Nos. 2018ZD09 and 2018MS039).

Z. Cai et al. (Eds.): NCTCS 2021, CCIS 1494, pp. 177–195, 2021.
https://doi.org/10.1007/978-981-16-7443-3_11

an Hamiltonian cycle (HC) whose distance meets $d(HC) \leq cd(OHC)$ where c is some fixed constant. There are a number of special classes of graphs where one can find the OHC in some reasonable computation time, see [1].

Karp [2] has shown that TSP is NP-complete in computation complexity. This means that there are no exact polynomial-time algorithms for TSP unless $P = NP$. The computation time of the exact algorithms for TSP is $O(a^n)$ for some $a > 1$. For example, Held and Karp [3], and independently Bellman [4] designed the dynamic programming algorithm to solve the TSP that required the $O(n^2 2^n)$ computation time. Integer programming techniques, such as either branch-and-bound [5,6] or cutting-plane [7,8], have been able to solve the TSP instances on thousands of points. In 2006, the VLSI application (Euclidean TSP) on 85,900 points has been solved with one improved branch-and-cut method on the networked computer system having 128 nodes [8]. In the 2019 ECOR conference, Cook [9] reported that they computed the optimal Hamiltonian cycle through 109,399 stars. Until now, they are the two largest TSP that was resolved by the exact method.

In recent years, researchers have developed the polynomial-time algorithms for TSP on the sparse graphs. The number of the HCs is greatly reduced with respect to a sparse graph. For example, given a sparse graph of average degree $d = 3$ or 4, Sharir and Welzl [10] proved that the number of the HCs is less than $e(\frac{d}{2})^n$, where e is the base of the natural logarithm. Gebauer [11] gave the lower bound of the number of the HCs roughly as $(\frac{d}{2})^n$ for a sparse graph of average degree 3. Furthermore, Björklund [12] proved that the TSP on a bounded degree graph could be resolved in time $O((2-\epsilon)^n)$, where ϵ depends on the maximum degree of the vertex in the graph. For the TSP on a cubic graph, Eppstein [13] introduced an exact algorithm whose running time is $O(1.260^n)$. This computation time was improved to $O(1.2553^n)$ by Liśewicz and Schuster [14]. Aggarwal, Garg, and Gupta [15], and independently Boyd, Sitters, Van der Ster, and Stougie [16] gave two $\frac{4}{3}$−approximation algorithms to solve the TSP on a metric cubic graph. For the TSP on a cubic connected graph, Correa, Larré, and Soto [17] proved that the approximation threshold was strictly below $\frac{4}{3}$. For the TSP on a bounded-genus graph, Borradaile, Demaine, and Tazari [18] gave the polynomial-time approximation scheme. In the case of the asymmetric TSP ($ATSP$) on a bounded-genus graph, Gharan and Saberi [19] designed the constant-factor approximation algorithm. For the TSP on a planar graph, the constant-factor is $22.51(1 + \frac{1}{n})$. Moreover, Svensson, Tarnawski, and Végh [20] first proved the 901-approximation polynomial-time algorithm for the local-connectivity $ATSP$ on a graph having two edge weights. They finally designed the 506-approximation algorithm for $\Delta - ATSP$ using the subtour partition cover under the local connectivity conditions [21]. Besides the improvement of the exact and approximation algorithms for TSP on sparse graphs, the heuristics are also accelerated. Taillard and Helsgaun [22] used the POPMUSIC method to find the candidate OHC edges. The experimental results demonstrated that the computation time of the basic LKH was greatly reduced for the big TSP instances. Thus, whether one is trying to find the exact solutions or approximations for the TSP, one has a variety of more efficient algorithms available if one can reduce a given instance of TSP to finding the OHC in a sparse graph.

According to the $k - opt$ *moves*, Hougardy and Schroeder [23] presented the sufficient condition for the useless edges out of all OHCs. They gave the 3-step combinatorial algorithm which trims many useless edges. According to the sparse graphs, the Concorde was accelerated more than 11 times for certain big TSP instances. Wang [24] introduced the frequency graphs as another way to reduce the number of edges that one has to consider for finding the OHC. At first, the frequency graphs are computed with the special optimal 4-vertex paths with given endpoints [24]. Let $\mathcal{OP}^4$ denote the set of all optimal 4-vertex paths in K_n. Then, the edge-frequency $f(A, B)$ of an edge $(A, B) \in K_n$ is the number of the optimal 4-vertex paths which contain (A, B) as an edge. Through studying many real-world TSP instances [24], the edge-frequencies of the OHC edges are much higher than those of most of the other edges. This suggests that we can safely eliminate the edges of low frequency and the OHC will be kept intact. The hope is that after the edges of low frequency are eliminated, we can be left with a certain sparse graph so that the techniques for either finding or approximating the OHC for sparse graphs can be applied.

In the following, Wang and Remmel [25] computed the edge-frequencies with the frequency quadrilaterals. They assumed that a quadrilateral $ABCD$ contains six optimal 4-vertex paths. Then, the frequency quadrilateral $ABCD$ is computed with the six optimal 4-vertex paths in the quadrilateral $ABCD$. Based on the orders of the three distance sums determined by the edges' distances in $ABCD$, six frequency quadrilaterals are derived for $ABCD$. According to the six frequency quadrilaterals, they computed the probability $p_5(e)$, $p_3(e)$ and $p_1(e)$ that an edge e has the edge-frequency $f(e) = 5,\ 3$ or 1 in a frequency quadrilateral. In addition, they formulated one binomial distribution $\mathcal{B}(N, p_{\{3,5\}}(e))$ for evaluating the average edge-frequency of edges computed with the frequency quadrilaterals in K_n. Based on the binomial distribution, Wang and Remmel [28] designed one iterative algorithm to cut $\frac{1}{3}$ of the edges with the smallest edge-frequencies at each iteration until some sparse graph is computed. Moreover, Wang and Remmel [29] presented one new binomial distribution considering the negative correlation between the edge-frequencies related to two adjacent edges. Based on the new binomial distribution, they cut $\frac{1}{2}$ of the edges with the smallest edge-frequencies at each iteration for computing a certain sparse graph. The experiments for the TSP instances in $TSPLIB$ illustrated that the two iterative algorithms computed the sparse graphs containing $O(n \log n)$ edges. Furthermore, the sparse graphs are connected and they contain the OHC for most of the TSP instances. As a few known OHC edges are cut, the preserved graphs become even sparser and they generally contain good approximations.

Although the binomial distribution works well to reduce a TSP on K_n to the TSP on sparse graphs, the intrinsic reason why the OHC edges are still preserved when we cut $\frac{1}{3}$ or $\frac{1}{2}$ of the edges with the smallest edge-frequencies is not disclosed. The experimental results indicate that the OHC edge-frequencies are bigger than the eliminated $\frac{1}{3}$ or $\frac{1}{2}$ of the edge-frequencies. However, the distributions of all edge-frequencies and OHC edge-frequencies are not studied in the previous papers. In this research, we shall study the distribution functions which cultivate the edge-frequencies computed with frequency quadrilaterals for all edges and the OHC edges. Based on the distribution of edge-frequencies, one can estimate the percentage of the preserved edges as they are eliminated according to a given frequency threshold. The research illustrates that the OHC edges will be preserved even though a big percentage of edges are cut according to edge-frequencies.

The outline of this paper is as follows. First in Sect. 2, we shall study the distribution function for all edge-frequencies computed with frequency quadrilaterals. In Sect. 3, the distribution of the OHC edge-frequencies are analyzed. In Sect. 4, we will do experiments to verify the two distributions with the real-world TSP instances. In the last section, the conclusions are drawn and the possible future research directions are given.

2 Distribution of All Edge-Frequencies

As the edge-frequencies are computed with frequency quadrilaterals, one can cut the edges with the small edge-frequency according to a given frequency threshold. If the special frequency quadrilaterals are chosen for the OHC edges, one can use the big frequency threshold [27]. In general, the frequency quadrilaterals are chosen at random for computing the edge-frequencies. In this case, the average edge-frequency is a good choice as the frequency threshold [28]. The distribution of the edge-frequencies is significant to estimate the percentage of the eliminated edges according to the frequency threshold. Moreover, the distribution of the OHC edge-frequencies illustrates how many OHC edges will be cut according to the frequency threshold.

An edge e is contained in $\binom{n-2}{2}$ quadrilaterals $ABCD$ in K_n. Each quadrilateral can be converted into one of the six frequency quadrilaterals [25]. Therefore, there are corresponding $\binom{n-2}{2}$ frequency quadrilaterals containing e. e has an edge-frequency $f(e)$ =1, 3, or 5 in a frequency quadrilateral containing e. As we choose N frequency quadrilaterals containing e to compute its edge-frequency, the total edge-frequency $F(e) = \sum_{i=1}^{N} f_i(e)$ where $f_i(e)$ equals 1, 3, or 5 in the ith frequency quadrilateral. The average edge-frequency of e is computed as $\bar{f}(e) = \frac{1}{N}\sum_{i=1}^{N} f_i(e)$. The average frequency of e is used in this study since it is bounded to the interval $[1, 5]$. For convenience, we call the average edge-frequency as edge-frequency in the following sections. We are interested in the distribution of the edge-frequencies $\bar{f}(e)$ of all of edges. $F(e)$ conforms to the similar distribution as $\bar{f}(e)$.

Since $f_i(e) \in \{1, 3, 5\}$, the edge-frequency $\bar{f}(e) \in [1, 5]$. Given an edge e, N edge-frequencies $f_i(e) \in \{1, 3, 5\}$ are independently selected. We assume each of the edge-frequencies 1, 3, and 5 occur with the probability $\frac{1}{3}$ based on the six frequency quadrilaterals in paper [25]. The expected frequency is 3 and the corresponding variance is $\frac{8}{3}$. If the frequencies $f_i(e) = 1$, 3, and 5 of all edges e

are independent to each other, the edge-frequency $\bar{f}(e)$ will conform to the normal distribution based on the central limit theorem. Unfortunately, the edge-frequencies $f_i(e) = 1$, 3, and 5 of any two vertex-joint edges in a frequency quadrilateral have the negative correlations. For example in a frequency quadrilateral $ABCD$, the frequencies $f(A, B)$ and $f(A, C)$ of two adjacent edges (A, B) and (A, C) have the three cases $\{1, 3\}$, $\{1, 5\}$, and $\{3, 5\}$, respectively. Every edge e is adjacent to $2(n-2)$ edges in K_n and each pair of adjacent edges are contained in $n-3$ quadrilaterals. Thus, the edge-frequencies $f_i(e) = 1$, 3, and 5 of the adjacent edges in the frequency quadrilaterals are not independent to each other. It means that the edge-frequencies $\bar{f}(e)$ of the $\binom{n}{2}$ edges in K_n will not accurately conform to the normal distribution.

There are $\binom{n}{2}$ edge-frequencies $\bar{f}(e_i)$ with respect to the edges e_i $\left(1 \le i \le \binom{n}{2}\right)$ in K_n, and each frequency $\bar{f}(e_i) \in [1, 5]$. We order the $\binom{n}{2}$ frequencies $\bar{f}(e_i)$ from small to big values. An edge-frequency sequence is formed as $\left(\bar{f}(e_1), \bar{f}(e_2), \cdots, \bar{f}\left(e_{\binom{n}{2}}\right)\right)$ for some fixed ordering of edges. The first edge-frequency $\bar{f}(e_1)$ is the smallest and the last edge-frequency $\bar{f}\left(e_{\binom{n}{2}}\right)$ is the biggest. The edge-frequency $\bar{f}(e_i)$ is monotone increasing according to the edge index i. In the edge-frequency sequence, an edge-frequency $\bar{f}(e_i)$ will rise smoothly to another edge-frequency $\bar{f}(e_{i+k})$ as k is a small number. Thus, the Theorem 1 is given as below.

Theorem 1. *In the ordered edge-frequency sequence* $\left(\bar{f}(e_1), \bar{f}(e_2), \cdots, \bar{f}\left(e_{\binom{n}{2}}\right)\right)$, *each edge-frequency* $\bar{f}(e_i)$ $\left(1 \le i \le \binom{n}{2}\right)$ *is nearly equal to its two adjacent edge-frequencies* $\bar{f}(e_{i-1})$ *and* $\bar{f}(e_{i+1})$ *for big number* n.

Proof. There are $\binom{n}{4}$ frequency quadrilaterals in K_n, and each quadrilateral contains six edges. There are one pair edge-frequency 1 s, 3 s and 5 s, respectively, in each frequency quadrilateral. The number of each of the edge-frequencies 1, 3, and 5 is equal to $2\binom{n}{4}$ in K_n, respectively. Given a number $i \in \left[1, \binom{n}{2}\right]$, if $\bar{f}(e_i)$ is much bigger than $\bar{f}(e_{i-1})$, the following edge-frequencies $\bar{f}(e_j)$ $(j > i)$ will rise to 5 quickly since $\bar{f}(e_{i+1}) \ge \bar{f}(e_i)$. It implies there will be bigger than $2\binom{n}{4}$ frequency 5 s with respect to all frequency quadrilaterals. It violates the restriction of the frequency quadrilaterals in K_n. Therefore, the two adjacent edge-frequencies $\bar{f}(e_{i-1})$ and $\bar{f}(e_i)$ do not have much difference.

Among the $\binom{n}{2}$ edge-frequencies $\bar{f}(e_i)$, most of them will be a value near to 3 since the expected frequency of edges is 3. If we line the edge-frequency $\bar{f}(e_i)$ according to the edge index i, an edge-frequency curve will be obtained. As n rises, the edge-frequency curve will become flatter according to i since the number of edges increases as $O(n^2)$ whereas $\bar{f}_i \in [1, 5]$. Based on the edge-frequency sequence, we assume $\frac{\bar{f}(e_i)}{\bar{f}(e_{i-1})} = 1 + x_i$ where $x_i \in [0, 1]$ is a random number. There is a sequence of independent random values $x_i \in [0, 1]$ which make the formula (1) hold, where $\bar{f}(e_0)$ is the smallest edge-frequency. Here, we assume the independent values $1 + x_i$ have an identical distribution.

We apply the logarithm operation to $\bar{f}(e_i)$ and obtain the formula (2). Since we assume the independent random values $(1+x_k)$s conform to the same distribution, the sum $\sum_{k=1}^{i} \log(1+x_k)$s conform to the normal distribution according to the central limit theory. It indicates the edge-frequency $\bar{f}(e_i)$ conforms to the log-normal distribution $\mathcal{LN}(\mu, \sigma^2)$. Moreover, since $\log \bar{f}(e_i)$ is limited to the interval $[0, \log 5]$, the Beta distribution is better to describe the logarimatic edge-frequency $\log \bar{f}(e_i)$s. In reverse, the edge-frequency $\bar{f}(e_i)$ will conform to the log-beta distribution $Log-Beta(\mu, \sigma^2)$. Here, the expected value μ and variance σ^2 are computed based on the normalized $\log \bar{f}(e_i) \in [0,1]$. It mentions that the edge-frequencies $\bar{f}(e_i)$ of the $n-1$ edges containing a vertex v also conform to some log-beta distribution.

$$\bar{f}(e_i) = \bar{f}(e_0) \prod_{k=1}^{i} (1+x_k). \tag{1}$$

$$\log \bar{f}(e_i) - \log \bar{f}(e_0) = \sum_{k=1}^{i} \log(1+x_k). \tag{2}$$

In the following, we compare the log-normal distribution and log-beta distribution for the edge-frequencies. A log-normal distribution is determined by the expected value μ and standard deviation σ related to the edge-frequency sequence $\left(\log \bar{f}(e_1), \log \bar{f}(e_2), \cdots, \log \bar{f}\left(e_{\binom{n}{2}}\right)\right)$. Given a TSP instance on K_n, one first computes the edge-frequency $\bar{f}(e_i)$ for every edge e_i using the frequency quadrilaterals. Then, the logarithm operation is applied to each edge-frequency $\bar{f}(e_i)$ for computing the corresponding value $\log \bar{f}(e_i)$. Using the statistical methods, the μ and σ can be computed. If the natural logarithm base is used, the mean of the log-normal distribution is represented as $\exp\left(\mu + \frac{\sigma^2}{2}\right)$ and the variance of the log-normal distribution is computed as $(\exp \sigma^2 - 1) \times \exp(2\mu + \sigma^2)$. Based on the derivation and experimental results in paper [25], the mean and variance of the edge-frequencies $\bar{f}(e_i)$ are 3 and 0.52, respectively. Thus, we build the formulae (3) and the parameter values $\mu \approx 1.07$ and $\sigma^2 \approx 0.056$ can be derived. The edge-frequency $\bar{f}(e)$ approximately conforms to the log-normal distribution $\mathcal{LN}(1.07, 0.056)$. The probability density curves of the log-normal distribution $\mathcal{LN}(1.07, 0.056)$ and normal distribution $\mathcal{N}(3, 0.52)$ are shown in Fig. 1. It mentions that the edge-frequency $\bar{f}(e)$ is restricted to the interval $[1, 5]$. To show the difference between the log-normal distribution $\mathcal{LN}(1.07, 0.056)$ and normal distribution $\mathcal{N}(3, 0.52)$, we draw their probability density curves according to $\bar{f}(e) \in [0, 6]$ in Fig. 1. Obviously, the accumulative probability $Pr(f \leq 3)$ of the log-normal distribution is bigger than $Pr(f \leq 3)$ of the normal distribution. If we use the frequency threshold 3 to cut the edges with the edge-frequency below 3, more than half edges will be eliminated.

$$\begin{aligned} \exp\left(\mu + \frac{\sigma^2}{2}\right) &= 3 \text{ and} \\ (\exp \sigma^2 - 1) \times \exp(2\mu + \sigma^2) &= 0.52 \end{aligned} \tag{3}$$

Let's see the log-beta distribution for the edge-frequencies. As we know, the random variable x of Beta distribution is restricted to $[0,1]$. After the edge-frequency sequence $\left(\log \bar{f}(e_1), \log \bar{f}(e_2), \cdots, \log \bar{f}\left(e_{\binom{n}{2}}\right)\right)$ is computed, a linear transformation (4) is used to transfer each logarimatic edge-frequency $\log \bar{f}(e_i)$ to one value $x_i \in [0,1]$. The linear transformation does not change the distribution of the $\log \bar{f}(e_i)$. In this case, the variables x will conform to the beta distribution $x \sim Beta(\alpha, \beta)$. Since $\log \bar{f}(e_i)$s approximately conforms to the normal distribution, we assume the beta-distribution is symmetric and $\alpha = \beta > 1$. A Beta distribution $Beta(\alpha, \beta)$ is controlled by two positive shape parameters α and β. Given a beta distribution $x \sim Beta(\alpha, \beta)$, the mean value of x is computed as $E[x] = \frac{\alpha}{\alpha+\beta}$ and the variance is noted as $var[x] = \frac{\alpha\beta}{(\alpha+\beta)^2(\alpha+\beta+1)}$. Since $\alpha = \beta$, the $E[x]$ and $var[x]$ are simplified as formulae (5). Based on the formulae (4) and (5), we derive the formula (6). The relationships of means and variances between log-beta distribution and beta distribution are built according to those for normal distribution and log-normal distribution in formulae (3). We assume the smallest edge-frequency $\bar{f}(e_1) > 1$ and the biggest edge-frequency $\bar{f}\left(e_{\binom{n}{2}}\right) = 5$. Using the mean value 3 and variance 0.52 of the edge-frequencies $\bar{f}(e_i)$, the $\alpha = \beta = 2.09$ and $\bar{f}(e_1) = 1.70$ are derived. Thus, $x = \frac{\log \bar{f}(e) - \log \bar{f}(e_1)}{\log \bar{f}\left(e_{\binom{n}{2}}\right) - \log \bar{f}(e_1)}$ conforms to the beta distribution $Beta(2.09, 2.09)$. According to the formula (5), the $E[x] = 0.5$ and $var[x] = 0.0482 \approx 0.048$ hold. In view of the formula (4), the edge-frequency

$$\bar{f}(e) = \exp\left(\left(\log \bar{f}\left(e_{\binom{n}{2}}\right) - \log \bar{f}(e_1)\right) x + \log \bar{f}(e_1)\right) = \exp((\log 5 - \log 1.70)x + \log 1.70).$$

Using the linear transformation $\frac{\bar{f}(e) - \bar{f}(e_1)}{\bar{f}\left(e_{\binom{n}{2}}\right) - \bar{f}(e_1)}$, $\bar{f}(e)$ is normalized to a value in the interval [0,1]. The normalized edge-frequency $\bar{f}(e)$ conforms to the log-beta distribution $Log - Beta(0.5, 0.048)$. The probability density curves of the beta distribution $Beta(2.09, 2.09)$ and the log-beta distribution $Log - Beta(0.5, 0.048)$ are illustrated in Fig. 2.

$$x = \frac{\log \bar{f}(e) - \log \bar{f}(e_1)}{\log \bar{f}\left(e_{\binom{n}{2}}\right) - \log \bar{f}(e_1)} \tag{4}$$

$$E[x] = \frac{\alpha}{\alpha+\beta} = \frac{1}{2} \text{ and}$$
$$var[x] = \frac{\alpha\beta}{(\alpha+\beta)^2(\alpha+\beta+1)} = \frac{1}{4(2\alpha+1)} \tag{5}$$

$$\mu = E[\log \bar{f}(e)] = \frac{1}{2}\left(\log \bar{f}\left(e_{\binom{n}{2}}\right) + \log \bar{f}(e_1)\right) \text{ and}$$
$$\sigma^2 = var[\log \bar{f}(e)] = \frac{\left(\log \bar{f}\left(e_{\binom{n}{2}}\right) - \log \bar{f}(e_1)\right)^2}{4(2\alpha+1)} \tag{6}$$

Since the edge-frequencies are restricted to the interval [1, 5], the beta distribution is better to describe the variable $\log \bar{f}(e_i)$ and the log-beta distribution will be more suitable for cultivating the edge-frequencies $\bar{f}(e_i)$. It is clear the log-beta distribution is unsymmetrical. For example, the expected frequency $\mu = 3$ is normalized to 0.394 but not 0.5 in view of the log-beta probability density curve in Fig. 2. According to the normalized edge-frequency $\bar{f}(e) \in [0, 1]$, the small edge-frequencies below the expected frequency 3 occupy the bigger percentage than those having the edge-frequencies above 3. If we use the frequency threshold 3 to cut the edges of the smaller edge-frequencies, more than 54% edges will be eliminated. The probability models [28, 29] illustrate that the edge-frequency of the OHC edges is generally bigger than the expected frequency 3. Thus, at least 54% edges will be cut according to the frequency threshold 3 and the OHC edges are kept intact.

The mean 3 and variance 0.52 of the edge-frequencies $\bar{f}(e_i)$s are used to derive the log-normal distribution $\mathcal{LN}(1.07, 0.056)$ and log-beta distribution $Log - Beta(0.5, 0.048)$. For different TSP instances, the variance will slightly deviate from 0.52 due to the number of equal-weight edges and computation errors. For the log-normal distribution, if the real variance 0.52 becomes a little bigger, the parameter σ^2 will increase accordingly but the mean μ will decrease by a small value. For log-beta distribution, if the variance 0.52 becomes bigger, the smallest edge-frequency $\bar{f}(e_1)$ and $\alpha = \beta$ will decrease by a bit.

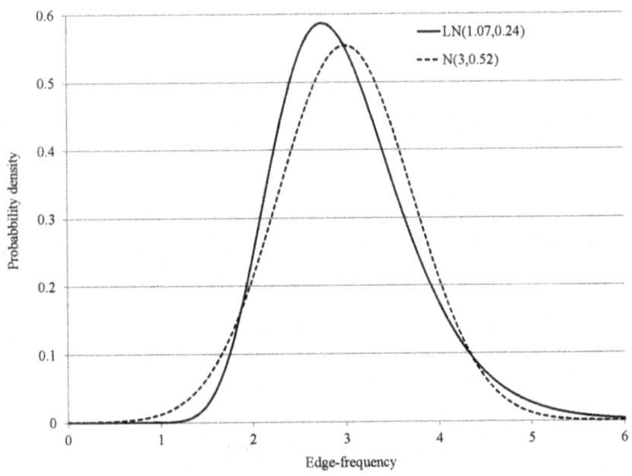

Fig. 1. The log-normal and normal distributions for edge-frequencies

3 Distribution of the *OHC* Edge-Frequencies

For the OHC edges, the distribution of the edge-frequencies will be different from that for all edges. Based on the probability models [25, 29], each OHC edge will have a big edge-frequency above 3. Moreover, Wang proved that an OHC

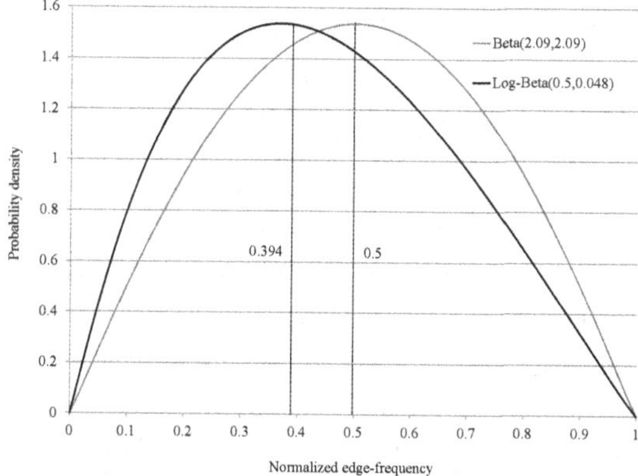

Fig. 2. The log-beta distribution and beta distribution for edge-frequencies

edge-frequency $\bar{f}(e)$ approaches 5 as n is big enough [30]. It means most edge-frequencies of the OHC edges will be near to 5. The edge-frequency far away from 5 has the small probability. If the OHC edge-frequencies are ordered from small to big values, there will be a small number of the small edge-frequencies. Moreover, the adjacent small edge-frequencies generally have a big difference because they rise to 5 quickly. For the big edge-frequencies close to 5, the two adjacent edge-frequencies $\bar{f}(e_i)$ and $\bar{f}(e_{i+1})$ will be nearly equal, i.e., $\frac{\bar{f}(e_{i+1})}{\bar{f}(e_i)} \approx 1$. Thus, the distribution function for all edge-frequencies is not suitable for the OHC edge-frequencies. We assume each OHC edge-frequency is bigger than $5-\delta$ and $\delta \geq 0$ is a small value. Since the OHC edge-frequencies are constrained to the small interval $[5-\delta, 5]$, the probability function will be zero everywhere except in $[5-\delta, 5]$. In this case, the probability density function will degenerates to some Dirac delta function as $\delta \to 0$.

In actual applications, the scale of the TSP instances is limited. Most of the OHC edge-frequencies will be restricted to an interval $[5-\delta, 5]$. If δ is assigned a small value, such as $\delta < 0.5$, there will be a few OHC edges whose edge-frequencies are smaller than $5-\delta$, especially for some small and medium size of TSP instances. The experiments in the next section will illustrate that the number of the OHC edges with the small edge-frequency is very small. Thus, we can use a given big frequency threshold to cut the other edges according to the edge-frequencies.

4 Experiments and Analysis

certain TSP instances to show the distributions of the edge-frequencies. Many experiments are done but only part of the experimental results are illustrated for saving pages. Before the experiments, the OHC of these TSP instances are computed with Concorde Solver [31]. We show the distribution of the OHC edge-frequencies with respect to the known OHC for these TSP instances.

4.1 Change of the Edge-Frequencies

Firstly, we show the change of the edge-frequencies $\bar{f}(e_i)$ according to the edge index $i \in \left[1, \binom{n}{2}\right]$ for four small TSP instances ail535, att532, si535 and u574. The four small TSP instances represent four types of TSP instances where the distances are computed based on different functions. Since the scale of these TSP instances is small, we compute the edge-frequencies with the $\binom{n}{4}$ frequency quadrilaterals. The edge-frequencies are ordered from small to big values to form the edge-frequency sequence $\left(\bar{f}(e_1), \bar{f}(e_2), \cdots, \bar{f}\left(e_{\binom{n}{2}}\right)\right)$. We lined the edge-frequency $\bar{f}(e_i)$ according to the edge index i. For each instance, the n OHC edge-frequencies are ordered to form the other edge-frequency sequence. We also line the OHC edge-frequencies from small to big values according to i. The edge-frequency curves for the four TSP instances are illustrated in Fig. 3.

The left picture in Fig. 3 shows the edge-frequency curves for all edges and the right picture illustrates the edge-frequency curves for the OHC edges for the four instances, respectively. In the left picture, the minimum edge-frequency is near to 1 and the maximum edge-frequency is 5. The edge-frequency $\bar{f}(e_i)$ rises smoothly from the minimum edge-frequency to 5 according to $i \in \left[1, \binom{n}{2}\right]$. Although the four TSP instances have different types of edges' distances, their edge-frequency curves are similar. It indicates the frequency quadrilaterals are useful to various types of TSP instances. Moreover, the edge-frequency rises faster on both curve ends and increases slower in the middle. Thus, the edges owning the small or big edge-frequency far away from 3 occupy the small percentage whereas the edges with the edge-frequency close to 3 have the big percentage. In addition, the edge-frequency curve becomes flatter in the middle for the bigger TSP instances. For example, the edge-frequency curve of u574 is flatter than that of att532, ail535 and si535 in the middle, respectively.

In the right picture of Fig. 3, the OHC edge-frequency $\bar{f}(e_i)$ rises from one smallest value above 3.5 to 5. The OHC edge-frequencies are bigger than the expected frequency 3 even for the small TSP instances. As the edge index i rises, the OHC edge-frequency curve becomes flatter. It says most OHC edge-frequencies tend to 5. Thus, the OHC edges with the big edge-frequency close to 5 have the big probability whereas the edges having the edge-frequency far away from 5 occupy a very small percentage. One sees the edge-frequency curves for the three TSP instances ail535, att532 and u574 are nearly identical. The edge-frequency of *si*535 rises to 5 faster than that of the other three TSP instances. si535 has many equal-weight edges in K_n, which is different from ail535, att532 and u574. Given a quadrilateral $ABCD$ containing the equal-weight edges, the three distance sums $d(A,B)+d(C,D)$, $d(A,C)+d(B,D)$ and $d(A,D)+d(B,C)$ or two of them are usually equal. In this case, it is hard to choose the right optimal four-vertex paths with respect to the OHC for computing the high edge-frequencies for some OHC edges. In our algorithm to compute the edge-frequencies, we choose the optimal four-vertex paths according to the vertex lexicographic orders. For example for endpoints A, B in quadrilateral $ABCD$, if the four-vertex paths (A,C,D,B) and (A,D,C,B) have the equal distance, (A,C,D,B) is taken as an optimal four-vertex path and (A,D,B,C)

is neglected. This choice is not always right with respect to the known OHC, which may decrease the OHC edge-frequencies for some TSP instances. For si535, this choice works well to compute the high edge-frequencies for the known OHC edges. For the TSP instances without many equal-weight edges, such as ail535, att532 and u574, their edge-frequency curves are very close. For the four small TSP instances, there are a few edges with the small edge-frequency below 4. Most OHC edges have a high edge-frequency close 5. For example, the OHC edges with $\bar{f}(e_i) \geq 4.5$ occupy an absolutely big probability.

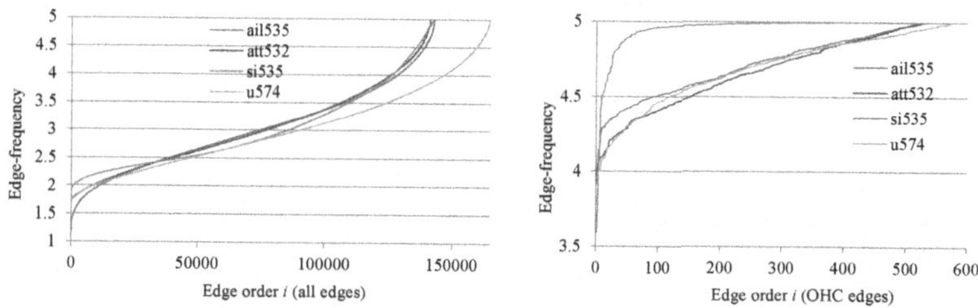

Fig. 3. The changes of edge-frequencies for four small TSP instances

4.2 Distribution of the Edge-Frequencies

According to the first experiments, we know the edge-frequencies of the OHC edges are generally bigger than those of most of the other edges. In this subsection, we will demonstrate the distribution of edge-frequencies for certain benchmark TSP instances. As we use the big frequency threshold to cut the edges with the smaller edge-frequency, one can estimate the number of eliminated edges based on the distribution. First, we compute the edge-frequencies for four medium scale of TSP instances pr2392, pcb3038, fnl4461 and rl5934 and show the distributions of their edge-frequencies. It is time-consuming to compute the edge-frequencies with all frequency quadrilaterals. To save computation time, we randomly choose 1000 frequency quadrilaterals containing each edge to compute the edge-frequency $\bar{f}(e_i)$. The statistical method is used to compute the probability of $\bar{f}(e_i)$s according to an appointed interval. Since $\bar{f}(e_i) \in [1,5]$, the whole interval $[1,5]$ is divided into 200 small intervals $[f_j, f_{j+1}]$ where $0 \leq j \leq 199$. The span of each interval is 0.02, i.e., $f_{j+1} - f_j = 0.02$. Given an edge-frequency $\bar{f}(e_i)$, it will belong to one of the 200 intervals $[f_j, f_{j+1}]$. If the number of $\bar{f}(e_i)$s in an interval $[f_j, f_{j+1}]$ is N_j, the probability of the edge-frequency $\bar{f}(e_i) \in [f_j, f_{j+1}]$ is computed as $P(\bar{f}(e_i)) = \frac{N_j}{\binom{n}{2}}$. For convenience, an edge-frequency $\bar{f}(e_i)$ is normalized to a value in [0,1] using the linear transformation $\frac{\bar{f}(e_i) - \bar{f}(e_1)}{\bar{f}\left(e_{\binom{n}{2}}\right) - \bar{f}(e_1)}$. The $P(\bar{f}(e_i))$s are lined according to the normalized frequency $\bar{f}(e_i) \in [0,1]$. One will have an overview of the distribution of the edge-frequencies. In addition, the logarithm operation is applied to the edge-frequencies $\bar{f}(e_i)$. In the same manner, the values $\log\bar{f}(e_i)$ are normalized to [0,1] and their probabilities are also computed and lined. The distributions of the normalized edge-frequency $\bar{f}(e_i)$ and logarithm edge-frequency $\log\bar{f}(e_i)$ are shown in Fig. 4. The left picture in Fig. 4 illustrates the distribution of the edge-frequency. The right picture in Fig. 4 shows the distribution of the logarithmatic value $\log\bar{f}(e_i)$. For comparisons, the Beta distribution $Beta(2.09, 2.09)$ is also illustrated. For the TSP instances without many equal-weight edges, the log-beta distributions of $\bar{f}(e_i)$s are nearly identical. After $\bar{f}(e_i)$ is changed into $\log\bar{f}(e_i)$, the distribution of the $\log\bar{f}(e_i)$ is close to the beta distribution $Beta(2.09, 2.09)$.

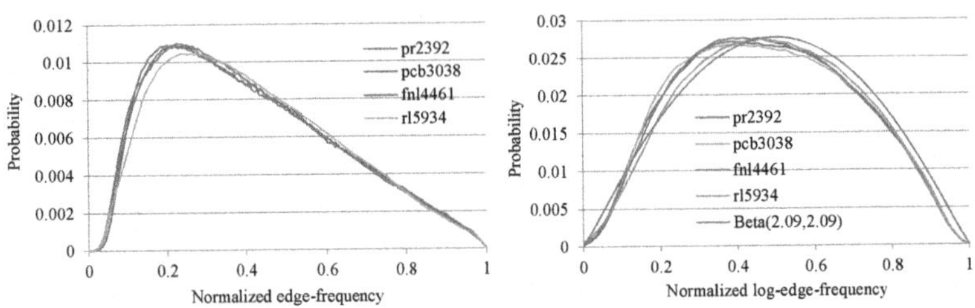

Fig. 4. The distributions of edge-frequency and logarithm edge-frequency for four medium TSP instances

In the second experiments, we shall show the distributions of edge-frequency $\bar{f}(e_i)$ for four large TSP instances brd14051, d15112, d18512 and pla33810. For each edge e_i, the 1000 random frequency quadrilaterals containing e_i are chosen to compute the $\bar{f}(e_i)$. Since the 1000 quadrilaterals for each edge are too small for the large TSP instances, $\bar{f}(e_i)$s of some edges will not accurately reflect their expected edge-frequencies. The distributions of the normalized frequency $\bar{f}(e_i)$ and $\log\bar{f}(e_i)$ for the four large TSP instances are illustrated in Fig. 5. In the left picture of Fig. 5, as $\bar{f}(e_i)$ is small, the four distribution curves are not as close as those in Fig. 4. Once $\bar{f}(e_i)$ becomes big, the four distribution curves gather together gradually. The right picture illustrate the distributions of $\log\bar{f}(e_i)$ for the four large TSP instances. Even though there are computation errors due to the equal-weight edges and the usage of the small number of random frequency quadrilaterals, these $\log\bar{f}(e_i)$s approximately conform to the beta distribution $Beta(2.09, 2.09)$.

Simultaneously, the distribution of the OHC edge-frequencies is also computed according to the designed small intervals. Since the number of the OHC edge-frequencies are much smaller than that of all edge-frequencies, we use a big value 0.1 as the frequency span, i.e., $f_{j+1} - f_j = 0.1$, for computing the probability of the OHC edge-frequencies. The distributions of the OHC edge-frequencies for the four medium TSP instances and the four large TSP instances are shown in Fig. 6, respectively. One sees the minimum edge-frequency $\bar{f}(e_i)$ of the OHC edges is generally bigger than 4 for the medium and large TSP instances. Thus,

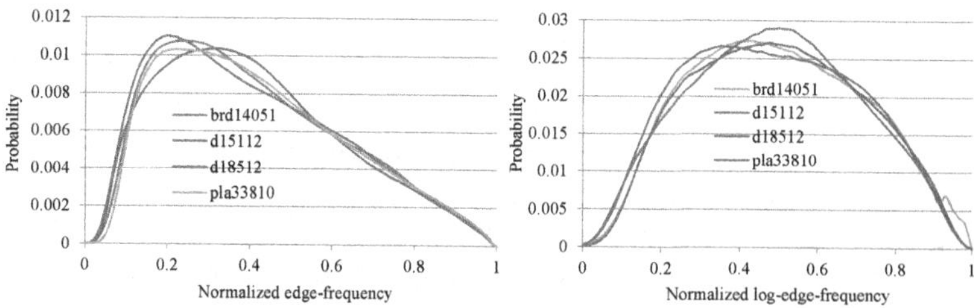

Fig. 5. The distributions of edge-frequency and logarithm edge-frequency for four large TSP instances

one can use the frequency threshold above 4 to cut the edges with the smaller edge-frequency as he or she searches an OHC. In addition, the smaller edge-frequencies have the smaller probability and the big edge-frequencies occupy the bigger percentage. It means the number of the OHC edges having the small edge-frequency is limited. Moreover, as n rises, more and more OHC edge-frequencies approach 5. Wang has proven that an OHC edge-frequency will tend to 5 as n is big enough [30]. In theory, the distribution of the OHC edge-frequencies will degenerate to an approximate Dirac delta function which has the probability 1 around 5 and zero elsewhere.

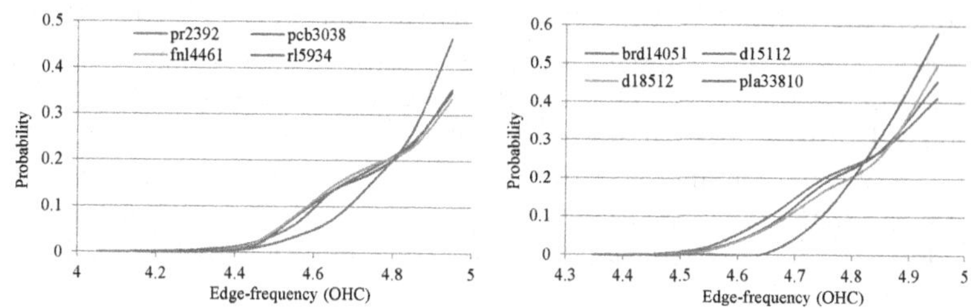

Fig. 6. The distributions of the OHC edge-frequencies for eight TSP instances

4.3 Edges Elimination According to the Edge-Frequencies

Since the OHC edge-frequencies are much bigger than most of the other edge-frequencies, we can cut the other edges according to the minimum OHC edge-frequency as we resolve TSP. After many edges are cut, the search space of the OHC will be greatly reduced. For certain small and medium TSP instances, Wang and Remmel [25] have computed the sparse graphs according to the minimum edge-frequency of the OHC edges. In this section, we show the experimental results for more TSP instances, especially for the TSP instances of large size. One will see that the big percentage of edges will be eliminated according to the minimum OHC edge-frequency. The known OHC of each TSP instance is computed with the branch-and-cut method. The TSP datum are downloaded from the websites [31] and [26]. They include National TSPs, VLSI TSPs and the other various types of TSPs in $TSPLIB$. For each TSP instance, 1000 random quadrilaterals are selected for each edge to compute its frequency. Thus, the computation time is $O(n^2)$. As the frequency of each edge is computed, the minimum edge-frequency of the known OHC edges is used to cut the edges having the smaller edge-frequency. The experimental results are illustrated in Table 1.

In the table, $\bar{f}_{min}$ is the minimum OHC edge-frequency, the number of edges with the edge-frequency above $\bar{f}_{mim}$ is noted as N, and $r = \frac{N}{\binom{n}{2}} \times 100\%$ is the percentage of the edges with the edge-frequency above $\bar{f}_{min}$. To show the change of the OHC edge-frequencies according to n, the average OHC edge-frequency is computed as $\mu = \frac{1}{n}\sum_{i=1}^{n} \bar{f}(e_i)$ and the standard deviation is computed as $\sigma = \sqrt{\frac{1}{n-1}\sum_{i=1}^{n}(\bar{f}(e_i) - \mu)^2}$. One sees the $\bar{f}_{min}$ is bigger than 4 for most of these examples, especially for TSP instances of big size. The results verify the probability model [25] and the theories [30] for the OHC edges. As the edges with the edge-frequency below $\bar{f}_{min}$ is cut, a small percentage of edges are preserved, see the percentage $r(\%)$ in Table 1. For most small and medium TSP instances, greater than 80% or 85% of edges are eliminated. For the big TSP instances, greater than 90% or 95% of edges are cut from K_n. These results approximate those computed based on the functions $\mathcal{LN}(1.07, 0.056)$ and $Log - Beta(0.5, 0.048)$. The values of $r\%$ demonstrate the edge-frequencies conform to the log-beta distribution $Log - Beta(0.5, 0.048)$. As $\bar{f}_{min}$ is close to 5, a big percentage of edges can be cut according to $\bar{f}_{min}$ and the OHC will be preserved. One can use the algorithms to find the OHC in the preserved graphs after many edges are cut. In addition, μ becomes bigger and σ becomes smaller according to n. It means more and more OHC edges will have the edge-frequency close to 5 as n rises. The experimental results illustrate the distribution of the OHC edge-frequencies will tend to some Dirac delta function as n is big enough. Thus, one can use the bigger frequency threshold to cut the edges with the small edge-frequency for the bigger size of TSP instance. It mentions that some TSP instances contain many $ABCD$s where the three distance sums $d(A, B) + d(C, D)$, $d(A, C) + d(B, D)$ and $d(A, D) + d(B, C)$ are equal or two of them are equal. In this case, the experimental results will deviate from the log-beta distribution due to the wrong selection of the optimal four-vertex paths. For example in a $ABCD$, if $d(A, B) + d(C, D) = d(A, C) + d(B, D) < d(A, D) + d(B, C)$, (A, B), (C, D), (A, C), (B, D) will have the same frequency 5 in the frequency $ABCD$ computed with our program codes. If many such $ABCD$s appear for a TSP instance, the number of edges with the big frequency will increases and $r(\%)$ will become bigger.

In 2014, Hougardy and Schroeder [23] provided the 3-step algorithm to eliminate the edges out of OHC based on $3-opt$ move. We compare our results with those after the first step of the 3-step algorithm. The comparisons of the experimental results for some TSP instances are shown in Table 2. For most TSP

instances, the 3-step algorithm computes the sparser graphs than our method. However, the percentages of the preserved edges have much difference for distinctive TSP instances. Thus, the performance of the three-stage algorithm relies on the structures of TSP instances. On the other hand, the percentages of the preserved edges for these TSP instances have small difference based upon frequencies of edges. It hints the frequency quadrilaterals have the nearly equal function for various TSP instances. Moreover, the frequency of the OHC edges increases according to n so that the percentage of the preserved edges becomes smaller and smaller. Based on the properties of the frequencies of the OHC edges, the iterative algorithm [28] was designed to eliminate more other edges out of OHC for computing the sparse graphs for TSP.

4.4 Experiments for TSP on the Preserved Graphs

According to the edge-frequencies, one can cut the big percentage of edges out of the OHC and compute a certain sparse graph for TSP. In this section, the Concorde Online is used to resolve some TSP instances on the preserved graphs. Concorde resolves an instance of TSP using the exact method of branch-and-cut. Since many edges are eliminated from K_n, the search space of the OHC will be greatly reduced. In current stage, the Concorde only resolves the TSP on K_n. To use the Concorde Online, the eliminated edges are assigned the maximum distance of edges in each K_n. In fact, the Concorde resolves a variation of the initial TSP. We shall compare the computation time with that used by Concorde for resolving the original TSP. As many eliminated edges are assigned the big weight, the distance matrix file of a large scale of TSP instance will be much bigger. The Concorde Online only accepts the TSP distance file below 16MB. Thus, certain moderate scale of TSP instances are selected for the experiments.

Seven TSP instances in $TSPLIB$ are tried. These instances are shown in Table 3. Given a TSP instance, the edge-frequency of each edge is computed with 500 randomly selected quadrilaterals. All edge-frequencies are ordered and more than 82% of the edges are cut according to their edge-frequencies. For each preserved graph, the eliminated edges are given the maximum distance in the original graph. Given each changed TSP, we did ten experiments with the Concorde Online. We also did ten experiments for the original TSP. The optimal solution and computation time of each experiment are recorded. In Table 3, N notes the number of edges in one preserved graph, OHC is the optimal solution found based on the changed and original TSP graphs, t_p and t_o are the average computation time of Concorde Online for resolving the changed and original TSP, respectively. To show the difference between t_p and t_o, the ratio $p = \frac{t_p}{t_o} \times 100\%$ is computed.

The experimental results illustrate that the preserved graphs contain the original OHC although a big percentage of edges are eliminated. It says the OHC edges generally have the bigger edge-frequencies than most of the other edges. Thus, the TSP on these preserved graphs is equal to that on K_n. The experimental results in Table 1 also demonstrate the facts for most TSP instances. Moreover, the average computation time t_p is generally smaller than t_o for all of

Table 1. Edges elimination for certain medium and large TSP instances

TSP	n	μ	σ	$\bar{f}_{min}$	$r(\%)$	TSP	n	μ	σ	$\bar{f}_{min}$	$r(\%)$
pr439	439	4.703	0.214	3.952	10.53	bgb4355	4355	4.844	0.129	4.224	7.52
d493	493	4.652	0.245	3.906	12.78	fnl4461	4461	4.806	0.142	4.322	5.587
att532	532	4.650	0.241	4.010	10.88	rl5915	5915	4.861	0.120	4.292	6.147
ali535	535	4.706	0.206	3.872	13.36	rl5934	5934	4.857	0.123	4.278	6.057
si535	535	4.951	0.142	3.617	19.69	tz6117	6117	4.847	0.133	3.988	11.9
pa561	561	4.772	0.187	3.962	12.17	xsc6880	6880	4.858	0.119	4.214	7.83
d657	657	4.730	0.211	3.928	13.42	eg7146	7146	4.829	0.129	4.008	11.71
gr666	666	4.701	0.164	4.098	8.71	pla7397	7397	4.858	0.106	4.104	10.82
lim963	963	4.770	0.182	4.068	10.51	lap7454	7454	4.854	0.120	4.28	6.037
pr1002	1002	4.759	0.185	3.910	13.99	ym7663	7663	4.844	0.116	4.084	10.19
u1060	1060	4.702	0.241	3.924	11.81	ida8197	8197	4.861	0.116	4.118	8.925
vm1084	1084	4.755	0.199	3.882	14.19	ei8246	8246	4.852	0.118	4.292	6.229
pcb1173	1173	4.756	0.183	4.020	11.12	ar9152	9152	4.879	0.124	4.244	6.697
d1291	1291	4.798	0.156	3.964	12.32	kz9976	9976	4.825	0.153	3.956	11.53
rl1304	1304	4.806	0.164	3.906	13.74	gr9882	9882	4.859	0.111	4.332	5.37
rl1323	1323	4.800	0.172	4.032	11.15	xmc10150	10150	4.870	0.108	4.292	5.792
dka1376	1376	4.791	0.164	4.10	9.885	fi10639	10639	4.849	0.120	4.238	6.721
dca1389	1389	4.756	0.198	4.01	10.41	usa13509	13509	4.837	0.124	4.320	5.216
u1432	1432	4.758	0.176	4.102	9.84	xvb13584	13584	4.881	0.100	4.392	4.897
dja1436	1436	4.718	0.231	3.692	8.29	brd14051	14051	4.851	0.112	4.444	4.045
icw1483	1483	4.763	0.192	4.02	10.29	mo14185	14185	4.833	0.142	3.968	10.62
fl1577	1577	4.831	0.132	3.760	12.37	xrb14233	14233	4.877	0.102	4.346	5.176
rbv1583	1583	4.798	0.164	3.972	12.66	ho14473	14473	4.917	0.119	4.346	5.402
rby1599	1599	4.80	0.160	3.964	12.79	d15112	15112	4.863	0.106	4.368	4.994
vm1748	1748	4.797	0.171	4.148	8.90	it16862	16862	4.848	0.121	4.310	5.355
djc1785	1785	4.799	0.162	4.058	10.63	xia16928	16928	4.810	0.165	3.944	11.09
u1817	1817	4.784	0.169	3.818	15.36	pjh17845	17845	4.875	0.113	4.268	7.421
rl1889	1889	4.820	0.162	3.898	14.04	d18512	18512	4.873	0.104	4.434	4.337
dcc1911	1911	4.787	0.171	4.032	10.52	frh19289	19289	4.897	0.0945	4.354	6.136
djb2036	2036	4.818	0.149	4.08	10.19	fnc19402	19402	4.894	0.0983	4.270	6.927
dcb2086	2086	4.816	0.152	4.046	11.25	ido21215	21215	4.901	0.0865	4.386	6.121
d2103	2103	4.819	0.043	4.442	4.35	fma21533	21533	4.871	0.106	4.338	6.045
u2152	2152	4.788	0.163	4.064	9.72	bbz25234	25234	4.899	0.0854	4.462	4.129
bva2144	2144	4.729	0.221	3.796	14.44	fyg28534	28534	4.902	0.0776	4.480	3.443
xqc2175	2175	4.804	0.159	4.174	8.041	pbh30440	30440	4.890	0.0903	4.324	5.019
bck2217	2217	4.771	0.193	4.050	9.79	xib32892	32892	4.894	0.0919	4.372	4.347
u2319	2319	4.761	0.172	4.274	6.61	fry33203	33203	4.887	0.0968	4.316	4.929
pr2392	2392	4.811	0.148	4.104	9.63	pla33810	33810	4.905	0.075	4.470	4.047
irw2802	2802	4.786	0.177	3.914	12.19	bby34656	34656	4.913	0.0793	4.476	4.307
dbj2924	2924	4.823	0.145	4.142	8.81	pba38478	38478	4.919	0.0827	4.482	6.476
pia3056	3056	4.815	0.154	4.154	8.332	ics39603	39603	4.903	0.099	4.31	5.934
pcb3038	3038	4.810	0.145	4.194	8.05	rbz43748	43748	4.914	0.0978	4.326	7.826
xqe3891	3891	4.845	0.130	4.214	7.621	dan59296	59296	4.936	0.0944	4.206	7.937

Table 2. The results computed with our method and paper [23]

TSP	n	$r(\%)$	$r(\%)$ [23]	TSP	n	$r(\%)$	$r(\%)$ [23]
pr1002	1002	13.99	8.502	rl1889	1889	14.04	11.595
u1060	1060	11.81	7.819	d2103	2103	4.35	7.550
vm1084	1084	14.19	6.978	u2152	2152	9.72	5.056
pcb1173	1173	11.12	4.733	u2319	2319	6.61	0.807
d1291	1291	12.32	14.759	pr2392	2392	9.63	4.249
rl1304	1304	13.74	14.662	pcb3038	3038	8.05	2.072
rl1323	1323	11.15	12.219	fnl4461	4461	5.587	1.292
u1432	1577	9.84	2.144	brd14051	14051	4.045	2.697
vm1748	1748	8.90	9.476	d15112	15112	4.994	1.492
u1817	1817	15.36	6.610	d18512	18512	4.337	0.846

these TSP instances. It means enlarging the distances of the edges out of OHC will accelerate the algorithms based on branch-and-bound for resolving TSP. Thus, one can use the big numbers to replace the distances of eliminated edges for reducing the computation time of algorithms for TSP.

Table 3. Comparisons of the computation time of Concorde for some changed and original TSP instances

TSP	n	OHC	N	t_p(s)	t_o(s)	$p(\%)$
pr1002	1002	259045	84891	3.3	3.8	85.94
d1291	1291	50801	142342	1136.8	1960.8	57.97
rl1304	1304	252948	146098	21.7	24.4	88.85
u1432	1432	152970	176310	8.3	15.5	53.50
fl1577	1577	22249	212351	206.7	499.1	41.42
d1655	1655	62128	228590	18.7	27.9	66.98
vm1748	1748	336556	260252	96.5	145.3	66.43

5 Conclusions

As we compute the edge-frequencies with the frequency quadrilaterals, all edge-frequencies conform to the log-beta distribution. The OHC edge-frequencies conform to the approximate Dirac delta distribution. Since the OHC edge-frequencies are much bigger than those of most of the other edges, we can use a given big frequency threshold to cut many other edges with the smaller edge-frequency. The percentage of the preserved edges can be estimated based on the log-beta distribution. The log-beta distribution of edge-frequencies gives the foundation to design the iterative algorithms for cutting edges having the small edge-frequencies. That is, the edge-cutting process can be always executed until some OHC edge-frequencies become zero or very small in a certain preserved sparse graph. As the distances of the eliminated edges are replaced with a very big number, the experiments demonstrate the computation time of the algorithms based on branch-and-bound is reduced. It indicates enlarging the distances of the edges out of OHC will accelerate the algorithms for TSP. The following two questions will be studied in the near future. First, we will design algorithms based on the sparse graphs for resolving TSP. The second question is what kind of approximation we can find according to the preserved graphs if a few OHC edges are lost.

References

1. Gutin, G., Punnen, A.P.: The Traveling Salesman Problem and Its Variations. Springer, New York (2007). https://doi.org/10.1007/b101971
2. Karp, R.M.: On the computational complexity of combinatorial problems. Networks (USA) **5**(1), 45–68 (1975)
3. Held, M., Karp, R.M.: A dynamic programming approach to sequencing problems. J. Soc. Ind. Appl. Math. **10**(1), 196–210 (1962)
4. Bellman, R.E.: Dynamic programming treatment of the travelling salesman problem. J. ACM **9**(1), 61–63 (1962)
5. Carpaneto, G., Dell'Amico, M., Toth, P.: Exact solution of large-scale, asymmetric traveling salesman problems. ACM Trans. Math. Softw. (TOMS) **21**(4), 394–409 (1995)
6. de Klerk, E., Dobre, C.: A comparison of lower bounds for the symmetric circulant traveling salesman problem. Discrete Appl. Math. **159**(6), 1815–1826 (2011)
7. Levine, M.S.: Finding the right cutting planes for the TSP. ACM J. Exp. Algorithmics (JEA) **5**, 1–16 (2000)
8. Applegate, D., et al.: Certification of an optimal TSP tour through 85900 cities. Oper. Res. Lett. **37**(1), 11–15 (2009)
9. Cook, W.: The traveling salesman problem: postcards from the edge of impossibility (Plenary talk). In: The 30th European Conference on Operational Research, Dublin, Ireland (2019)
10. Sharir, M., Welzl, E.: On the number of crossing-free matchings, cycles, and partitions. SIAM J. Comput. **36**(3), 695–720 (2006)
11. Gebauer, H.: Enumerating all Hamilton cycles and bounding the number of Hamiltonian cycles in 3-regular graphs. Electr. J. Comb. **18**(1), 1–28 (2011)
12. Björklund, A., Husfeldt, T., Kaski, P., Koivisto, M.: The traveling salesman problem in bounded degree graphs. ACM Trans. Algorithms **8**(2), 1–18 (2012)
13. Eppstein, D.: The traveling salesman problem for cubic graphs. J. Graph Algorithms Appl. **11**(1), 61–81 (2007)
14. Liśkiewicz, M., Schuster, M.R.: A new upper bound for the traveling salesman problem in cubic graphs. J. Discrete Algorithms **18**, 1–20 (2014)
15. Aggarwal, N., Garg, N., Gupta, S.: A 4/3-approximation for TSP on cubic 3-edge-connected graphs. Computing Research Repository-CORR abs/1101.5 (2011)
16. Boyd, S., Sitters, R., van der Ster, S., Stougie, L.: The traveling salesman problem on cubic and subcubic graphs. Math. Program. **144**(1–2), 227–245 (2014)

17. Correa, J.R., Larré, O., Soto, J.A.: TSP tours in cubic graphs: beyond 4/3. SIAM J. Discrete Math. **29**(2), 915–939 (2015)
18. Borradaile, G., Demaine, E.D., Tazari, S.: Polynomial-time approximation schemes for subset-connectivity problems in bounded-genus graphs. Algorithmica **68**(2), 287–311 (2014)
19. Gharan, S.O., Saberi, A.: The asymmetric traveling salesman problem on graphs with bounded genus. In: SODA 2011, pp. 967–975. ACM, New York (2011)
20. Svensson, O., Tarnawski, J., Végh, L.A.: Constant factor approximation for ATSP with two edge weights. Math. Program. Ser. B **168**, 1–27 (2017)
21. Svensson, O., Tarnawski, J., Végh, L.A.: A constant-factor approximation algorithm for the asymmetric traveling salesman problem, pp. 1–64. https://arxiv.org/pdf/1708.04215.pdf (2019)
22. Taillard, É.D., Helsgaun, K.: POPMUSIC for the traveling salesman problem. Eur. J. Oper. Res. **272**(2), 420–429 (2019)
23. Hougardy, S., Schroeder, R.T.: Edge elimination in TSP instances. In: Kratsch, D., Todinca, I. (eds.) WG 2014. LNCS, vol. 8747, pp. 275–286. Springer, Cham (2014). https://doi.org/10.1007/978-3-319-12340-0_23
24. Wang, Y.: An approximate method to compute a sparse graph for traveling salesman problem. Expert Syst. Appl. **42**(12), 5150–5162 (2015)
25. Wang, Y., Remmel, J.B.: A binomial distribution model for the traveling salesman problem based on frequency quadrilaterals. J. Graph Algorithms Appl. **20**(2), 411–434 (2016)
26. Reinelt, G.: http://comopt.ifi.uni-heidelberg.de/software/TSPLIB95/. Accessed 12 Aug 2019
27. Wang, Y.: An improved method to compute sparse graphs for traveling salesman problem. Int. J. Ind. Manuf. Eng. **12**(3), 92–100 (2018)
28. Wang, Y., Remmel, J.: A method to compute the sparse graphs for traveling salesman problem based on frequency quadrilaterals. In: Chen, J., Lu, P. (eds.) FAW 2018. LNCS, vol. 10823, pp. 286–299. Springer, Cham (2018). https://doi.org/10.1007/978-3-319-78455-7_22
29. Wang, Y., Remmel, J.B.: An iterative algorithm to eliminate edges for traveling salesman problem based on a new binomial distribution. Appl. Intell. **48**(11), 4470–4484 (2018). https://doi.org/10.1007/s10489-018-1222-2
30. Wang, Y.: The sufficient and necessary conditions for an edge e in the optimal Hamiltonian cycle based on frequency quadrilaterals. J. Optim. Theory Appl. **181**(2), 671–683 (2019)
31. Mittelmann, H.: NEOS Server for Concorde. http://neos-server.org/neos/solvers/co:concorde/TSP.html. Accessed 26 Oct 2020

Evaluating Performance, Power and Energy of Deep Neural Networks on CPUs and GPUs

Yuyang Sun, Zhixin Ou, Juan Chen(✉), Xinxin Qi, Yifei Guo, Shunzhe Cai, and Xiaoming Yan

College of Computer, National University of Defense Technology, Changsha, China
{sunyuyang,ouzhixin16,juanchen,qixinxin19,guoyifei18,caishunzhe, yanxiaomingnudt}@nudt.edu.cn

Abstract. Deep learning has achieved accuracy and fast training speed and has been successfully applied to many fields, including speech recognition, text processing, image processing and video processing. However, the cost of high power and energy comes together with the high accuracy and training speed of Deep Neural Network (DNN). This inspires researchers to perform characterization in terms of performance, power and energy for guiding the architecture design of DNN models. There are three critical issues to solve for designing a both accurate and energy-efficient DNN model: i) how the software parameters affect the DNN models; ii) how the hardware parameters affect the DNN models; and iii) how to choose the best energy-efficient DNN model. To answer the three issues above, we capture and analyze the performance, power and energy behaviors for multiple experiment settings. We evaluate four DNN models (i.e., LeNet, GoogLeNet, AlexNet, and CaffeNet) with various parameter settings (both hardware and software) on both CPU and GPU platforms. Evaluation results provide detailed DNN characterization and some key insights to facilitate the design of energy-efficient deep learning solutions.

Keywords: Convolutional neural network · Deep learning · Performance characterization · Power characterization · Energy characterization

1 Introduction

Recent years, deep learning develops rapidly and has been widely used. A variety of Deep Neural Network (DNN) models, including Convolutional Neural Networks (CNNs) and Recurrent Neural Networks (RNNs) have been developed. Specifically, LeNet [17], one of the earliest CNNs, promotes the development of the field of deep learning. AlexNet [16] and GoogLeNet [25] are the champion

Y. Sun and Z. Ou contributed equally to this work and should be considered as co-first authors.

Z. Cai et al. (Eds.): NCTCS 2021, CCIS 1494, pp. 196–221, 2021.
https://doi.org/10.1007/978-981-16-7443-3_12

models of ILSVRC (ImageNet Large-Scale Visual Recognition Challenge) [3] over the past years, and proved to be successful models. These DNN models are successfully used in plenty of fields, such as text processing, speech recognition, image, video processing [18], etc.

Hardware and software development breaks through a main bottleneck of DNN model, the large amount of training calculations. High-performance processors and more sophisticated neural network architecture brings higher accuracy and faster training speed to DNN models. GPUs and CPUs with higher throughput and stronger computing power are constantly introduced in order to improve training speed. There is a constant release of new software frameworks such as the cuDNN primitives, which run on NVIDIA Graphics Processing Units (GPUs), and the Intel Deep Learning Framework (IDLF) from Intel that runs on CPUs to accelerate the training of complex DNNs. In addition, the accuracy of DNN models has been increased thanks to the unremitting efforts of researchers. The accuracy of the champion model in the 2015 ILSVRC (ImageNet Large-Scale Visual Recognition Challenge) has surpassed human recognition ability (by about 5% [3]).

However, the power and energy cost becomes higher together with higher accuracy and training speed, which may result in system instability and extra cooling costs. Despite the high energy of DNN training, researchers are faced with the challenge of designing accurate and energy-efficient neural network architecture. This is not possible without a comprehensive analysis of DNN performance, power and energy. The following issues must be solved in order to design a DNN model that is both accurate and energy-efficient.

- How software parameters affect the performance, power and energy behavior in DNN training? For instance, what is the power and performance trends for different acceleration libraries and deep learning framework? How the super-parameter settings affect the performance, power and energy behavior?
- How hardware parameters affect the performance, power and energy behavior in DNN training, such as what is the impact of the number of cores of a CPU on the performance and power of DNN training? And what is the impact of the CPU frequency on DNN training? How CPU and GPU affect the performance, power and energy behavior of DNN training?
- What is the difference in performance and power behaviors when applying different DNN models?

There are several studies focusing on performance characterization on GPUs [19,22]. However, little exists in the literature that deals with power and performance characterization simultaneously of both CPU-based and GPU-based DNN training.

To answer the above issues, we conduct a systematic and in-depth characterization of DNN training in terms of power, performance and energy. To evaluate the impact of software configurations on DNN training, we alternate different super-parameters, optimization libraries and training framework to find out the most energy-efficient configurations. Additionally, we apply five DNN models (i.e., LeNet, GoogLeNet, AlexNet, CaffeNet, and AlexNet-MNIST) on both CPU and GPU platforms to capture and analyze the performance, power and energy behaviors in model training, digging out the difference of CPU-based training from GPU-based training. Finally, we evaluate different DNN models and offer a comparative analysis. We make the following key contributions:

1. We provide a thorough and systematic characterization of performance, power and energy behaviors during DNN training period on the target CPU based and CPU-GPU based platform, including Intel Xeon X5-2650 v3 and Nvidia Tesla K80.
2. We offer recommendations on hardware and software parameter settings, as well as different DNN frameworks. We also offer suggestions on what optimization policies to adopt for better performance and energy efficiency.
3. We give some key insights about energy efficiency gained from evaluation of DNN models executed in both CPUs and GPUs. Software parameters contributes to energy efficiency in application layer, while hardware parameters affect energy efficiency in architecture layer.

The rest of the paper is organized as follows. Section 2 introduces the background of DNN and related studies. Section 3 introduces the platforms, benchmarks, data sets involved in the experiments, as well as the CNN models and training framework. Section 4 characterizes the performance, power and energy behaviors of CPU-based and GPU-based DNN training. Section 5 discusses and summarizes the key insights proposed in evaluation. Section 6 details related works. Section 7 concludes this paper.

2 Background

2.1 Deep Neural Network

Deep learning is an important branch in the field of machine learning research. Due to its effectiveness in many applications, deep learning has been widely used in academia and industry. Convolutional Neural Networks (CNNs) and Recurrent Neural Networks (RNNs) are two of the most successful deep neural network models and have been applied in various fields such as computer vision and speech recognition [18].

Convolutional Neural Network (CNN): CNNs better simulate the way the human brain processes and recognizes images, and they are actually multi-layer perceptrons. A multi-layer perceptron is a multi-layer neural network, which consists of an input layer, an output layer and multiple hidden layers in between. Each hidden layer represents a function between its input and output, and the function is defined by the parameters of the layer. The hidden layer of a CNN is mainly composed of a convolutional layer, a pooling layer and a fully connected layer. Each layer contains thousands to millions of neurons. A single neuron receives input, calculates their weighted sum, and sends the output to the neuron in the next layer. In this way, different layers apply different operations to inputs and produce outputs for the layers below.

Table 1. Specifications of hardware platform

Name	CPU	GPU
Processor	Intel® Xeon X5-2650 v3	Nvidia Tesla k80
# cores/node	20	4992
Frequency	2.3 GHz	2.5 GHz
Memory size	64 GB	11 GB (global memory)
LLC size	25 MB	–

Recurrent Neural Network (RNN): RNNs are artificial neural networks that process sequence or time-series data, which are commonly used to solve sequential or temporal problems, as in language translation [24], natural language processing (NLP), speech recognition, and image captioning. Like feed-forward and CNNs, RNNs also learn from training data. It takes information from past inputs and outputs to generate current inputs and outputs. The output of RNN depends on the elements that came before it, contrary to the traditional DNN, where the input and output are independent.

2.2 Performance/Power Characterization of Neural Network

There exist some studies devoted to performing performance and power characterization of different CNN models on CPU and GPU. For example, Li et al. [19] evaluated CNN models on different processor architectures, such as Intel Xeon CPU, Nvidia Kepler and Maxwell GPU. Rodrigues et al. [22] proposed a evaluation framework, using ARMs streamlined performance analyzer combined with standard deep learning frameworks such as Caffe and cuDNNv5, to measure the energy and performance of deep neural networks. However, little exists in the literature that deals with power and performance characterization simultaneously of both CPU-based and GPU-based DNN training.

3 Experiment Setup

In this section, we describe the hardware, software and evaluation metrics used in the experiments. It also mentions the kinds of experiments that are needed to characterize DNN models as far as performance, power and energy.

3.1 Hardware

The experimental platform includes both CPU and GPU, which supports CPU-based DNN training and GPU-based DNN training. Table 1 gives the configuration. CPU supports frequency scaling and three processor frequency levels (maximum, medium, minimum) are set for the experimental platform. Three frequency levels are Max_{freq} = 3.8 GHz, Mid_{freq} = 3.4 GHz, and Min_{freq} = 2.8 GHz (turbo-off) respectively.

3.2 Software

System Software: We use the same system software to compile applications. The operating system is Centos 7. The driver, library and framework used in the experiment are CUDA10.2 and CUDNNv7.6.5 respectively.

DNN Models: We use the open source benchmark test set, Convnet [1], including most publicly accessible CNN models. We select four ImageNet champion neural network models: AlexNetv2, OverFeat, VGG_A and GoogleNet. Then we use Text Classification with CNN and RNN [11] from github to compare the difference of performance, power and energy between RNN and CNN.

Benchmark: We use two classic benchmark suites: one is the CUDA version of linpack provided by NVIDIA, and the other is a program that uses CNN and RNN for text classification, to compare the DNN models in terms of performance, power and energy.

Data Set: For GPU training in text classification, we use the THUC (THU Chinese Text Classification) [20] data set, which is a Chinese text classification toolkit launched by the Natural Language Processing Laboratory of Tsinghua University, which can automatically and efficiently implement user-defined text classification corpus training, evaluation, and classification functions. THUCTC has good universality for long texts in the open field, does not depend on the performance of any Chinese word segmentation tools, and has the advantages of high accuracy and fast testing speed.

Measurement: The Intel's Running Average Power Limiting (RAPL) [15] is used to record the CPU power usage at 1000 ms interval. The power of GPU is obtained through Nvidia System Management Interface (Nvidia smi) [4].

3.3 Metrics

We use running time (s), Power (W) and Energy (KJ) to evaluate performance, power and energy relatively. Also, we use Energy-Delay Product (EDP) to evaluate energy efficiency of GPUs, because When considering both high performance and low power, EDP is a commonly used indicator. EDP calculates the product of energy and time spent to complete a computational task. Besides the metric used in this paper, there are other metrics to evaluate energy efficiency. The Green500 list [10] uses GFlops/W to evaluate the computing power per watt.

3.4 Types of Experiments

We perform three types of comparative experiments to examine how software parameters, hardware parameters and different DNN frameworks correlate with

DNN training. Additionally, we conduct a set of comparative experiments to evaluate the difference of CNN and RNN training in terms of performance, power and energy.

1. Software:
   - Using the acceleration libraries or not (see Sect. 4.1).
   - Different deep learning frameworks (see Sect. 4.1).
   - Different superparameters (see Sect. 4.1).
2. Hardware: Different frequency levels (see Sect. 4.2).
3. Different DNN frameworks: RNN and CNN (see Sect. 4.3).

4 Experimental Results and Analysis

4.1 Comparison of Different Software Parameters

With or Without GPU Acceleration Library: This section compares the differences in terms of performance, power and energy in DNN training with-/without cuDNN acceleration library. The cuDNN library realizes the acceleration of some specific operations. DNN training without the cuDNN library means using the original implementation version of the framework on the GPU.

Figure 1 gives the comparisons of performance, power and energy of the two versions. In Fig. 1, CNoff means not using the cuDNN library, and CNon means using the cuDNN library. LT, GN, AX, CFT, AX-MNIST represent five different CNN models, namely LeNet, GoogleNet, AlexNet, CaffeNet, and AlexNet-MNIST, respectively. These five CNN models all contain 10,000 forward and backward propagation iterations, and *batch_size* is set as 128.

From Fig. 1, it can be seen that using the cuDNN library, compared with not using the cuDNN library, has an average performance increase of 3.72%, an average increase in GPU power by 0.56% and an average reduction in energy by 3.91%. The following analyzes the reasons for using the cuDNN library to cause higher GPU power and lower energy. In the version that uses the cuDNN library, GPU utilization and computing efficiency are greatly improved, which accelerates some operations in neural networks, and increases GPU power. The performance benefit brought by GPU acceleration is greater than the disadvantage brought about by the increase in power, so the whole energy is reduced. Note that the cuDNN library is used by default in all subsequent experiments. In addition to GPU power, the proportion of CPU power cannot be ignored. In most cases, GPU power is between 60 W and 70 W, while CPU power is between 5 W and 7 W, and CPU power accounts for about 10% of total power. This inspired us to study how to make the CNN framework more reasonable use of CPU and GPU in the training phase.

Different CPU Acceleration Libraries: This section discusses CPU performance, power and energy of the AlexNet model running on the Caffe framework with: 1) different CPU configurations (OpenBLAS, MKL and OpenMP), and 2)

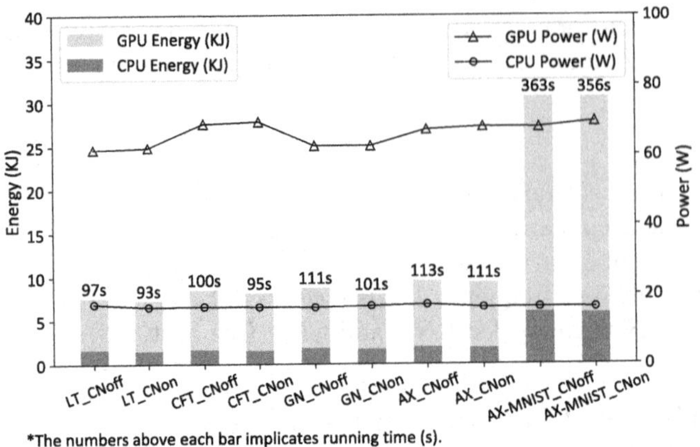

Fig. 1. Comparison in performance, power and energy of five DNN models with and without cuDNN library. (*CNoff means not using the cuDNN library, and CNon means using the cuDNN library).

different amount of processor cores. When merely using the CPU for computing, the GPU is in idle state and its energy is negligible. Therefore, mainly consider the performance, power and energy characteristics of the CPU and DRAM.

Figure 2 mainly compares the power and energy of CPU processor and DRAM. Figure 2 shows that when using different CPU acceleration libraries, the average CPU power varies from 20.08 W to 22.03 W, and the average DRAM power varies from 15.23 W to 16.28 W. The average CPU energy ranges from 6.43 KJ to 10.62 KJ, and the average DRAM energy ranges from 4.69 KJ to 7.92 KJ. Compared with the average CPU power (21.36 W) for all CPU acceleration libraries, the average power consumed by DRAM is relatively small (15.7 W), but it cannot be ignored.

In the case of using the same number of processor cores, the MKL library has the best performance and the lowest power among three CPU acceleration libraries. When we use one core, the performance of MKL is 40.5% higher than that of OpenMP, the energy is 38.7% lower. Compared with using one core, using four cores improves the performance and energy of MKL by 7.2% and 5.3%, relatively.

To conclude, more processor cores for CNN model may not improve performance and reduce energy, because there exists a trade-off between higher computing ability and higher communication overhead [7]. The communication overhead may be higher than the benefits brought by multi-core computing power. For example, when using OpenMP library acceleration, the performance and energy of using all four processor cores are not as good as using fewer cores. When using the MKL library, although one processor core is the slowest when performing calculations, it has the lowest energy.

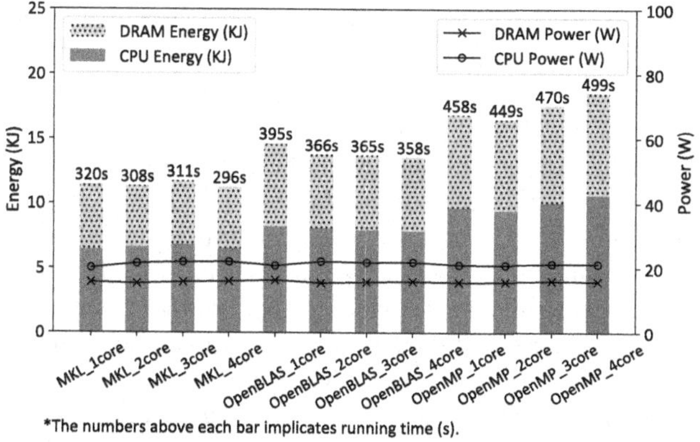

Fig. 2. The power and performance comparison under different frameworks, when merely using CPU to run AlexNet. (*Contents in X-axis represent the settings: MKL, OpenMP, OpenBLAS represents the chosen CPU acceleration library, and the following x core (x = 1, 2, 3, 4) is the number of processor cores under chosen acceleration library).

Different DNN Framework: We apply five popular deep learning frameworks (Caffe [14], Torch [9], TensorFlow [5], MXNet [8] and CXXNet [2]), and compare performance, power and energy characteristics among them. The default *batch_size* is 128.

Figure 3 gives the comparisons of DNN training with different deep learning frameworks. As shown in Fig. 3, the deep learning framework with the best performance and the least energy is CXXNet. In comparison, Torch and TensorFlow have poor performance and high average power.

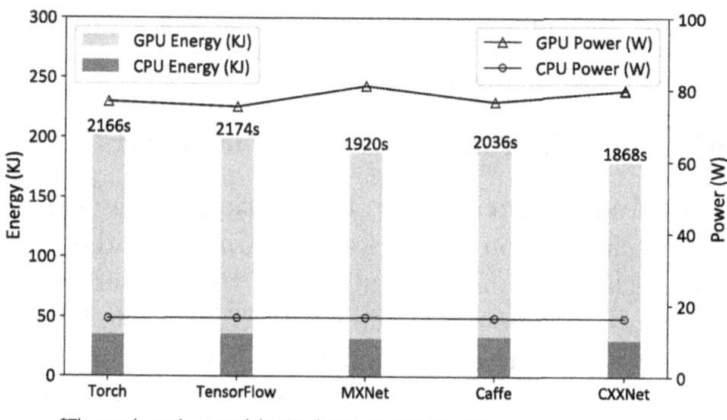

Fig. 3. Compare the power and performance of AlexNet under different frameworks on GPU.

Different *batch_size*: As an important parameter for training CNNs, *batch_size* not only affects the training speed and accuracy of model in GPU as is generally believed, but also influences the performance, power and energy of CPU.

We compared the power and energy changes of AlexNet on GPU and CPU when *batch_size* increased from 8 to 256. As shown in Fig. 4, with the increase of batch_size, the power of CPU and GPU is basically unchanged, while the average energy required to train each image is reduced (from 1.11 J to 0.24 J).

The size of *batch_size* affects the average energy of training each CNN image. When the *batch_size* is larger, it means that more images are packed into a batch and sent to the network for training in one iteration. Normally, we think that larger *batch_size* allows higher data-level parallelism and can reduce energy. However, a larger *batch_size* requires more memory to store data, which may exhaust the limited GPU memory, when the *batch_size* increases to a certain extent, the reduction in energy is not obvious.

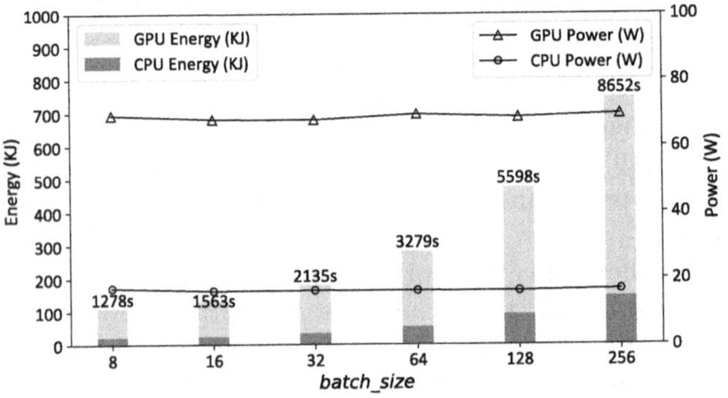

Fig. 4. AlexNet power and performance comparison under different *batch_size*.

4.2 Comparison of Different Hardware Parameters

Enable Overclocking or Turbo-Off: This section discusses the effect of turning on/off CPU overclocking on the performance, power and energy of the CNN model. CPU overclocking technology can change the frequency of the CPU and affect the performance and power of the CPU [27,28]. The CPU of our experimental platform turns on the overclocking at 3.8 GHz by default, and all the previous experimental results adopt this default setting. In addition, we set up three overclocking situations to compare the effects of turning on/off overclocking on the results, including 3.8 GHz overclocking (maximum overclocking set as 3.8 GHz), 3.4 GHz overclocking (maximum overclocking set as 3.4 GHz) and turbo-off (frequency set without overclocking as 2.8 GHz). The following

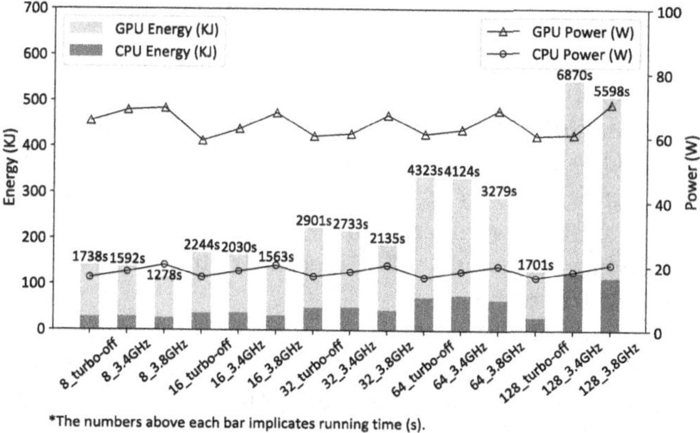

Fig. 5. Comparison of running CNN with GPU acceleration under three overclocking settings.

compares the differences in CNN model performance, power and energy in these two cases.

1. *Comparison of turning on/off overclocking on the CPU-GPU platform.* Figure 5 shows the comparison of CNN performance, power and energy under three different overclocking settings. We firstly analyze the effect of overclocking when *batch_size* is fixed at 128 (see in the last three bars in Fig. 5), the difference in overclocking settings influences the performance, power and energy greatly. On the basis of not using overclocking (using the normal frequency of 2.8 GHz), overclocking will shorten the execution time, increase the power of the CPU and GPU, reduce the energy of the GPU, and increase the energy of the CPU. Specifically, under 3.4 GHz overclocking and 3.8 GHz overclocking settings, performance increases by 3.3% and 21.2%, GPU power increases by 1.6% and 20.1%, and CPU power increases by 22.0% and 68.0% respectively, GPU energy was reduced by 1.7% and 5.3%, and CPU energy was increased by 17.9% and 32.3%.

   Figure 5 also gives a comparison of overclocking when *batch_size* is other groups of values. The result shows a similar phenomenon - if overclocking is not used as a benchmark, overclocking will shorten the execution time, while CPU and GPU power increase, GPU energy decreases and CPU energy increases. The following analyzes the reasons for the performance improvement and GPU energy reduction caused by overclocking. A higher overclocking limit is conducive to the improvement of CPU utilization and computing efficiency, thereby improving performance and GPU power. At the same time, the performance gains brought by GPU acceleration are greater than the disadvantages caused by increased power, and energy is the product of power and time, so GPU energy has been reduced.

2. *Comparison of enabling/disabling CPU overclocking on the CPU platform.* Figure 6 shows the comparison of CNN performance, power and energy under three different overclocking settings. Take the MKL library as an example. If we take no overclocking (frequency set as 2.8 GHz) as a benchmark, when setting the 3.4 GHz and 3.8 GHz overclocking upper limits, the performance increases by 13.8% and 15.7%, respectively; the DRAM power increases by 2.8% and 3.9%, CPU power increased by 8.9% and 16.9%, respectively; CPU energy increased by 6.1% and 1.4% respectively, and DRAM energy increased by 11.3% and 12.4%, respectively.
In addition to using the MKL library, we also compared the results of three different overclocking settings when using other CPU acceleration libraries, and the results are mostly similar to using the MKL library. We use performance, power and energy without overclocking (using the 2.8 GHz normal frequency) as benchmark values. Each CPU acceleration library will improve performance after overclocking. Both DRAM and CPU power will increase, CPU energy will increase while DRAM energy will decrease (this is different from the MKL library).

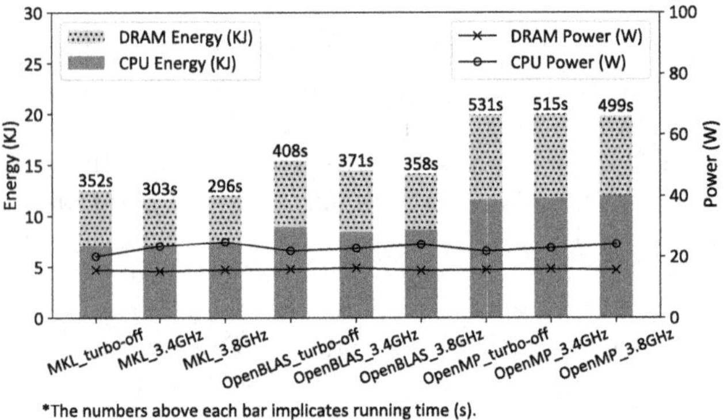

Fig. 6. Comparison of running CNN with CPU under different overclocking settings. The number above each bar indicates running time.

Additionally, we discuss the impact of turning on/off overclocking on different deep learning frameworks. We use the AlexNet neural network, *batch_size* is set to 128, GPU acceleration is used, and the same three different overclocking limit settings are used to compare different frameworks.

Figure 7 shows the comparison results of performance and energy under different overclocking settings. As shown in Fig. 7, energy varies with CPU frequency under different frameworks, and the increase in frequency does not always lead to an increase in energy. Under the framework of Caffe and CXXNet, energy increases first and then decreases with the increase of frequency, while under the framework of Torch, TensorFlow, and MXNet, energy will increase with the increase of frequency.

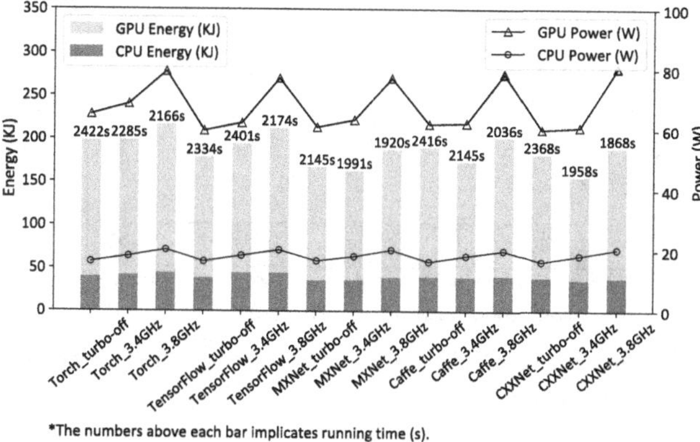

Fig. 7. Use GPU to accelerate the power and performance of different frameworks with overclocking turned on.

4.3 Comparison of Two Code Implementations: RNN and CNN

Overall Comparison of RNN and CNN: Firstly, we discuss the performance and power difference for two neural networks implementations (CNN and RNN). We use an efficient Chinese text classification toolkit [11], which contains both RNN and CNN implementation, to measure performance and power of two code implementations. Due to the number of iterations for RNN implementation is much less than that for CNN implementation, the execution time of RNN implementation is much less than that of CNN implementation. But the average total power values of RNN and CNN have very little difference, 87.6 W (RNN) and 85.5 W (CNN). The average power comparison results for different *batch_size* are almost the same.

Furthermore, we compare the results of the two implementations by testing five different values of *batch_size*, including 8, 16, 32, 64 and 128. For the same *batch_size*, the average power values are almost the same (broken lines in Fig. 8), but the execution time (numbers above each bar in Fig. 8) and energy (the bar in Fig. 8) are quite different. Figure 8(a) shows the execution time, power, and energy of RNN, and Fig. 8(b) shows the same result of CNN.

Because the CNN energy is much higher than the RNN energy, we define *Energy Gap* as the energy efficiency evaluation metric. *Energy Gap* calculates how many times the RNN energy is the CNN energy (see the height of the bar in Fig. 8(c)). Numbers above each bar indicate how many times the RNN running time is the CNN execution time. As *batch_size* increases, the *Energy Gap* and the *running time gap* (evaluate performance similar to energy efficiency) between RNN and CNN grow larger.

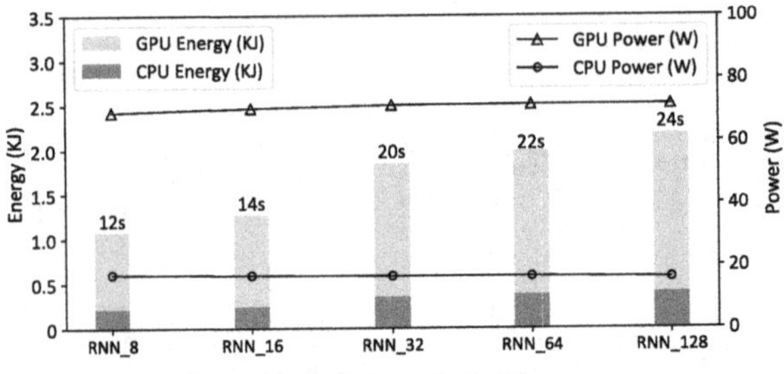

(a) Comparison of execution time, power and energy for RNN with five *batch_size*

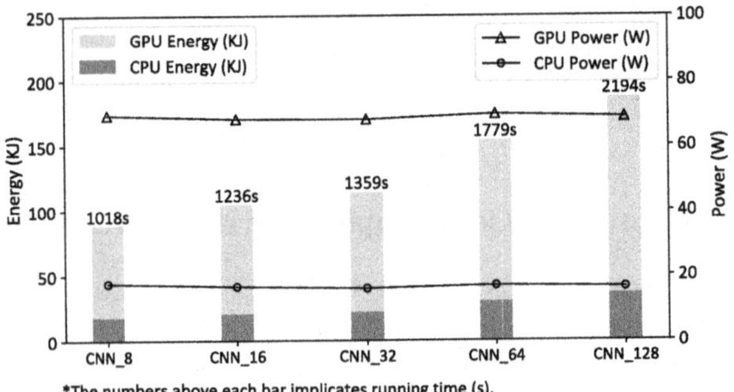

(b) Comparison of execution time, power and energy for CNN with five *batch_size*.

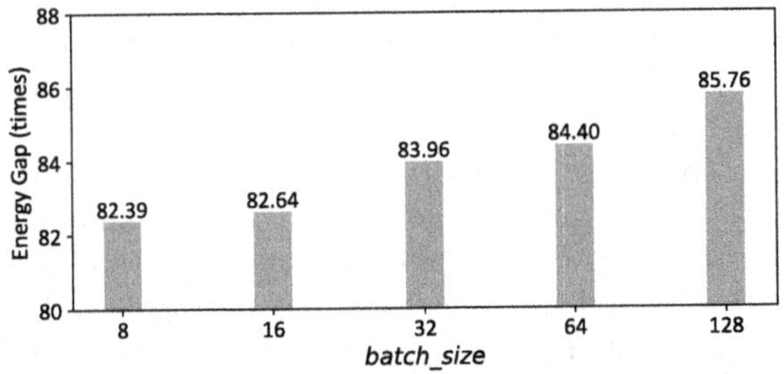

(c) Comparison of RNN and CNN under different *batch_size*. The Energy Gap is calculated by how many times the CNN energy is the RNN energy.

Fig. 8. Comparison of two code implementation: RNN and CNN.

RNN Code Implementation Analysis: The code implementation of the RNN model can be divided into two stages: the first stage is preprocessing, which converts the original data set into acceptable input for the RNN model; the second stage is model training, which uses input data to train the weight of the neural network. These two types of code implementation have separate behaviors, leading to power diversity in running programs. The Pseudo-code 1 shows RNN code implementation.

Pseudo-code 1. RNN code implementation

Input: original text files
Output: RNN model

```
 1: preprocessing
 2: while epoch < num_epoch do
 3:     some RNN layers
 4:     full connection layer
 5:     dropout layer
 6:     relu layer
 7:     calculate accuracy and loss
 8:     if (accuracy − last_accuracy) < threshold then
 9:         earlystopping
10:     end if
11:     epoch ← epoch + 1
12: end while
```

Figure 9 presents the power of CPU and GPU during RNN model establishment. A significant turning point appears around the 20 s, after which the main component of power changes from CPU power to GPU power. Combined with the code implementation to analyze the behaviors of these two stages, line 1 in Pseudo-code 1 is the preprocessing stage, corresponding to the first 20 s in Fig. 9. Preprocessing is executed in CPU, so CPU is relatively active and consumes much power (around 18.5W) in this period while GPU consumes limited power(around 40W). From the 20th second, preprocessing is finished and model training (line 2–12 in Pseudo-code 1) starts. We use TensorFlow as the deep learning framework in this stage. GPU undertakes most of the work of model training, while CPU is not involved in much. When performing iterative operations, GPU power is as high as about $90W$, and it continues until the end of the program.

To further explain the difference of GPU power in the two stages, we draw Fig. 10 to show the utilization rate of GPU in different stages. Utilization rate of GPU and GPU power are roughly matched. The higher the utilization rate of GPU, the higher the corresponding GPU power, as shown in Fig. 10.

CNN Code Implementation Analysis: Similar to RNN, the CNN code implementation is also divided into two parts: preprocessing and model training (see in Pseudo-code 2).

Since the overall behavior of RNN and CNN are similar, the power curves obtained during the operation of the two are also very similar (see in Fig. 11). Both of RNN and CNN are composed of two parts: data preprocessing and training. There are two reasons for the difference that the training time required for

Pseudo-code 2. CNN code implementation

```
Input: original text files
Output: RNN model
preprocessing
while epoch < num_epoch do
    CNN layer
    global max pooling layer
    full connection layer
    dropout layer
    relu layer
    calculate accuracy and loss
    if (accuracy − last_accuracy) < threshold then
        earlystopping
    end if
    epoch ← epoch + 1
end while
```

CNN is longer than RNN. On the one hand, historical information is considered in the RNN model, so RNN is more suitable for text processing tasks that are obviously related to the text before and after. On the other hand, analyzing from the model itself, the calculation of the convolutional layer is more complicated, so the amount of calculation per second during CNN training is greater, and the average power per second during CNN training is higher.

Figure 12 shows the utilization rate of GPU in different stages of CNN model. The trend of GPU utilization is similar to the trend of GPU power. In preprocessing stage, the utilization of GPU is nearly 0, while in the model training stage, the number is as high as 100%.

5 Discussion for Three Key Questions

This section discusses the following three questions:

- **Q1:** How software parameters affect the performance, power and energy behavior in DNN training?
- **Q2:** How hardware parameters affect the performance, power and energy behavior in DNN training?
- **Q3:** What is the difference in performance and power behaviors when applying different DNN frameworks?

5.1 Analysis of Influential Factors on Energy Efficiency

To quantify the impact of different parameters (including both hardware and software parameters) on energy efficiency, we calculate the EDP under different parameter settings listed in Table 2.

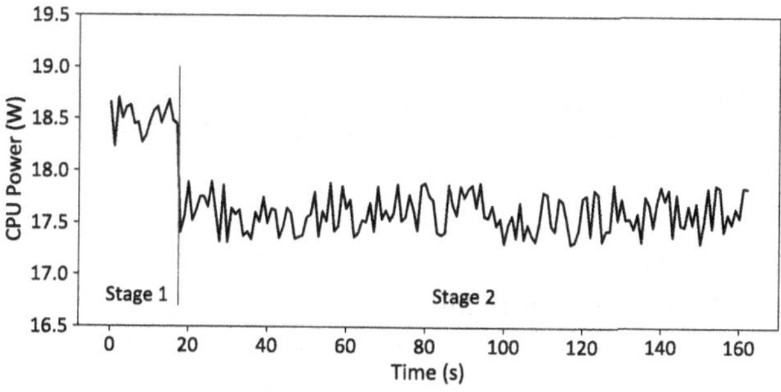

(a) Realtime CPU power for preprocessing and training RNN model.

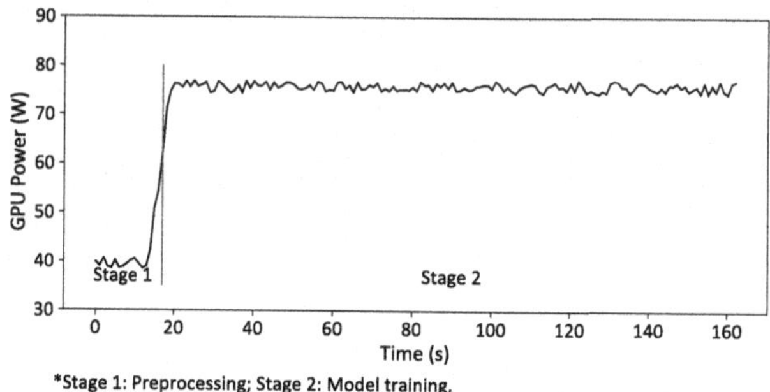

(b) Realtime GPU power for preprocessing and training RNN model.

Fig. 9. Realtime power of CPU and GPU for preprocessing and training RNN model.

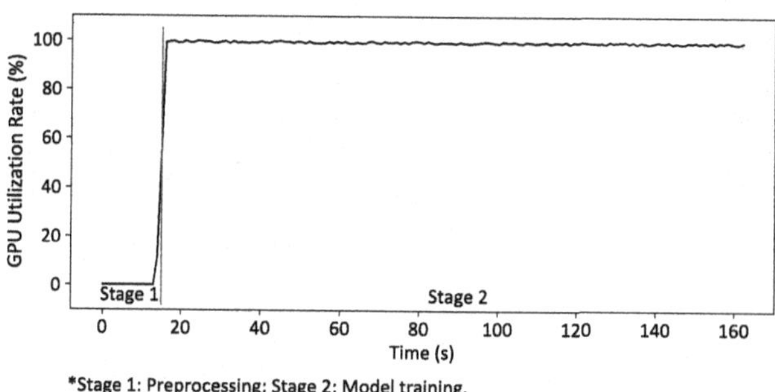

Fig. 10. GPU utilization rate for preprocessing and training RNN model.

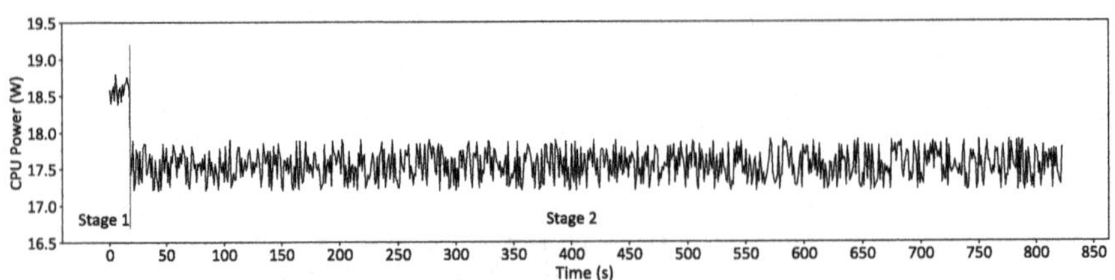

(a) Realtime CPU power for preprocessing and training CNN model.

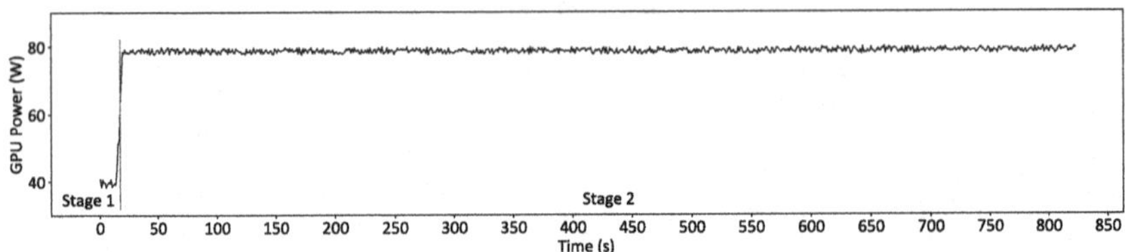

(b) Realtime GPU power for preprocessing and training CNN model.

Fig. 11. Realtime power of CPU and GPU for preprocessing and training CNN model.

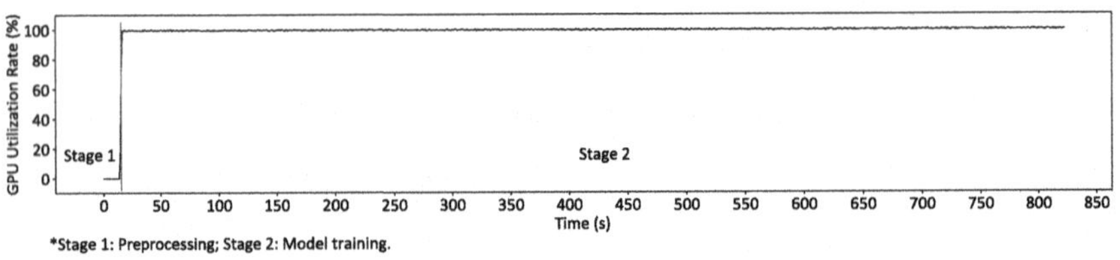

Fig. 12. GPU utilization rate for preprocessing and training CNN model.

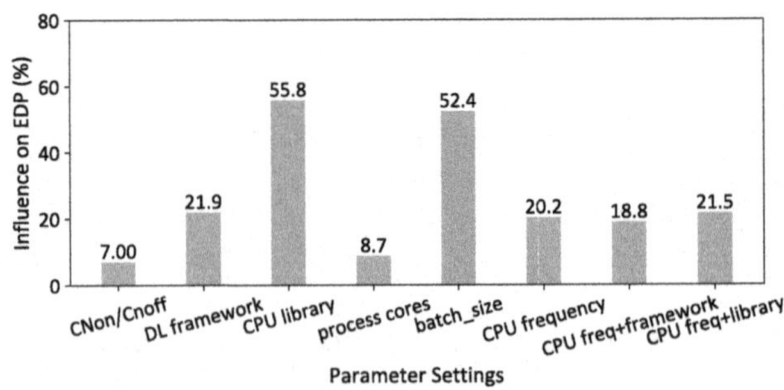

Fig. 13. The influential degree on energy efficiency (EDP) of different parameter settings.

Table 2. Consideration of different parameters

Software parameters	cuDNN library	CNon/CNoff
	Deep learning framework	Caffe/Torch/TensorFlow/ MXNet/CXXNet
	CPU acceleration library	MKL/OpenMP/OpenBLAS
		Processor cores: 1/2/3/4
	batch_size	8/16/32/64/128
Hardware parameters	Overclocking	2.8 GHz (turbo-off)/3.4 GHz/3.8 GHz
		CPU/CPU-GPU platform
		CPU acceleration libraries
DNN framework	CNN/RNN	

The Impact of Software Parameters (Q1): As shown in Fig. 13, the importance order of software parameters are: CPU acceleration library > Batch size > DL framework > cuDNN library. Obviously, the selection of CPU acceleration libraries has the most significant impact on energy efficiency among all software parameter settings (see Fig. 13). There is a huge difference in the energy efficiency when choosing different CPU acceleration libraries. For example, compared with TensorFlow, the EDP of MKL is 55.8% lower, which means MKL has a much higher energy efficiency than TensorFlow. Besides, a proper number of cores also helps to increase energy efficiency. Using 4 cores brings an extra 8.7% increase for MKL than using 3 cores in energy efficiency. Additionally, different deep learning frameworks also have a great influence on energy efficiency. CXXNet framework shows the best energy efficiency in this paper, which is 21.9% higher than TensorFlow, who performing the worst in energy efficiency. GPU acceleration library also contributes to energy efficiency. Adapting cuDNN increases energy efficiency by a factor of 7% as compared with not using cuDNN.

The reason why adapting CPU acceleration libraries performs best among all software parameters is that the absolute CPU power are relatively low, which contributes more improvement in EDP when the performance are almost similar. In addition, the adopt of cuDNN accelerates the GPU computing, and GPU utilization and computing efficiency are greatly improved, which improves performance but increases GPU power. The performance benefit brought by GPU acceleration is greater than the disadvantage brought about by the increase in power, so the whole energy is reduced. The size of *batch_size* affects the average energy of each image of CNN. When the *batch_size* is larger, it means that more images are packed into a batch and sent to the network for training in one iteration. Normally, we think that larger *batch_size* allows higher data-level parallelism and can reduce energy. Different DNN framework and whether applying cuDNN or not have low impact on the energy efficiency. These evaluation results are the same as reference [19].

The Impact of Hardware Parameters (Q2): As shown in Fig. 13, the importance of hardware parameters on energy efficiency improvements are almost the same. his is because the influence of overclocking on energy efficiency depends on platform architectures. In CPU-GPU platform, enabling overclocking brings an increase in performance, while decreasing power of GPU and raising power of CPU. Considering the proportion of CPU and GPU power, the total power of platform decreases, together with a 18.8% decrease in EDP in the best condition. In CPU platform, overclocking increases performance while causes extra power in different components, which leads to an uncertainty on energy efficiency analysis.

An important observation can be obtained from Fig. 13 - applying overclocking has a significant impact on energy efficiency improvement and is far more effective than modifying software parameters. It's noted that the impact of overclocking on GPU platform are the same as reference [19] stated. On the basis of the same experiment, we also did several sets of extended experiments (see Sect. 4.2). A similar conclusion was also reached in the extended experiment.

The Impact of DNN Framework (Q3): In addition, we also compare the difference between the two DNN frameworks, CNN and RNN. According to results and analysis in Sect. 4.3, as for different DNN framework, there are not many differences in power. However, their performance is very different, and so is the overall energy. Figure 8 shows that when *batch_size* is set as 128, the energy of CNN is up to 88.6 times than that of RNN.

When taking EDP (see definition in Sect. 3.3) to evaluate energy efficiency, Fig. 8 in Sect. 4.3 shows the difference between the two DNN frameworks in EDP.

5.2 Comparison Between Influential Factors of Energy Efficiency and Influential Factors of Performance

Some of the parameters shows consistent effects in both performance and energy efficiency (Sect. 5.2-**Consistency**), while some of them behave different in performance and energy efficiency (Sect. 5.2-**Difference**).

Consistency: The parameters with consistent effect in performance and energy efficiency can be divided into the following two types.

The first type of parameters mainly include software parameters, which affect energy efficiency by improving performance without significantly influencing power. For example, the use of CPU and GPU acceleration libraries can bring performance improvements. Although power increases due to higher processor utilization, it can bring energy efficiency gains as a whole. For another example, using different deep learning frameworks and neural network frameworks leads to different speeds up while has a relatively slight impact on power. Therefore, shorter running time leads to lower EDP. As shown in Fig. 14, the higher the performance, the higher the corresponding energy efficiency. *batch_size* affects energy efficiency by affecting the degree of data-level parallelism. The larger the amount of data, the higher the parallelism, which makes the average energy per unit of data smaller and thus improve energy efficiency.

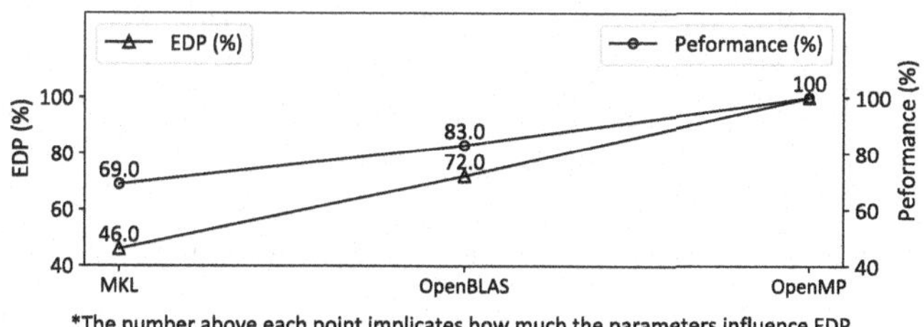

Fig. 14. Different trends on performance and energy efficiency with different CPU acceleration libraries.

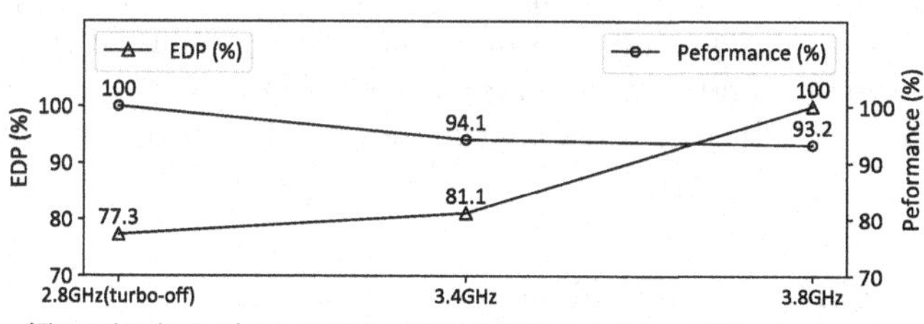

Fig. 15. Different trends on performance and power with different CPU frequency.

The second type of parameters mainly include hardware parameters, which affect energy efficiency by influencing both performance and power significantly. For example, using different overclocking settings results in a huge change in performance and power, which can be seen from the power curve in Fig. 6 and 5 that under the same configuration. When considering the influence in EDP, Fig. 15 shows that as the frequency increases, EDP decreases accordingly. Although the power has an obvious upward trend, while the running time decreases, the overall effect on EDP is positive.

Difference: Specially, some parameters show different effect on performance and energy efficiency. To be more detailed, some parameter settings improve performance (decrease running time) or energy efficiency (decrease EDP) while decrease the other one. Taking processor core number as an example (See in Fig. 16). When using CPU acceleration library OpenMP, the best setting for performance (3 processor cores) is different from that for energy efficiency (2 processor cores); when using CPU acceleration library MKL, the best setting for performance (2 processor cores) also differs from that for energy efficiency

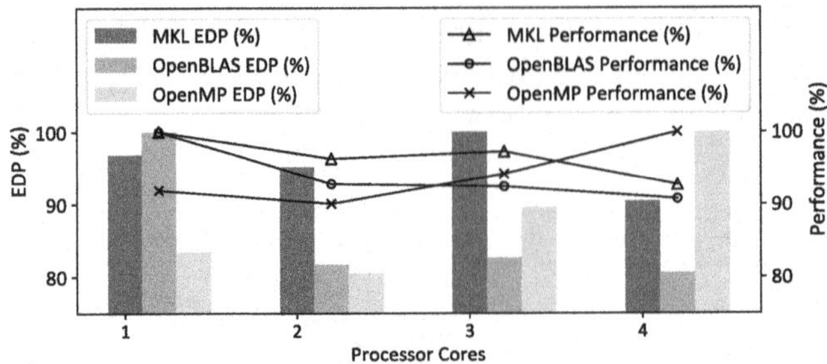

Fig. 16. Different trends in performance and energy efficiency with different processor cores.

(4 process cores). Meanwhile, when using CPU acceleration library OpenBLAS, 4 processor cores can bring best performance and energy efficiency at the same time.

The reason why processor core numbers cannot ensure a better performance and higher energy efficiency at the same time is that, adding core numbers will increase performance and power simultaneously. Thus, when we multiply time by energy to get EDP, it is hard to say whether it is better to use more processor cores or not.

5.3 Key Insights for Optimization

These analysis and discussions can help guide energy efficiency optimization in two layers. As for optimization in application layer, attentions should be given to software parameters that are closely related to energy efficiency. Using CPU acceleration libraries, like MKL, and GPU acceleration libraries, like cuDNN, always contributes to energy efficiency, since the acceleration libraries can coordinate various components better and significantly reduce running time. Frameworks with better performance also implies higher energy efficiency, such as deep learning framework CXXNet and neural network framework RNN, because more efficient frameworks cost fewer time to solve similar problems, and help to increase energy efficiency in many case. Another parameter, *batch_size*, is worth noting, whose impact on energy efficiency differs in separate platforms due to varies in Cache, DRAM and other architectures.

As for architecture layer, hardware parameters brings different effects on separate platforms. Using overclocking is benefit to energy efficiency in general, because it significantly speeds up the calculations. However, the highest overclocking degree not always implies the best energy efficiency, since overclocking also increases power, and the overall effect depends on unique architectures. As for process core number, it is hard to find a number that can brings best effect in both performance and energy efficiency, because performance and power simultaneously, leading to an uncertain effect in EDP. The diversity in architectures needs further attempts to find suitable parameter settings.

6 Related Work

6.1 DNN Characterization

There exist some studies devoted to performing performance and power characterization of different CNN models on CPU and GPU. D. Li et al. [19] evaluated the performance and power characteristics of different CNN models on CPU and GPU. They evaluated different processor architectures (i.e. Intel Xeon CPU, Nvidia Kepler, and Maxwell GPU) and discussed the impact of acceleration libraries and various hardware settings on CNN performance and power. At the same time, they studied how the network topology, batch size, and hardware parameters (hyperthreading, ECC, and DVFS) settings affect the performance and power of CNN.

Yao [30] also studied the energy efficiency of CNN on high-performance GPU. They have studied the impact of GPUD VFS on the energy consumption and performance of deep learning based on experience through a large number of comparative experiments on GPU architecture, DVFS settings and DNN configurations.

Rodrigues [22] considered the energy when migrating current deep learning applications from high-end GPUs or servers to low-power heterogeneous devices (such as mobile devices). This is because deep neural networks require additional processing steps to be deployed on low-power devices. These steps include using compression techniques to reduce network size or provide efficient device-specific software implementations. Due to the lack of tools and the inability to accurately and consistently measure power and performance between devices, migration is further exacerbated. They proposed a new evaluation framework, using ARMs streamlined performance analyzer combined with standard deep learning frameworks such as Caffe and cuDNNv5, to measure the energy and performance of deep neural networks, and applied this framework to study the extrusion network in Maxwell of NVidia Jetson TX1. The behavior of performing image classification tasks on the GPU and showing the performance and power characteristics of a specific layer of the neural network.

Tang [26] studied the impact of GPU DVFS on the energy and performance of deep learning. Hodak [13] studied the influencing factors of energy efficiency in data centers from a hardware perspective. Ou [21] observed that in multicore platform, using different number of processor cores may results in varies in CPU power and DRAM power, thus leading challenges to power modeling.

6.2 Guideline for Power Modeling

One way to model the energy of neural networks is to calculate the number of multiplication and accumulation (MAC) [12] to simulate the number of floating-point operations of the CPU or GPU, and to calculate the weight of the number of main memory accesses to simulate the pre-training model. As compared with MAC operations, weights must be loaded from DRAM, which has a higher relative energy cost. Therefore, a lot of research work (such as pruning, compression, etc.) focuses on reducing the number of weights or parameters of neural network models.

Calculating the number of weights is considered too simple, so some studies have further tried to improve the energy modeling method by combining the energy costs of different types of data at different levels of the memory hierarchy. T.-J. Yang [29] established an energy estimation model by calculating the number of times that each data value was reused in the memory hierarchy using the optimization process. The memory hierarchy is divided into four levels: DRAM, global buffer, array and register file. The energy of each level is extracted from the 65nm processor. The energy estimation model is used to map any shape of neural network model to its specific application accelerator (such as Eyeiss).

Research work on modeling energy at the application level using performance counters for general-purpose processors has also begun to appear. NeuralPower [6] uses regression-based methods to model GPU power and execution time. These models are built for the three main layers of CNNs, namely the convolutional layer, the pooling layer, and the fully connected layer. They use real values of power and time to build a predictive model of average power and runtime. Real power value on NVidia GTX1070 GPU is captured by NVidia smi. NeuralPower uses application layer features, such as core size, number of layers, etc., as input to the power estimation model, and eliminates the effects of voltage and frequency scaling by keeping the GPU in a fixed state. The output of the power prediction model is combined with the output of the runtime model to estimate the energy of each layer. The estimated values of each layer are then added to obtain the estimated power of the entire CNN.

DeLight [23] establishes a simple feedforward neural network energy model in the training phase. In a distributed training environment, the researchers model the use of energy based on basic arithmetic operations and communication of shared weights. Also, they establish two types of operation models: multiplication and addition and activation functions. The former being two adjacent layers a function of the number of connections between neurons, while the latter is a scalar multiplication. The communication energy is a function of the number of shared weights. By running a microbenchmark on the CUDA core of the Nvidia TK1 embedded platform, the modeling coefficients of these operations are obtained.

7 Conclusion and Future Work

7.1 Conclusion

For better designing accurate and energy-efficient DNN models, it is very important to understand the performance, power and energy characteristics under different parameter settings. This paper focuses on three critical issues for designing a both accurate and energy-efficient DNN model, i.e.

- how the software parameters affect the DNN models;
- how the hardware parameters affect the DNN models;
- how to choose the best energy-efficient DNN model.

To answer the above three issues, we apply five DNN models (i.e., LeNet, GoogLeNet, AlexNet, CaffeNet, and AlexNet-MNIST) on both CPU and GPU platforms to capture and analyze the performance, power and energy behaviors when using different hardware and software parameter settings, as well as different DNN models. Evaluation results provide detailed DNN characterization and useful insights to facilitate the design of energy-efficient deep learning solutions.

7.2 Future Work

Our future exploration directions are as follows:

1. Up to now, our characterization of energy efficiency characteristics is based on computing nodes, computing units and computing frameworks. This kind of coarse-grained energy efficiency characterization can provide guidance for the architecture design of neural networks. At the same time, we noticed that the computational characteristics of different layers of the neural network are different. If we perform more fine-grained feature characterization and further explore the performance, power and energy characteristics of different network layers, the results analysis can provide more refined architecture design and more accurate guidance.
2. With the continuous development of CNN, there will be more and more application scenarios for CNN. For example, some embedded systems begin to use CNN for training and prediction. We only conducted experimental tests on the energy efficiency of the CNN model on the CPU and GPU platforms. In the future, we plan to test on computing platforms such as FPGA and ASIC to analyze the energy efficiency behavior of the CNN model on different platforms.
3. Most GPU applications can utilize almost all the resources of the GPU, including both video memory and cores. And GPU power is always in a high state, reaching 90% of TDP most of the time.
4. Currently, GPU is almost the most commonly used computing core. In this article, we merely select one GPU platform, while more amount of GPUs and other different GPU platforms may bring different results. The energy efficiency behavior of GPUs of different architectures may be very different, so it is necessary to conduct energy efficiency testing and analysis on GPUs of different architectures.
5. Our experiments run on a small number of nodes, while multi-node operations in a distributed environment are more common in neural networks and cloud computing environments. Therefore, the energy efficiency research of CNN under multiple nodes is another issue we will consider in the future.

References

1. Convnet. https://github.com/soumith/convnet-benchmarks
2. cxxnet. https://github.com/dmlc/cxxnet

3. Imagenet large-scale visual recognition challenge. http://image-net.org/challenges/LSVRC
4. Nvidia system management interface. https://developer.nvidia.com/nvidia-system-management-interface
5. Abadi, M., et al.: TensorFlow: large-scale machine learning on heterogeneous distributed systems. ArXiv abs/1603.04467 (2016)
6. Cai, E., Juan, D.C., Stamoulis, D., Marculescu, D.: NeuralPower: predict and deploy energy-efficient convolutional neural networks. In: The 9th Asian Conference on Machine Learning (ACML 2017) (2017)
7. Chen, J., et al.: Analyzing time-dimension communication characterizations for representative scientific applications on supercomputer systems. Front. Comput. Sci. **13**(6), 1228–1242 (2019)
8. Chen, T., et al.: MXNet: a flexible and efficient machine learning library for heterogeneous distributed systems. ArXiv abs/1512.01274 (2015)
9. Collobert, R., Kavukcuoglu, K., Farabet, C.: Torch7: a matlab-like environment for machine learning. In: NIPS 2011 (2011)
10. Committe, G.: Green500. https://www.top500.org/lists/green500/. Accessed 20 May 2021
11. Guassic: Text classification with CNN and RNN. https://github.com/gaussic/text-classification-cnn-rnn
12. Han, S., Pool, J., Tran, J., Dally, W.J.: Learning both weights and connections for efficient neural networks. In: Twenty-ninth Conference on Neural Information Processing Systems (NIPS 2015) (2015)
13. Hodak, M., Gorkovenko, M., Dholakia, A.: Towards power efficiency in deep learning on data center hardware. In: 2019 IEEE International Conference on Big Data (Big Data) (2019)
14. Jia, Y., et al.: Caffe: convolutional architecture for fast feature embedding. ArXiv abs/1408.5093 (2014)
15. Khan, K.N., Hirki, M., Niemi, T., Nurminen, J.K., Ou, Z.: RAPL in action: experiences in using RAPL for power measurements. ACM Trans. Model. Perform. Eval. Comput. Syst. **3**(2), 1–26 (2018)
16. Krizhevsky, A., Sutskever, I., Hinton, G.: ImageNet classification with deep convolutional neural networks. Adv. Neural Inf. Process. Syst. **25**(2), 1097–1105 (2012)
17. LeCun, Y., Boser, B., Denker, J.S., Henderson, D., Howard, R.E.: Backpropagation applied to handwritten zip code recognition. Neural Comput. **1**(4), 541–551 (1989)
18. LeCun, Y., Kavukcuoglu, K., Farabet, C.: Convolutional networks and applications in vision. In: Proceedings of 2010 IEEE International Symposium on Circuits and Systems, pp. 253–256 (2010). https://doi.org/10.1109/ISCAS.2010.5537907
19. Li, D., Chen, X., Becchi, M., Zong, Z.: Evaluating the energy efficiency of deep convolutional neural networks on CPUs and GPUs. In: 2016 IEEE International Conferences on Big Data and Cloud Computing (BDCloud), Social Computing and Networking (SocialCom), Sustainable Computing and Communications (SustainCom) (BDCloud-SocialCom-SustainCom), pp. 477–484 (2016)
20. Sun, M., Li, J., Guo, Z.: THUCTC: an efficient Chinese text classification toolkit. http://thuctc.thunlp.org/
21. Ou, Z., Chen, J., Zhang, Y., Dong, Y., Yuan, Y., Wang, Z.: Power modeling for Phytium FT-2000+/64 multi-core architecture. In PPoPP 2020 Workshop: Principles and Practice of Parallel Programming 2020, Workshop: Benchmarking in the Datacenter, 7 p. (2020)

22. Rodrigues, C.F., Riley, G., Luján, M.: Fine-grained energy profiling for deep convolutional neural networks on the Jetson TX1. In: 2017 IEEE International Symposium on Workload Characterization (IISWC), pp. 114–115 (2017)
23. Rouhani, B.D., Mirhoseini, A., Koushanfar, F.: DeLight: adding energy dimension to deep neural networks. In: International Symposium on Low Power Electronics & Design (2016)
24. Sutskever, I., Vinyals, O., Le, Q.V.: Sequence to sequence learning with neural networks. In: Proceedings of the 27th International Conference on Neural Information Processing Systems, NIPS 2014, vol. 2, p. 3104–3112. MIT Press, Cambridge (2014)
25. Szegedy, C., Liu, W., Jia, Y., Sermanet, P., Rabinovich, A.: Going deeper with convolutions. IEEE Computer Society (2014)
26. Tang, Z., Wang, Y., Wang, Q., Chu, X.: The impact of GPU DVFs on the energy and performance of deep learning: an empirical study. In: The Tenth ACM International Conference (2019)
27. Thomas, D., Shanmugasundaram, M.: A survey on different overclocking methods. In: 2018 Second International Conference on Electronics, Communication and Aerospace Technology (ICECA), pp. 1588–1592 (2018)
28. Wu, F., et al.: A holistic energy-efficient approach for a processor-memory system. Tsinghua Sci. Technol. **24**, 468–483 (2019)
29. Yang, T.J., Chen, Y.H., Sze, V.: Designing energy-efficient convolutional neural networks using energy-aware pruning. In: 2017 IEEE Conference on Computer Vision and Pattern Recognition (CVPR) (2017)
30. Yao, C., et al.: Evaluating and analyzing the energy efficiency of CNN inference on high-performance GPU. Pract. Exp. Concurr. Comput. **33**, e6064 (2020)

Proving Mutual Authentication Property of 5G-AKA Protocol Based on PCL

Tong Zhang(✉), Meihua Xiao, and Ri Ouyang

East China Jiaotong University, Nanchang 330013, China
zt422zt@163.com

Abstract. The authentication function of the mobile network is the foundation to ensure the legitimacy of the network and user identities and provide security services. The authentication function of the network is realized by the network authentication protocol. Authentication protocol's safety directly affects the communication security of the network and users. Protocol Combination Logic PCL is an formal method to make a description of protocol state transition together with algorithm in concurrent and distributed networks, which can be used to prove the security of network protocols. This paper studies the authentication mechanism of the 5G network authentication protocol 5G-AKA, and conducts formal analysis and security certification of the 5G-AKA protocol through Protocol Combination Logic (PCL). We arrive at the conclusion that the protocol has the function of mutual authentication property guarantee among entities participated Home Net HN and User Equipment UE . Protocol Combination Logic PCL can be applied to the formal analysis of similar mobile network protocols.

Keywords: 5G-AKA protocol · PCL · Authentication property · Formal analysis

1 Introduction

Mobile users make up 2/3 of the worldwide population including almost five billion people [1]. USIM cards are utilized to make connection into mobile networks and these users are under the protection from security mechanisms regulated by 3GPP group. Since 2000, the introduction of network generations such as 3G and 4G is completed by a variant of the 3GPP standardized AKA. Since 2016, the 3GPP group has been standardizing on the next generation of mobile communications (5G), also through an AKA protocol. These protocols involve a user with a device (UE), a service network (SN) with a base station in the vicinity of the user, and a home network (HN) corresponding to the user operator. The user uses his USIM-equipped cell phone (UE) to link with the base station operated by the SN through an unsecured wireless channel. the SN communicates with the user's operator (HN) on the right side through an authenticated (wired) channel.

Supported by National Natural Science Foundation of China under Grant 61962020.

Z. Cai et al. (Eds.): NCTCS 2021, CCIS 1494, pp. 222–233, 2021.
https://doi.org/10.1007/978-981-16-7443-3_13

With the arrival of the 5G era, the impact of mobile communication networks on human society will rise to an unprecedented level, and the security of 5G networks will become more important than ever. However, the new architecture, technology, services, and protocols of 5G networks pose new challenges to 5G network security, especially the correct operation of 5G networks needs to rely on a complex and huge protocol system, and these protocols are difficult to guarantee absolute security. In a wireless open network environment, the authentication key agreement protocol can ensure mutual authentication between users and establish a secure communication channel. Therefore, the authentication key agreement protocol has practical significance and is one of the important topics in the formal research field. When it comes to measuring the safety of wide range, real-world protocols of safety, for instance, protocols [2] of entity authentication together with TLS 1.3 [3–5], messaging [6]. Official approaches are on the basis of rigorous mathematical concepts and languages with distinct semantics and expressions, which allow discovering vulnerabilities in protocols. Theorem proving is one of the most successful approaches in official means, which describe a security protocol as an axiomatic system and the expected property as a theorem to be proved [7]. Theorem proving has been studied intensively by many scholars and has made great progress. PCL is a logic for proving the security properties of network protocols [8], which is chiefly utilized to confirm the authentication and confidentiality of protocols under public key cryptosystems.

In this paper, based on PCL , we study the theory of PCL and try to apply it to mobile communication networks. We explore the security of the 5G-AKA protocol which provides mutual authentication between HN and UE in 5G network and draw the conclusion that the protocol is possible to satisfy a strong authentication property and prevent replay attacks. Our proof approach based on PCL could be utilized to design and analysis of such mobile networks mutual authentication protocols.

The framework of this article is as follows. The corresponding research is introduced in Sect. 2 Sect. 3 covers 5G-AKA protocol and Sect. 4 describes the proof system of PCL. In Sect. 5, security proof of 5G-AKA protocol will be discussed in depth. As for Sect. 6, our conclusions together with future work are demonstrated.

2 Related Work

Authentication protocol, acting as defense in the first line of defense in the field of mobile communication network, is one of the important areas of mobile communication network protocol security research. Official approached have been adopted to AKA protocols in past days, but due to the limitations of using strong abstraction, protocol simplification, and analytical properties, previous work can only provide weak guarantees.

The primal AKA protocol established for 3G was nonautomatically confirmed by 3GPP by means of TLA and improved BAN logic [9]. Analysis of TLA paid more attention to functional properties such as ability of the protocol to recover from desynchronization. The short paper-and-pencil proof given in the improved BAN logic offers weak guarantees due to the limitations of the logic, e.g., regarding key agreement and confidentiality. The logic especially does not take into consideration, for instance, including disadvantages of agents and type, and it has had soundness issues previously [10]. Furthermore, the proof considers a simplified protocol without SQN concealment or resynchronization, since SQNs are invariably considered to be synchronized. This avoids, for instance, the privacy attacks which are on the basis of desynchronized misinformation that we have observed. Arapinis et al. [11] discovered a linkability attack flaw in the 3G identity authentication protocol. Attackers are able to use this flaw to determine whether the target user is in a certain area. Ravishankar et al. [12] discovered a logical flaw in the AKA protocol, which had the possibility to be utilized to follow location of users and analyze user communication behavior. Changhee et al. [13] discovered the flaws of linkability attacks in LTE networks and put forward a valid scheme. An attack that uses objective user registration request messages to discern whether the objective user exists was introduced in [14], and the author proposes a systematic solution. 5G AKA is a new identity authentication protocol used in 5G networks. It is necessary to study it to verify whether it has defects. If it does exist, it needs to be repaired lightly and efficiently.

3 5G-AKA Protocol

3.1 Protocol Introduction

AKA stands for Authentication and Key Agreement. The protocol of AKA uses a question answering mechanism to accomplish authentication between the user and the network, while a communication key is agreed upon on the basis of the authentication. 5G mobile communication criterions are being completed and are of availability at present in draft form [15]. These standards describe protocols designed to provide security for users together with service providers. AKA protocol is one of the most significant protocols, which enables users together with their service providers to set up shared secret keys authentically.

The 5G network is mainly composed of user terminal equipment (UE), service network (SN), along with home network (HN). The user's authentication function is mainly completed by them. The service network mainly implements user access management, session management and other functions. The duty of home network is chiefly user identity authentication together with management of identity message. Network of 5G supports more application scenarios on the original basis, and penetrates into the Internet of Things fields such as smart home, car networking, and drones.

In order to allow SN and users to set up a safe channel with mutually authenticate, 3GPP has stipulated 2 authentication approaches: 5G AKA together with EAP-AKA'. Since the focus of our study is the 5G AKA authentication approach, these differences will not be described in-depth here.

3.2 Protocol Process and Simplification

According to the 5G security standard, the interaction process of the 5G-AKA protocol is shown in Fig. 1, and its complete implementation process is described as follows [15].

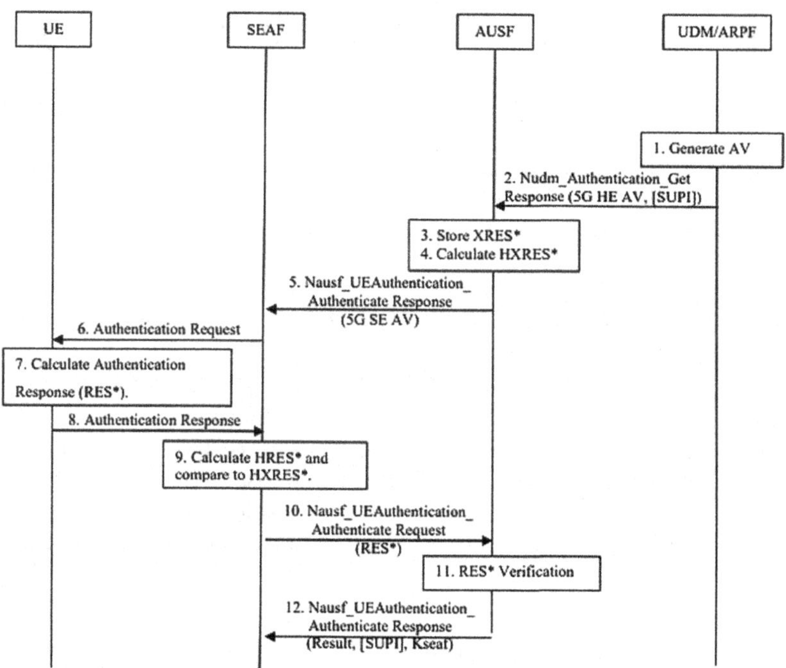

Fig. 1. The interaction process of the 5G-AKA protocol

In this paper, our focus is on the authentication property of the 5G-AKA protocol. From the above interaction flow, it is clear that the function of the SN is simply to pass the information received from the UE to the HN. Besides, if there is a base station from HN located nearby UE, then the HN and the SN are the identical subject. Therefore, the SN can be built into the HN and abstractly model both as a whole. In this case, the 5G-AKA protocol has the identical safety as the simplified 5G-AKA protocol shown in Fig. 2. A practical execution of protocol is described as follow. practical execution of protocol is described as follow.

(1) The UE starts the protocol by discerning itself to the HN, which enables to use the HN public key pk_N together with the fresh randomness n^e to send its hidden permanent identity $\{SUPI\}^{n^e}_{pk_N}$.
(2) After receiving the identification message, HN uses its sk_N to retrieve the permanent identity $SUPI$, and then recovers SQN_N and the key k related to

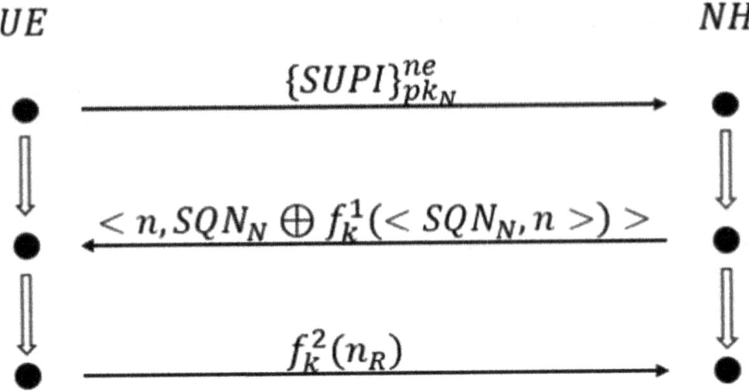

Fig. 2. The simplified 5G-AKA protocol

the identity $SUPI$ from its record. Then HN produces a new random number n. It masks the sequence number SQN_N by XOR with $f_k^5\ (n)$, and performs MAC processing on the message by calculating $f_k^1\ (< SQN_N\ ,\ n >)$. Then it sends the message $< n\ ,\ SQN_N\ \oplus\ f_k^5\ (n)\ , f_k^1\ (< SQN_N\ ,\ n >) >$.

(3) Upon receipt of information, the UE computes $f_k^5\ (n)$. It will unmask the SQN_N and check the authentication of the message by recalculating $f_k^1\ (< SQN_N\ ,\ n >)$ and verifying whether it is equivalent to the third element of the information. Then, it sends $f_k^2\ (n)$ to prove the knowledge of k to the HN.

3.3 Authentication Properties

From an agent A's point of view, four levels of authentication between two agents A and B [16]: firstly, aliveness, which just make sures that B has been running the protocol before, but not necessarily with A; secondly, weak agreement, which make sures that B has been running the protocol before with A, but not necessarily using the same data; thirdly, non-injective agreement, which make sures that B has been running the protocol before with A and both of them agree on the data; and fourthly, injective agreement, which additionally makes sure that every protocol operation of an agent has a uniquely matched operation of other agents, and prevents replay attacks.

The mutual authentication between subscribers and HNs is described formally as follows. First, users must make sure that only SNs authorized by their HN can be successfully authenticated. And then, the user must obtain the non-injective agreement on SNname with its HNs after confirming the key.

4 Protocol Composition Logic (PCL)

In September 2005, A. Datta and others of the Information Security Laboratory of Stanford University put forward the Protocol Composition Logic PCL

(Protocol Composition Logic) [17, 18], which provides a new form of formal verification and analysis of safety protocols and can be utilized for automated proof of protocol attributes.

PCL is a logic which is adopted to prove the safety properties of network protocols which apply public and symmetric key encryption technology. The design of logic concentrates on process computation, whose initiatives include probable protocol procedures such as producing new random numbers, message sending and receipt, and conducting decryption and digital signature confirmation initiatives. The proof system contains axioms and inference rules for a single protocol action, and generates assertions about the protocol comprising various procedures. Assertions are merely recorded according to the protocol steps, but their logic is sound in a strong sense. Every provable assertion that contains a sequence of actions applies to all protocol executions, including specific and extra initiatives of the malicious adversary. Through this manner, safety properties of the attacked protocol can be proved, while at the same time reasoning only regarding of the behavior of honest parties in the protocol. PCL is in favor of combinatorial reasoning over complicated safety protocols and has been adopted in several industry criteria such as Kerberos V5, SSL/TLS and IEEE802.11i.

At present, Protocol Combination Logic has been successfully used in the formal analysis and verification of multiple network security protocols. For example, A. Datta et al. applied this logic to the protocol defined in ISO-9798-3, and found some security flaws in the protocol.

4.1 Syntax

Formula for PCL is offered through syntax in Table 1, in which S can stand for any chain. Here, t and P stand for a term and a thread separately. φ and ψ was utilized to denote the predicate formulas, while m denotes the generic term as "message". Messages take the following shape (content, source, target, protocol identifier), and in addition to the message content, a unique protocol identifier is provided for each message source and target field. The source area of information perhaps cannot be able to trace the specific sender because an intruder is able to fake the original address. In the same way, the subject which is discerned by the target field perhaps unable to accept the information since an intruder may block tackle it. However, the origin and target fields in the information are possible to help describe and prove authentication properties, while the protocol identifier is used to prove the properties of the protocol. Most protocol proofs use formulas of the form $\theta\,[P]_X\,\varphi$, which stands for that later than performing action P in thread X, the resultant state of formula φ is true for X begining from the state in which formula θ is true.

When running an authentication protocol, one formula can be false or true. More precisely, the main semanteme relation, $Q,\ R \mid =\ \varphi$, can be read as, "the formula φ holds for run R of protocol Q. [18]" In this relevance, R is an intact run, in which all sessions opened in the run have finished, or an incomplete run in which several subjects wait for extra information to finish several sessions. We suppose Q is a protocol, while $\bar{Q}$ is accordingly the set of all original structures

Table 1. The formulas of PCL.

Action formulas:
$a ::= Send\,(X,t)\vert Receive\,(X,t)\vert New\,(X,t)\mid$ Encrypt $(X,t)\mid$ Decrypt $(X,t)\vert Sign\,(X,t)\vert$ Verify (X,t)
Formulas:
$\phi := a\vert a < a\vert Has\,(X,t)\vert Fresh\,(X,t)\vert Gen\,(X,t)\mid$ FirstSend $(X,t,t)\mid$ Honest $(N)\vert t = t\vert Contains\,(t,t)\vert\phi\wedge\phi\vert\neg\phi\vert\exists x\cdot\phi\vert Start\,(X)$
Modelling formulas:
$\Psi := \phi S \phi$

of protocol Q, and every containing a probable intruder cord. Then $Runs(Q)$ is the set of all runs of Q with intruder, he set of all runs of with intruder, each starting from an original structure in $\bar{Q}$ series of reaction procedures inside a cord space. We suppose that φ has free variables, then $Q,\ R \mid = \ \varphi$ if we have $Q,\ R \mid = \ \sigma\varphi$ for all substitutions σ that eliminate all the free variables in φ. We write $Q \mid = \ \varphi$ if $Q,\ R \mid = \ \varphi$ for all $R \in Runs(Q)$.

4.2 Proof System

The proof system for protocol combinatorial logic consists of logical axioms and proof rules for protocol behavior, sequential reasoning, together with a special honesty rule. The axioms and proof rules include protocol action axioms, holding axioms, timing axioms and rules, encryption and signature axioms, hold axioms, and honesty rules. Some of the axioms which are used in this work as following.

Axioms of Prorocol Actions. As a result of performing some action (or not performing some action), the axioms of the protocol operation state property remain in the state. We use a in the axiom to denote a random action, while a to stand for the related statement in the logic. T stands for true in the value of Boolean.

AA 1 $T\,[a]_x$ a
AA 2 $Start\,(X)\,[]_X\neg a\,(X)$
AA 3 $\neg Send\,(X,t)\,[b]_x\neg Send\,(X,t)$ if $\sigma send\,(X,t) \neq \sigma$ for all substituti ons σ
AA 4 $T\,[a;\cdots,b]_X$ a $< b$
AN 1 $New\,(X,t)\wedge New\,(Y,t)\supset X = Y$
AN 2 $T[$new $x]_x$ Has $(Y,t)\supset(Y = X)$
AN 3 $T[$new $x]_x$ Fresh($X,t)$
AN 4 Fresh($X,t)\supset Gen\,(X,t)$

Possession Axioms. [17] The possession axiom describes the terms available to the principal when it has certain other terms.

$$\text{ORIG } New(X,t) \supset Has(X,t)$$
$$\text{REC } Receive(X,t) \supset Has(X,t)$$
$$\text{TUP } Has(X,t) \wedge Has(X,m) \supset Has(X,(t,m))$$
$$\text{ENC } Has(X,t) \wedge Has(X,k) \supset Has\,(X,\text{ENC}_k\,\{|t|\})$$
$$\text{PROJ } Has(X,(t,m)) \supset Has(X,t) \wedge Has(X,m)$$
$$\text{DEC } Has\,(X,\text{ENC}_k\,\{|t|\}) \wedge Has(X,k) \supset Has(X,t)$$

Axioms and Rules for Temporal Ordering. [17] The following 2 axioms offer a method to derive temporal ordering between initiatives of distinct threads.

$$FS1\;\; Fresh\,(X,t)\left[Send\; t^{'}\right]_X \;\; FirstSend\left(X,t,t^{'}\right) \;\; where\; t \subseteq t'$$
$$FS2\;\; FirstSend\left(X,t,t^{'}\right) \wedge a\left(Y,t^{''}\right) \supset Send\left(X,t^{'}\right) < a\left(Y,t^{''}\right) \tag{1}$$
$$where\; X \neq Y,\; and\; t \leq t^{''}$$

Preservation Axioms. [17] The below axioms describe that the truth values of some statements proceed to keep later than some more distant initiatives.

$$P1\;\; Persist\;\; (X,t)\,[a]_X\;\; Persist\;\; (X,t)\, for\;\; Persist\;\; \in \{\; Has, FirstSend, a, Gen\;\}$$
$$P2\;\; Fresh\;\; (X,t)\,[\text{ a }]_x\;\; Fresh\;\; (X,t)\;\; where\; t \approx a$$

4.3 Strong Authentication

In order to prove a more intensive authentication property, we should claim the temporal ordering among Alice and Bob actions. From our earlier statement, the ultimate authentication property is supposed to declare that each message sent by $\hat{X}$ is received by $\hat{Y}$ and vice versa, that before the corresponding receiving event, each sending event occurs, and furthermore, that the information from each principal $(\hat{X} or \hat{Y})$ appear in the same order in both records. In the same way, the initiator role whose the formal property proved about is $\vdash Q_{AKA}\; T\,[Init_{AkA}] \times Honest\left(\hat{Y}\right) \wedge \hat{Y} \neq \hat{x} \supset \phi_{auth}$, but ϕ_{auth} now models the stronger property.

4.4 Proof Procedures

We can complete the proof in three steps.

(1) Prove that Alice performs her sending and receiving actions in a certain order. This step can be done by looking at the sequence of Alice's actions in her role.

(2) Assuming that Bob is honest, we can reason that Bob performs the sequential actions of sending and receiving actions. This can be achieved in two steps. Firstly, based on the properties of cryptographic primitives (e.g., encryption or signature), we can deduce that only Bob can perform a particular initiative such as producing his own signature. Afterwards, the honesty rule is used to build the temporal relation between Bob's actions (e.g., then the honesty rule is utilized to establish temporal relationship between Bob's actions (e.g., Bob sending message msg2 to Alice occurs after Bob receives message msg1 from Alice).
(3) Finally, using timing rules to establish temporal order between Alice and Bob send and receive actions, this timing relationship is often established using the freshness of the data contained in the message.

5 Formal Analysis of 5G-AKA Protocol

5.1 Protocol Formal Representations

Roles of the 5G-AKA Protocol

$$
\begin{aligned}
&Init_{AKA}\\
&\quad \equiv(\hat{Y}[\\
&\quad new\ n_{x_1} : m_{x_1} enc(SUPI,\ n_{x_1}),\ \hat{Y};\\
&\quad send\ \hat{X},\ \hat{Y}m,\ m_{x_1},\ ID_{HN},\ SN_{name};\\
&\quad receive\ AK,\ MAC,\ CONC,\ SQN_{HN},\ m_{Y_2},\ n_{Y_1};\\
&\quad verify\ m_{Y_2},\ (AK,\ MAC,\ CONC,\ SQN_{HN}),\ \hat{Y};\\
&\quad match\ MAC/MAC';\\
&\quad match\ f_1(k,\ < SQN_{HN},\ n_{Y_1} >)/MAC'';\\
&\quad match\ Challenge(K,\ n_{Y_1})/RES;\\
&\quad send\ RES;\\
&\quad]_X()
\end{aligned}
$$

$$
\begin{aligned}
&Resp_{AKA}\\
&\quad \equiv()[\\
&\quad receive\ \hat{X},\ \hat{Y}, m_{X_1}, ID_{HN}; m_{Y_1} = dec\ m_{X_1}, \hat{Y}; new\ n_{Y_1}\\
&\quad match\ f_1(k,\ < SQN_{HN},\ n_{Y_1} >)/MAC;\\
&\quad match\ f_5(k,\ n_{Y_1})/AK;\\
&\quad match\ (SQN_{HN} \oplus AK)/conc;\\
&\quad match\ challenge(K,\ n_{Y_1})/xRES\\
&\quad m_{Y_2} SIGN(AK,\ MAC,\ CONC, SQN_{HN}),\ \hat{Y};\\
&\quad send\ AK,\ MAC,\ CONC, SQN_{HN},\ m_{Y_2}, n_{Y_1};\\
&\quad receive\ RES;\\
&\quad]_Y()
\end{aligned}
$$

where $Init_{AKA}$ is the action sequence for the initiator role (corresponding to UE) and $Resp_{AKA}$ is the action sequence for the responder role (corresponding to HN).

5.2 Detailed Proving Process

According to the Protocol Combination Logic PCL, the formal representation of the authentication of the initiator role session to be proved is as follows.

$$\vdash Q_{AKA}\ T\left[Init_{AkA}\right]_X\ Honest\left(\hat{Y}\right) \wedge \hat{Y} \neq \hat{X} \supset \phi_{auth}$$

$$\begin{aligned}\phi_{auth} \equiv Y.\ ((&Send\,(X,\ msg_1) < Receive\,(Y,\ msg_1))) \bigwedge \\ &(Receive\,(Y,\ msg_1) < Send\,(Y,\ msg_2)) \bigwedge \\ &(Send\,(Y,\ msg_2) < Receive\,(X,\ msg_2)) \bigwedge \\ &(Receive\,(X,\ msg_2) < Send\,(X,\ msg_3)) \bigwedge \\ &(Send\,(X,\ msg_3) < Receive\,(Y,\ msg_3))\end{aligned}$$

$$msg_1 \equiv \left(\hat{X},\ \hat{Y},\ m_{X_1}, ID_{HN}\right)$$

$$msg_2 \equiv \left(\hat{X},\ \hat{Y}, AK,\ MAC,\ CONC,\ SQN_{HN}, m_{Y_2}, n_{Y_1}\right)$$

$$msg_3 \equiv \left(\hat{X},\ \hat{Y},\ RES\right)$$

When the above equation holds, the initiator role of the 5G-AKA protocol is able to guarantee session authentication. In this paper, only the proof process at the UE side is given, and the case of the proof process at the HN side is similar.

1) AN2 $\quad T\left[new\ n_{x1}\right]_X\ Has\,(Y, n_{x1}) \supset\ (Y\ =\ X)$
2) AA1,FS1 $\quad T\left[Send\ m_{x1}\right]_X\ FirstSend\,(X, m_{x1}, msg1)$
3) 1),2),P1 $\quad T\left[Init_{AKA}\right]_X\ FirstSend\,(X, m_{x1}, msg1)$
4) 3),FS2 $\quad T\left[Init_{AKA}\right]_X\ Receive\,(Y, msg1) \wedge \hat{Y} \neq \hat{X} \supset$
$(Send\,(X, msg1) < Receive\,(Y, msg1))$
5) AA1 $\quad T\left[Verify\ \ m_{Y2}, (AK, MAC, CONC, SQN_{HN})\right]_X$
$FirstSend\,(X, m_{x1}, msg1)$
6) 5),P1,SEQ $\quad T\left[Init_{AKA}\right]_X\ Verify$
$(X, SIG_{\hat{Y}}\,\{AK, MAC, CONC, SQN_{HN}\})$
7) 6),VER $\quad T\left[Init_{AKA}\right]_X\ \exists Y, t.\ \ Send\,(Y, t) \wedge$
$Contain\,(t, SIG_{\hat{Y}}\,\{AK, MAC, CONC, SQN_{HN}\})$
8) HON_{QAKA} $\quad \left(Honest\left(\hat{Y}\right) \wedge Send\,(Y, t) \wedge\right.$
$\left.Contain\,\left(t, SIG_{\hat{Y}}\,\{AK, MAC, CONC, SQN_{HN}\}\right)\right) \supset$
$(New\,(Y, n_{X1}) \vee (Receive\,(Y, msg1) < Send\,(X, msg2))$
9) 7),8) $\quad T\left[Init_{AKA}\right]_X\ Honest\left(\hat{Y}\right) \supset (\exists Y.New\,(Y, n_{X1})) \vee$
$(Receive\,(Y, msg1) < Send\,(X, msg2))$

10) AA1 $T\left[new\ n_{x1}\right]_X\ New\left(X, n_{x1}\right)$
11) 10),P1,SEQ $T\left[Init_{AKA}\right]_X\ New\left(X, n_{x1}\right)$
12) 9),11),AN1 $T\left[Init_{AKA}\right]_X\ Honest\left(\hat{Y}\right) \wedge \hat{Y} \neq \hat{X} \supset$ $\left(\exists Y.Receive\left(Y, msg1\right) < Send\left(X, msg2\right)\right)$
13) HON_{QAKA} $\left(Honest\left(\hat{Y}\right) \wedge Receive\left(Y, msg1\right) \wedge Send\left(X, msg2\right)\right) \supset$ $FirstSend\left(Y, n_{Y2}, msg2\right)$
14) AA1,AR3,SEQ $T\left[Init_{AKA}\right]_X\ Receive\left(X, msg2\right)$
15) 13),14),FS2 $T\left[Init_{AKA}\right]_X\ Honest\left(\hat{Y}\right) \wedge \hat{Y} \neq \hat{X} \wedge \left(Receive\left(Y, msg1\right)\right.$ $\left.\wedge\, Send\left(X, msg2\right)\right) \supset \left(Send\left(Y, msg2\right) < Receive\left(X, msg2\right)\right)$
16) AA4,P1 $T\left[Init_{AKA}\right]_X\ Receive\left(X, msg2\right) < Send\left(X, msg3\right)$
17) HON_{QAKA} $\left(Honest\left(\hat{Y}\right) \wedge Receive\left(Y, msg2\right) \wedge Send\left(X, msg3\right)\right) \supset$ $FirstSend\left(Y, msg3\right)$
18) AA1,AR3,SEQ $T\left[Init_{AKA}\right]_X\ Receive\left(Y, msg3\right)$
19) 18),FS2 $T\left[Init_{AKA}\right]_X\ Receive\left(Y, msg3\right) \wedge \hat{Y} \neq \hat{X} \supset$ $\left(Send\left(X, msg3\right) < Receive\left(Y, msg3\right)\right)$
20) 4),12),15),16),19) $\vdash Q_{AKA}\ T\left[Init_{AkA}\right]_X\ Honest\left(\hat{Y}\right) \wedge \hat{Y} \neq \hat{X} \supset \phi_{auth}$

According to the above proof procedures, the security 5G-AKA protocol is proved, which is guaranteed to satisfy a strong authentication property. The strong property prevents replay attacks.

6 Conclusion

In this paper we perform the analysis and proof for the security of 5G-AKA protocol and the proof shows that the 5G-AKA protocol satisfies a strong authentication property and prevent replay attacks. Although this paper has successfully proved the security of mutual authentication, in future work we will extend corresponding rules of PCL for the security analysis of cryptographic protocols with more complex primitives.

References

1. GSMA Global Mobile Trends 2017. https://www.gsma.com/globalmobiletrends/. Accessed 6 May 2018
2. Kobeissi, N., Bhargavan, K., Blanchet, B.: Automated verification for secure messaging protocols and their implementations: A symbolic and computational approach. In: Automated Verification for Secure Messaging Protocols and their Implementations: A Symbolic and Computational Approach. IEEE (2017)
3. Bhargavan, K., Blanchet, B., Kobeissi, N.: Verified models and reference implementations for the TLS 1.3 standard candidate. In: 2017 IEEE Symposium on Security and Privacy (SP). IEEE (2017)
4. Cremers, C., Horvat, M., Hoyland, J., et al.: A comprehensive symbolic analysis of TLS 1.3. In: ACM SIGSAC Conference, pp. 1773–1788. ACM (2017)

5. Cremers, C., Horvat, M., Scott, S., et al.: Automated analysis and verification of TLS 1.3: 0-RTT, resumption and delayed authentication. In: EEE Symposium on Security and Privacy (SP). IEEE (2016)
6. David, B., Cas, C., Simon, M.: Provably repairing the ISO/IEC 9798 standard for entity authentication. J. Comput. Secur. **21**(6), 817–846 (2013)
7. Wang, J., Zhan, N.J., Feng, X.Y., Liu, Z.M.: Overview of formal methods. J. Softw. **1**(30), 33–61 (2019)
8. Datta, A., Derek, A., Mitchell, J., et al.: A derivation system for security protocols and its logical formalization. In: Proceedings of 16th IEEE Computer Security Foundations Workshop, pp. 109–125. IEEE (2003)
9. Li, X., Zhang, X.: Formal verification for EAP-AKA protocol in 3G networks. In: 2009 International Conference on Computational Intelligence and Software Engineering. IEEE (2009)
10. Boyd, C., Mao, W.: On a limitation of BAN logic. In: Helleseth, T. (ed.) EUROCRYPT 1993. LNCS, vol. 765, pp. 240–247. Springer, Heidelberg (1994). https://doi.org/10.1007/3-540-48285-7_20
11. Arapinis, M., Mancini, L., Ritter, E., Ryan, M.: New privacy issues in mobile telephony: fix and verification. In: Proceedings of the 2012 ACM Conference on Computer and Communications Security, pp. 205–216. ACM, New York (2012)
12. Borgaonkar, R., Hirschi, L., Park, S., Shaik, A.: New privacy threat on 3G, 4G, and upcoming 5G AKA protocols. Proc. Priv. Enhanc. Technol. **2019**(3), 108–127 (2019)
13. Hahn, C., Kwon, H., Kim, D., Kang, K., Hur, J.: A privacy threat in 4th generation mobile telephony and its countermeasure. In: Cai, Z., Wang, C., Cheng, S., Wang, H., Gao, H. (eds.) WASA 2014. LNCS, vol. 8491, pp. 624–635. Springer, Cham (2014). https://doi.org/10.1007/978-3-319-07782-6_56
14. Hu, X., Liu, C., Liu, S., You, W., Zhao, Y.: A Systematic analysis method for 5G non-access stratum signalling security. IEEE Access **pp**(99), 125424–125441 (2019)
15. TS 33.501: Security architecture and procedures for 5G system. https://www.tech-invite.com/3m33/tinv-3gpp-33-501.htmls. Accessed 2 Aug 2020
16. Basin, D., Dreier, J., Hirschi, L., Radomirovic, S., Sasse, R., Stettler, V.: A formal analysis of 5G authentication. In: Proceedings of the 2018 ACM SIGSAC Conference on Computer and Communications Security, pp. 1383–1396. ACM, Toronto (2018)
17. Datta, A., Roy, A., Mitchell, J., et al.: Protocol composition logic (PCL). Electron. Notes Theor. Comput. Sci. **172**(1), 311–358 (2007)
18. Datta, A., Derek, A., Mitchell, J. et al.: Secure protocol composition. In: Proceedings of the 2003 ACM Workshop on Formal Methods in Security Engineering, pp. 11–23. ACM (2003)

Research on the Model Transformation Method and Application of Formal Model Driven Engineering (FMDE)

Ya Liu[1,2], Jinyun Xue[1(✉)], Zhiheng Zhang[1,2], Yang Liu[1,2], and Hongwen Hu[1,2]

[1] National-Level International Science and Technology Cooperation Base of Networked Supporting Software, Nanchang, China

[2] School of Computer Information Engineering, Jiangxi Normal University, Nanchang 330022, China

Abstract. MDE is a software development method with UML modeling and model conversion as the main approach. MDA is a concrete and partial realization way of MDE, and it is a model-driven development framework mainly based on UML. For the graphical modeling language UML, there are problems such as complex and cumbersome language mechanisms, inaccuracy and ambiguity in concepts, lack of formal description and formal derivation, making it difficult to guarantee reliability. Based on the framework of practical formal method (PAR) and model-driven engineering, this paper proposes a new algorithm development method FMDE model transformation method and application research. The model, meta-model, algorithm model and program model proposed by FMDE make model-driven software development more efficient. The grammatical and semantic definitions of the formal modeling languages SNL, Rdal, Apla and the BNF description facilitate the formal derivation and correctness verification of the algorithm program, SNL demand model → Radl algorithm model transformation converts the SNL function requirements of the algorithm problem into Radl algorithm specifications, uses Radl algorithm model → Apla program model transformation to convert the algorithm to Apla program, uses Apla program model → executable code model transformation to convert Apla program It is automatically converted into an executable language program, and finally the correctness of the model transformation is proved through a case, which improves the efficiency, correctness and reliability of algorithm development.

Keywords: UML · Formal modeling language · PAR · Model transformation · FMDE

1 Introduction

Software development is a complex and difficult task. How to develop high-quality software efficiently and at low cost has always been the focus of attention and research in the field of computer software development. The use of abstract methods, namely model modeling, is a concrete and practical method to solve software development

Z. Cai et al. (Eds.): NCTCS 2021, CCIS 1494, pp. 234–254, 2021.
https://doi.org/10.1007/978-981-16-7443-3_14

problems. Model-driven engineering (MDE) takes the model as the primary software product, constructs the business model of the software system through modeling as the problem domain, and then relies on model transformation to drive software development, (semi-)automatically produce the final complete application program [1]. MDA is a model-driven development framework mainly based on UML modeling. Model-driven architecture (MDA) is a partial and specific implementation approach of MDE, while UML is the core element of the MDA software development framework. UML is a universal standardized modeling language suitable for all stages of software development, but it lacks precise semantic information, so it is difficult to verify directly, and reliability cannot be guaranteed. The formal method is a method strictly based on mathematical logic. It has the transparency of mathematical logic. Its formal language is machine-processable, which is convenient for formal verification to ensure reliability. Therefore, it is extremely important to use formal methods with strict mathematical foundations for system development, especially for integrity systems that require formal proof of safety. At the seminar in 2011, European MDE leader Jean Bézivin pointed out that Model Driven Engineering (MDE) with UML modeling language as its core has missed its best development period, and MDE has come to a standstill [2].

One of the main goals of Model Driven Software Engineering (MDSE) is to automatically generate code through models [3] to improve productivity. However, the actual application of code generation is still relatively slow and limited to small-scale applications. More experience shows that the reason is: lack of code generation modeling language and reliable automatic code generation tools and platforms [4, 5]. PAR [6] is a unified software formal development method and supporting development platform, which can significantly improve the efficiency and reliability of algorithm and software development.

Xue Jinyun's team proposed the framework of formal model-driven engineering (FMDE) in the article "Methodology and Platform of IS Code Generation" published on ACM in 2020. [7] FMDE is a new software development method and architecture based on the combination of practical formal methods (PAR methods) and model-driven engineering (MDE) [4, 8].

2 FMDE Related Concepts and Methods at Home and Abroad

2.1 Model Driven Engineering (MDE)

MDE is a branch of software engineering. The basic view of MDE is that the entire software development process is a certain activity around the model: modeling, model conversion, model "execution" or "interpretation" and code generation, model-based The back and forth and so on. MDE is a software development method with UML modeling and model conversion as the main approach. MDE is not a pure new concept or idea, but more of the practice and theory around "models and modeling" in the field of software development. Generalized or generalized. Under this understanding, all modeling theories and techniques in software development can be summarized as its specific content. For example, domain modeling and domain model-driven development (DDD), domain-specific models and languages (DSM/DSL), and many computer languages, especially semantic work, can be explained or better from the standpoint or perspective of this MDE Positioning. For example, from the standpoint of MDE, MDA and MDD are a partial and specific way of realizing MDE.

Model-driven engineering (MDE) and model-driven software development (MDSS) are an important direction of software engineering development. Modeling and modeling are the mainstays of software development. Compared with other software development methods, the characteristics of model-driven development methods are mainly used to display domain models and build software systems based on these models, and complete the transition from design to implementation through continuous (semi-automatic) conversion, thereby completing the development of the entire system.

2.2 Unified Modeling Language UML

Proposal of UML

UML is a universal modeling language, a language used to visually model software systems. Since OMG adopted UML as its standard modeling language in 1997, UML has received widespread attention from people from all walks of life and has been widely used, but it has also been criticized from different angles from users, tool developers, scholars and educators all the time. At present, people from all walks of computer have put forward various opinions on UML, and focus on several commonly recognized issues: streamlining, defining the core, extending the mechanism, and formal semantics.

Advantages and Disadvantages of UML

a. Advantages of UML modeling language:
   UML unifies the different views of various methods on different types of systems, different development stages and different internal concepts, thereby effectively eliminating unnecessary differences between various modeling languages. It is actually a general modeling language, which can be widely used by many users of object-oriented modeling methods.
b. Disadvantages of UML modeling language:

(1) There are still many problems in the development of UML. Scholars believe that it lacks a refined core and well-defined periphery, and some semantic definitions are not precise enough and are ambiguous [9]; Modeling practitioners believe that it lacks a mechanism to support their own domain modeling requirements; tool developers have deviations in understanding due to the uncertainty of the specification, and self-interpretation of UML may mislead users.
(2) The key problem of UML is that it is too large and complex, and there are theoretical flaws in language architecture, semantics, etc. [10]. the semantics are bloated, and it has standard elements of vague and sparse semantics.
(3) The Unified Modeling Language has become a part of software engineering courses in many universities worldwide, but due to the complexity of UML, students find it difficult to learn and use [11]. Usually, students think that UML diagrams are useless and can only be used as documents that no one reads [12].

3 Formal Models Drive Engineering Concepts

In the fields of computer science and software engineering, formal methods based on strict mathematical foundations are suitable for the description, development and verification of software and hardware systems [13]. Formal methods are used in software and hardware design, and appropriate mathematical analysis can be used. Improve the reliability of the design [14], especially for highly reliable systems that require formal proof of safety [15]. Professor Xue Jinyun's team proposed a formal model-driven engineering (FMDE) framework.It follows the technical route defined by FMDE, which combines practical formal method (PAR method), PAR platform prototype and MDA to realize software system development. PAR is composed of requirements modeling language SNL (metamodel), algorithm modeling language Radl, abstract program modeling language Apla, a set of model conversion rules and a set of automatic conversion tools. This tool can realize several conversions from the demand model to the algorithm model, to the abstract program model, and finally to the executable program. The goal of conversion is to generate executable programs. Here, we only introduce a few main contents of the PAR platform. More information about PAR can be found in [6, 16, 17].

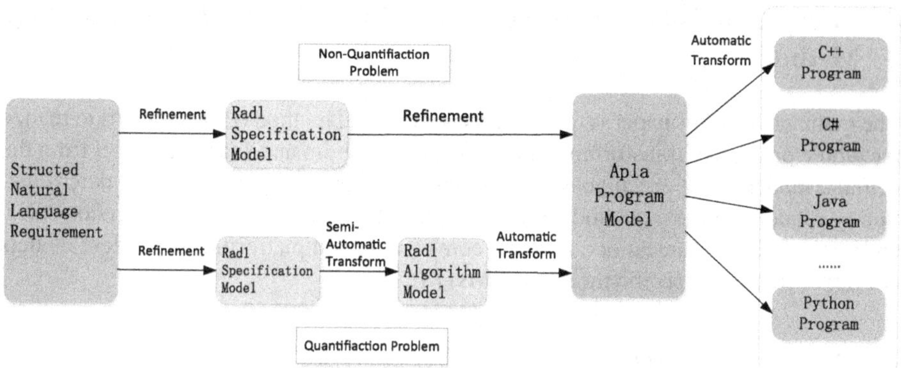

Fig. 1. PAR platform architecture

The architecture of the PAR platform is shown in Fig. 1. There are two ways to generate code. The first one is to deal with quantization problems. The PAR platform can automatically transform the SNL demand model into the Radl standard model, semi-automatically into the Radl algorithm model, and then into the Apla abstract program model, and finally into the executable program. The second method is to deal with non-quantitative problems. The user can directly design the Apla program manually, formally prove it, and then convert it into an executable program.

The goal of Model Driven Software Architecture (MDA) is to automatically generate executable program codes through the conversion of software models. This is a very challenging large-scale research [4, 18].

Model-driven engineering is the automatic generation of software products from abstract models of structure and function. It is possible to automate the development process by using model conversion, coding domain knowledge and implementation strategy code generators for specific system types.Using this method, the correctness of a complex software system can be answered by analyzing abstract models of lower complexity, provided that the conversion and generator used are correct. This model-driven approach makes it easier to achieve correct design and correct implementation.

FMDE is a new software development method and architecture based on the combination of practical formal methods (PAR methods) and model-driven engineering (MDE) [4, 8]. MDE is a software development method that focuses on creating and using domain models. MDE technology pays more attention to the architecture and automation. It maintains, analyzes, simulates by upgrading the model to a first-level artifact, and finally converts it into code or other models, thereby generating a higher level of abstraction in system development.

4 Theoretical Issues Involved in the FMDE Model Transformation Method

The main work of this paper is to use a practical formal method (PAR method) to realize the whole process of transforming the algorithm, program and software model from the demand model to the executable program model. This process involves the determination of related theories, methods, formal modeling languages, model conversion rules, and finally the mechanical or automatic conversion from platform-independent models (PIMs) to platform-specific models (PSMs) [3].

4.1 Model and Meta-model

PAR is the general term for PAR method and PAR platform. In PAR, there are 2 new definitions of modeling:

Regarding the definition of the model: A model is an abstract representation of system functions.

The abstract representation of the system model can be system requirements, algorithm abstract programs, executable language programs, etc., depending on the abstract level and specific characteristics of the system. The demand model, algorithm model and abstract program model are platform independent (PIMs); The executable language program models are platform specific models (PSMs). The constraints of all models can be described by the formal specification language Radl. The system model is composed of subsystem models. Subsystems correspond to system components. In PAR, the system models of different abstract levels in the same system are functionally equivalent. Compared with other modeling systems, PAR makes model-driven software development easier and more convenient.

About the definition of meta-model: Meta-model is the functional specification of the system.

Other models in the system can be obtained by gradually refinement (formal derivation or automatic model conversion) from the standard model. The meta-model defines the specification describing a certain model, specifically, the elements that make up the model and the relationship between the elements. The meta-model is a concept relative to the model, and the original model is meaningless without the model. Meta-modeling refers to the process of establishing a meta-model. Therefore, meta-model modeling includes: analysis, construction and development of a set of frameworks, rules, constraints, models and theories for modeling certain types of specified problems. All the constraints of the meta-model can be described by the requirements modeling language SNL. The meta-model is used to define a common language in the software development field to discuss and describe software development problems and solutions.

4.2 Algorithm Model and Program Model

The program calculus developed by Dijkstra [19] and Griess [20] regards the program and the algorithm as the same thing. The development of the program is equivalent to the development of the algorithm. The algorithms and programs we developed have some similarities with them. However, our focus is different: we separate the algorithm (recursively expressed) from the program, and then pay special attention to the formal deduction of the algorithm, not the program calculus. The algorithm expressed by the recurrence relation is just a set of mathematical formulas, which is mathematically transparent. Therefore, it can be directly obtained by formal derivation with some simple mathematical tools. After getting the correct algorithm expressed by recursion, it is a simple task to convert it into the correct program.

Regarding the definition of the algorithm model: the algorithm model is an abstract representation equivalent to the function of the algorithm.

Regarding the definition of the program model: The program model is an abstract representation equivalent to the program function.

About the definition of algorithmic program: Algorithmic program is an algorithm described in executable programming language or abstract programming language. Algorithm program and algorithm function are equivalent.

4.3 Data Types and Actions in PAR

(1) Standard data type
The standard data types mentioned in this article are data type sets, character types, floating point types, Boolean types, etc. in general executable programming languages (such as C++ and Java).

(2) Pre-defined combination data type
These types are stored in the component library in the form of abstract data types (ADT) designed by the system designer, and can be used as standard data types. Pre-defined data types such as system pre-defined sets, lists, packages, binary trees, graphs, and relational data. The two realization methods of each predefined data are predefined.

(3) Custom abstract data types
The PAR platform provides a custom abstract data type language mechanism for building system models. The above three data types can be used as generic parameters of the modeling language.

(4) Custom action
Custom actions: subroutines, functions, procedures, methods, subsystems, transactions, services, threads, etc. The above actions can be used as generic parameters of the modeling language.

(5) Predefined actions
In PAR, the predefined actions include several quantifiers. Assuming that θ represents a binary operator that satisfies the commutative law and the associative law, then

$$(\theta\, i \;:\; r(i) \;:\; f(i))$$

It means the amount obtained by performing operations on the function f(i) in the range of r(i). We put the binary operator +, ·, ∧ , ∨ , ◇(Minimum), ◆(maximum), ∩ (pay), ∪ (and) and ↑ The qualifier is written as Σ, Π, ∀, ∃, ◇, ◆, ∩, ∪ and ↑.

4.4 Formal Modeling Language SNL

Requirements Modeling Language SNL
The structured natural modeling language, SNL, is based on the characteristics of algorithm specifications and the ambiguity of natural language expressions. It limits natural language and defines a natural language based on mathematical formulas, basic quantifiers and calculations. Algorithm specification description language for abstract data types. We can describe the formal requirements of various typical algorithms and applications. Based on these formal requirements, we can use the change rules of logical expressions such as quantifiers to achieve system function refinement and data refinement, and obtain a system model that is closer to the executable program language model, that is, the algorithm model. SNL is the source language for SNL → Radl algorithm model conversion.

The maximum and demand model described by SNL is as follows:

```
AlgorithmName:maxsum;
IN A[0..n-1]: Array of Integer,0≤n;
OUT A[n]: Array of Integer;
Satisfy: s=(MAX i,j:0≤i≤j≤n:(∑k:i≤k≤j:a[k]));
```

4.5 Formal Modeling Language Radl

Radl language is an algorithm modeling language based on recursive relations defined to realize the formalization and semi-automatic development of algorithm programs. Radl is designed to describe the statute of the problem, the statute transformation rule and the description algorithm specification. Radl is the front-end language of Radl → Apla program converter, and it is also the target language of SNL → Radl.

Algorithm Modeling

Radl provides standard data types, custom data types, predefined ADT and custom ADT mechanisms. Such as arrays, sets, sequences, binary trees and graphs. The most important concept in the PAR method is the recurrence relation of solving the problem sequence, referred to as recursion. On the basis of recursion, the core of the algorithm is defined as a set of recursions. An algorithm is a set of mathematical formulas. It is more convenient for formal derivation and proof. After obtaining the efficient and correct algorithm, the final program is obtained through simple transformation.

The Radl language design algorithm makes the logic of the algorithm correspond to the algorithm in the process of derivation and verification, and the running logic of the final generated executable program is consistent, which is conducive to improving the readability and verifiability of the algorithm and code, and is used for efficient and correct development. The algorithm program. Using the Radl language to design an algorithm only needs to focus on the characteristics of the algorithm itself, highlight the ingenuity in the algorithm design, and not pay too much attention to other insignificant details, restore the logic of the algorithm to deal with the problem as much as possible, and show more steps to solve the problem.

Demand Modeling

Using the data types and operations provided by the Radl modeling language, we can describe the formal requirements of various typical algorithms and applications. Based on these formal requirements, we can use the change rules of logical expressions such as quantifiers to implement system function refinement and data refinement, and obtain a system model closer to the executable program language model. That is, the algorithm model and the abstract programming model.

Statute Conversion Rules

Statute conversion rules are mostly quantifiers, which have been proved in [14, 21]. The following is used in this article. We use θ to represent the binary operator that satisfies the commutative law and the associative law, that is, there

$$(\theta\, i \; : \; r(i) \; : \; f(i))$$

It means the amount obtained by performing operations on the function f(i) in the range of r(i). The associative law, commutative law and its quantifier θ have the following properties:

a. Cross product properties

$$(\theta\ i, j: r(i) \wedge s(i, j): f(i, j)) = (\theta\ i: r(i):(\theta\ j: s(i, j): f(i, j)))$$

b. Scope split nature

$$(\theta\ i: r(i): f(i)) = (\theta\ i: r(i) \wedge b(i): f(i))\ \theta\ (\theta\ i: r(i) \wedge\neg\ b(i): f(i))$$

c. Single point split

$$(\theta\ i: 0 \leq i < n + 1: f(i)) = (\theta\ i: 0 \leq i < n: f(i))\ \theta\ f(n)$$

d. Generalized associative law and commutative law

$$(\theta\ i: r(i): s(i)\ \theta\ f(i)) = (\theta\ i: r(i): s(i))\ \theta\ (\theta\ i: r(i): f(i))$$

4.6 Abstract Program Modeling Language Apla

Apla language is an abstract programming language defined in order to realize the PAR method of formal development. The design of Apla fully embodies the language mechanism of data abstraction and function abstraction. That is, using the program development method of top-down gradual refinement, first design abstract programs based on abstract functions and data; then gradually refine the abstract functions, Until you can use executable statements to describe. Apla language supports abstract data types, provides basic data types, abstract data types, and a custom ADT mechanism to facilitate program development and shorten code length while ensuring legibility. Apla is the target language of Radl → Apla program converter and the source language of Apla → executable language program automatic conversion system.

Apla's BNF Description

a. Program and program body

<Pan-parameter table>::=<type parameter>{<process parameter>}

<type parameter>::=sometype <identifier>{","<identifier>}";"

<process parameter>::= somefunc <identifier> ([<type parameter>]): <type>

b. Declarations and definitions

<Custom ADT type declaration>::="define ADT" <identifier>(<parameter part>{;<formal parameter part>});{<procedure header>|<function header>}" enddef;"

<variable description>::= "var" <variable definition> {";"<variable definition>}";"

<variable definition>::= <identifier>{ ,<identifier>} ":" <type>

c. Process description

<procedure header>::= "procedure" <identifier>; |"procedure" <identifier>(<formal parameter part>{;<formal parameter part>});

<subroutine body>::= [<constant description>][<type description>][<variable description>][<procedure description>] [<function description>]"begin"<compound statement> "end;"

d. Function description

<function header>::= "function" <identifier>":" <return type>;|"function" <identifier>(<formal parameter part>{;<formal parameter part>}):<return type> ;

e. Instantiation part

<The instantiation of the program>::=
"program"<identifier>":new"<identifier>"
("<instantiation argument table>");"{"program"<identifier>": new" <Identifier>" ("<Instantiated Argument Table>");"}

f. Statement section

<conditional statement>::= "if" <Boolean expression> "->"<compound statement>{"[]"Boolean expression>"->"<compound statement>}"fi;"

<do statement>::="do" <Boolean expression>"→ "<compound statement>{"[]"<Boolean expression>"->"<compound statement>}"od;"

<foreach statement>::="foreach("<variable group>:<constant>|<variable> "≤"|"<"<variable group> "≤"|"<" <constant>|<variable>:< Statement>)

<input procedure statement>::= "read(" <read parameter table>");" | "readln(" <read parameter table> ");"

5 Case Study

5.1 In-Order Traversal of Binary Tree

A new algorithm design method FMDE is used to derive a non-recursive algorithm program that traverses a binary tree in order, and then a formal proof is given using the Dijkstra-Gries standard program proof method.

Let T be a finite binary tree, In(T) represents a series of node sequences generated by the in-order traversal of T. We use the binary tree abstract data types and sequences given by SNL, Radl and Apla to describe the program specification and develop algorithms program.

Step 1. Describe the demand model with SNL

```
AlgorithmName: scantree
IN:  T:Tree;
OUT: p: Sequence;
satisfy: p=INTree(T);
```

Step 2. Use the SNL → RADL model conversion tool to convert the SNL function requirements of the algorithm problem into the RADL algorithm specification:

```
| [X: list(Integer); T: btree;] |
PQ1: Given is a finite binary tree T
PR1: X=In (T)
```

Step 3. Based on the method of FMDE, the algorithm is derived formally from Radl's formal function specification. According to the post-condition PR1 and the law of algebra, we have:

(1) Divide the original problem and get:

$$\text{In(T)} = \text{In(T.1)} \uparrow [\text{T.d}] \uparrow \text{In(T.r)}$$

(2) Looking for the recurrence relationship, the general strategy of the non-recursive algorithm for traversing the binary tree in the middle order is obtained. In order to obtain a non-recursive algorithm program, we carry out the following derivation:

```
In (T)
= In(T.l)↑[T.d]↑In(T.r)
= In(T.l.l)↑[T.l.d]↑In(T.l.r)↑[T.d]↑In(T.r)
=In(T.l.l.l)↑[T.l.l.d]↑In(T.l.l.r)↑[T.l.d]↑In(T.l.r)↑[T.d]↑In(T.r)
=In(T.l.l.l.l)↑[T.l.l.l.d]↑In(T.l.l.l.r)↑[T.l.l.d]↑In(T.l.l.r)↑[T.l.d]
↑In(T.l.r)↑[T.d]↑In(T.r)
```

This derivation gives a general strategy for designing non-recursive pre-sorting algorithms. That is to introduce 3 variables: X, q, S, among them, the sequence variable X is used to store the visited node flag sequence, such as T.d↑T.l.d↑T.l.l.d…;q is used to store the subtree of T to be visited, such as T.l.l; S is a sequence variable, which is used as a stack to store the right subtree of T to be traversed, such as In(T.l.l.r)↑In(T.l.r)↑In(T.r); in order to develop a loop invariant, we define A function F(S)is as follows:

$$F([]) = []$$
$$F(q \uparrow S) = q.d \uparrow In(q.r) \uparrow F(S)$$

Step 4. Generate cycle invariant based on FMDE:

$$I : X \uparrow In(q) \uparrow F(S) = In(T)$$

Step 5. Use the Radl → Apla model conversion tool to convert the algorithm to the Apla program:

```
Procedure Inorder(T:btree(char,50);var X:list(char,50));
{
  PQ: Given is a finite binary tree T
  PR:X=In(T)
}
Var S: list(char,50);
Var q:btree(char,50);
BegIn
X, q, S:=[],T,[];
{
  I: In(T)=X↑In(q)↑F(S);
}
do q ≠% → q, S:= q.l,q↑s;
[] q =% ∧S ≠[] → q,S,X:=s[h].r, s[h+1…t],X↑[s[h].d];
od;
end.
```

Step 6. Using Apla → executable code model conversion tool, Apla programs can be automatically converted into executable language programs, such as C++, Java, etc.

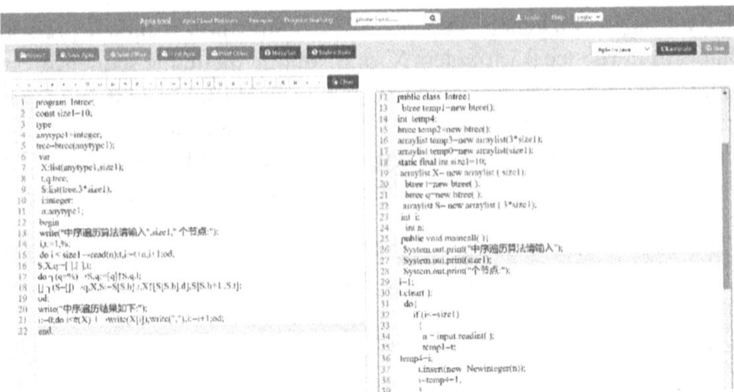

Fig. 2. The middle-order traversal Apla program is converted to a Java program.

Java programs can be completed through our Apla-Java program converter. Figure 2 shows the result generated by the converter. The left window of the figure is the Apla program of middle-order traversal, which gives a binary tree, visits each node in the tree in middle-order, and prints out the order of the nodes in the tree. The right window in the figure is part of the Java code generated by the converter. Obviously, the number of lines of Java code is much more than that of Apla. After pressing the "RUN" button, the converter calls the Java compiler to compile the Java code into machine code, and then runs the machine code.

Here, we use Dijkstra-Gries' standard procedure proof method to prove the correctness of the model transformation.

The proof is divided into four steps:

(1) Prove that I is true before the loop is executed.
wp(x,q,s:=[],T,[],I)
≡[]↑In(T)↑F([]) =In(T) [wp definition]
≡In(T) =In(T)
≡ true

(2) Prove that I is indeed a loop invariant
1> Condition c1 is q≠%
The statement s1 is q,s:=q.l,q↑s
I∧q≠% => wp(s,q:=q↑s,q.l,I)
≡I∧q≠% => X↑In(q.l)↑F(q↑s) =In(T) [wp definition]
≡I∧q≠% => X↑In(q.l)↑q.d↑In(q.r)↑F(s) =In(T)
≡I∧q≠% => X↑In(q)↑F(s) =In(T)
≡I∧q≠% => I
≡true
2> The condition c2 is q=%∧s≠[]
The statement s2 is q,s,x:=s[h].r,s[h+1..t],X↑[s[h].d]
I∧q≠%∧s≠[]=>wp(q,s:=s[h].r,s[h+1..t],I)
≡I∧q≠%∧s≠[]=>x↑[s[h].d]↑In(s[h].r)↑F(s[h+1..t]) =In(T) [wp definition]
≡I∧q≠%∧s≠[]=>x↑F(s[h]↑s[h+1..t]) =In(T)
≡I∧q≠%∧s≠[]=>x↑F(s) =In(T)
≡I∧q≠%∧s≠[]=>I [predicate calculus]
≡true

(3) The post-proof assertion that PR must be true when the loop terminates
I∧┐(q=%∧s≠[]∨q≠%) => x=In(T)
≡I∧q=%∧s=[] => x=In(T)
≡x↑In(q)↑F(s)=In(T) => x=In(T)
≡x↑In(%)↑F([])=In(T) => x=In(T)
≡ x=In(T) => x=In(T) [predicate calculus]
≡true

(4) The termination of the cycle is clearly established

Based on the formal method, a non-recursive algorithm program for traversing the binary tree in order is derived. The correctness of the model transformation is guaranteed.

5.2 Calculate the Maximum Sum of the Array Segment

Question: Given an integer array a[0:n-1], try to calculate the maximum sum of adjacent elements in a. Assume that the sum of the hollow segments in a is zero.

Step 1. Describe the demand model with SNL:

AlgorithmName:maxsum;
IN A[0..n-1]: Array of Integer,0≤n;
OUT A[n]: Array of Integer;
Satisfy: s=(MAX i,j:0≤i≤j≤n:(∑k:i≤k≤j:a[k]));

Step 2. Use the SNL → RADL model conversion tool to convert the SNL function requirements of the algorithm problem into the RADL algorithm specification:

AQ2:Given is an Intrger a[0:n-1], let maxsum(a[0:n-1]) represent the maximum sum of array a

AR2: $\mathrm{maxsum}(a[0:n-1]) = (\max i, j : 0 \le i \le j < n : \mathrm{sum}(i, j))$, in

$\text{if } i \ge j,\ \mathrm{Sum}(i, j) = 0$

$\text{if } i < j,\ \mathrm{Sum}(i, j) = \sum (k : i \le k < j : a[k])$

Step 3. Based on the method of FMDE, the algorithm is derived formally from Radl's formal function specification. According to the post-condition AR2 and the law of algebra, we have

(1) In order to obtain a fast algorithm, we divide the original problem into:

$$\mathrm{maxsum}(a[0:n-1]) = F(\mathrm{maxsum}(a[0:n-2], a[n-1]))$$

$$\text{That is}: \ \mathrm{maxsum}(a0:m-1) = F(\mathrm{maxsum}(a[0:m-2], a[m-1])) \quad 0 \le m \le n$$

(2) Find the recurrence relationship F

maxsum(a[0:m])
=(MAX i,j:0≤i≤j≤m:sum(i,j))
= Cross product properties
=(MAX j:0≤j≤m:(MAX i:0≤i≤m:sum(i,j)))
={令(MAX i:0≤i≤m:sum(i,j))=ms(j)}
=(MAX j:0≤j≤m:ms(j))
= Range split and single point range
=max((MAX j:0≤j≤m:ms(j)),ms(m))
=max(maxsum(a[0:m-1]),ms(m))

So, get:

Recurnence 1. $\mathrm{maxsum}(a[0:m]) = \max(\mathrm{maxsum}(a[0:m-1]), \mathrm{ms}(m)) \quad 0 \le m \le n$

Repeat (1) and (2) to find the recurrence relationship between ms(m) and ms(m-1)

ms(m)
=(MAX i:0≤i≤m:sum(i,m))
=(MAX i:0≤i≤m:∑(k:i≤k<m:a[k]))
={ Range split and single point range}
(MAX i:0≤i≤m:∑(k:i≤k<m:a[k])+a[m])
={ Definition of general distribution rate and sum (i, j) }
(MAX i:0≤i≤m:sum(i,m-1)+a[m])
={ Range split and single point range }
max((MAXi:0≤i≤m:sum(i,m-1)),sum(m,m-1)+a[m])
={ Definition of ms(m) }
max(ms(m-1),0)+a[m]
=max(ms(m-1])+a[m],a[m])

So there is:

Recurnence 2. $ms(m) = max(ms(m-1]) + a[m], a[m])$

Obviously when $m = 0$, $ms(m-1) = 0$, $maxsum(a[0:m-1]) = 0$, so

Initiation 1. $m = 0 \wedge ms(m-1) = 0 \wedge maxsum(a[0:n-1])$

Combining Initiation 1. Recurnence 1 and Recurnence 2, we get the following algorithm for the maximum sum problem:

```
ALGORITHM: maxsum(a[0:n-1])
|[a:array(0:n-1,Integer);m,maxsum,ms:Integer]|
{AR∧AQ}
BEGIN:m=0++1;ms(m-1)=0:maxsum(a[0:m-1])=0
TERMINATION:m=n
RECUR:maxsum(a[0:m])=max(maxsum(a[0:m-1]),ms(m))
ms(m)=max(ms(m-1])+a[m],a[m])
END
```

Based on this algorithm, let the initial value of m be 0, we can calculate the value of maxsum(a[0:m-1]) step by step, and get the desired result when m = n.

Step 4. Generate cycle invariant based on FMDE.

Let the variables s and c store the values of maxsum(a[0:m-1]) and ms(m) respectively, then the following loop invariant AI can be obtained:

$$AI \quad s = maxsum(a[0:m-1]) \wedge c = ms(m-1) \wedge 0 \leq m \leq n$$

Step 5. Use Radl → Apla model conversion tool to convert algorithms and algorithm invariants into Apla programs:

```
Program maxsum(a[0:n-1])
{PQ: Given a integer array a(0： n-1,Integer)}
{PR:s=maxsum(a[0:n-1])}
Var m,s,c:Integer;a:array(0:n-1,Integer);
m,s,c:=0,0,0;
{LI:s=maxsum(a[0:m-1]∧c=ms(m-1)∧0≤m≤n)}
do m≠n -> c:=max(c+a[m],a[m]);
        s:=mIn(s,c);
        m:=m+1
od
```

Step 6. Using Apla → executable code model conversion tool, Apla programs can be automatically converted into executable language programs, such as C++, Java, etc.

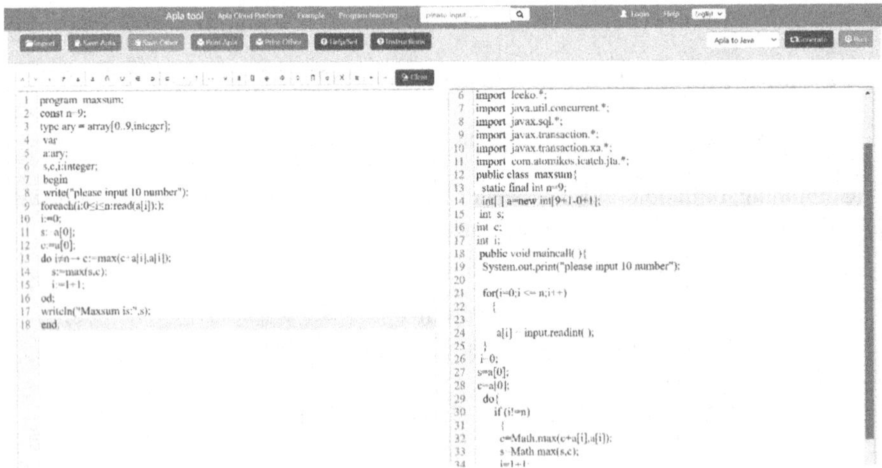

Fig. 3. Maxsum and Apla program conversion Java program

Figure 3 is the result of running step 6. The left window is used to store the Apla program model, and the right window is used to store the executable program model (Java program). Obviously, perform step 2 and step 5. Will get similar results.

Based on the formal method, the maximum sum of adjacent array segments is derived. The reliability of the PAR platform has been rigorously tested. Therefore, the result of the Java program is correct.

6 Comparison of Related Work

FMDE is an emerging software development method that reflects the idea of MDE. Through the analysis of the case in Sect. 4, it can be concluded that the FMDE algorithm development method in this article is a software development method with SNL demand modeling, Radl algorithm modeling, and Apla program modeling as the main approaches.

Use SNL → RADL model transformation to convert the SNL function requirements of algorithm problems into RADL algorithm specifications, use Radl → Apla model transformation to convert algorithms to Apla programs, and use Apla → executable code model transformation to automatically convert Apla programs into executable language programs. And finally prove the correctness of the model transformation through a case. Compared with the traditional software development method that uses UML modeling and model conversion as the main approach, the FMDE algorithm adopted in this article obviously has more efficient development efficiency. It is once again proved that the theory and application of the FMDE method can improve the efficiency and correctness of algorithm development and reliability.

Oxford Jim Davis proposed a formal model-driven software engineering method. The modeling language of this method is called Booster. It can develop key information systems based on the MDE framework. This paper introduces a model-driven engineering method, FMDE, which is particularly suitable for the development of key information systems. Both the model language and the converted language are suitable for formal analysis, and the conversion strategy and related development methods are designed to maintain the integrity and usability of the system. Event-B [22] is a formal modeling language for reactive systems and a formal software development method. In this method, the software system is initially conceived in a very abstract way, and then Refined into code.

The PAR method is a practical formal method. The PAR platform [14, 23] is a platform developed to support the PAR method, which improves the correctness and conciseness of the program. The PAR method and the PAR platform include key technologies such as new definitions and new development strategies of loop invariants, unified algorithm programming methods and new algorithm representation methods, custom algorithm design languages and abstract programming languages, which can greatly increase development complexity. The efficiency and reliability of the algorithm program. The PAR method and PAR platform consist of a requirement modeling language SNL, an algorithm modeling language Radl for algorithm specifications and a description algorithm language, an abstract program modeling language Apla for formal development, a set of model conversion rules and a set of automatic conversion tools. These tools can realize the conversion from the SNL requirement model to the RADL algorithm model, then to the APLA program model, and finally to the executable program model. The goal of the conversion is to generate an executable program. FMDE is a new software development method and architecture based on the combination of practical formal method (PAR method) and model-driven engineering (MDE).

7 Conclusion

7.1 Gives Definitions of Models, Meta Models, Etc

This paper defines the model and meta-model, algorithm model and program model in the formal model-driven engineering (FMDE) modeling process, which improves the efficiency and correctness of algorithm program development.

7.2 Gives the Syntax and Semantic Definition of the Formal Modeling Language

This paper presents the grammatical and semantic definitions of formal modeling languages SNL, Radl, and Apla. Using the data types and operations provided by the Radl modeling language, a system model closer to the executable programming language model is obtained. Using the data types and operations provided by the Radl modeling language, I can describe the formal requirements of various typical algorithms and applications. The purpose of using Apla is to perfectly realize function abstraction and data abstraction in program development, so that any Apla program is simple enough, easy to understand, formal deduction or proof.

7.3 Gives FMDE Model Transformation Method and Application Research

The FMDE algorithm development method in this article is a software development method with SNL demand modeling, Radl algorithm modeling, and Apla program modeling as the main approaches. Use SNL $\rightarrow$ RADL model transformation to convert the SNL function requirements of algorithm problems into RADL algorithm specifications, use Radl $\rightarrow$ Apla model transformation to convert algorithms to Apla programs, and use Apla $\rightarrow$ executable code model transformation to automatically convert Apla programs into executable language programs. Finally, a case is used to prove the correctness of the model transformation, which improves the efficiency, correctness and reliability of algorithm development.

References

1. Ma, X., et al.: Review and prospect of software development method development. J. Softw. **30**(01), 3–21 (2019)
2. Weizhong, S., Yanbing, J., Zhiyi, M.: Existing problems and development path of UML. Comput. Res. Dev. **04**, 509–516 (2003)
3. Kurtev, I.: State of the art of QVT: a model transformation language standard. In: Schürr, A., Nagl, M., Zündorf, A. (eds.) AGTIVE 2007. LNCS, vol. 5088, pp. 377–393. Springer, Heidelberg (2008). https://doi.org/10.1007/978-3-540-89020-1_26
4. Gargantini, A., Riccobene, E., Scandurra, P.: Combining formal methods and MDE techniques for model-driven system design and analysis. Int. J. Adv. Softw. **3**(1 and 2), 1–18 (2010)
5. Sommerville, I.: Software Engineering (Tenth Edition), Pearson Education Limited 2016, pp. 159–162 (2016)
6. Xue, J., Zheng, Y., Hu, Q., You, Z., Xie, W., Cheng, Z.: PAR: a practicable formal method and its supporting platform. In: Sun, J., Sun, M. (eds.) Formal Methods and Software Engineering. ICFEM 2018. LNCS, vol. 11232, pp. 70–86. Springer, Cham (2018). https://doi.org/10.1007/978-3-030-02450-5_5
7. Xue, J., Cheng, Z., Yang, Q., You, Z., Hu, Q., Xie, W.: Methodology and platform of IS code generation. In: Proceedings of the 2020 International Conference on Big Data in Management (ICBDM 2020), pp. 49–57. Association for Computing Machinery, New York, NY, USA (2020)
8. Adesina, O.: Integrating formal methods with model-driven engineering. In: International Conference on Model-Driven Engineering Languages and Systems, At Ottawa, Canada (2015)
9. Lange, C.F., Chaudron, M.R.: Effects of defects in UML models. In: ICSE '06 Proceedings of the 28th International Conference on Software Engineering (2006)

10. Raghuraman, A., et al.: Does UML modeling associate with lower defect proneness? A preliminary empirical investigation. In: 2019 IEEE/ACM 16th International Conference on Mining Software Repositories (MSR). IEEE (2019)
11. Chren, S., Buhnova, B., Macak, M., Daubner, L., Rossi, B.: Mistakes in UML diagrams: analysis of student projects in a software engineering course. In: Mistakes in UML Diagrams (2019). https://doi.org/10.1109/ICSE-SEET.2019.00019
12. Boberic-Krsticev, D., Tesendic, D.: Experience in teaching OOAD to various students. Inform. Educ. **12**(1), 43–58 (2013)
13. Butler, R.W.: What is Formal Methods?. 2001-08-06 [2006-11-16]. (Original Content Archived on 08 December 2006)
14. Holloway, C.M.: Why engineers should consider formal methods (PDF). 16th Digital Avionics Systems Conference (27–30 October 1997). (Original Content (PDF) archived on 16 November 2006)
15. Archer, M., Heitmeyer, C., Riccobene, E.: Proving invariants of I/O automata with TAME. Autom. Softw. Eng. **9**, 201–232 (2002)
16. Xue, J.Y.: PAR method and its supporting platform. In: Proceedings of in International Workshop on Formal method for Developing Software, Annual Report, No. 348, Macao: UNU-IIST (2006)
17. Jinyun, X.: PAR: a model driven engineering platform for generating algorithms and software. In: Symposium on Programming: Logics, Models, Algorithms and Concurrency on April 29th and 30th, 2016 to recognize Jayadev Misra's accomplishments, at the University of Texas. https://www.cs.utexas.edu/symposium
18. Berramla, B., Deba, E,A., Benhamou, D.: Model transformation generation a survey of the state-of-the-art. In: International Conference on Information Technology for Organizations Development, pp. 1–6 (2016)
19. Dijkstra, E.W.: A Discipline of Programming. Prentice Hall, New Jersey (1976)
20. Gries, D.: The Science of Programming. Springer-Verlag, New York (1981)
21. Jinyun, X.: A unified approach for developing efficient algorithmic programs. J. Comput. Sci. Technol. **12**(4), 314–329 (1997)
22. Rivera, V., Cataño, N., Wahls, T., Rueda, C.: Code generation for Event-B. Int. J. Softw. Tools Technol. Transfer **19**(1), 31–52 (2015). https://doi.org/10.1007/s10009-015-0381-2
23. Jinyun, X.: Two new strategies for developing loop invariants and its applications. J. Comput. Sci. Technol. **8**(3), 147–154 (1993)
24. Davies, J., Milward, D., Wang, C.W., Welch, J.: Formal model-driven engineering of critical Information systems. Sci. Comput. Program. **103**, 88–113 (2015)
25. Liu, Z., Xue, J., Xia, J., Wang, X.: The research on concurrent distributed transaction processing mechanism in PAR platform and its application. J. Jiangxi Norm. Univ. (Nat. Sci.) **43**(6), P649-854 (2019)
26. Xue, J., Gries, D.: Developing a Linear Algorithm for Cubing a Cycle Permutation, Science of Computer Programming, vol.11 (1988)
27. Xue, J., Davis, R.: A derivation and proof of Knuth's binary to decimal program. Softw. Concepts Tools **18**, 149–156 (1997)
28. Xue, J., Yang, B., Zuo, Z.: A linear in-situ algorithm for the power of cyclic permutation. In: Preparata, F.P., Wu, X., Yin, J. (eds.) FAW 2008. LNCS, vol. 5059, pp. 113–123. Springer, Heidelberg (2008). https://doi.org/10.1007/978-3-540-69311-6_14
29. Xue, J.: Genericity in PAR platform. In: Liu S., Duan Z. (eds.) Structured Object-Oriented Formal Language and Method. SOFL+MSVL 2015. LNCS, vol. 9559, pp. 1–12. Springer, Cham (2016). https://doi.org/10.1007/978-3-319-31220-0_1
30. Zheng, Y.J., Ling, H.F., Xue, J.Y., Chen, S.Y.: Population classification in fire evacuation: a multiobjective particle swarm optimization approach. IEEE Trans. Evol. Comput. **18**(1), 70–81 (2014)

31. Zheng, Y.J., Ling, H.F., Chen, S.Y., Xue, J.Y.: A hybrid neuro-fuzzy network based on differential biogeography-based optimization for online population classification In earthquakes. IEEE Trans. Fuzzy Syst. **23**(4), 1070–1083 (2014)
32. Zheng, Y.J., Chen, Q.Z., Ling, H.F., Xue, J.Y.: Rescue wings: mobile computing and active services support for disaster rescue. IEEE Trans. Serv. Comput. **9**(4), 594–607 (2016)
33. Zheng, Y.J., Sheng-Yong, C., Yu, X., Jin-Yun, X.: A Pythagorean-type fuzzy deep de-noising auto-encoder for industrial accident early warning. IEEE Trans. Fuzzy Syst. **25**(6), 1561–1575 (2017)
34. Kent, S.: Model driven engineering. In: Butler, M., Petre, L., Sere, K. (eds.) IFM 2002. LNCS, vol. 2335, pp. 286–298. Springer, Heidelberg (2002). https://doi.org/10.1007/3-540-47884-1_16
35. Bézivin, J.: Model driven engineering: an emerging technical space. In: Lämmel, R., Saraiva, J., Visser, J. (eds.) GTTSE 2005. LNCS, vol. 4143, pp. 36–64. Springer, Heidelberg (2006). https://doi.org/10.1007/11877028_2

Author Index

Printed in the United States
by Baker & Taylor Publisher Services